CONTRASTS —
Gospel Evidence
and
Christian Beliefs

by
Roger P. Booth, LL.B., B.D., Ph.D., A.K.C.
Solicitor

Paget Press

By the same author —
Jesus and the Laws of Purity. (JSOT Press, Sheffield, 1986).

To Adam, Alistair and Philip.

Published by Paget Press,
202 Manor Way, Aldwick, Bognor Regis, W.Sussex.

Printed by J.W. Lambert & Sons,
Station Road, Settle, North Yorkshire.

Copyright © Roger P. Booth, 1990.

ISBN 0-9515220-0-0

PREFACE.

The purpose of this book is to exhibit some contrasts between the evidence of the Gospels (and other NT writings) and orthodox Christian belief—orthodox, that is, in the sense of conformity to the ancient creeds of the Church or to traditional Christian rite.

The book is a practical application of our view that the historian and the lawyer should follow a similar method in assessing the available evidence regarding 'what happened' at a particular time, whether ancient or modern, and place, whether Eastern or Western: in assessing ancient Eastern traditional evidence, such as the Gospels, the method allows for less weight to be given to the evidence because of the greater danger of distortion in transmission, and the greater credulity of the ancients. This method was applied in a narrower sphere in my book 'Jesus and the Laws of Purity' in 1986, and is here applied to Gospel assertions more central to Christian faith and practice.

In the following pages we use our forensic method in an attempt to assess, as a lawyer would, the assertions of the Evangelists concerning words and deeds of Jesus and the Apostles. We analyse the Gospel assertions, and then weigh against that evidence, any evidence which may tend to deny the accuracy of the assertions.

But like a judge in a court of law, our judgement is only that *on a balance of probability* the assertion of the Evangelist is true or untrue *according to the available evidence.* We believe that this approach to the evidence is pursued by the historian but in a less formal way. Neither the historian nor the judge *knows* what happened on a past occasion, but this reflection should not deter us from making a decision based on probability, for we take decisions in the affairs of daily life relying on data which are only probably correct; there are few things about which we possess certainty.

Where our conclusions show a cleavage between Christian belief or practice and the teaching or intent of Jesus as evidenced by the Gospels, then Christians being nomine ipso followers of Jesus rather than e.g. Paul, should presumably wish to return to the teaching of Jesus. Sometimes the path back to such conformity is self-evident but occasionally, as in the case of the liturgy and the priesthood, we have doffed the mantle of the historian and hazarded a guess at the manner of worship, fellowship and organisation which Jesus would have intended for his followers if he had foreseen the non-arrival of the kind of Kingdom, and of himself as Son of Man, which he had thought to be so imminent.

We now address the academic reader on the notes to the main text. While some of these notes make minor points supplementing the arguments in the text, a majority cite Biblical or other authority for the statements in the text. The references to other writers, particularly recent writers, are comparatively sparse. We think that the only other reason justifying us in referring the reader to further writings is that they offer significant new insight for or against our assertions in the text. Some academic works deluge the reader with references to a plethora of books and articles which certainly display the author's erudition and breadth of reading, but of which many are either marginal to the content of the main text or are essentially only re-stating the views of another writer. A pound of new insight is worth a peck of new packaging!

In particular, we have tried to avoid listing recent articles or books just because they are the most recent writing on a topic. Literature's right to publicity depends not on its youth or age, but its merit, i.e. does it significantly increase our understanding of the NT? It is arguable that even to-day the student will receive more help towards that understanding from the creative thought of Albert Schweitzer, F.C. Burkitt, R. Bultmann, M. Dibelius, V. Taylor and T.W. Manson than from the meticulous dissection of Gospel verses which he may admire in current theological journals.

The consummate cleverness which is attributed to Mark by some current critics, would surely have amazed him. For example, in the parable section at 4,1-34 J. Dewey and others have found a five-part concentric structure (a technique by which Mark is thought to inter-relate and contrast his material), but G. Fey has detected such a structure in seven parts! (CBQ, Vol. 51, pp.65-81).

Be that as it may, swollen notes, and references to words hot from the printer earn favour in the groves of Academe, and since many publishers are reluctant to risk investment without the imprimatur of a University elder, so the bulging bustles of academic fashion prevail, especially with scholars who need to publish to nurture University careers.

The law don has weightier reason for his pre-occupation with the most recent emissions from the presses. For the latest law-reports which he avidly devours in order to write case-notes or articles thereon for the legal periodicals, do possess some importance. Although the principle in a recently reported case may have been much better expressed in a purple passage of Sir George Jessel or Lord Atkin many years ago, yet the judge's decision last month, however pedestrian, may pursuant to the doctrine of stare decisis create new law by applying the old principle to a new set of circumstances. The danger of this concern with the latest decisions is that the don may infect his student with an enthusiasm for the 'wilderness of single instances' rather than with an appreciation of the development of legal principle which may be gained from a study of the classic Bowen-type judgments of the past.

Finally, a word to the non-academic readers who justifiably complained that one of the features which rendered my last book less than limpid, was my use of theological terms and 'inside' jargon without explanation to the reader on the 'outside'. This time I have tried to include in a glossary at the end all expressions and names which might pose a difficulty to the non-specialist reader. I hope that this book will help to close the chasm which now 'yawns' between the scholar's study and the worshipper's pew.

PREFATORY NOTES.

1. Texts and Translations

Hebrew words have been transliterated.

The text of the New Testament which is adopted, is that published in Nestle-Aland, Novum Testamentum Graece, Deutsche Bibelstiftung Stuttgart, 1979. The text used of the Hebrew Bible is that of Biblia Hebraica Stuttgartensia, and that of the Septuagint is the edition by A. Rahlfs, Stuttgart, 1935. The translation used of the Old and New Testaments is the Revised Standard Version.

The Hebrew text of the Mishnah used is that published by Philip Blackman in Mishnayoth, Second Edition, Gateshead, 1977, and the English translation used is that by Herbert Danby in The Mishnah, Oxford, 1933. The English translation of the Babylonian Talmud used is that edited by I. Epstein, The Soncino Press, London, 1938. The English translation of the Dead Sea Scrolls used generally is that by Geza Vermes in The Dead Sea Scrolls in English, London, 1962.

2. Abbreviations

The following abbreviations are used:

Aland	Nestle-Aland Novum Testamentum Graece (as above).
Bauer	A Greek-English Lexicon of the NT and Other Early Christian Literature, E.T. and edited by W.F. Arndt and F.W. Gingrich, Chicago, 1957.
B-D	A Greek Grammar of the NT and Other Early Christian Literature by F. Blass and A. Debrunner, 9th-10th edition, E.T. by R.W. Funk, Chicago, 1961.
CBQ	Catholic Biblical Quarterly.
BDB	A Hebrew and English Lexicon of the OT edited by F. Brown, S.R. Driver and C.A. Briggs, Oxford, 1907.
Danby	The Mishnah, Oxford, 1933.
Danby's Appendix	Appendix (III) of Rabbinical Teachers in the Mishnah, to Danby's above translation.
E.T.	English translation.
ExpT.	Expository Times.
GK	Gesenius' Hebrew Grammar, as edited and enlarged by E. Kautzch, Oxford, 1910.

Heb.	Hebrew
Jastrow	A Dictionary of the Targumim, the Talmud Babli and Yerushalmi, and the Midrashic Literature, New York, 1957, by M.A. Jastrow.
JBL	Journal of Biblical Literature.
JJS	Journal of Jewish Studies.
JQR	Jewish Quarterly Review.
JNTS	Journal of New Testament Studies.
JTS	Journal of Theological Studies.
LXX	The Septuagint.
Blackman	Translation of Hebrew Text in Mishnayoth above.
NT	The New Testament.
OT	The Old Testament.
RSV	The Revised Standard Version.
Soncino Rabbinical Index	The Index of Rabbis mentioned in the Babylonian Talmud, which is contained in the Index volume of the English translation mentioned above.
TDNT	Theological Dictionary of the New Testament, Grand Rapids, 1964-76.
Transl.	Translated.
X	Codex Sinaiticus.
ZNW	Zeitschrift für die neutestamentliche Wissenschaft.

TABLE OF CONTENTS

PREFACE	I
PREFATORY NOTES	IV
TABLE OF CONTENTS	VI
CHAPTER I — GOSPEL ASSERTIONS AND THE RESURRECTION	**1**
I — The Forensic Model	1
II — The Resurrection	11
A. The Evidence in the NT	12
B. Circumstantial Evidence	13
C. Source Criticism	16
D. The Nature of the Resurrection	22
III — Conclusions	38
Notes	39
CHAPTER II — 'DEMONS CROSS TO CENTRE'	**46**
I — History of Demons	47
II — Jesus and Demons	51
A. The Temptation	51
B. Exorcisms and the Kingdom	53
C. Satan in the Teaching of Jesus	57
D. The Tribulation envisaged by Jesus	57
E. Jesus and the End-time	59
F. The Vicarious Victim of Satan	61
G. Jesus as the Isaianic Suffering Servant	63
H. The Suffering Servant as a Ransom to Satan	65
J. Jesus as Suffering Servant *and* Son of Man?	66
III — Conclusion	67
Notes	68
CHAPTER III — SHOULD CHRISTIANS BE 'KOSHER'?	**71**
I — Introduction	71
II — Jesus' Intent regarding Mission to Gentiles	72
III — Jesus' possible attitude to Gentile Law-observance	75
A. Evidence of the Pentateuch	75
B. Evidence of Rabbinic Tradition	78
C. Evidence of first Palestinian Jewish followers	81
D. Review of Evidence and Conclusions	95
IV — Consequences for Christians To-day	101
Notes	102

CHAPTER IV — THE LAST SUPPER — TO BE REPEATED? 112
   I — The NT Evidence 112
      A. Routes in Delivery of Tradition 112
      B. Evidence common to Mark and Paul 116
      C. Evidence opposed to Mark and Paul 118
      D. Gospel Traditions other than common Mark and Paul 121
      E. Evidence opposing the 'Covenant' reference 130
      F. Conclusion on words and actions at Last Supper 134
   II — Jesus' Intention for the Future 135
      A. The Theme of the Supper 135
      B. The disciples' dining customs 136
      C. The Influence of the Mystery Religions 140
      D. The Symbolism of the Bread and Wine 141
      E. Conclusion 142
   III — The Consequences for Worship To-day 142
      A. and B. Attendance at Temple and Synagogue 142
      C. Common Meals 147
      D. Private Prayer 148
      E. Conclusion 148
      Notes 148

CHAPTER V — WHY PRIESTS? 155
   I — Jesus and Priesthood 155
   II — Ministerial Exclusivity 158
      A. The Functions 158
      B. The Defence of Exclusivity—the Apostolic Succession 159
   III — Conclusions 164
      Notes 165

CHAPTER VI — IS JESUS GOD? 167
   I — The Titles of Jesus 168
      A. Prophet 168
      B. Teacher 172
      C. Lord 173
      D. Son of God 174
      E. The Servant of the Lord 178
      F. The Christ/Messiah 181
      G. Son of Man 182
   II — Signs of Jesus' Status in his Ministry 187
   III — Estimates of Jesus held after his death 189

IV — Conclusions	193
Notes	195
CHAPTER VII — REPRISE	199
EXCURSUS I — Mark on Washing—ignorant or malicious?	201
NOTES	216
EXCURSUS II — Why are some Spirits described in the Synoptic Gospels as unclean?	218
NOTES	223
EXCURSUS III — Authenticity of the Korban pericope: an historico-legal view.	225
NOTES	231
INDEX OF ANCIENT PASSAGES CITED	234
INDEX OF MODERN AUTHORS	242
INDEX OF SUBJECTS	245
GLOSSARY	251

CHAPTER I.

Gospel Assertions and the Resurrection

In 'Jesus and the Laws of Purity' we used a forensic model as a means for determining the authenticity of statements by the Evangelists.[1] We submitted that the scepticism of those who, like Käsemann and McArthur,[2] impose a presumption of inauthenticity on those statements, is too severe, since the Gospel text (no matter who wrote or amended it) represents assertions by *somebody* that Jesus and others said and did various things. Those assertions are, according to our forensic model, evidence that those things were said and done, and those who deny their accuracy, must bring as strong evidence to that effect. The burden of proof of the probable authenticity of an assertion should lie on the Evangelist as in a Court case, but if the assertion is not opposed by contrary evidence, the evidence constituted by the assertion usually discharges the burden. This is straightforward—the difficulty lies in deciding what may constitute contrary evidence. We suggested that any factor which indicates unlikelihood that Jesus spoke the meaning of the words concerned (not the ipsissima verba) or did the act alleged by the Evangelist, would constitute opposing evidence, and we would include within that category (a) a conflicting Gospel statement, (b) an established trend of the thought or behaviour of Jesus which is inconsistent with the Gospel statement, (c) a physical phenomenon alleged in the Gospel statement which is contrary to the natural laws, (d) a likelihood that the early church has written back into the life of Jesus later polemic, knowledge or experience, as in the case of Mark 8, 34, and (e) acknowledged editorial practices of the Evangelist, such as Mark's summarizing sentences. If a Gospel statement is opposed by such counter-evidence, then judgment upon its authenticity will be governed by the balance of probabilities as in the civil forensic model.[3]

We intend in this Chapter to consider issues affecting this forensic model, and then to apply it to an investigation of the resurrection.

I. THE FORENSIC MODEL

It may be argued that the forensic model is not suitable to an investigation into the authenticity of ancient literature since the credulity of the ancients was greater, and their concern for historical accuracy less, than that prevailing to-day.[4] These differences can be admitted, and they will either affect the weight which we allow to some Gospel assertions, or will appear as counter-evidence. The model can thus make adjustments for these differences.

But it is also argued that the legal approach leads to a mistaken view of the Gospels "as direct evidence of some historical reality" whereas the nature of the Gospels is narrative, which "suggests greater caution in making historical inferences."[5] Our method does, indeed, treat the statements of the Evangelists as evidence that the acts or speech related actually happened, because that is what the Evangelists are claiming. This is implicit in the very manner in which they write—they are not purporting to be fictional story-tellers, but recorders of events which allegedly happened at a certain time and place. Luke expressly communicates his historical purpose in his first four verses. This does not mean that what they write is accurate history, but it does mean, in our view, that we should treat their statements as of the genre which they intend them to be, namely allegations of fact.

We do not regard the statements of the Evangelists as 'direct' evidence in the sense of 'first-hand' or 'eye-witness' testimony, because, as oral tradition, they have generally passed through many tradents before reaching the Evangelist, except, for example, evidence which Mark may have received from Peter. For this reason we are willing to judge the evidence of the Evangelist to be overborne by less weighty opposing evidence than we would allow to succeed were the Evangelist giving evidence to-day about an event which had recently occurred and which he had witnessed himself. We have given examples of such opposing evidence above.

However, radical critics presume the statements of the Evangelists not to be reports of genuine incidents in the life of Jesus but to be stories created by the early Church. To reach that judgment without first appraising all the available evidence for and against the authenticity of the specific statement in issue, and giving some weight as evidence to the Evangelist's statement, appears to be unscientific. Some statements have, we concede, been invented by early Christians; for example, we think it probable that the reference to Jesus 'taking up his cross' at Mark 8, 34 was influenced by the manner of Jesus' death. But does such post-Easter interpolation even of whole stories justify the historian in presuming that *all* the witness says is false, unless it is shown otherwise? Do we know anybody in daily life who is so dishonest that we presume *everything* he says to be false (and few would deny at least the honest intent of the Evangelists)? It seems to us more rational to weigh the evidence for and against the Gospel statement rather than to presume it to be false, or too remote to be verifiable. After all, even a positive verdict for authenticity is only a conclusion that on a balance of probabilities the statement is authentic; on this earth we cannot *know* that a Gospel statement is true, but neither does a judge in Court to-day *know* that one party rather than the other is telling the truth — he also will judge the issue on a balance of probability, except in criminal cases.[6]

However, H.K. McArthur claims that "there is enough dubious material in the Gospels to justify the conviction that the burden of proof rests with those who affirm the authenticity of specific events or motifs."[7] He notes that ancient historians revised their tradition with a freedom foreign to modern historians, and that the early Christian writers did so more than others because of (a) the transforming effect of the Easter experience, (b) the non-professional character of the community, and (c) the rapid movement of the tradition from its original cultural situation (Palestinian Judaism) into quite different cultural situations (Hellenistic Judaism, Gentile Hellenism etc.).

The Easter experience would no doubt make the disciples look back on Jesus' acts and teaching in a new light, but we do not think it would cause them, imbued as they would be with his moral teaching, to falsify events of his life beyond embroidery with detail.

Modern sociological criticism would probably take issue with McArthur's description of the community as non-professional, for certainly there were early Christians who were educated — Luke and Simon of Cyrene are examples. But even if the tradition was passed on by unliterary Palestinians, their reverence for the life and teaching of their Lord, and possibly their memory-training in the synagogue schools, would, we think, reduce the normal amount of intentional or accidental distortion of the tradition. We admit that in the writing of his editorial matter, such as explanatory parentheses, Mark was liable to betray his prejudice and, perhaps, ignorance, and in Excursus I we study examples, but such explanations and summaries are readily recognisable as redactional, and should not, of themselves, be allowed to impugn the authenticity of the traditions which Mark records.

The movement of the tradition into new cultural situations would clearly cause it to be 'dressed' in different language and adjusted concepts; thus the Jewish 'Messiah' understood by Jews as the one anointed by God to bring in the New Age, became in Asia Minor the Greek 'Christ', a title without meaning to Hellenism. But this clothing of the tradition in Greek language and thought did not necessarily distort in it the substance of the events and teaching of Jesus' life.

The illustrations which McArthur uses to show the Evangelists' freedom in revision demonstrate how minor may have been the consequences of that freedom: — Matthew at 26,1f. writes, as a logion of Jesus, Mark's own note at 14,1 that it was two days before the Passover.

Luke at 24,6. alters the Marcan words of the young man at the tomb at 16,7 that the women should tell the disciples that Jesus is going before them to Galilee, into an injunction that the women remember what Jesus told them while he *was* in Galilee. Matthew at 18,16 mentions the Jewish need for two or three witnesses, and has perhaps consequently increased Mark's Gadarene demoniacs to two; Matthew alone mentions 'two' witnesses against Jesus, and alone pairs the list of the Twelve. Yet Matthew's alteration of the Marcan note of the date, and his duplication of certain numbers, appear almost immaterial and without effect on the substance of the respective narratives. Luke's alteration of the information that the risen Jesus will go to Galilee, is of more importance, but since Luke's tradition recorded non-Galilean appearances, the alteration is understandable, and hardly affects the substance or nature of his evidence of the resurrection. In short, it is submitted that the Evangelists' freedom with their tradition rarely affects the essence of the event recorded.

This burden of proof of authenticity, imposed by the radical critics, will be discharged if compliance with authenticating criteria can be shown. N. Perrin has argued for three criteria, those of dissimilarity, coherence, and multiple attestation.[8] The criterion of dissimilarity insists that the speech attributed to Jesus in the Gospels is only genuine if its thought is found neither in Jewish teaching nor in the teaching of the early Church. This criterion must exclude much genuine Jesus-material, for what is more likely than that (a) having been brought up in a Jewish family and educated as a Jew, Jesus' teaching will have been influenced by Jewish teaching, and that (b) the early Christians' teaching and faith will have been influenced by the teaching of the founder of that faith? The criterion of coherence accepts as authentic, traditional material which is consistent with material authenticated by the criterion of dissimilarity; being dependent upon that criterion, it is tainted with the same defects.

The criterion of multiple attestation accepts as genuine Jesus-material, Gospel statements which are attested by more than one of the independent witnesses of Gospel traditions, i.e. Mark, 'Q', special Lucan source (L) and special Matthean source (M). This criterion is based on the common-sense view that statements which are supported by the evidence of another independent witness are thereby shown to be more probably true than those which rest on the evidence of one unsupported witness. That principle is an essential part of our forensic approach, but we think that it is incorrectly employed by the radical critics. For those independent traditions are separate witnesses for the authenticity of the Gospel statement, and should be balanced against the weight of the evidence opposing authenticity of the kinds we have outlined. To pit these witnesses against a presumption of inauthenticity is contrary to the way we approach issues of credibility in ordinary life. We weigh the strength of the statements for and against, and then decide—we don't start off with an inbuilt prejudice against the credibility of the assertion. We do apply in this book the forensic rule that the burden of proof of a fact is on the party who asserts it, but this is of little practical effect here, since the statement of the witness will usually prove the assertion if unopposed, and if opposed, will depend on a balance of probability.

Nor does our method deprive itself of the insights of form and redaction criticism, for each may produce counter-evidence to the evidence of the Evangelists' statements. Form criticism may show that the original form of an oral traditional story embodied in the Evangelists' statements has been altered by the early Christians to serve their own purposes; J. Jeremias has shown how the target of some parables was moved as the audience became not Jesus' listeners but the Church's members, and as the opponents of the message became not the rich and ungodly, but the Jews generally.[9] Redaction criticism may show that the Evangelist has added to or altered the traditional stories which he has received, or by placing a particular story in a particular context in the Gospel, has affected the meaning. Thus the counter-evidence produced by each literary tool may render it more probable that the evidence of the Evangelist is inauthentic in whole or in part. But we believe that the correct rôle for the results of this criticism is as counter-evidence to the evidence of the Evangelist rather than as evidence to support an unrealistic presumption of falsity.

Both lawyer and non-lawyer scholars have found the forensic analogy appropriate. N. Anderson, a former Director of the Institute of Advanced Legal Studies, writes, "If, for example, [the scholar] takes the view that the Gospels were at least intended as an honest account of what the current tradition attributed to the historical Jesus, that this tradition can be shown (at least in part) to go back to a very early date, and that there are clear indications that much of it (again to speak with caution) must be regarded as authentic, then he will, presumably, apply [the legal rules for the interpretation of documentary evidence, the hearsay rules and the balance of probability criterion] or some adaptation of them, on the basis that the account should be accepted as prima facie reliable unless there is evidence to show that the opposite is the case."[10] We would demur only on Anderson's point that a pre-condition of applying a forensic model is that there are clear indications that much of the tradition must be regarded as authentic, for this seems to pre-suppose favourable judgment on the majority of the material. V.A. Harvey, a theologian, often notes[11] the similar approach of the historian and the lawyer in his book, 'The Historian and the Believer', and writes, ". . . historical judgments may be compared to judgments in law courts or in everyday life. To be sure, the analogy is not a strict one because the procedures of law courts are very formalised, and the overall aim is to bring a conclusion under a prior definition laid down by law. Nevertheless, there is a sense in which arguments in law and in history are analogous."[12] We would only disagree with his two qualifications on the analogy. Firstly, the formalities of law-court procedures can be abandoned in historical inquiries, and the essence applied mutatis mutandis. Secondly, the evidentiary rules affecting the proof of facts (with which the historian is concerned) are applied before and in isolation from the later inquiry whether the facts, as proved, fit within that 'prior definition laid down by law', e.g. of some wrong or injury.

We stress here that we do not suggest that any superior wisdom is contained in the forensic rules of evidence; the rules which lawyers have devised for determining what a witness in a civil (i.e. non-criminal) dispute may tell the Court are only the embodiment in formal language of the principles of common-sense which ordinarily intelligent people would almost unconsciously follow in deciding whether a person was telling the truth. For the principal criterion governing the admissibility of evidence in a Court is relevance—does the evidence sought to be given render it more or less likely that the fact in issue happened?

Consequently, the application of the forensic rules to Gospel statements is not an attempt to force the Gospels into the straight-jacket of an artificial and alien rule-world; it is simply the application mutatis mutandis to historical records of the canons of common-sense (concerning such questions as the duty to prove a fact in issue and the relevance of other facts to that fact in issue) which have been marshalled by lawyers into rules which assist the search for truth in the disputes of daily life.[13] The value to the historian of this forensic system of rules is that it encourages him to assess the admissibility and relevance of the Gospel statements as historical evidence, to weigh this evidence against the counter-evidence, similarly assessed, and to reach a judgment on authenticity, based on a balance of probabilities.

It may be argued that in enquiries into the authenticity of the Gospel statements we should apply the rules of evidence prevailing in the Jewish or Roman courts of that era—the 1st century A.D. But it is the interested people of to-day to whom the authenticity or otherwise of the Gospels is relevant, so that it is the forensic standards of proof accepted in their day and culture which seem more appropriate for use.

Perhaps a more correct evaluation of the authenticity of the records of Jesus' life might be obtained if we were to include in our examination all the non-canonical documents. The Gospels outside the canon, however, generally do not contain independent traditions (let alone traditions emanating from fresh witnesses), but rather purvey seemingly fanciful embellishments of the earlier stage of the traditions as presented in the NT. But where relevant secular history is available as in, say, Josephus, it should be utilised and treated in the same forensic manner, as should any Christian remains outside the NT, such as the agrapha, which appear to contain independent traditions.

Again, it may be said that the judgments on authenticity reached with the aid of the forensic tool are arbitrary because so much evidence of Jesus' words and deeds must have been lost in the handing down of the oral traditions, and in the loss of written records (as the lost Gospel to the Hebrews and Mark's allegedly lost ending exemplify). But the historian's perception is always limited by the extent and quality of his materials whatever methodology he may employ to assess their evidence. He cannot say at the end, 'This is what happened', but only, 'This is what the evidence available to me indicates, on a balance of probabilities, to have happened.' And then it is only his opinion.

We think that the reason why the historian and the lawyer should follow a similar methodology in their search for truth was accurately expressed by A.O. Lovejoy, an historian, —". . . though the inquiries of the historiographer, especially if they relate to events remote in time, are often more difficult, and sometimes at a lower level of probability, than the inquiries of courts, they have the same implicit logical structure, which is simply the structure of all inquiry about the not-now-presented; and if they are historical inquiries, and not criticism or evaluation, their objective is the same—to know whether, by the canons of empirical probability, certain events. . . happened at certain past times, and what, within the existential limits of those times, the characters of those events were."[14]

As stressed above, the legal methodology does not produce an absolute judgment on authenticity, but only a qualified conclusion that on the evidence adduced it is more likely that an event happened than that it did not. This compares with the historian's inquiry whether "by the canons of empirical probability" an event happened. It is important in the case of the Gospel record of Jesus' words to clarify what is meant by the inquiry into whether an event happened. Regarding Jesus' words the inquiry is whether the Evangelist's report that Jesus *uttered* the substance of the words is on a balance of probabilities correct, not whether the substance of the words *is true*. The 'event' is the uttering of the substance of the words. Thus, the strict English common law rule of hearsay does not prevent the consideration of the Evangelist's statement of what the eye or ear-witness told him, or even more remote tradition, because the Evangelist's statement is only being used to prove *what* Jesus (or the Pharisees or anybody else) said, not the truth of it.[15] Therefore, the Evangelist's statements are usable by the historian for he is only asking, "What did Jesus say?", not, "Is the content of what Jesus said, correct?" The accuracy of the content is usually more the concern of the theologian and the religious enquirer. It will sometimes be determined by the fulfilment or otherwise of predictions; for example, the content of Jesus' prediction at Matthew 10,23 that the disciples in their first mission would not have gone through all the towns of Israel before the Son of Man came, is shown to be incorrect by the failure of the Son to arrive within that period. The truth of the content of other statements is only discernible by the eye of faith; thus at Matthew 11,28-30 Jesus promises that he will give rest to the heavy laden since his yoke is easy and his burden light, but the historian cannot probe the fulfilment of this promise. In short, the historian's aim is to investigate only *what* Jesus said, and the forensic model is intended to serve only that end.

In the examples of opposing evidence which we enumerated above, it is the physical phenomena contrary to the natural laws whose validity and weight as evidence are most controversial. By "natural laws" we generally mean the laws of physics and biology whose operation we experience in our daily lives.[16] Thus, the evidence of the laws of nature will generally be the same as the evidence of man's present experience, since science derives its laws from observation. The second of E. Troeltsch's three principles of critical historical enquiry was the principle of analogy whereby we are able to make judgments on a balance of probability only if we presuppose that our own present experience is not radically dissimilar to the experience of past persons.[17] Following this principle, we would admit against Mark's evidence that Jesus walked on the water (6,48-49), the counter-evidence from the laws of nature, namely the laws of density in physics which attest that a body of greater density than water will fall through the water. Moreover, this evidence equates with our present experience that if we attempt to walk on the surface of water, we will sink, and common sense tells us that this must also have been the experience of the ancients; indeed, Mark tells us that this was the experience of his time in that he records the belief of the disciples that Jesus so walking was a ghost (v.49). Also we have reports of death by drowning from the earliest times and the ancient deluge myth relating Noah's need to build an ark to be saved. However, the evidence from the laws of physics and the evidence of our present experience do not have cumulative weight, since the reason for their coincidence is that in essence they are the same evidence—the laws are derived from the observation of experience.

F.H. Bradley argued that the universality of law (i.e. the universal operation of the laws of nature) and the causal connection (i.e. the law of cause and effect) are the ultimate presuppositions of critical history,[18] and Marc Bloch wrote that "the universe and society possess sufficient uniformity to exclude the possibility of overly pronounced deviations."[19] The natural law of cause and effect also coincides with our experience that nothing happens unless something causes it to happen, or, as St. Thomas Aquinas insisted, 'nothing moves without a mover.'[20] This law is counter-evidence against some miracles; thus against the evidence of Mark at 11, 14 and 20 that Jesus' curse caused the fig tree to wither, we would place the counter evidence that the effect of the withering of a tree must have a biological cause. D.F. Strauss' concept of myth rests on the view that "all things are linked together by a chain of causes and effects, which suffers no interruption."[21] R. Bultmann stressed the importance of this principle in connection with miracles, ". . . the historical method includes the presupposition that history is a unit in the sense of a closed continuum of effects in which individual events are connected by the succession of cause and effect"—a continuum which "cannot be rent by the interference of supernatural transcendent powers. . ."[22]

The admission of these natural laws which equate with our experience, as counter-evidence, will generally result in the judgment that on a balance of probabilities the phenomenon asserted by the Evangelist which contravenes these laws, is not authentic. This judgment is almost a foregone conclusion if the counter-evidence is the universal and uniform application of these laws, or is the evidence of our present unvarying experience. But does it accord with a truly scientific spirit of historical enquiry to exclude the possibilities that (a) there may be rare exceptions to these universal laws, and that (b) although our present experience, even when interpreted as the experience of men in general, has not included an astonishing event, like the re-vivification of a corpse, yet it might have happened?

R.G. Collingwood considered that Bradley's dogma of universal laws made true historical thinking impossible, for the historian must be free to consider all possibilities. Collingwood claimed that all truly historical events are unique, and that neither natural law nor present experience can constitute an adequate standard by which to test their authenticity.[23] Thus, the alleged miracles of the NT share "in the arbitrariness, irrationality and independence which characterize all events to some degree."[24]

We can agree with Collingwood that all historical events are unique in their particularity i.e. in the sense that any act is only done once by that actor in that time and place, but this uniqueness surely has little importance. Unlike events which contravene the laws of nature, i.e. 'miracles', other historical events are not unique since the nature or essence of that event can, and probably will, be repeated. 'A person died at noon to-day in bed A43 in a London hospital.' Nobody else can die at that time and date in that bed, but the event of death is continually repeated. In contrast, the resurrection of Jesus is rightly alleged to be unique, if historical, because, despite other alleged instances, the essence of the event, the re-vivification of a corpse, has not, so far as we know, happened at any other time, and is unlikely to be repeated.

It can readily be appreciated that proof of the existence of just one occasion of a breach of the natural laws would be of immense importance; in that the breach would destroy the principle of the immutability of the laws of nature, the counter-evidence constituted by those laws against the Evangelists' evidence of miracles would be much weakened. The creation of the world is interesting in this context. Does this constitute a precedent for unique events which contravene the laws of nature, in this case, the law of cause and effect? The world has been created by some force, and its creation to that extent accords with the law of cause and effect. But if we ask who created that force, and repeat the question again and again, is the final answer an effect (a creator) which did not have a cause, i.e. a self-existent creator? If so, the Self-Existent is a unique event which contravenes a natural law, that of cause and effect. And if one event has broken natural laws, why, in logic, cannot others? The Big Bang theory of creation appears to require the same series of questions, since the atmospheric or other elements which caused it, have presumably been created.

It can, however, be objected that we should not apply to an enquiry into the cause of creation, natural laws belonging to the nature of a created and finite world, since the rules governing the creation of that world—an act which was prior to and outside the world—may be different, so that the cause and effect of creation may, under those laws, recede into infinity. For either the succession of creators recedes back into infinity, or there is an ultimate self-existent creator whose existence, in that he has not been made, partakes of the infinite.[25] It seems difficult to answer this objection satisfactorily. Admittedly, the mind of man which is finite in that it has a biological beginning and end, is yet able to contemplate the infinite, as is shown by our above remarks.[26] Therefore, it may be said, there is not this unbridgeable qualitative gap between the finite and the infinite; the same natural laws may apply in both with the exception of the unique breach of the law of cause and effect by either the Self-Existent, or an infinite series of creators. However, from finite man's ability to understand the concept of infinity which is abstract, it does not follow that the laws governing the nature of the tangible world should apply in the sphere of the infinite. The difference between the finite and the infinite strikes us as so fundamental that the laws governing their respective natures must be different. We conclude that a breach of the law of cause and effect involved in the creation of the world is not a breach of the laws of nature prevailing in that world, since the creation occurred before and outside the world. Nor are we aware of any other proved breach of the laws of nature.

A further argument raised against the presupposition of universal laws of nature is that modern science no longer employs the idea of immutable laws, but speaks rather of probabilities and statistical generalisations. Although this argument may particularly refer to aspects of the physical world such as the structure of atoms—aspects far removed from the NT phenomena such as the virgin birth and the re-animation of corpses, yet it does make a general point. F.G. Downing writes, "The scientist can test again and again what he says . . . And he deals with very large numbers of very similar things and happenings, which makes what he says very much more certain. To be fair it does not make what he says absolutely certain: he cannot propound laws that shall never be broken. He can mostly talk about things as being very very probable or very very improbable . . . But he has a very high degree of practical certainty."[27]

We are, moreover, impressed by the claim that it conflicts with the critical spirit of historical enquiry to refuse to consider the possibility of an event which breaches the laws of nature. We consequently feel that our forensic model must take account of this possibility. Accordingly, we will treat a breach of the natural laws as counter-evidence against the authenticity of the event alleged, but that evidence will not be allowed to outweigh in our judgment the Evangelists' evidence of the event, if that evidence is strong and consistent.

II. THE RESURRECTION

We will now apply our forensic model to the examination of the authenticity of the NT reports of the most important miraculous event, the resurrection of Jesus. We will examine the evidence supporting the appearances of Jesus after death, without considering, at this stage, whether those appearances were external to the disciples and objective,[28] or internal and subjective.

A. The Evidence in the NT.

The statements of the Evangelists which constitute evidence for the resurrection fall under the following heads:

1. **The Empty Tomb.** The dead body of Jesus was laid in a tomb (Mark 15,46; John 19,42). When Mary Magdalene and others came to the tomb later, it was empty (Mark 16,6; John 20,6,8).

2. **The Appearances of Jesus after death.** The NT writers testify as follows:-

Mark.

In the first eight verses of Ch. 16 which are considered to form part of his original Gospel,[29] no appearance of Jesus is reported; there is only the report of his promise at 14,28, repeated by the young man at the tomb (16,7), that after he was raised up, he would go before them to Galilee.

Matthew.

Jesus appears to the women as they run from the tomb to tell the disciples the news of the resurrection (28,9, 'M' material). At 28, 16-20 (also 'M') Jesus appears to the eleven on the mountain in Galilee.

Luke/Acts.

Jesus makes three appearances, and the reports are all from Luke's special source ('L'). At Luke 24,13-31 Jesus appears to Cleopas and his friend on their way to Emmaus. At 24,36-51 he appears to the eleven in Jerusalem, and leads them to Bethany.[30] The third appearance is at Acts 1,4-11 where after a summary of his appearances during forty days (v.3) Luke reports that Jesus was staying with the disciples at Jerusalem, and that, after a final speech, he was 'lifted up' at Mount Olivet.

In Luke's reports of the preaching of the kerygma in Acts, there are six references to Jesus being raised up; five of those references mention the apostles as witnesses of the risen Jesus, and one adds that Jesus ate and drank with the apostles.[31] We cannot, however, treat these reports as additional evidence of the resurrection, since they probably only constitute repetitions by Luke in summary form of the detailed evidence proffered in his Gospel.

John.

Jesus appears to Mary Magdalene at the tomb at John 20,14-17. Secondly, he appears to the ten disciples (Thomas being absent) at vv.19-23. Thirdly, he appears to the disciples (including Thomas) at vv.26-29. Fourthly, at Ch.21 (although at 21,14 John calls it the third appearance) Jesus appears to seven of the disciples on the beach at Tiberias.[32]

Paul.

At 1 Corinthians 15,5-8 Paul records the tradition received by him, that Jesus appeared to Peter, then to the twelve, then to more than five hundred of the brethren at once, then to James, then to all the apostles, and lastly 'as to one untimely born', to himself.

B. Circumstantial Evidence.

It is often claimed[33] that the survival of the Church despite persecution, and its massive growth from tiny beginnings, are evidence for the resurrection of Jesus. The argument runs that the Church would not have survived or grown to that extent if the early followers of Jesus had not been convinced that God had raised Jesus from the dead. But the conclusion that God raised Jesus, does not flow logically from the fact of the church's survival and growth. There are other possible causes for the survival and growth, such as leaders like Paul, who would probably have been dynamic, even if not motivated by Jesus' resurrection. Other religions, such as Islam, have survived early difficulties, and achieved massive growth from small beginnings without the impetus of a resurrection. Following our forensic approach, we concede that proof of a fact in issue may be effected by the proof of other facts; the evidence of those other facts is called 'circumstantial' evidence. Those other facts must, however, be relevant in that they render the existence of the fact in issue more or less probable, otherwise they are not admissible. Relevance is thus a matter of logic, common sense and human experience, rather than of law.[34] In this instance, the 'other' facts of the Church's survival and growth do not, in our opinion and for the reasons mentioned above, render more or less likely the 'fact in issue', that Jesus rose from the dead. Consequently we cannot accept this evidence in proof of Jesus' resurrection.

Two other pieces of theoretical evidence for the resurrection are mentioned by A.M. Hunter. Firstly, the existence of the NT. Hunter writes, "Who would have troubled to write these documents if Jesus had ended his career as a crucified revolutionary? Every written record made about Him was made by men who believed in a risen Lord."[35] This evidence, however, would seem to duplicate the NT evidence. The reports of the resurrection giving rise to the faith of the NT authors seem likely to have originated with the witnesses whose accounts underlie the traditions in the Gospels, Acts 1 and 1 Corinthians which we have summarised at A. above and whose authenticity and strength as evidence we will examine hereafter. We cannot count the same evidence twice.

Secondly, Hunter cites the existence of the Lord's Day, and argues that no Christian Jew would have changed the sacred day from Saturday to Sunday if that had not been the day on which Jesus was first seen risen. (In fact, Jewish Christians **added** a sacred day, for they continued to honour the sabbath on Saturday and began to honour the Lord's Day on Sunday.) We do not know whether this observance of the Lord's Day was started by Jewish Christians who had *independent* knowledge of the resurrection either by their own witness of it or by access to a witness, in each case not represented in the Gospel traditions. If it was not started by Jewish Christians with such independent knowledge of the resurrection, then this observance arose from a belief in the resurrection based upon the Gospel traditions which we will shortly examine, and it provides no new testimony to the resurrection. The earliest reference cited by Hunter to 'the first day of the week' is at 1 Corinthians 16,2[36] where Paul mentions that he had previously directed the Galatians to make a contribution on that day. Dating 1 Corinthians at 53/54,[37] that direction to the Galatians was probably given not earlier than 52 A.D. It is impossible to deduce from this reference whether the observance of the first day was initiated by independent witnesses of the resurrection appearances or persons who otherwise were relying directly or indirectly on witnesses underlying traditions not represented in the Gospels: if they were not relying on a witness extraneous to the NT traditions, then the observance of the Lord's Day does not provide new evidence of the resurrection appearances, since the first observers of Sunday would in that event be dependent upon the witnesses whose traditions underlie the NT accounts.

We are also not sure that Christian observance of the first day of the week rather than the Jewish sabbath was due primarily to the occurrence of the resurrection on that day. The writer of the Epistle of Barnabas (c. 130 A.D.), interpreting Isaiah 1,13, states, "You can see what he is saying here: 'It is not these sabbaths of the present age that I find acceptable, but the one of my own appointment: the one that, after I have set all things at rest, is to usher in the Eighth Day, the commencement of a New World' (And we too rejoice in celebrating the eighth day; because that was when Jesus rose from the dead . . .)"[38] The prime reason for the observance of the first day of the week is here stated to be an eschatological one, namely that a new world started on that day. Justin (c. 150 A.D.) writes in his Apology at 67,29f., "Now we all hold our meeting together on the day of the Sun, because it is the first day on which God having changed the darkness and matter, made the world, and Jesus Christ our Saviour on the same day rose from the dead."[39] Here again the *prime* reason for the first day is that it was the first day of creation. G. Dix writes of Sunday, "It is only secondarily a memorial of the historical fact of the resurrection of Jesus."[40]

These two areas of doubt persuade us that it would be unwise to treat the honouring of the first day of the week as resurrection evidence independent of the witnesses underlying the traditions in the Gospels.

Evidence for the resurrection which is probably independent of the Gospel traditions of it, lies, in our view, in the records in the Gospels and Acts of the change of heart in the disciples before and after Jesus' death. According to Mark's evidence at 14,31 all the disciples at Olivet assured Jesus that they would rather die than deny him, but on his arrest, they all forsook him and fled (14,50), and Peter denied him three times (14,66-72).[41] We do not know of any counter-evidence against this. Yet, about fifty days' later Peter is preaching the resurrection of Jesus at Pentecost (Acts 2), Peter and John are arrested for such preaching not long afterwards (Acts 4,3), and then the apostles generally are arrested for their preaching and healing (Acts 5,18). While the detailed accuracy of Luke's reports in Acts of Peter's speeches may be challenged, there is no counter-evidence against his reports that Peter and the other apostles 'gave their testimony to the resurrection of the Lord Jesus' (Acts 4,33) even though they must all have known the risk of imprisonment and persecution.

We consider that this psychological change in the eleven from fear and cowardice to courage is admissible circumstantial evidence of the resurrection: something unusual must have happened to the eleven to cause this change, in the time between their fear on his arrest and their courage and faith shortly after his death. The evidence of this change, in our view, renders it more likely that the risen Jesus had appeared to them, for this is, indeed, 'something unusual' which could have caused the transformation. We must note, however that this evidence, like all circumstantial evidence, is less strong than direct evidence, i.e. evidence originating in a witness of an appearance of Jesus, because not only may the evidence be untrue, but also the inference from the fact of which circumstantial evidence is given, to the fact in issue, may be incorrect: all inferences are the application of the results of human observation of what *usually* happens, and in any case the *un*usual may have happened. Cross and Wilkins give an example—"People who surreptitiously possess themselves of poison are frequently up to no good, but there is always the possibility that the particular purchaser was merely seeking to acquire scientific knowledge . . . "[42] Thus not only may the witnesses lying behind the traditions in the Gospels and Acts of the disciples' change of heart have been mistaken, but the inference that the change of heart was due to the appearance of Jesus, may be incorrect.

Nevertheless, this circumstantial evidence, albeit weaker than direct evidence will support direct evidence of the appearances, but will not, alone, be strong enough to prove the appearances.

We think that circumstantial evidence *opposing* a bodily resurrection of Jesus lies in the failure of the nearly contemporary secular historians who mention Jesus, to refer to his resurrection. The omission is strange because if Jesus rose with any kind of material body, it would surely have excited widespread attention, notwithstanding the limited communications of the ancient world, and the comparative remoteness of Judaea. It is particularly strange since for Paul, the principal publicist of Christianity to the outside world, the resurrection was the foundation of his preaching (1 Corinthians 15, 14; cf. Acts 17,18). If the resurrection had been proclaimed as a subjective visionary experience of Jesus' followers, then it would presumably have attracted little interest from the outside world, but the church preached it as objective, $\dot{\epsilon}\mu\phi\alpha\nu\eta$ (Acts 10,40). Josephus, in about A.D. 93 describes Jesus as a wonder-worker and wise teacher who was crucified, but his reference to the resurrection is generally agreed to be a Christian interpolation (Antiquities XVIII,iii,3). Tacitus, writing about A.D. 115-7 mentions the death sentence by Pontius Pilate but not the resurrection (Annales XV, 44); nor does Suetonius in his comments on the banishment by Claudius from Rome of the Jews who made a great disturbance because of 'Chrestus' (Claudius 25). Even Pliny the Younger writing in A.D. 111, who had as proconsul of Bythinia questioned accused Christians in Court, only seems to have discovered about Jesus that they sing a hymn to Christ as to a God (Epp. X. 96).

Admittedly, there was much greater credulity in the ancient world,[42A] and stories of the appearance after death of religious heroes were not uncommon, as we discuss below; nevertheless the fact that the resurrection is mentioned only in the Church's own writings must be classed as relevant opposing evidence. It is not strong evidence, however, since it is both circumstantial and an 'argument from silence'.

C. Source Criticism

Having summarised the NT evidence for Jesus' resurrection at A. above, we will now consider the strength of that evidence as measured by the number of separate appearances and the number of witnesses attesting each appearance. For each NT account of an appearance may be (a) the only report of that appearance, or (b) a report of an appearance also reported in another Gospel, but which emanates from the same witness, and differs from the other report only through distortion in the delivery of either or both reports by tradents, or (c) a report of an appearance which is reported in another Gospel, and which differs from the other report because it has been handed down from a different witness of that appearance. Depending on whether it is external or internal, and individual or collective, an appearance reported in two Gospel accounts which have been handed down from different witnesses of the appearance may be considered as strongly attested. We will first consider the traditions for the empty tomb and then those testifying to the appearances of Jesus after death.

The Empty Tomb

In the story of the women at the tomb Matthew (28, 1-8) and Luke (24,1-12) follow Mark (16,1-8) with variations. John's account at 20,1-18 contains such important differences, e.g. the introduction of Peter and 'the other disciple', and the command not to touch Jesus, that this impresses us as a separate tradition. We thus have two traditions, the Markan and the Johannine testifying to the empty tomb. The Pharisees did believe that at the general resurrection on the Day of Judgment the righteous would rise bodily from their graves,[43] so that the disciples, believing that Jesus had risen, might well without further enquiry have assumed the grave to be empty. However, we do not think there is sufficient nexus between the fact of this Jewish belief and the fact in issue, namely the emptiness of Jesus' tomb for us to admit the belief as circumstantial evidence against the Gospel assertions within the principle of relevance discussed at B. above.

We accordingly accept the evidence of the empty tomb.

The Appearances of Jesus after death

a. An appearance at or near the tomb is recorded by Matthew (28, 9-10) who has added it to his story of the women at the tomb, which story otherwise follows Mark, although it heightens the miraculous element in Mark, e.g. there was a great earthquake (28,2) and the guards through fear of the angel who rolled the stone away, 'became like dead men' (28,4). John's account of the appearance at the tomb (20,14-17) is very different from Matthew's. In Matthew Jesus meets the two Marys as they run from the tomb; they clutch his feet and worship him, and Jesus tells them to tell his brethren to go to Galilee where they will see him. In John Jesus speaks to Mary Magdalene *at* the tomb, and she thinks he is the gardener. When she recognises Jesus, he tells her *not* to hold him, as he has not ascended to the Father. She then tells the disciples.

These two accounts are so different, that we think they are separate traditions, i.e. John has not redacted Matthew or the tradition on which Matthew is based. Indeed, C.H. Dodd writes concerning reports of the resurrection appearances, "In so far as there are resemblances between the Johannine and the Synoptic pericopae, they are not such as to require the hypothesis of literary dependence for their explanation."[44] However, against Matthew's evidence that Jesus met the two Marys, there is the intrinsic unlikelihood of the incident. It seems unlikely that the immediate reaction of the women would be to worship Jesus as a divine figure rather than flee in terror, and the injunctions in v.10 not to be afraid, and to tell the disciples to go to Galilee, indicate that the appearance of Jesus has been inserted by Matthew, for these injunctions duplicate the injunction by the angel in vv.5 and 7 (taken from Mark). Apparently, Mark contained no appearance by Jesus in his presumed lost ending—at least such is the inference to be drawn from his 'they said nothing to anyone' in v.8 which seems to close his version of the tomb incident. Moreover, Luke, who probably had the full-length Mark before him, does not include the appearance.

Since we therefore assign the Matthaean tomb appearance to redaction, its contradiction with John's account in relation to the handling of Jesus (takes place in Matthew—forbidden in John) is not relevant. We are left with John's account which seems to contain no internal difficulties, but is opposed by the negative evidence of the absence of the appearance in Mark which, exceptionally for negative evidence, seems to us very strong, because any report of the tomb incident would have mentioned the vital fact of Jesus' appearance, if the witness had believed it to have occurred. Paul does not mention this appearance in his list at 1 Cor. 15, but we deem this negative evidence to be of little weight since Paul's list is probably not comprehensive—it does not mention the appearance to Cleopas and friend reported by Luke.

John's evidence of the appearance is thus opposed mainly by Mark's negative evidence. Following our forensic model, the burden of proof lies on John, and since Mark's negative evidence is in our opinion of equal, if not greater, weight, we conclude that John has not discharged the burden of proof, and we cannot accept the appearance at the tomb.

b. An appearance to Cleopas and his friend on the way to Emmaus is reported at Luke 24,13-31. The appearance reported here is quite distinct from the other reported appearances, for neither in the external circumstances (apart from the eating with Jesus, cf. John 21, 12-13) nor in the content of the discourse is there any point of contact with the other appearances. Luke's evidence is only opposed by Paul's negative evidence at 1 Cor. 15 which, being of little weight as mentioned above, is outweighed by Luke.

c. An appearance at Jerusalem to the disciples is reported by Luke at 24,36-51, and John reports two Jerusalem appearances, separated by eight days, at 20, 19-23 and 26-29. The theme of Jesus offering the handling of his body in order to prove that he has the same human body as before death, is present in both Luke at vv. 38-40 and in John at vv. 20 and 24-28. Luke's vv. 36-39 (or 40) where Jesus stood among them (ἐστη ἐν μεσῳ αὐτων), re-assured them and invited handling, are similar to John's vv.19-20 where Jesus stood among them (ἐστη εἰs το μεσον), greeted them, and showed them his hands and his side. The theme of disbelief is present at Luke vv.41-43 where Jesus eats broiled fish to prove his rising with a human body, while at John vv. 24-29 Thomas's doubt and subsequent belief through the invitation to handle, express the same theme. But the differences show that John has not copied Luke, and those differences in the two traditions also convince us that the stories at Luke's vv.36-43 and John's vv.19-20 and 24-29 originate in different witnesses of the same appearance (or appearances) in Jerusalem. The evidence of these separate witnesses behind Luke and John is not opposed by counter-evidence and we accept it.

d. An appearance by the sea of Tiberias, Galilee, to the disciples is recorded at John 21. There seems to be no identity with any other appearance since the eating of fish here is on the beach in quite different circumstances from Jesus eating fish at Luke 24, 42-3; there Jesus eats in Jerusalem to prove his bodily identity while in John he prepares and gives the disciples fish and bread on the beach in Galilee, but not in order to prove his identity since they know that (vv.7 and 12) before he gives the food to them (v.13). Similarly, the fishing, the eating on the beach and the content of the discourse preclude any link with Matthew's report of the appearance on the mountain in Galilee (28, 16-20). Again, we accept this unopposed tradition.

e. An appearance with final commissioning is reported at Luke 24, 44-51 (in Jerusalem/Bethany) and at Matthew 28, 16-20 (in Galilee), and with these reports Jesus' speech (in Jerusalem) at John 20, 21-23 is strikingly similar.[4][5]

In John Jesus sends out the disciples (into the world), confers the Holy Spirit, and authorises them to forgive sins. In Luke Jesus tells them that the prophecy must be fulfilled that he should suffer and rise on the third day, and repentance and forgiveness of sins be preached to all nations; they are to be the witnesses of these things, and he will send the Father's promise on them, but they are to stay in Jerusalem till clothed with power from on high (ἐνδυσησθε ἐξ ὑψουs δυναμιν).

In Matthew it is on a mountain in Galilee that Jesus tells the disciples that all authority has been given him, and they are to make disciples of all nations, baptizing and teaching them, and that he will be with them always. At Acts 1,4-5 and 8 after a summarising statement by Luke of appearances over forty days, Luke almost exactly repeats the order from Jesus at Luke 24 that the disciples are to stay in Jerusalem to await the promised Holy Spirit from the Father; they will receive power from the Holy Spirit, and will be his witnesses to the end of the earth. At 1, 6-7 Jesus replies to a question from the disciples, that it is not for them to know the time which the Father has fixed for the restoration of the kingdom to Israel. Apart from these two verses the passages in Luke 24 and Acts 1 are so similar that this evidence of similarity outweighs in our view Luke's evidence of separate appearances at Jerusalem/Bethany and Olivet, and we conclude that in the two passages Luke has used and redacted one tradition.

In view of the evidence that Luke (in two statements) and John have placed the final commissioning appearance in Jerusalem, we think that Matthew's evidence of Galilee is outweighed, particularly since there is further counter-evidence in that this is the only appearance not near the tomb which is recorded by Matthew, and he may have placed this appearance in Galilee because of the Marcan evidence that Jesus would appear in Galilee.

The content of Jesus' words in all these four reports is so similar that we think they were spoken on one occasion which, notwithstanding their position in Luke's Gospel and in John, we think was the final mission-charge appearance, as indicated in Matthew and Acts; this was probably also the occasion of the Ascension. There are sufficient differences in the content, however, and in the external circumstances of the reports to show that no Evangelist has copied another — there are three separate traditions. Further, these differences are so significant that, not without some hesitation, we think them to arise from stories from different witnesses rather than from distortions in the transmission through different hands of a story from one witness (see pp. 112-116 infra).

f.   An appearance to Peter is reported by Paul at 1 Corinthians 15,5. The other evidence for such an appearance is Luke's indirect report at 24,34 where the eleven tell Cleopas and friend that the Lord has appeared to Simon. The order at Mark 16, 7 of the young man at the tomb to the women to tell his disciples 'and Peter' that Jesus is going before them to Galilee, does not seem to infer a special appearance to him. There is however, no counter-evidence to this early evidence of Paul, nor is there reason to think that Luke's report is based on Paul. But since the reports of both Paul and Luke in essence only state the bare fact of the appearance (to Peter), there is no evidence upon which a judgment that the two reports emanated from separate witnesses (i.e. persons to whom Peter announced his vision), can be based (although Luke's information that the eleven (and others) at Jerusalem told Cleopas and friend of Peter's vision, suggests a tradition independent of Paul's account). Yet even if these two reports were originated by one witness we have no cause to doubt them, for there is no counter-evidence.

g. Other appearances. Paul also mentions at 1 Cor.15 appearances to the twelve (eleven?), to more than five hundred brothers at once, to James and then to all the apostles. His evidence of the appearance to the twelve is early supportive evidence of the later Gospel evidence, and since Paul follows it with other appearances, this evidence supports the first appearance at Jerusalem rather than the final commissioning appearance. However, we cannot attribute Paul's evidence of the appearance to the twelve to a separate witness or even to a separate tradition on the basis of this bare statement of the appearance. And we are unwilling to place any weight on the evidence of the other alleged appearances when no surrounding circumstances are given; the appearances to the large number and to the apostles might be references to Pentecost.[46]

Finally, Paul mentions the appearance to himself, which creates difficulties, as we shall discuss later (infra pp. 27-9). Luke at Acts 1,3 mentions many 'proofs' of Jesus being alive, and his appearances over forty days, but here also we are unwilling to place weight on summarising comments without specificity.

Our source-critical enquiry into the strength of the evidence for the resurrection has shown a preponderance of evidence in favour of the following appearances of the risen Jesus, and we have placed alongside the appearances the number of separate witnesses underlying the traditions: —
1. To Cleopas and friend on the road to Emmaus (b. above). One witness — reported by Luke.
2. To eleven disciples at Jerusalem (c. above). Two witnesses — reported by Luke and John respectively.
3. To seven disciples (including Peter, James and John) by sea of Tiberias (d. above). One witness — reported by John.
4. To eleven disciples (final commission) at Jerusalem (e. above). Three witnesses — reported by Matthew, Luke and John respectively.
5. To Peter (f. above). One witness — reported by both Paul and Luke.

All these appearances are already proved in accordance with our forensic model, so that it is unnecessary to consider the additional evidence of the empty tomb. The circumstantial evidence for the appearances derived from the disciples' change of heart discussed in section B. above, is offset by the circumstantial evidence of the silence of secular historians.

The two Jerusalem appearances are attested by two and three witnesses respectively, but whether the evidence of more than one witness for those appearances is admissible, and whether the evidence for each appearance of the five, can constitute supporting evidence for the other four, is examined at p.33-7 infra.

D. The Nature of the Resurrection.

Resurrection in this context means rising again from the dead. But what kind of 'rising again' of Jesus does the evidence prove? The proved fact of the empty tomb indicates that the Evangelists assert that Jesus appeared after death with his original human body. Let us examine the evidence for and against this assertion.

For a human bodily resurrection.

The fact of the empty tomb is *admissible* as circumstantial evidence in our view to support the bodily resurrection of Jesus because, pursuant to the criterion of relevance mentioned at B. above, it renders Jesus' resurrection with his original human body more likely according to the canon of commonsense. However, the empty tomb evidence is of *little weight* as circumstantial evidence due to the possibility that the body of Jesus might have been removed from the tomb,[47] and there are pieces of Gospel evidence suggesting that this might have happened. At John 19,41-2 it is related that Jesus' body was placed temporarily in a new tomb close to Golgotha because there was little time; it was nearly the start of the Day of Preparation for the Passover, on which no work might be done. Luke's account of the burial at 23,53-4 is consistent with this hasty placing of the body in another's tomb (although Matthew at 27,60 states that it was placed by Joseph in his own new tomb). The trespassing corpse might thus have been removed by the owner of the new tomb. The other hint that the corpse might have been removed is in stories of Matthew at 27,62-66 and 28,11-15. In the former passage the chief priests and the Pharisees ask Pilate if the sepulchre can be made secure until the third day lest the disciples steal the body and claim that Jesus has risen from the dead. In the latter, the chief priests bribe the soldiers to tell the people that the disciples stole Jesus' body while they were asleep. It is only a possibility that these stories may have been Matthew's attempt to impeach the credibility of a rumour that the body had been removed by the disciples. Matthew at 28,15b writes, '. . . and this story [theft of the body by the disciples] has been spread among the Jews to this day'—a story, not, perhaps, of a theft by the disciples, but by others.[48]

Stronger evidence in favour of a human bodily resurrection is the evidence of physical actions by the risen Jesus.[49] We look seriatim at the

proved appearances (apart from that to Peter which contains no detail):—
1. On the road to Emmaus Jesus walked and talked with Cleopas and friend (24,15f.). He sat at table with them, broke bread and gave it to them (v.30).
2. In Jerusalem, according to Luke, Jesus invites the disciples to handle his hands and feet, 'for a spirit has not flesh and bones as you see that I have' (24,39). He then eats a piece of broiled fish (vv.42-3). At John 20 (in addition to talking) Jesus shows them his hands and side (v.20), and invites Thomas to handle his hands and side (v.27).
3. By the sea of Tiberias it is implied in John 21 that Jesus prepares a charcoal fire, and fish and bread on it (vv.9 and 12). He then takes the bread and fish and gives it to them (v.13).
4. At the final commissioning in Matthew he walks and speaks (28,17f.). In Luke he speaks (24,44f.), and walks (v.50), and at Acts 1,4-5 and 7-8 he talks. At John 20,21f. he talks.

The strongest evidence here is the evidence of Jesus eating at 2 (and it may be implicit that he ate, at 1 and 3), and the evidence of him inviting handling of his body at 2. Although we have rejected the evidence of the appearance at the tomb (p. 18 supra), those accounts do contain evidence that Matthew and John believed Jesus' resurrection to be bodily, for the women hold Jesus' feet at Matthew 28,9, and at John 20,17 Jesus tells Mary not to hold him (which would be an illogical command if Jesus did not have bodily substance).[50]

Against a human bodily resurrection
There is the following counter-evidence that Jesus did not possess his human body after rising:-

I. THE INTERNAL EVIDENCE

We consider the evidence in the records of the same above appearances:-
1. On the road to Emmaus, Cleopas and friend do not recognise Jesus (Luke 24,16) and only recognise him at the end of the journey in the breaking of bread (v.31). Jesus then vanishes (ibid.).
2. In Jerusalem, according to Luke, he 'stood among them' (24,36), and the report that the disciples were startled and frightened and thought they saw a spirit (v.37), indicates an abnormal arrival without the physical limitations of a human body. Similarly, at John 20,19 Jesus 'came and stood among them' despite the doors being shut 'for fear of the Jews'. Eight days later the same non-bodily appearance occurs—'The doors were shut, but Jesus came and stood among them,. . . .'(v.26).
3. By the sea of Tiberias Jesus stood on the beach but apparently not with a normal human body, for the disciples do not recognise him (John

21,4). However, he may not have been near enough to be recognised easily, for the boat was about a hundred yards off (v.8). John recognised Jesus (v.7) presumably when the boat came nearer the beach. At v.12 we read that none of the disciples dared to ask Jesus who he was for 'they knew it was the Lord'. This indicates that Jesus did not possess his usual pre-death body since if he had, the thought of asking him who he was, would not have arisen; as it was, they did not ask him because, although not looking as before death, they recognised him.

4. After the final commissioning, the nature of Jesus' departure at Bethany, according to Luke 24,50-51 is uncertain. His parting from them at v.51 (διεστη ἀπ'αὐτων) is consistent with a human body, but the addition και ἀνεφερετο εἰς τον οὐρανον (and he was taken up into heaven) is not consistent with a human body. There is good textual evidence both for the inclusion and the exclusion of this addition.[51] Although we have concluded (supra p. 19-20) that Luke 24,44-51 and Acts 1,4-5 and 8 are redacted versions of the same tradition, and that there was consequently only one ascension we prefer to include this addition, because at Acts 1,2 Luke refers back to this incident, writing that after commanding the apostles through the Holy Spirit, Jesus was taken up (ἀνελημφθη, from the same verbal root ἀναφερ- as ἀνεφερετο). Also inconsistent with a human body is the description of the ascension at Acts 1,9 where Jesus is again lifted up (ἐπηρθη), and 'a cloud took him out of their sight'.

The evidence of Paul also runs counter, in our view, to a resurrection of Jesus with his pre-death body. We do not intend to adduce that evidence at this stage, however, for it can be used more fittingly later (infra pp.27-29), and we think the above counter-evidence shows, by comparison with the NT evidence supporting a human bodily resurrection, how serious are the inconsistencies in that evidence; for while Jesus eats and invites handling of his body, he also arrives through closed doors, vanishes, and is lifted up into the sky.

II. THE LAWS OF NATURE

The re-animation of a corpse conflicts with the biological laws of nature. Obviously, millions of bodies have been buried in the course of history, but we are not aware of any well-attested case of a corpse regaining life. Nor, following our dismissal of the possible precedent of creation, are we aware of any well-attested exception to the immutability of the laws of nature.

Nevertheless, we decided above (p.9f.) that it did not accord with the proper critical spirit of the historian to outlaw any possibility from consideration, and that consequently the counter-evidence of a breach of the natural laws would not be allowed to outweigh in our judgment the

Evangelist's positive evidence of a supernatural event if that evidence was strong and consistent. However, in this case, the Evangelists' evidence that the original human body of Jesus was re-vivified, is opposed by counter-evidence of the clear inconsistencies in the Gospel evidence concerning the nature of Jesus' risen body, quite apart from the conflict with natural laws. Thus, the evidence for the Evangelists' assertion is so weakened by its internal inconsistencies, that it is not strong enough to justify a favourable judgment which would involve the acceptance of a unique breach in the laws of nature.[51A]

Since we have concluded that the evidence does not on a balance of probability when weighed against the counter-evidence, prove the Gospel assertion that Jesus' original human body was resurrected, the remaining possibilities seem to be (a) that Jesus appeared after death with a body which was not his human body, but was recognisable, (b) that Jesus appeared only in visionary form, or (c) that Jesus was after his death present to his disciples and others in the same qualitative sense as other dead human beings may be 'present' to their relatives and friends, and if famous, to others, after their death.

(a) Appearance with a Spiritual body.

Paul believed that at the general resurrection of Christians on the return of Christ the resurrected would have bodies different from their human bodies. To a questioner who asks at 1 Corinthians 15,35 with what bodies the dead are raised, he replies (inter alia) in vv. 39-44, ''. . . For not all flesh is alike, but there is one kind for men, another for animals . . . There are celestial bodies and there are terrestrial bodies; . . . It is sown a physical body, it is raised a spiritual body. If there is a physical body, there is also a spiritual body.' Although Paul writes a few verses earlier of the order of resurrection as being, '. . . Christ the first fruits, then at his coming those who belong to Christ.' (15,23), it should not be inferred that Paul believed that Christ had a spiritual body, since Paul is asserting in this verse only that Christ's rising is the guarantee of the future rising of Christians—but not necessarily with the same kind of body as Christ—and is only asserting at v. 44 that *at the general resurrection* the risen will have a spiritual body, not their human body.[52] However, in view of Paul's estimate of the general resurrection body and Philo's perception in the Genesis creation accounts of the heavenly archetypal man,[53] it is quite possible that some did consider that *Jesus* rose with an objective spiritual body.

If the evidence in the Gospels/Acts 1 be adduced to support an assertion that Jesus rose not with a physical body but with a recognisable spiritual body, that assertion is met by the following counter-evidence which is the converse of that opposing the human bodily assertion:

1. Some Gospel evidence seems to support Jesus' possession of a spiritual i.e. recognisable but non-material, body after death. For he enters through closed doors, is not recognised at first by the disciples, vanishes, and ascends into the clouds. But since we have no evidence of what the powers and limitations of a spiritual body are, we are no more able to affirm that it could enter through closed doors and vanish than to deny that it could walk, talk, prepare food and eat. What we can judge is that Jesus' concern that the disciples should handle his hands and feet or side so as to be convinced by the feel of his flesh and wounds that his body was the same as his human body, is evidence against his having a spiritual body. Since the historian also has not evidence upon which to assess whether a spiritual body may both pierce closed doors and yet feel like, and have the marks of, his previous body, he cannot categorically deny the possibility of consistency in the evidence, but on a balance of probabilities, he must judge against consistency.

2. Paul's equation of his own visionary experience with the appearances to the disciples as discussed infra pp.27-9, is inconsistent with Jesus' possession of any form of body discernible outside visions or dreams, even a spiritual body, although the conflict does not seem so great as with a human body.

3. The possession by an identifiable personality existing outside dreams or visions, of a non-material body, conflicts with our present experience and the laws of nature. Although we decided that the creation of the universe did not involve a breach with the laws of nature because creation was before and outside the world, a vital aspect of Jesus' resurrection body is that it appeared *in* the world. Its non-material nature would therefore breach the natural laws, and since the evidence favouring a non-material body is inconsistent, we do not consider it strong enough to support a unique exception to those laws, and we judge that the NT evidence is outweighed by the counter-evidence.

Against assertions of the Evangelists that Jesus appeared after death with either his human body or another kind of body, we would, if it were needed, adduce the further evidence of the aforementioned (p.1) credulity of the ancients before and after the 1st century A.D. and their less scientific approach to historiography. Relevantly to this, Philostratus writes of reports that Apollonius continued his teaching after his death, and appeared to a sceptic to persuade him of the immortality of the soul and that he, Apollonius, was still alive.[54] And Livy reports how Romulus, who passed from earth in a thick cloud, shortly afterwards returned from the sky declaring heaven's will that Rome be the world's capital, and that Romans should cherish the art of war.[55] There seems to have been a similar credulity among Jews. Enoch and Elijah, according to the Bible[56] were taken up to heaven alive, and, at the other end of the time spectrum, in the Talmud (Taanith 22a), Elijah appears to a Rabbi in a market-place, and they discuss the world to come. And in III Enoch Metatron, 'the Prince of the Presence', identifies himself as Enoch, and leads Rabbi Ishmael to a vision of the Merkabah.[57]

(b) Appearance in a visionary form

We now consider the possibility that Jesus only appeared to the disciples in an internal, visionary form. Although the NT evidence does not in our view prove an assertion that Jesus appeared with any human or other external form of body, it does prove, as concluded on p.21 supra that he did appear to one or more of his disciples on five occasions *in some way*. The evidence shows that the appearances were very active and pictorial in that Jesus ate, walked, prepared a meal and broke bread. For this reason we think the evidence indicates a presence in visionary form rather than a presence of the kind that the bereaved commonly experience of the loved one being 'with them' after death, and we discuss this fully below (pp.37-8).

It may be argued that if the NT accounts are to be interpreted as reporting the appearances of the risen Jesus in a visionary form, that evidence cannot be assessed by the historian because it is internal and subjective and incapable of corroboration by independent testimony; only the seer and persons to whom the seer has reported the vision ('hearsay') witnesses)[58] can, by its nature, give evidence of it. We will discuss the possibility of corroboration for evidence of visions later (infra pp.34-7), but whether or not corroboration is possible, we must, following our forensic model, admit the Evangelists' statements as evidence that the disciples had visions, and weigh that evidence against the counter-evidence. Just as it is unscientific for the historian to refuse to assess evidence because it conflicts with the laws of nature, so it is also unscientific to close the eyes to evidence of a vision because it may be impossible to corroborate it.

For a visionary nature of the appearances

The evidence attesting a visionary nature of the appearances to the disciples is as follows: —

I. Paul's First Letter to the Corinthians, which contains the earliest NT account of the resurrection appearances, was written c.53-4 A.D.,[59] some twenty years after the appearances and about fifteen years before the earliest Gospel account, in Mark. The tradition received by Paul is much briefer and simpler than the traditions of the appearances which are recounted in the Gospels. The Gospel traditions, in turn, contain much less dramatic detail than the reports in the later uncanonical Gospels:[60] it seems that detail accumulates in the delivery of the tradition. According to Paul's tradition at I Corinthians 15,5-8 Jesus appeared to many more people than are recorded in the Gospels; to Peter, then to the twelve (eleven?), then to more than five hundred followers at once, then to James, then to all the apostles, and finally, 'as to one untimely born', to Paul himself.

Paul refers to the appearance to himself by the same verb, $\overset{\text{\'{}}}{\omega}\varphi\theta\eta$, as he uses three times in connection with the appearances to the others. This verb, the aorist passive of $\overset{\text{\'{}}}{o}\varrho\alpha\omega$ — 'I see' — is used intransitively with the dative to mean 'appeared (to)' and it does not signify whether the appearance is perceptible by the senses or not.[61] By its constant use respecting the other appearances and respecting the appearance to himself, Paul seems to indicate that he regards the appearance to himself to be of the same nature as the appearances to the others. On the other hand, Paul might have known that the traditions relating to the other appearances testified to a bodily resurrection, but may have placed the appearance to himself in the same category in order to bolster his apostolic authority. But in the resurrection passage 15,1-11 this is hardly his motivation, since he says at v.9, 'For I am the least of the apostles and am unfit to be called an apostle, because I persecuted the Church of God.

His own experience to which he refers, is almost certainly the appearance on the Damascus Road (since he was not a disciple of Jesus at the time of the resurrection) and the preponderance of evidence shows that experience to be of an internal visionary nature.[62] Admittedly, his own descriptions of the appearance are ambiguous. At 1 Corinthians 9,1 he asks in proving his apostolic credentials, 'Have I not seen the Lord?' — '$\overset{\text{\'{}}}{\varepsilon}o\varrho\alpha\kappa\alpha$' is again neutral concerning the nature of the 'seeing'. But at 2 Corinthians 12,1 Paul speaks of his 'visions and revelations of the Lord' — $\overset{\text{\'{}}}{o}\pi\tau\alpha\sigma\iota\alpha\varsigma$ $\kappa\alpha\iota$ $\overset{\text{\'{}}}{\alpha}\pi\sigma\kappa\alpha\lambda\upsilon\psi\varepsilon\iota\varsigma$. $\overset{\text{\'{}}}{o}\pi\tau\alpha\sigma\iota\alpha$ per Bauer, s.v. is used of a vision of God or of the Lord, and the root $\overset{\text{\'{}}}{\alpha}\pi\sigma\kappa\alpha\lambda\upsilon\pi\tau$ — generally means in this context a revelation not perceptible to the senses, but intelligible to the mind. Paul then describes (12,2-4) an ecstatic vision which he had fourteen years previously, but this can hardly be his Damascus Road experience, since the Letter was written c. 54-5 A.D.[62i] which is more than fourteen years after that experience. However, at Galations 1,12 and 16 Paul almost certainly refers to that experience. At 1,12 he states that the gospel which he preached came through a revelation ἀποκαλυψεως—of Jesus Christ, and at 1,16 he writes that when God was pleased to reveal—ἀποκαλυψαι—his Son to him[63] 'in order that I might preach him among the Gentiles, I did not confer with flesh and blood'.

Clearly, Paul is the best witness on whether Jesus' appearance to himself was external or visionary, and we think the correct interpretation of his evidence in Galations 1 in the light of his visions and revelations reported at 2 Corinthians 12, 1-4 (and 7) is that it was visionary.

What Luke reports concerning Paul's Damascus Road experience must depend for authenticity on Luke having received correct information either directly from Paul or through a tradent. Subject to this, Luke's evidence that Paul's conversion experience was visionary, carries weight. At Acts 26,19 Paul in describing to Agrippa his Damascus journey, mentions his 'heavenly vision' —τῃ οὐρανιῳ ὀπτασιᾳ. This coheres with Luke's detailed description of Paul's conversion experience at Acts 9,3f. (cf. Acts 22 and 26) where Paul relates that a light from heaven flashed about him, and he heard the voice of Jesus, whereas those with him only heard the voice (cf. 22,9). The evidence of Paul himself, supported by that of Luke, plainly shows that Jesus' appearance to Paul on the Damascus Road was visionary.

Thus Paul's use at I Corinthians 15 of the same verb ὠφθη to describe the appearances to the others as to describe the appearance to himself, indicates his opinion that the tradition(s) he received of the other appearances of Jesus, described those appearances as visionary like his own.[64] This conclusion must be subject to a caveat, for it involves the assumption that the Aramaic word in the original Palestinian tradition received by Paul, which has been translated by Paul or an earlier tradent by the Greek ὠφθη bore the same neutral nuance in regard to perceptibility by the senses. Our conclusion also involves the assumption that ὠφθη had in Paul's day that neutral nuance which modern lexicography allots to it.

Paul's evidence of the appearances of Jesus being in visionary form is not opposed by the Evangelists' evidence of appearances in a bodily form since we have judged that evidence on a balance of probability to be incorrect. We think that Paul's evidence of 500 persons having a vision of Jesus at the same time is probably an exaggeration in the tradition which he received; surely such a publicly experienced vision would have received notoriety and been mentioned by the Roman historians or Josephus. Admittedly, group hallucinations are not unknown,[65] so that the appearances to the eleven are not to be doubted on that ground.

II. Paul's evidence that Jesus appeared in a vision may be supported by the report of the Transfiguration at Mark 9,2-8. Some scholars hold this to be a resurrection appearance which has been brought back into the ministry of Jesus.⁶⁶ We find it significant that this transformation of Jesus which, since it is accompanied by an appearance of Moses and Elijah, is almost certainly visionary, is not described as such by Mark, but is related as a physical manifestation in external circumstances: after six days Jesus led Peter, James and John up a high mountain, and Jesus was transfigured before them—μετεμορφωθη ἐμπροσθεν αὐτων. Bauer s.v. defines the use of μετεμορφωθη here as a transformation that is outwardly visible. Mark makes no mention of visions or revelations, and Paul's neutral verb ὤφθη is used for the appearance of Moses and Elijah to the disciples. Peter even offers to make tents for Jesus, Moses and Elijah which emphasises the down-to-earth nature of the occasion.

The probability that the Transfiguration which Mark described as an external event, was an internal vision, is supported by Matthew's report at ch.17 where in vv. 1-5 he follows Mark closely, but afterwards when Jesus and the disciples are coming down the mountain, and Mark reports Jesus' command to the disciples not to tell anybody what they had seen—ἁ εἰδον—Matthew reports a command not to tell the vision—ὁραμα—to anybody (17,9). Bauer s.v. ὁραμα defines it as 'in our literature, of supernatural visions whether the person who had the vision be asleep or awake', and in addition to this Matthaean use, cites (inter alia) its use by Luke at Acts 7,31 respecting the appearance to Moses in the burning bush, and at Acts 10,17 respecting Peter's vision of the animals on the sheet. The meaning of ὁραμα as a vision, contrasting with reality, is illustrated at Acts 12,9 where Luke writes that Peter 'did not know that what was done by the angel was real (ἀληθες), but thought he was seeing a vision (ὁραμα).

Luke, like Mark, describes the Transfiguration as an external event. At 9,32 he stresses the disciples' alertness when they saw Jesus' glory and the two with him: 'Now Peter and those who were with him were heavy with sleep but kept awake—διαγρηγορησαντες—and they saw his glory...' Admittedly, Luke reports the appearance of Moses and Elijah 'in glory'—ἐν δοξῃ—(v. 31 cf. v. 32), and that a cloud—νεφελη overshadowed them (v.34); although δοξα can mean simply brightness or splendour, Bauer s.v. notes that it can indicate the state of being in the next life e.g. Luke, 24,26, and also notes that νεφελη is used as a sign of God's presence.⁶⁷ But in view of the expressed alert state of the disciples, this heavenly connotation should not detract from the external nature of the event as described by Luke.

Mark and Luke's description of the appearance of Moses and Elijah at the Transfiguration as external when, as indicated by Matthew, it was almost certainly an internal collective vision, is, we think, supporting evidence for the proposition that Jesus' resurrection appearances which the Evangelists and Paul also describe as external events, were, in fact, internal visions.

Further evidence indicating that the appearances of Jesus may have been in visionary form, is contained in the reports of the incident at the tomb. In Mark, a young man dressed in white is sat at the tomb (16,5). Matthew and Luke use Mark's version, but embroider it. In Matthew an angel descended from heaven, rolled back the tombstone and sat on it, and 'His appearance was like lightning, and his raiment white as snow.' (28,2-3). In Luke two men stood at the tomb 'in dazzling apparel' (24,4). In John, Mary saw two angels in white in the tomb (20,11-12). The young men in white or dazzling raiment can be equated with angels, and angels are commonly in attendance in visions as the messengers of God's word. In the same way that angels announced the resurrection at the tomb, so an angel appeared to ($\overset{\text{'}}{\omega}\phi\theta\eta$) Zechariah, and told him that Elizabeth would bear a son (Luke 1,11-13). This incident is described as a vision—$\delta\rho\alpha\mu\alpha$—at 1,22. Similarly, it was the angel Gabriel who announced to Mary that she was to bear Jesus (Luke 1,26-38). Now in Matthew and John Jesus also appears at or near the tomb, and since the Evangelists presumably believed all the appearances of the risen Jesus to be of the same nature, these indications that they considered the appearances of the young men/angels, and therefore Jesus, at the tomb to be visionary, constitute evidence that they considered all the appearances of Jesus to be visionary. Our earlier conclusion that the accounts of Jesus' appearance at the tomb were inauthentic, does not affect the admissibility of those accounts as evidence of the Evangelists' subjective assessment of the nature of the appearances of Jesus after his resurrection.

Against a visionary nature of the appearances.

We now examine the evidence opposed to the evidence attesting the appearances to the disciples to be in a visionary form. Unlike the assertions of a bodily resurrection, this evidence of visionary appearances is not opposed by evidence of a conflict with the laws of nature since, as discussed below, both individual and collective visions are scientifically explicable. However, although visions can and do occur, they *rarely* occur, so the well-known fact of their comparative rarity is relevant counter-evidence in that it renders less likely the visionary appearances according to the dictates of common-sense; that which rarely happens, is less likely to have happened in a particular instance than a commonly occurring event is likely to have happened in a particular instance. Nevertheless, the strength of this counter-evidence of rarity will be reduced by any factors which render visions more likely to have been experienced in the particular instances. It is these factors which we now investigate with regard to the appearances to the disciples.

The psychiatric term for the 'seeing' of something which has no reality outside the seer is an hallucination. The Swiss psychiatrist E. Bleuler defined hallucinations as "perceptions without corresponding stimuli from without."[68] Hallucinations are not as rare as might be thought. In 1889 the English Society for Psychical Research issued a questionnaire with the following query, 'Have you ever, when believing yourself to be completely awake, had a vivid impression of seeing or being touched by a living being or inanimate object or of hearing a voice; which impression so far as you could discern, was not due to any external physical cause?' To this 17,000 replies were received, of which over 2,000 stated that, under the conditions indicated, figures had been seen, or, less frequently, voices had been heard.[69] And when Edmund Gurney investigated these cases by correspondence and interview, he found that the great majority of accounts had been provided by contributors who were manifestly sane, and had been healthy at the time.[70]

The disciples were in psychological situations which were likely to render them susceptible to hallucinations. As discussed more fully in our next Chapter, we think that the disciples believed with Jesus, that his death, as a substitute for the pre-Messianic tribulation of sinners, would enable the Messianic Kingdom to arrive immediately, and that Jesus, as he told the High Priest (Mark 14,62), would come on the clouds of heaven as the Son of Man.[71] When Jesus' grave is found empty, they are convinced that he has risen so as to return any moment as that Son of Man. In this crisis of expectation, we believe, the disciples have their visions of the risen Jesus.

L.J. West writes that although the rôle of expectation (mental set) continues to be studied in relation to perception, there can be no doubt of the significance of psychological factors in determining the nature of hallucinated objects.[72] He discusses the effect of excessive excitation, and states, "The functions of consciousness apparently reach an optimal point in relation to the level of arousal, beyond which they disorganise progressively as arousal increases excessively. The presence of marked arousal (produced for example by extreme anxiety or by chemical stimulation of the brain) is accompanied by marked disturbance of concentration. Again, contact with external stimuli is impaired this time by excessive input that 'jams the circuit' in which case spontaneous dissociative experiences may occur. Finally, as arousal reaches high proportions, the hallucinations of full-blown delirium or psychotic excitement may appear with frightening vividness, intensity and emotional accompaniment'.[73]

Although we think that the emotional arousal in the case of the disciples was principally caused by their expectation (induced by Jesus' prophecy and the empty tomb) of Jesus' arrival as Son of Man, we think that anxiety and fear were contributory elements. For Mark tells us that at Jesus' arrest all the disciples abandoned him and fled (14.50). It seems natural that their fear of action against them by the High Priest, the Sanhedrin or Pilate would continue for a few weeks, although John is the only Evangelist specifically to report that the doors were shut for fear of the Jews (20,19 and 26).

West also mentioned loss of sleep and sensory deprivation as inducing hallucinations.[74] He writes that progressive sleep loss appears to decrease one's capacity for integrating perceptions of the external environment, and that hallucinations will probably occur in anyone if wakefulness is sufficiently prolonged. Significantly, he adds that the excessive arousal of anxiety is likely to hasten or enhance hallucinatory production. In Mark, Jesus upbraids the disciples thrice for sleeping in Gethsemane (14,37,40,41), but the horror of the arrest may have prevented further sleep that night, and they probably slept little on the night of the crucifixion or on the Saturday night. Two or three nights without sleep can produce the susceptibility to hallucinations, but we can only speculate on the amount of sleep lost by the disciples. West mentions that when people are kept in isolation (i.e. sensory deprivation) information input via the senses (e.g. hearing and sight) is depatterned or reduced. If such a person remains alert, he is likely to experience vivid fantasies and perhaps hallucinations.[74] However, the indications in the Gospels (e.g. Luke 24,33; John 20,19,26) are that the disciples, apart perhaps from Thomas, stayed together most of the time, and a person is presumably only deprived of external stimuli, when in solitary confinement.

An hallucination shared by more than one person (a collective vision) is much less common than an individual one, and as all the visions which we have found to be authentic in the Gospels,[75] are collective, the weight of the counter-evidence of rarity is thereby increased. However, collective visions do occur; C.G. Jung,[76] discussing the multiple witnessing of unidentified flying objects (UFOs), writes, "It is closely akin to the collective visions of, say, the crusaders during the siege of Jerusalem, the troops at Mons during the first World War, the faithful followers of the Pope at Fatima, Portugal etc. Apart from collective visions there are on record cases where one or more persons see something that physically is not there. . . Even people who are entirely compos mentis and in full possession of their senses can sometimes see things that do not exist." West finds a possible explanation of collective visions when describing the cause of an hallucination; he writes, "It may be that the psychophysiological basis for recognition (of an external object, by the mind) requires the unconscious preparation of a perceptual engram (the physically stored memory of a previously seen object, for example) against which to match incoming sensory information for identification, significance and meaning in terms of past experience. If some external object is present but inadequately recognised, an incorrect perceptual engram may be activated to be perceived as an illusion; in the absence of an external stimulus such an engram is perceived as a hallucination. This theoretically may account for the specificity of collective visions. . . Among lifeboat survivors at sea, for example, several people who share similar expectancies (mental sets) may see the same nonexistent ship projected against the blank screen of empty sea and sky. Such an experience may persist in some of the people for many minutes, even after a logical belief in its impossibility has been communicated to all.[77] But in the case of the appearance of Jesus there seems no reason why the disciples' belief that they had seen him should not (as it apparently did) persist indefinitely; the shipwrecked would soon realise that a ship was not approaching them, whereas the disciples, it seems, received no subsequent perception to indicate that Jesus had *not* been present to them.[78]

The above evidence of the probable susceptibility of the disciples to hallucinations on account of their states of excitement, fear and perhaps sleeplessness, and the evidence of the occurrence of collective visions amongst groups possessing a common expectation, much reduces the weight of the counter-evidence of the rarity of visions. Nevertheless, since that opposing evidence still remains, we must attempt to assess how strong the evidence supporting hallucinatory appearances is.

As mentioned supra (p.21) the strength of the evidence for each appearance depends on how many admissible witnesses there are for each appearance, and on whether the proved fact of one appearance is supporting evidence for the occurrence of the other appearances. These questions will depend on whether the appearances are to be regarded as external objective events in the sense that 'Jesus physically appeared to Peter' or as internal subjective events in the sense that 'Peter had a vision of Jesus'. If the appearances are to be regarded as external events, then the law governing the admission of 'similar facts' as evidence will permit evidence of appearances by Jesus to other persons to be considered as evidence supporting the evidence of the appearance by Jesus which is in issue (i.e. being examined). In non-criminal cases the English courts will receive evidence of similar facts provided (as in the case of all evidence) it is relevant, and provided that it is not oppressive or unfair to the other side.[79] This latter proviso means in practice that the opposing party must have fair notice of the intention to adduce evidence of similar facts to a fact in issue, and thus does not apply in our literary context. The similar fact must be relevant in the sense that it must make the fact in issue more or less probable. Now A's evidence of the similar fact that Jesus post mortem objectively appeared to him does, according to the canons of common-sense, render more likely the fact in issue, namely that on another occasion Jesus post mortem objectively appeared to B. Of course, if Jesus externally appeared to both A and B on the same occasion, then we are not concerned with 'similar fact' evidence—both A and B are valid witnesses to the same event.

Thus, if the appearances were external bodily appearances, the other four of the five proved appearances listed on p.21 supra would be admissible similar facts to prove the appearance in issue. Moreover, in the two collective (group) appearances there listed, of which source criticism indicated that there were traditions originating in more than one independent witness (numbers 2 and 4), those witnesses would be valid witnesses to the same event. All the appearances would then be strongly proved.

If, on the other hand, the appearances are to be regarded as internal subjective experiences (i.e. visions), then B's experience on one occasion of seeing Jesus in a vision is not receivable as evidence of a similar fact to support A's evidence of the fact in issue, namely A's vision of Jesus on another occasion. For evidence of similar facts is admissible in civil cases for the reason that it is more likely as a matter of human experience (see supra p.34) that, for example, A did a certain act (the fact in issue) this week because A, the same person, did a similar act last week. But in the case of visions, the fact that B experienced a vision of Jesus last week does not render it more likely that A experienced a vision of Jesus this week, since the fact in issue is not, whether Jesus, as the actor (or 'mover' in philosophic language) appeared to A this week, but whether A, as the actor, experienced a vision of Jesus this week: the other fact that B experienced a vision of Jesus last week is not a similar fact because it does not render A's vision more likely: A and B are different actors and the likelihood of A's vision of Jesus depends on A's psychological state, not on whether Jesus had been the object of B's experience on another occasion.

Nor is B's vision of Jesus last week circumstantial evidence of A's vision of Jesus this week since it does not render A's vision more probable: A and B are likely to have different psychological states and external circumstances. A difference between evidence of similar facts and circumstantial evidence is that circumstantial evidence, where relevant (i.e. making the act in issue more or less probable) can testify to an act done by a different person than the doer of the act in issue, whereas similar fact evidence must relate to an act done by the doer of the act in issue.

However, if a disciple's internal subjective experience of seeing Jesus after his death was collective in the sense that the vision was experienced by more than one disciple together at the same time, then the possibility of proving that disciple's visionary experience is greater. Similar fact evidence of the experiences of the other disciples in the group is not admissible since they are not the same actors as the disciple concerned, but circumstantial evidence is admissible. Pursuant to the principles discussed above, B's evidence of his experience of a vision of Jesus is admissible circumstantial evidence of the fact in issue, namely A's experience of that vision, since, as A and B were together and experienced the same vision at the same time, B's experience of it renders it, in common sense, more likely that A experienced it.

Thus, although the evidence of the vision of one disciple on one occasion is not admissible to support the evidence for the visions of the other disciples on other occasions, since, being experienced by a different actor, it is not a similar fact, the evidence of the other disciples who experienced a **collective** vision, **is** admissible circumstantial evidence to support each member of the group's evidence of his experience of it. Therefore, the visionary experience of the disciples in Jerusalem (number 2 in our list supra p.21) can properly be attested by each of the two separate witnesses from whom we think the separate traditions sprang, and who had accordingly participated in that collective vision; similarly, the visionary experience of the final commission to the disciples (number 4) can be attested by three such witnesses. We accordingly judge that the evidence testifying that those two appearances of Jesus were visionary, outweighs the counter-evidence of rarity of visions, and they are proved to be visionary.

We treat evidence of other visions experienced by *the same person* as relevant evidence of similar facts to prove the vision in issue, and consider that evidence to be stronger if the other visions are of the same object, e.g. Jesus. For the evidence that A experienced a vision of Jesus last week renders it in common sense more likely that he experienced one this week because it shows his psychological propensity. Thus, the evidence of the visionary experiences of Peter, Thomas, James and John at Tiberias (no. 3) and of Peter alone (no. 5) are supported by the evidence of their other experiences at Jerusalem (no. 2) and of the final commissioning (no. 4). The evidence of the single witnesses who participate in the collective visions at nos. 3 and 5 and originated the traditions concerning them, when supported by this 'similar fact' evidence outweighs, we think, the counter-evidence of rarity, and we accept those appearances also as visionary.

Although the appearance of Jesus at Emmaus (no. 1) has been previously proved to have taken place, the single witness's evidence for it being visionary is not supported by similar fact evidence of other appearances to Cleopas, and we do not know who the other disciple was. Consequently, the evidence of the single witness underlying the Lucan tradition, supporting the visionary nature of the appearance, is opposed by the counter-evidence of rarity, albeit reduced in cogency by the factors described above. If there were no other evidence we would have to judge the visionary nature of that appearance unproved, since the burden of proof is on the asserter of its visionary nature, and in view of the balance of probability as we see it, that burden seems undischarged. However, since we have previously concluded that the appearances were not with a human or other kind of external body, and that the other four appearances were visionary, it would be obtuse not to accept these conclusions as relevant additional evidence that the Emmaus appearance too, was visionary, and we accordingly consider the counter-evidence to be overborne, and accept the Emmaus appearance also as visionary.

(c) **Presence of Jesus like that of loved one to bereaved**

Our conclusion that Jesus was present in visionary form to his disciples after his death, suggests that the nature of his presence was different from the nature of the presence of their loved one sometimes experienced by bereaved relatives.

Evidence supporting the difference between the visionary experience of the disciples and the bereavement experience, lies in the dramatic psychological change in the disciples. As discussed above (p.15) the disciples forsook Jesus and fled on his arrest, yet at Pentecost and afterwards they preached the kerygma notwithstanding persecution and arrest.

This evidence of psychological change does not support or oppose the visionary nature of the appearances to the disciples, but it does support the suggestion that Jesus' personality was present to the disciples in a way differing from the presence of the loved one to bereaved relatives. Relatives and friends are sometimes comforted, and strengthened to continue living with fortitude, by the felt presence of the departed dear one,[80] and unknown devotees of their deceased heroes are sometimes inspired by the 'presence' of the great man or woman,[81] but for neither category would it be claimed that the effect of the 'presence' is so cataclysmic as to inspire a continuing course of conduct so contrary to past character, as did the appearances of Jesus to the disciples.

The comparative emotional intensity of different experiences is, being internal and subjective, very difficult to assess, but we are inclined to think that the disciples' visions of Jesus, the mystical presence of Jesus experienced by the devout Christian, and the presence of the departed loved one or hero, felt by relatives and friends, or devotees, differ from each other in reducing degrees of intensity rather than in nature.[82] Jesus did not, so far as we know, make a resurrection appearance to Stephen, yet Stephen no doubt experienced the mystical presence of Jesus (he is described at Acts 6, 3 and 8 as 'full of Spirit' and 'full of power'), and finally, immediately before death, he has a vision of the Son of Man at the right hand of God (Acts 7,55-6). Similarly, those religious mystics, including the OT prophets, who have felt God, Jesus or Mary to be very close, have in several instances experienced visions of God,[83] Jesus or Mary, so perhaps the vision is a more intense experience of the mystical presence of the revered, which in turn, is a more intense example of the presence of the loved one felt by the bereaved.[83A]

III. CONCLUSIONS

To summarise our discussion in this Chapter, we determined that:

1. A forensic model is appropriate and adaptable to an historical inquiry.
2. The fact that a Gospel assertion involves a breach of the natural laws should form counter-evidence to the evidence provided by the assertion.
3. The counter-evidence of the natural laws should prevail unless the evidence supporting the Gospel assertion is strong and consistent. Openness to the possibility of a breach of those laws is the correct attitude of the historian, notwithstanding that, so far as we know, there has not (even in the case of creation) been a proved breach of those laws.
4. Respecting the Resurrection, the NT evidence[84] does establish an appearance of some kind by Jesus after death.
5. The evidence is not sufficiently strong and consistent to outweigh, on a balance of probabilities, the counter-evidence of the natural laws, and to establish that Jesus' body after his death was his human body, or was another body which was externally recognisable.
6. The NT evidence establishes that the appearances by Jesus were of a visionary nature.
7. Through application of the forensic rules governing the admissibility of similar facts and circumstantial evidence, it was shown that the evidence for the visionary nature of all the appearances by Jesus, except the appearance on the road to Emmaus (no.1), was strong.

Postscript.

If an historian may be permitted a theological afterthought, albeit a controversial one, it seems unfortunate for the peace of mind of 'honest doubters' that belief in an external bodily resurrection of Jesus has, apparently since the time of the Apostles' Creed, formed a corner-stone of orthodoxy. Paul supplied proof-texts for this dogma at 1 Corinthians 15,12-19, of which we may take v.14 as typical—"if Christ has not been raised, then our preaching is in vain, and your faith is in vain." (This has historically been understood as referring to Jesus' bodily resurrection, although, following our interpretation, supra, of vv.1-8, we think Paul meant visionary resurrection, as on the Damascus Road.) But why should our faith be in vain if Jesus was raised in the same way as Christians hope to be raised, i.e. in soul, leaving their human bodies on earth? The primitive confession, 'Jesus is Lord' (1 Cor.12,3) in the sense of arbiter of a man's life can conscientiously be made without belief in a bodily resurrection of Jesus. John the Evangelist saw Jesus' glory primarily in his crucifixion rather than his resurrection.[85]

If we crave a special, because bodily, resurrection for Jesus on the ground that it will demonstrate God as putting his seal of approval on Jesus' life and death, are we not like the Pharisees, seeking a sign when we should be using our God-given faculty of reasoning? Why should the appearances and teaching of Jesus in visions be considered less authoritative and significant than if they were by a bodily Jesus? G. Thiessen has well said, "He appeared to many people after his death. And what if those appearances were fantasies and hallucinations?! Why shouldn't God use fantasies and hallucinations to address a message to us?"[86] Whether or not Jesus revealed to men God's will as to how they should live, can safely be left to man's judgment based on the Gospel records of the loving and self-sacrificial nature of his life and death.

NOTES

1. Sheffield, 1986.
2. **Op. cit.** pp15-16.
3. **Op. cit.** pp15-18.
4. Convincing evidence of this credulity is the success of the 2nd century A.D. religious charlatans, Alexander of Abonuteichos and Peregrinus or Proteus described by Lucian of Samosata, and discussed in **The Myth of God Incarnate**, ed. J. Hick, London, 1977, pp.89-92. Lucian writes of Peregrinus who at one stage joined the Christians in Palestine, "He was prophet, cult-leader, head of the synagogue, and everything all by

himself... and they revered him as a god... next after that other whom they still worship, the man crucified in Palestine..."(p.90).

Regarding the attitude to factual accuracy, what H.J. Cadbury in **The Making of Luke-Acts**, London, 1958, wrote at pp.319-20 of the 'professional' Luke is probably even truer of the other Evangelists:- "The ideals of verification or research that we count so important, his contemporaries largely ignored... In the fiction of speeches, in indifference to dates and to other minor data, in objectivity and in many other traits... Luke belongs to the ancient rather than to the modern standards."

5. J. Dewey in **The Catholic Biblical Quarterly**, Vol. 49 No. 4 October 1987, p. 664.
6. To secure in England a conviction in a criminal case, it is necessary to show that the accused is guilty 'beyond reasonable doubt.'
7. 'The Burden of Proof in Historical Jesus Research', **Expository Times** 82 (1972) pp.116-119 at p.118.
8. **Rediscovering the Teaching of Jesus**, London, 1967, Ch.1.
9. **The Parables of Jesus**, London, 1972^3, passim.
10. **A Lawyer among the Theologians**, London, 1973, p.24.
11. On pp.55, 58, 60, 61, 62, 77-8, 112, 120 etc.
12. **The Historian and the Believer**, London, 1967, p.72.
13. Cf. Booth, op. cit. p.226, n.16. However, contrary to the impression which I may have given in that note, I do not think that the hearsay rule would exclude evidence of the Gospel reports of Jesus' words which, of course, are remote hearsay in many cases, having been handed down by several tradents before reaching the Evangelist. For hearsay evidence is only barred if A is reporting what B told him in order to establish the **truth** of what B said; the historian is only using the Evangelist's reports of Jesus' words as evidence to prove that Jesus **said** those words—that they are authentic; whether they are true or not (e.g. whether he was the Son of Man and would come on the clouds of heaven) is left to the judgment and faith of the reader.
14. 'Present Standpoints and Past History' in **The Philosophy of History in our Time**, ed. H. Meyerhoff, New York, 1959.
15. Cf. N. Anderson, op. cit. p.115, and see n.5A supra.
16. F.G. Downing writes in **The Church and Jesus**, London, 1968, p.138, "... it is accepted that the events which interest historians happen 'in the setting of 'natural events' that fall within the scope of various sciences' general laws... Men could not carry their severed heads... and stones did not float in air—nor in wells."
17. See his **Gesammelte Schriften** II, pp.729-753.
18. **Collected Essays**, Oxford, 1935, Vol. I, p.21.

19. **Op. cit.** p.115.
20. **Summa Theologica,** Book i, The Five Ways.
21. **The Life of Jesus Critically Examined,** E.T., G. Eliot, 5th edn. London, 1906, Sec. 14.
22. **Existence and Faith,** ed. S.M. Ogden, New York, 1961, pp.291-2.
23. **The Idea of History,** Oxford, 1946, p.139.
24. R.R. Niebuhr, **Resurrection and Historical Reason,** New York, 1957, p.171.
25. Aquinas, ibid., rejects a series of movers ad infinitum, and insists that there must at some stage be an unmoved mover; this, however, is the application of the laws of this world to the realm of the infinite.
26. But cf. Descartes who argues (**Meditations** 3, 37) that the ability of himself, a finite being, to hold the idea of God, an infinite being, must have been implanted by that infinite being (and therefore God existed).
27. **Op. cit.** p.136.
28. C.F.D. Moule, quoting G.W.H. Lampe in **The Significance of the Message of the Resurrection for Faith in Jesus Christ,** London, 1968. at p.3 calls 'objective' in this context "question-begging". We think 'external' and 'internal' (to the disciples) are clearer, but 'objective' and 'subjective' are similar in meaning, and are well-known terms.
29 B.M. Metzger's Committee in **A Textual Commentary on the Greek NT,** London/New York, 1971 at pp.122-6 concludes that the original Gospel ended at v.8. The unfulfilment in either the first eight verses or the longer ending, of the promised appearance in Galilee which the reader naturally expects to be reported later in view of its essential importance, persuades us that the end of Mark's Gospel was lost, more than does the conflicting linguistic views of scholars over whether ἐφοβουντο γαρ could form a grammatically correct end to the Gospel. Although evidence for the longer ending comes from the first half of the second century, the traditions in it disclose little new evidence beyond that in the other Gospels, and we consider them secondary.
30. We discuss infra pp.19-20 whether Jesus is first 'lifted up' here.
31. See the synoptic chart at the end of C.H. Dodd's **The Apostolic Preaching and its Developments,** London, 1936.
32. Scholars differ over whether chapter 21 which, in view of the peroration at the close of chapter 20, is clearly an appendix, was an afterthought of the Evangelist or the work of another. This appendix was issued as part of the Gospel from the earliest times, being quoted by Tertullian (**Scorp.** 15) and treated by Origen in his **Commentary** as equal with the other chapters. See further J.H. Bernard, **John,** ICC, Edinburgh, 1928, pp.687-8. Since ch. 21 is thus early, and contains new traditions, its inclusion in the Gospel evidence is, in our opinion, justified.

33. E.g. by A.M. Hunter, **The Work and Words of Jesus,** London, 1950, p.129, and J. Hick, op.cit. p.170.
34. See **Halsbury's Laws of England,** London, 1979^4, Vol.17, para.3 and Cross and Wilkins, **Outline of the Law of Evidence,** London, 1981^5, p.217; also Hart v. Lancashire & Yorkshire Railway, 1869, 21 L.T. 261 wherein lies Baron Bramwell's delightful dictum, "Because the world gets wiser as it gets older, it was not therefore foolish before."
35. Ibid.
36. Other NT references to 'the first day of the week' are at Acts 20,7 and Revelations 1,10.
37. See C.K. Barrett, **1 Corinthians,** London, 1968, p.5, "the early months of 54, or possibly towards the end of 53."
38. Translated by M. Staniforth, **Early Christian Writings,** London, 1968, p.215.
39. Our translation.
40. **The Shape of the Liturgy,** London, 1945, p.337, and see J.A. Jungmann, **The Early Liturgy,** E.T. London, 1959, p.19-24.
41. John records that after the Crucifixion they were gathered behind closed doors 'for fear of the Jews' (20,19).
42. Cross and Wilkins, op.cit. p.18.
42A. Seen n. 4 supra and M. Bloch, **The Historian's Craft,** E.T. Manchester, 1954, pp.134f.
43. G.F. Moore, **Judaism,** New York, 1971, Vol I, pp.379-81. The Sadducees probably reflect the bodily resurrection view of the Pharisees (since the Sadducees themselves did not believe in the general resurrection) in their question to Jesus at Mark 12, 19-23.
44. **Historical Tradition in the Fourth Gospel,** Cambridge, 1963, pp.144-5.
45. R. Bultmann in **The History of the Synoptic Tradition,** E.T. Oxford, 1972, at p.288 identifies two motifs which are found separately or together in the resurrection stories — the proof of the resurrection by the appearances of the risen Lord, and the missionary charge of the risen Lord.
46. See E.W. Burton, **Galations,** ICC, Edinburgh, 1920, p.434.
47. See H. Kung, **Eternal Life,** E.T. London, 1984, pp.130-1.
48. A Greek inscription dating from the last years of Augustus or somewhat later, found in Palestine, is an edict (enforceable by death) against removing buried bodies. See Josephus, **Jewish Antiquities,** Loeb edn. Vol. p.27, note d.
49. Physical actions are, of course, reported of angels, e.g. Genesis 19, 1-22 and Isaiah 6,1-8, but we incline to treat such apparitions as visionary: see infra pp.29-31.

50. Cf. B. Lindars, **John**, London, 1972, p.607.
51. See Metzger, op. cit. pp.189-90.
51A. E. von Dobschütz, **The Apostolic Age**, London, 1909, p.16, writes, "The materialistic features which are ascribed to [the appearances] by the Gospels and the Acts of the Apostles are due to later elaboration. Men wished to have them thus palpable because it seemed that only in this way was it possible to make certain of their reality. To us, on the contrary, the spiritual element, which distinguishes the Pauline conception, but of which traces are seen in other accounts too, is a proof that something real was here experienced, although the age had no adequate form in which to represent it.
52. This is consistent with Jesus' own teaching at Mark 12,25, 'For when they rise from the dead, they neither marry nor are given in marriage, but are like angels in heaven.'
53. **Legum Allegoriae**, i,31.
54. **Life of Apollonius**, viii, 30-end.
55. **Annales** I,16.
56. Genesis 5,24; 2 Kings 2,11.
57. For further examples of this credulity in both the Hellenistic and Jewish worlds (although a sharp contrast cannot be drawn between the two in this respect) see **The Myth** supra, ch.5.
58. As discussed above (p.40 n.13) the evidence of a 'hearsay' witness is admissible to prove what the person whom he heard, said, but not to prove whether what that person said, is true. Thus, the evidence of the person to whom the seer has mentioned his vision, should not be admissible to show that the seer had a vision, but only to show that the seer **said** that he had a vision. However, in England 'first-hand hearsay' is now admissible to prove even the **truth** of what the witness was told. (Civil Evidence Act, 1968).
59. See n.37.
60. See e.g. Gospel of Nicodemus, ch.15.
61. See W. Michaelis, **TDNT**, Vol. V. Michigan, 1967, p.358 and on this verb generally W. Marxsen in **The Significance**, supra, at pp.26-8.
62. This is, we think, a minority view, see e.g. C.K. Barrett, **2 Corinthians** London, 1973, p.308.
62A. See Barrett, op. cit. pp.5 and 11.
63. The Greek here is '$\dot{\varepsilon}\nu\ \dot{\varepsilon}\mu o\iota$' – 'in me', but Burton, op. cit. pp.50-51 points out (inter alia) that if Paul had meant that God revealed his Son to others through Paul's preaching etc. that would have required '$\delta\iota\alpha\ \dot{\varepsilon}\mu o\upsilon$' or an addition such as $\tau\omega\ \kappa o\sigma\mu\omega$.
64. This also, we think, is a minority view, see e.g. G. Delling in **The Signicance**, supra at pp.84-5.

65. See Michaelis **op. cit.** Vol. V, p.354 and discussion on pp.33-4 infra.
66. A difficulty affecting this view is the then superfluous presence of Moses and Elijah in the story. For discussion, see V. Taylor, **Mark**, London, 1955, pp.386-8.
67. Cf. the pillar of cloud which led the Israelites (Exodus 13,21) and the cloud which took Jesus out of the apostles' sight (Acts 1,9).
68. Cited by L.J. West in **The New Encyclopaedia Britannica Macropaedia**, 15th edn. Chicago, 1985, Vol.25, p.492, s.v. 'Perception'.
69. Per Alexander Mair in **Encyclopaedia of Religion and Ethics**, Edinburgh, 1913, at p.483.
70. Per Brian Inglis in **The Unknown Guest**, London, 1987 at p.124.
71. Cf. A. Schweitzer, **The Mysticism of Paul the Apostle**, E.T. London, 1953^2, p.62 and **My Life and Thought**, E.T. London, 1933, p.52.
72. op.cit. p.495.
73. op.cit. p.494.
74. ibid.
75. Paul mentions individual appearances to Peter and James, and the appearance to Peter is also indirectly reported in Luke's Gospel at 24, 34.
76. **The Collected Works**, London, 1970^2, Vol. 10, p.314.
77. op.cit. p.495.
78. D.J. West in **Psychical Research Today**, London, 1962, at pp.54-55 gives religious and secular instances where belief in the experiences has persisted, and notes, "there is no doubt that collective religious visions have occured." A recent well-publicised series of collective visions are those of the Virgin Mary experienced over 2700 times over 7 years by teenagers in Medjurgorje, Yugoslavia.
79. Per Lord Denning in **Mood Music Publications Ltd., v. De Wolfe Ltd.** (1976), 1 A.E.R. 463, a copyright case, where the plaintiffs were held entitled to bring in evidence of other infringements by the defendants, similar to those alleged.
80. Agnes Whittaker notes in **All in the End is Harvest**, London, 1984, p.41 that dreams and day-time visions of seeing a person can be especially vivid in bereavement.
81. See letter from G.W.H. Lampe quoted in **The Significance**, supra, p.6. According to a B.B.C. wireless broadcast on a recent anniversary of the death of Elvis Presley, a fervent admirer of his singing still feels his presence with her, and in the Presley cult there are some who believe he is still alive.
82. Cf. Lampe cited ibid.
83A. H.W. Montefiore, in **Beyond Reasonable Doubt**, London, 1963, writes, at p.24 "The Resurrection appearances have something in

common with appearances of people shortly after their death (sometimes called "veridical hallucinations") which are recorded in the annals of the Society for Psychic Research. I do not know what would have happened if you or I had been present with a camera; but I suspect that Jesus' Resurrection appearances would not have shown up."

CHAPTER II.

'Demons cross to Centre'

The greater credulity of the ancients, mentioned in Ch.1, also affects the strength as evidence of the Gospel assertions concerning demons. The assertions there, express or implicit, that Satan, demons and unclean spirits (see Excursus II) conversed with Jesus, and were physically active (e.g. Matthew 4,5; Mark 5,13), are, like the Resurrection, opposed by the counter-evidence of the laws of nature or our experience of life (which, as we noted in Ch.1, generally co-incide). Our experience of life is that invisible personalities do not talk to us, or otherwise make themselves known to us, although spiritualist mediums and others would claim to converse with the spirits of the dead, for which there is also OT evidence (Saul and the witch of Endor, 1 Samuel 28).[1] We think, however, that the strength of spiritualist evidence is weakened by the possibility that the claimed contact with spirits may be only subjective experience, such as hallucination (see Ch.1), or may be induced by deception.[2] It is also our experience that personalities alien to ourselves (other than microbes etc.), be they corporeal or incorporeal, demonic or benevolent, do not inhabit our bodies. However, as argued by Collingwood, it would be unscientific for the historian to exclude any possibility, so we cannot deny the possibility that Satan and demons do exist. Consequently, if the Gospel evidence is strong and consistent, we should grant its dominance over the evidence of experience.

However, the Gospel evidence is not strong. For example, we discuss Jesus' temptation by Satan below, and the conversation between them, which is only reported in Q (Matthew and Luke), could, if authentic, only have been passed on by Jesus himself: it seems at least possible that Jesus or tradents presented as an external verbal exchange an inward temptation which Jesus naturally believed was the work of Satan.

Nor is the external evidence for the existence of demons strong. In some cases it is the demoniac who speaks to Jesus (e.g. Mark 5,6-7; 1,24), whereas in other cases the demon(s) inside the demoniac are reported as the speaker (e.g. Mark 1,26; 3,11; 5,11). Indeed, in both the exorcisms at Mark 1 and 5, first the demoniac is reported as crying out, and then the demons. The evidence is further confused by the fact that in one instance (the Gadarene demoniac) Mark reports the demoniac as speaking, while Matthew, altering Mark, puts the same question in the mouths of the demons. Probably the correct interpretation of the evidence is that the demoniacs addressed Jesus, but Jesus and the onlookers, due to the cultural beliefs of their day, attributed any eccentric speech of a demoniac to the demons.[3] We accordingly conclude that the rather confused Gospel evidence for the existence of Satan and demons, supported by the evidence of spiritualists, is outweighed by the evidence of our experience.

However, in this Chapter we are concerned not so much with the *reality* of the existence of Satan and demons, but rather with the extent of the influence which a subjective *belief* in their existence and powers exercised over the life and thought of Jesus.

Demons deserve the stage direction at the head of this Chapter rather than the waiting in the wings which they have endured in recent Biblical study.[4] J. MacQuarrie considers that belief in demonic powers "can hardly be said to be prominent in the NT",[5] and W. Foerster writes, "In the main it is astonishing how little the Synoptists depict the life and passion of Jesus as a battle against Satan, and how seldom Satan is mentioned at all in them."[6] However, we submit in this Chapter that not only do Satan and his demon underlings have important rôles in the healing ministry of Jesus, but that the destruction of them, being a pre-condition of the coming of the Kingdom of God, was the main purpose of Jesus' life and death. This was recognised by E. Hoskyns and N. Davey who wrote, "The purpose of Jesus was to work out in a single human life complete obedience to the will of God . . . But the obedience of Jesus was also a conscious conflict. It was a conflict with the prince of evil for the freedom and salvation of men and women. Upon the outcome . . . depended human freedom from sin."[7]

I. HISTORY OF DEMONS

Demons play a part at every stage of Jesus' career as portrayed in the NT. This is not surprising since in the time of Jesus Jews believed that Satan and his minions were responsible for most kinds of natural and voluntary evil in the world. This belief was of comparatively late origin. Before the Exile both good and evil were attributed to Yahweh. At Isaiah 45,7 Yahweh says, "I form light and create darkness, I make weal (Heb. shalom = peace) and create woe (Heb. *ra* = distress)".[8] At Amos 3,6 we read, "Does evil (Heb. *raah* — evil, distress)[8] befall a city unless the Lord has done it?"[9] However, during the period of domination by Persia (538-331 B.C.) and, perhaps, even during the Exile in Babylon, the Jews came into contact with the teaching of the prophet Zarathushtra (in Greek, Zoroaster) which regarded the one God Ahura Mazda and his six personified attributes as in perpetual battle with Angra Mainyu, the creator of all evil, and his retinue of inferior demons.[10] The Jews had previously ascribed both personal suffering and national disaster to their own lack of devotion to Yahweh. Thus, at Isaiah 1,5 Yahweh says, "Why will you still be smitten that you continue to rebel?" Also respecting national disaster, Yahweh says at Amos 2, 4, "For three transgressions of Judah, and for four, I will not revoke the punishment; because they have rejected the law of the Lord . . . " The same source is shown for personal suffering at Ezekiel 18,30, ". . . Repent and turn from all your transgressions lest iniquity be your ruin." But from Persia the Jews received the idea that sin and suffering arose from the direct interference of a malevolent spirit, in Hebrew *satan*. Thus, at Zechariah 3,1 Satan is the angelic accuser of Joshua, the High Priest who represents Israel. At Job 1,6f. Satan is again the accuser of Man in the Court of God, and with God's permission inflicts suffering on Job, to test him. However, Satan is acting in the OT only under the jurisdiction of, or with the authority of, God, and does not appear as a fallen spirit working against God.

While the Jewish belief in Satan may be attributed to the influence of Zoroaster, the Jews' acquaintance with demons and the like may have originated much earlier in the animistic beliefs of the primitive nomad. For he believed in the continued existence of the souls of the dead, and that certain stones, places and animals contained spirits for good or ill. Although the OT material appears to have been revised so as to show all creation and spiritual beings as subject to the one God, Yahweh, traces are still present of the old belief in spirits. E.O. James writes, ". . . the nomad Hebrews, like their Semitic kinsmen, had an elaborate demonology of jinn, afrit and ghul, however carefully a veil has been drawn over this aspect of their cult in the OT."[11] For example, at every sanctuary a stone (menhir) was set up and regarded as the abode of an indwelling el or supernatural being, and the menhir was anointed in order to renew the strength of the occupant spirit. Jacob, after his dream of the ladder to heaven and of God giving him the land, next morning set up a pillar, and anointed it with oil (Genesis 28, 1-10). Similarly, in that the stone set up by Joshua at 24,26 was announced by him to be a witness to all the words of the Lord, he apparently believed it had an indwelling personality. There are references to evil spirits also in sources which almost certainly originate in times long before the Exile. At 1 Samuel 16,14 we read, "Now the Spirit of the Lord departed from Saul, and an evil spirit from the Lord tormented him." The statement that the evil spirit is from God is repeated at vv.15,16 and 23, and it is at least arguable that this is later redaction to preserve monotheism. On the other hand, it does seem that the fact that the lying spirit was put into the prophets' mouths by God at 1 Kings 22,21, and that it was God who incited David to sin by numbering

Israel at 2 Samuel 24,1, are integral parts of those stories, and could hardly have been inserted later. Similarly, the sending by God of an evil spirit between Abimelech and the Shechemites at Judges, 9,23, does not bear the stamp of redaction. The 'spirit of jealousy' at Numbers 5,14 giving rise to the wife's ordeal by bitter waters does not seem to be connected with demonology, but rather to mean the impulse of jealousy. There is more connection with the old belief in spirits at Leviticus 16,10 where Yahweh directs that on the Day of Atonement a goat bearing all the sins of the people, is to be sent away to Azazel in the wilderness. Exactly who Azazel was, is not certain, but he was probably some kind of demon; at 1 Enoch 8-10 an Azazel is one of the fallen angels, teaches all unrighteousness to men and all sin is ascribed to him. The same concept of evil being transfered from humans to animals is shown at Leviticus 7, 14 and 53 where after the cleansing of a person or house from leprosy, a bird is sent out by the priest into the open field. Early Israelite belief in the spirits of the dead is attested by the recital at 1 Samuel 28,3 that Saul had put the mediums and wizards out of the land, and by the account later in the chapter of Saul visiting the witch of Endor, notwithstanding. In the Covenant Code at Exodus 22,18 ('E' material, 8th century) the death of every sorceress is required. Moreover, these spirits of the dead were not considered to be under the control of Yahweh; the Psalmist declares, "I am. . . like the slain that lie in the grave, like those whom thou dost remember no more, for they are cut off from thy hand." (88, 4-5). Therefore, respecting the influence of Persian demonology on the Jews, we tend to agree with J.H. Moulton, "It is only the naming and ranking of angels and the symmetrical framing of corresponding powers of evil that remind us of Parsi doctrine; the Jews always had both angels and demons, and all that is claimed is a possible encouragement from Parsi theology which developed what was latent already.[12]

Although, as mentioned above, in the OT Satan was under God's control, during the inter-testamental period this view of his rôle changed. The writers of 1 Enoch described a 'pandemonium under its king, ranged in opposition to Yahweh and the heavenly host.'[13] In that book the demons are ruled by a chief who is styled 'Satan' (54,6). They came into existence through 'fallen angels' who rebelled against God. In the words of R.H. Charles, "Their functions were three-fold: they tempted to evil (69,4 and 6); they accused the dwellers upon earth; they punished the condemned (53,3; 56,1; 63,1).[14] The myth of their origin is contained in a midrash on Genesis 6, 1-4 which describes how 'the sons of God' took to wife the daughters of men, and children were born to them. The midrash may also have been affected by 6,5 where God sees that the wickedness of man is great and the thoughts of his heart continually evil. The midrash is in chapters 6-11 of 1 Enoch which is itself from an earlier Book of Enoch, which Charles ascribes to 200-170 B.C.[15] It is related there how the angels swear a bond to descend to earth and marry women, and teach men all kinds of evil things. Azazel teaches how to make swords and other weapons, and ornaments, and how to beautify the eyes and make colouring tinctures. Other angels taught enchantments and astrology. They impregnated the women who 'bare great giants'. Among men, '. . . there arose much godlessness, and they committed fornication, and they were led astray, and became corrupt in all their ways.' (8,2). On the supplication of men, the holy angels intercede with God who tells Noah to hide, and brings a deluge upon the earth. (10,2-3). In chapter 15 (also pre-170 B.C.) God tells Enoch that evil spirits have issued from the bodies of the giants, and that these spirits work destruction on the earth and cause trouble, and will rise up against men, and against the women because they have proceeded from them. (vv.9-12).

In the Book of Jubilees which Charles dates at 109-105 B.C.,[16] at 4,15, in contrast to the motivation in Enoch, the angels ('the Watchers') descend to earth to instruct men and to do judgment and righteousness, but by v.22 they have sinned by union with the daughters of men. At chapter 5,1-3, the story of the union is related as in Enoch, for from this union 'all flesh corrupted its way', and so God sent the deluge, but Noah was saved. The cause of this destruction is re-told at chapter 7, 21-25, and then Noah tells his sons '. . . behold, the demons have begun their seductions against you and against your children', for he fears that his children will shed man's blood and eat the blood and flesh of animals after his death. Indeed, at 10,1-2, Noah's sons tell Noah that the unclean demons were leading astray and blinding and slaying their sons. Here God is believed to govern the demons, for Noah prayed to God, '. . . let them not rule over the spirits of the living; for Thou alone canst exercise dominion over them. . . let them not have power over the sons of the righteous. . . ' God then ordered them to be bound except for (on the pleading of their chief, Mastema) one tenth. Chapter 11,1-5 records how, later, the sons of Noah made war on each other, did evil and worshipped idols and 'malignant spirits assisted and seduced them into committing transgression and uncleanness.'

It is clear from the above passages that these writers attributed the whole panoply of man's temptation, disease, misery and death, to demons. In Jesus' healings madness, deafness, dumbness, blindness and epilepsy are attributed to demons, and Paul attributes his strange physical impediment to an angel of Satan (2 Cor. 12,7).

Reference to the sinning angels who were assigned to 'nether gloom' until judgment, is made at 2 Peter, 2,4 and at Jude 6, so in view of this persistence of the myth until at least the end of the first century, it seems almost certain that the Enochian view of the origin of the demons and evil was received by Jesus.

II. JESUS AND DEMONS

A. The Temptation

Jesus' first encounter with Satan in the synoptic Gospels is at his Temptation in the wilderness. In Mark's brief statement of the Temptation at 1,12-13 he specifically refers to του σατανα (Satan) while Luke always refers to ὁ διαβολος (the devil) and Matthew generally does, although he, too, mentions σατανα at 4,10 and ὁ πειραζων (the tempter) at 4,3. The account in Mark amounts to a general statement that Jesus was tempted in the wilderness by Satan for a substantial time. The accounts at Matthew 4,1-11 and Luke 4,1-13 follow Mark's general notice with slight additions and then, drawing on 'Q' material, add a description of the actual temptations. Since the publication of D.F. Strauss's 'The Life of Jesus Critically Examined' in 1834 many scholars have classed the Temptation story as legendary. Yet, employing the forensic standards of proof discussed in Chapter I, we treat Mark's general notice as evidence that Jesus did say that he had been tempted by Satan, for the source of a personal experience of this nature must have been Jesus himself. Similarly, we must treat the statements of Matthew and Luke as evidence that Satan tempted Jesus in the ways described. Against this *detailed* evidence of the temptations, however, we have to place the evidence proffered by our present experience of the intrinsic unlikelihood[17] that an evil person, corporeal or incorporeal led Jesus to the Temple and to a high mountain, uttered the tempting challenges, and offered him the kingdoms of the world. Against Mark's general notice we do not find any counter-evidence, for it is within our present experience that man is tempted to sin, and Mark's ascription of the cause of the temptation to a person, Satan, is only the product of the 1st century culture in which he lived. We therefore consider Mark's statement that Jesus was tempted by Satan for a substantial time to be proved. However, the Matthean and Lucan evidence of the detailed temptations is opposed by the counter-evidence of (a) the unlikelihood, already mentioned, of Satan's alleged physical actions and utterances, and (b) the unlikelihood, judged by our present experience, of the human Jesus believing that he *could* turn stones into bread or would be rescued by angels if he jumped off a pinnacle; if he did not have those beliefs, he could hardly have been tempted in those ways.

We judge this evidence to outweigh the Evangelists' evidence from 'Q' of the detailed encounter between Jesus and Satan, but if we pare away from that evidence the mythological form of description, we can interpret those Gospel statements as evidence that Jesus *believed* that he was tempted by Satan to use his powers and energies for selfish or vainglorious ends i.e. to acquire wealth, adulation and earthly empire. We see nothing opposed to that evidence.

It is noteworthy that in the third temptation in 'Q' Satan is able to offer Jesus all the kingdoms of the world and their glory; thus implying the belief of Jesus that they were under Satan's control. Against this dominion of Satan, the kingdom of this world, Jesus places the kingdom of God, and he sees the purpose of his life to be the bringing in of that kingdom, which involves the expulsion or destruction of Satan and his demons. The necessity for the destruction of Satan before, or simultaneously with, the arrival of the Kingdom, was probably learned by Jesus from the OT and from the elaboration of the theme in more contemporary literature. In the Beelzebul speech at Mark 3,27 Jesus says that nobody can enter a strong man's house and plunder his goods unless he first binds the strong man. By this Jesus means that a man possessed by a demon cannot be rescued until the demon is first expelled. This idea seems to be derived originally from Isaiah 49,24-5, "Can the prey be taken from the mighty, or the captives of a tyrant be rescued? Surely, thus says the Lord, 'Even the captives of the mighty shall be taken, and the prey of the tyrant be rescued, for I will contend with those who contend with you, and I will save your children." Although this originally referred to the rescue of the exiled Jews from Babylon, we think Jesus has re-interpreted it in the Marcan passage as referring to the rescue of men from the power of Satan. Hoskyns and Davey comment, "Thus Jesus wrestled with the terrible . . . power of evil in order that it might be compelled to disgorge its prey."[18]

The theme of the destruction of Satan in the kingdom of God is pursued in the Testament of the Twelve Patriarchs and in 1 Enoch, both of which may well have been known to Jesus since parts of them were found in the Qumran Library.[19] In the Testament of Simeon we read at 6,6, "Then shall all the spirits of deceit be given to be trodden under foot, and men shall rule over wicked spirits.", and at Testament of Levi 18,12, "And Beliar (Satan) shall be bound by him, and he shall give power to his children to tread upon the evil spirits." Also in the Assumption of Moses at 10,1 the two events are linked, "Then his Rule will be manifest through all his creation, and then the devil will be no more, and sorrow will be removed along with him."[19i] In 1 Enoch 10 God gives instruction to

Gabriel to destroy the "children of the Watchers (i.e. the demons), and then at 11,1-2 the Messianic bliss is described.[20] Such writings as these would form the background to Jesus' connection of the destruction of Satan with the arrival of the Kingdom.

B. Exorcisms and the Kingdom.

Jesus sees the onset of the Kingdom to be connected also with his release of sick people from the power of demons. Luke at 11,20 gives evidence from the 'Q' source (par. Matthew 12,28) at the end of the Beelzebul debate taken from Mark, that Jesus said, "But if it is by the finger of God that I cast out demons, then the kingdom of God has come upon you." Scholars have differed over whether the verb there, ἔφθασεν, means 'has actually arrived' or 'has almost arrived', but whether it represents realised or proleptic eschatology, the link in Jesus' mind between the expulsions and the kingdom is clear, and there is no evidence to counter that of the Evangelists that Jesus said this.[21] Again, Jesus connects healings with the arrival of the kingdom in the mission charge to the seventy at Luke 10,1-12 where at v.9 he says, 'heal the sick in it (a town) — θεραπευετε τους ἐν αὐτῃ ἀσθενεις — and say to them, "The kingdom of God has come near to you." τους ἀσθενεις probably means here the sick generally, but it would include those affected by demons (Bauer s.v.)

It was originally thought that demons attacked people from the outside, but by the 1st century A.D. the belief had arisen that people were 'possessed' internally by demons which over-rode their will and personality and, as discussed above, acted and spoke through the afflicted person. Only some of Jesus' healings are stated to be of the demon-afflicted, but those healings were probably the most conspicuous: Luke writes at Acts 10,38, "He went about doing good and healing all that were oppressed by the devil, for God was with him."

Although there are references in 'Q'—Luke 11,24, in 'M'— Matthew 7,22 and 10,8 and in 'L'—Luke 10,17-19, to the casting out of demons, the only exorcism reported in the Synoptics which is not derived from Mark, is the healing of a woman with 'a spirit of infirmity' at Luke 13,10-17, whom 'Satan bound for eighteen years'. Much the strongest evidence for the casting out of demons is in Mark. The healings of the man in the synagogue (1,23-26), the Gerasene demoniac (5,1-20), the Syrophoenician woman (7,24-30) and the deaf and dumb epileptic (9,14-29) were all effected by the expulsion of unclean spirits; in addition there are numerous general notices of such healings (e.g. 1,32-34 and 39).

That Jesus and others believed that in some of his healings Jesus expelled demons, seems proved by the above evidence. Admittedly, against this mainly Marcan evidence of exorcisms we have to place the evidence provided by our present experience which, as discussed above, posits the unlikelihood of persons, corporeal or incorporeal, inhabiting human bodies. Nevertheless, the Gospels reports are evidence that Jesus (and, indeed, the Pharisees in view of the Beelzebul incident, (3,22) *believed* that he expelled demons, and against that there is no contrary evidence. Moreover, there is supporting evidence in that other people of ancient times were believed to have cured affliction by expelling a demon from the subject. R. Bultmann[22] cites examples from both Jewish and Hellenistic literature. At Pesah 112b/113a it is told how Hanina b. Dosa (fl. A.D. c.80-120) exorcised Agrath a female demon, although on the terms that she could operate on Sabbath and Wednesday nights! The expulsion by Apollonius of a demon from a licentious young man is described by Philostratus.[23] Apollonius lived through most of the first Christian century. Lucian, a 2nd century Sophist, showed how widespread the belief in demon-possession was; he wrote, "I would greatly like to ask you what you think of all those who free demoniacs from the spirits that trouble them and so manifestly exorcise spectres. I do not need to go into details about them. Everyone knows about the Syrian from Palestine who understood such matters thoroughly. . . But the Syrian then used his exorcisms, and if the demon failed to respond, he would cast him out with threats. I have myself seen one come out, black and dark in colour."[24] The allegation that Jesus himself had an unclean spirit (Mark 3,30)[25] is hardly likely to have been invented by the early church, and is further evidence of the general belief in demon-possession.

There is more evidence also of the belief that Jesus expelled demons. The allegation at Mark 3,22 that Jesus cast out demons by the prince of demons, is again unlikely to have been invented, against Jesus' reputation, by the early church, and while it does not prove that Jesus *did* expel demons (because of the intrinsic unlikelihood, according to our present experience, of a personified demon even existing, let alone inhabiting a human body), it is strong evidence that the Pharisees *believed* that Jesus expelled demons. The authenticity of their allegation is also supported by the original quality of Jesus' argument in reply at vv. 23-27 concerning a divided kingdom and entry to a strong man's house.

The authenticity of the healing 'miracles'[26] (including the exorcisms) has been attacked on the grounds that (a) early Christians recollected the healing miracles of the prophets Elijah and Elisha i.e. the raising by Elijah of the dead child of the widow of Zarephath at 1 Kings 17, 8-24 and Elisha's bringing back to life of the Shunnamite's son at 2 Kings 4,18-37. They then believed that the greater prophet Jesus must have accomplished equally great things. (b) Stories of miracles collected round a hero thought to have divine powers, as in the case of Apollonius mentioned above.[27]. It has accordingly been argued that the stories of Jesus' miracles arose not because of their actuality but because of the felt need to show Jesus as doings things expected of the divine person which the early Christians considered Jesus to be.

Against this attack is to be set the fact that in Mark several of the healings are recounted as incidental to the main purpose of the stories. Thus, the story of the healing of the withered arm at Mark 3, 1-6 is to show Jesus' interpretation of the prohibition of 'work' on the Sabbath, and the hostility it created with the Pharisees. The healing of the Syrophoenician's daughter at 7, 24-30 is told not to show Jesus as a divine 'wonder-worker' but to demonstrate that while Jesus came first to the Jews, even Gentiles with sufficient faith can receive his grace. And the healing story of the epileptic at 9,14-29, has in addition to the theme of Jesus' superiority in healing over the disciples, another, perhaps more dominant, theme of the effectiveness of prayer and belief.[28] Some healing stories such as the healing of the man in the synagogue at 1,23-28 and the healing of the paralytic at 1,40-45 do appear to have as their 'point' the demonstration of Jesus' super-human powers, but those where the healing is an ingredient of secondary importance, constitute evidence that all the healings were not invented for the purpose of showing Jesus as a 'divine man'.

We consider that Mark's evidence supported by the evidence of the general belief in the expulsion of demons by other healers, outweighs the counter-evidence, and we accept that Jesus, his friends and his opponents did believe that he exorcised demons.

That Jesus saw his cures as an anticipatory sign of the onset of the Kingdom may well have been the result of the interpretation he placed on Isaiah 35,5-6 and 61,1 which describe the wonders to occur on the Day of the Lord. For when John the Baptist asks through his disciples whether Jesus is 'he who is to come', Jesus replies with words taken from those verses — 'Go and tell John what you hear and see; the blind receive their sight and the lame walk, lepers are cleansed and the deaf hear, and the dead are raised up, and the poor have good news preached to them.' (Matthew 11,4-5, par. Luke 7,22). Luke, from his own source, immediately before Jesus' quotation from those Messianic verses, shows his own belief in the link between the kingdom and (inter alia) demon-expulsion, with his brief notice, "In that hour he cured many of diseases and plagues and evil spirits, and on many that were blind he bestowed sight." (7,21). There seems to be no counter-evidence to oppose the 'Q' evidence that Jesus gave this reply to the Baptist's question; it certainly seems a very natural question for the Baptist to have asked.

Evidence that the early Christians or the Evangelists judged the coming of the Messiah or the Kingdom to involve the destruction of the demons may be contained in the exorcism stories at Mark 1,21-28 and at 5,1-13. For at 1,24, the demon, recognising Jesus, cries, "Have you come to destroy us? I know who you are, the Holy One of God." There is similar recognition and fear of consequent harm on the part of the Gadarene demoniac at 5,7—"What have you to do with me, Jesus, son of the Most High God? I adjure you by God, do not torment me." The link with their destruction at the coming of the Kingdom is more expressly marked by Matthew, who has altered the second Marcan sentence to "Have you come here to torment us *before the time?*". The intrinsic unlikelihood, judged by present experience, precludes acceptance of the Evangelists' evidence that the demons spoke thus, but the statements are evidence, without counter, that early Christians and/or the Evangelists connected the Kingdom and the destructions of the demons.

The centrality of demon expulsion in Jesus' thinking is indicated by his reply to the Pharisees at Luke 13,32 ('L' material), "Go and tell that fox, 'Behold, I cast out demons today and tomorrow, and the third day I finish my course." We accept this evidence constituted by the Lucan statement; in that it is in reply to an apparently friendly warning from the Pharisees that Herod wants to kill him, it conflicts with the 'tendenz' of Mark's attitude to the Pharisees, and there is thus no polemical or other motivation for Mark or others to have created it. The mission charges also show this centrality. At Mark 6,7 Jesus sends out the twelve and gives them authority over unclean spirits; their ministry comprised the preaching of repentance, the exorcising of demons and the anointing of the sick (vv.12-13). Although in the commissioning of the seventy reported at Luke 10,1-12 ('L' material) the expulsion of demons is not mentioned, yet Jesus may have granted such authority, for on the disciples' return they report that even the demons were subject to them in his name (10,17). Then Jesus again expresses the close relationship he sees between the expulsion of demons, the arrival of the kingdom and the destruction of Satan, when he replies (v.18), "I saw Satan fall like lightning from heaven." Whether the charge to the seventy is a variant tradition of the charge to the twelve, or is Lucan symbolism for a mission to the Gentiles, need not concern us, for there seems no reason to doubt Mark's evidence of a commissioning of the twelve with its grant of authority over unclean spirits, nor Luke's evidence of the apostles' delight at their power over the demons and of Jesus' experience of the consequent effect on Satan.

C. **Satan in the Teaching of Jesus.**

From what we have submitted above concerning the priority of the overthrow of Satan in the objectives of Jesus, it might have been expected that the subject of Satan and his wiles would have occupied a more prominent position in the general teaching of Jesus: part of the reason may be that the operations of Satan and his demons were already popular knowledge. However, their machinations do have some place in his general teaching. In his explanation of the parable of the sower at Mark 4, 13-20, Jesus explains that the seed which falls on the path represents the word which, when sown, is immediately taken away by Satan (vv.14-15). Against Mark's evidence that Jesus gave this explanation, we must place the evidence afforded by C.H. Dodd[29] and others that parables in the form of allegories were not a method of Jewish teaching but rather a Hellenistic means of conveying esoteric teaching. The fact that the idea expressed in 4,11-12 of parables intended to be understood only by those chosen for salvation, is couched in non-Synoptic language, and makes sense only as the early church's rationalisation of the Jewish rejection of Jesus' message, outweighs in our opinion Mark's evidence, and we do not accept this parable's explanation as historical. For similar reasons, we cannot accept Matthew's evidence at 13,36-43, of Jesus' explanation of the parable of the weeds, where he explains that the weeds are 'the sons of the evil one' (τοῦ πονηροῦ, the devil), and the enemy who sowed them is the devil (ὁ διάβολος). However, teaching of Jesus in 'Q' whose evidence seems to us unopposed, is the teaching about unclean spirits at Luke 11,24-26, which is tacked on to the Beelzebul pericope somewhat inconsequentially (par. Matthew 12,43-45). The warning that if a man does not fill his heart and mind which a demon has vacated, with faith in God (and other healthy interests?), he will soon find the vacuum thus created to be filled with more numerous demonic desires, seems to possess the concrete directness and originality peculiar to Jesus' thought. His belief in the future destruction of Satan and his demons as described in the Book of Enoch, is indicated at Matthew 25,41 ('M' material), and here also we have no cause to doubt the Evangelist's evidence.

D. **The Tribulation envisaged by Jesus.**

Jesus' principal concern seems to have been that the Kingdom of God should be brought in, and, as discussed above, his expulsion of Satan's minions, the demons, convinces him that the Kingdom is very near. Jesus probably believed, however, that a period of suffering, often called the 'pre-Messianic Tribulation', would have to be endured before the arrival of the Kingdom in its fulness. For at Mark 13,19 Jesus predicts a tribulation greater than any before, and that after it, the sun will be darkened and the heavenly powers shaken (vv. 24-5), and then the Son of Man will come with power and gather his Elect (vv. 26-7). While much doubt has been cast on the authenticity of the 'Little Apocalypse' of Mark 13, we do not see any strong counter-evidence to Mark's assertion that Jesus prophesied this tribulation: the assertion is supported by the 'Q' evidence of Jesus' woes upon Jerusalem at Matthew 23, 37-39 (par. Luke 13,34-35) and upon Chorazin, Bethsaida and Capernaum at 11,20-24 (par. Luke 10,13-15).

Indeed, it would be surprising if Jesus had not expected this tribulation since the concept had a long pedigree in Jewish literature. Some of the earlier authorities cited for this Jewish expectation, such as Hosea 13,3; Micah 5,10-15 and Isaiah 2,12-22 seem to speak, however, of God's future punishment of the sinful of Israel *on* 'the day of the Lord' rather than of this punishment being a *preliminary* to the 'day of the Lord'. The brief Book of Zephaniah, although written for the Israelites of the 7th Century B.C. could well have been interpreted by posterity as promising suffering at the end-time followed by God's glorious kingdom. The earliest clear prophesies of the *pre-Messianic* tribulation, though, appear in the Book of Daniel, where we read at 12,1, "At that time shall arise Michael, the great prince who has charge of your people. And there shall be a time of trouble such as never has been since there was a nation till that time; but at that time your people shall be delivered, every one whose name shall be found written in the book." And at 7,21-22 although the writer is probably thinking of Antiochus Epiphanes as the 'horn' referred to, the verses were probably interpreted subsequently as pointing to the suffering of a later end-time (indeed, 1 Enoch 62 can be construed as a midrash on Daniel 7); the verses read, "As I looked, this horn made war with the saints, and prevailed over them, until the Ancient of Days came, and judgment was given for the saints of the Most High, and the time came when the saints received the kingdom." And although II Baruch was probably written in the later half of the first Christian century, its description at chapters 25-30 of the tribulations followed by the bliss of the Messianic kingdom may well follow the thought of earlier times. The 23rd chapter of the Book of Jubilees also describes the suffering (here, at the hand of Gentiles) which would precede the study of the law and the peace of the Messianic kingdom. The tribulation is mentioned in Christian writings at Acts 14,22 and Revelation 1,9 and 7,14. A. Schweitzer wrote, "A time of unheard-of affliction must precede the coming of the Kingdom. Out of these woes the Messiah will be brought to birth. That was a view far and wide, in no other wise could the events of the last times be imagined . . . When Jesus speaks of suffering and persecution, it is a question of the afflictions which his followers must bear with him before the dawn of the kingdom. What is meant is the last desperate attack of the powers of this world at enmity with God, which shall sweep like a flood over those who in expectation of the Kingdom represent the divine power in the godless world."[30]

E. Jesus and the End-time.

Many scholars have argued that the predominance of the End-time in Jesus' thinking has been exaggerated by Schweitzer. Hugh Anderson insists that "we have to reckon with numerous other aspects of the gospel witness to him."[31] He mentions the Jesus of the parables, and the parables of the Kingdom in particular, and Jesus' teaching, as in the Sermon on the Mount, of God's providential care over all creation. Admittedly, there is a tension between Jesus' preaching of the urgency of repentance because of the pending Kingdom, and his teaching about present behaviour. But no apocalyptist can confine himself entirely to the coming crisis, for 'life does go on'. Therefore, he will perforce direct some teaching to an interim ethic, for the nature of the coming Kingdom predicates appropriate behaviour in the here and now rather than the irrelevance of morality which Paul condemned at I Thessalonians 4, and 2. Thess. 3. We think, though, that this interim teaching was subservient to the main message which was the need for repentance in face of the Kingdom which will arrive after the tribulation, and, is almost here, as shown by the initial defeat of Satan's minions in the exorcisms. Indeed, several parables of the Kingdom stress its imminent advent; the parables of the Defendant (Luke 12,57-59 par.), the Strong Man despoiled (Mark 3,27), the Waiting Servants (Mark 13, 33-37), the Ten Virgins (Matthew 25,1-12) and the Thief in the Night (Matthew 24,43-44 par.) all stress the immediacy of the Kingdom and (apart from the Strong Man) the need for decision now. This surely is the stuff of apocalyptic!

Anderson also opposes to Jesus' apocalypticism his rejection of cosmic signs and portents, and instances his refusal at Mark 8,12 to give the Pharisees a 'sign from heaven'.[32] We suggest, however, that this refusal arose from unwillingness, as in the Temptations, to seek acclaim in this way, for he was quite willing to point John the Baptist to his healing ministry as the sign of the Day of the Lord foretold by Isaiah at 35,5-6 and 61,1.

We accordingly believe that the placing of apocalyptic at the centre of Jesus' thought is justified. We think, however, that Jesus expected the prior tribulation to afflict not only the Elect, as Schweitzer claimed, but all men. For at Mark 13, 19-20 Jesus distinguishes between the Elect and 'all flesh' (πασα σαρξ) who would be killed in the great tribulation if the Lord had not shortened the days for the sake of the Elect (δια τους εκλεκτους). Jesus' belief that the tribulation would have affected 'men generally', is supported by his description of his blood as shed for 'many' (πολλων—meaning people generally) at Mark 14,24. However, we believe that these prophecies of general suffering and of the disciples' suffering were made before Jesus realised that he was to suffer vicariously, as described below.

As indicated above, Jesus thought that his expulsion of the demons signified that the Kingdom of God and therefore the destruction of Satan were imminent, and at Luke 10,18 he exclaims at the success of the disciples over demons, 'I saw Satan fall like lightning from heaven.' However, Jesus had also been expecting the onset of the prior tribulation followed by the arrival of the Son of Man to happen at any moment; he says at Matthew 10,23 ('M' material), to the commissioned disciples, '. . . you will not have gone through all the towns of Israel before the Son of Man comes.' We accept Matthew's evidence here for the early Church is unlikely to have invented a prophecy almost immediately proved false. For neither the tribulation nor the Son of Man appeared, and we agree with Schweitzer that it was as a result of the intense disappointment arising from the continued delay of the tribulation that Jesus concluded that God had decided to spare the sufferings of sinners in general.[33] Jesus had apparently envisaged this possibility for in the prayer he taught, he included "and lead us not into temptation (πειρασμον, Luke 11,4 par. Matthew 6,13). H. Seesemann writes on this petition, "What is at issue here is in no sense a test. The Lord is rather teaching his disciples to ask God not to withdraw His hand from them, but to keep them against temptation by ungodly powers. On the other hand, it is a mistake to think that the petition is grounded only in Jesus' imminent expectation of the end or to regard it merely as a request for preservation in the great eschatological tribulation."[34] We think, however, that the evidence in favour of the interpretation of this petition as a plea not to be submitted to the end-time suffering of the sinful, preponderates. For there is much textual evidence favouring the addition to Luke's version of the final petition in Matthew, αλλα ρυσαι ημας απο του πονηρου ("But deliver us from evil."[35] (6,13). του πονηρου should, we believe, be translated as 'the evil one' i.e. Satan, for the Jews thought in concrete terms, personifying abstract concepts such as evil. Lohmeyer considers this seventh petition to be authentic, and marks the "antithetic and yet climactic parallelism to the sixth petition;"[36] the meaning is 'do not lead us into the final tribulation, but keep us safe from Satan (who will inflict that tribulation).' Even if that seventh petition were *not* Jesus-material, it indicates that Matthew's church interpreted πειρασμον as eschatological tribulation.

F. The Vicarious Victim of Satan.

We also agree with Schweitzer that Jesus believed that God[37] had determined that he, Jesus, was to bear the tribulation in place of sinners in general.[38] He would, as the Suffering Servant of Isaiah 53, suffer the pre-Messianic tribulation on behalf of the many, and thus bring in the Kingdom. It seems likely that Jesus first told the disciples at Caesarea Philippi that he was to suffer in place of others. From Mark 8,27-28 we can assume that people generally and, perhaps, most of the disciples, thought that Jesus was a prophet, but he assents to Peter's declaration that he is the Christ (vv.29-30). Jesus thus acknowledged that he was the Messiah, the one anointed i.e. appointed, by God to bring in the Kingdom, and he then teaches that he will have to do this by suffering first. And here we see again how the defeat of Satan is pivotal to Jesus' thinking about the Kingdom, for when Peter rebukes Jesus for this acceptance of suffering, Jesus recognises Satan trying to persuade him, through Peter, not to suffer nor thereby introduce the kingdom in which Satan will be crushed: hence Jesus' words at 8,33. "Get behind me, Satan! For you are not on the side of God, but of men." This evidence of Mark concerning Caesarea Philippi is not opposed, in our view, by counter-evidence; indeed, there is supporting evidence in the Gospels for the popular rating of Jesus as a prophet,[39] and there must have been *some* occasion on which he told the disciples that he believed himself to be the Messiah, one appointed by God for a special task, probably a Danielic Messiah; hence the admission at the trial in the words of Daniel 7,13. Peter's rebuke and Jesus' fierce reply bear the hall-mark of authenticity—it is unlikely that the Church invented a dominical saying branding Peter as Satan!

Several speeches of Jesus indicate that he conceived his expected suffering and death as the tribulation which would bring in the Kingdom. From Luke's own source at 22,15 Jesus says, "I have earnestly desired to eat this passover with you before I suffer; for I tell you I shall not eat it until it is fulfilled in the kingdom of God." Also 'L' material is Jesus' saying at Luke 12,50, "I have a baptism to be baptised with; and how I am constrained until it is accomplished!". In the Marcan version of the Last Supper Jesus, after treating the broken bread as the symbol of his body, says of the cup, "This is my blood of the covenant which is poured out for many.", and adds the connection with the introduction of the kingdom, "Truly, I say to you, I shall not drink again of the fruit of the vine until that day when I drink it new in the kingdom of God." (14,24-5). While scholars may differ over the exact form of Jesus' words over the bread and wine, Mark's evidence of the linking of the elements with Jesus' suffering is supported by the independent evidence of Paul at 1 Corinthians 11,23-26. The counter-evidence that the consumption by early Christians of the flesh and blood of the divine hero resembles the consumption of the blood of the divine saviour in the Hellenistic mystery cults, and so might have been initiated after Jesus' death, is not as persuasive for us as the combined evidence of Mark and Paul, particularly as the ceremony easily fits into the procedure of the Jewish passover meal, and has clear Jewish features. For similar reasons, we see no good cause to doubt Luke's above evidence about suffering and the Kingdom. We discuss the Last Supper in more detail in Chapter IV infra.

V. Taylor finds links with the cosmic battle against Satan in Jesus' sayings in the Garden of Gethsemane according to Mark. He writes, "The references to 'the Hour' (14,35,41), the description of the Agony (33) and the sayings in 34, 36, 15,34, Luke 22,53b suggest that in one of its aspects the experience of Jesus was conceived as a conflict with Satanic powers; and if this inference is justified, it is probable that he thought the three disciples were exposed to similar perils and therefore in need of the injunction, 'Be vigilant, and pray.' These ideas are strange to the modern man, but not to the ancient world."[40] The Lucan evidence of Jesus' words to those arresting him at 22,53b is particularly relevant in showing how Jesus related the arrest to the cosmic battle, — "But this is your hour and the power of darkness." Admittedly, this Marcan evidence adduced by Taylor could only have been within the knowledge of Jesus and the three disciples, and the latter were hardly in a state of alertness! On the other hand, we would not expect the early Christians who considered Jesus to be divine, to have invented stories of his being distressed and praying that he might be allowed to avoid the suffering; nor to have invented reminiscences of the three leading disciples who neglected through sleep the dominical injunction to watch and pray. Accordingly, notwithstanding the limited accessibility to the evidence of Mark, we accept it, and there is no evidence to counter Luke's evidence concerning Jesus' complaint to his captors.

Thus Jesus, by his decision to take the road to Jerusalem, to suffer and die, was accepting the tribulation which was the rightful lot of men in general on account of their sins.[40A] At Isaiah 53,10-11 the prophet says of the Servant, "Yet it was the will of the Lord to bruise him; he has put him to grief; when he makes himself an offering for sin (Heb. *asham*), . . . he shall prolong his days; . . . by his knowledge shall the righteous one, my servant, make many to be accounted righteous; and he shall bear their iniquities. Therefore I will divide him a portion with the great,

. . . because he poured out his soul to death, and was numbered with the transgressors; yet he bore the sin of many. . . " That Jesus saw himself in this rôle of bearing the sins of others would be logical if he believed he had to do so in order to bring in the Kingdom. That he *did* see himself in this rôle, is supported by the Marcan and Lucan Supper sayings discussed above. This would also be supported by the ransom saying (Mark 10,45) which, as J. Jeremias points out,[41] is very closely connected with the eucharistic words. The saying reads, "For the Son of Man also came not to be served but to serve, and to give his life as a ransom for many.", but evidence against its authenticity is constituted by a similar saying of Jesus reported by Luke at 22,27, but which omits the references to the Son of Man and to giving his life as a ransom. The full verse reads, "For which is the greater, one who sits at table or one who serves? Is not the one who sits at table? But I am among you as one who serves." The teaching of humble service has the stamp of authenticity, and coheres with the washing of the disciples' feet at John 13,5, but Luke's omission of the 'ransom' part, and perhaps his omission of the reference to the Son of Man, constitute evidence that the 'ransom' part of the Marcan verse may be an addition of the early church. The following evidence, however, supports the 'ransom' words in Mark: 1. The Lucan verse seems to relate to a separate occasion — it comes at the end of a discussion about which of the disciples was the greatest, and forms the contrast with a rhetorical question about table-service, while the Marcan version comes at the end of a dominical speech about service following a request by the sons of Zebedee to sit next to Jesus in his glory. 2. Jeremias points out that $\lambda υ τ ρ ο ν$ (the Greek word translated 'ransom' at Mark 10,45) which in the LXX denotes the ransom money for the firstborn and for the liberation of slaves, has the wider meaning of substitutional offering, and thus repeats the function of the Servant described by *asham* in Isaiah 53,10.[42] 3. Jesus also states the purpose of his death in substitutional terms at the Last Supper, and the speech of Jesus in Luke, commending service rather than lordship, appears in his discourse following the Supper. In view of Jesus' words over the bread and wine at the Last Supper, the authenticity of 10,45 is not vital to our thesis, but on the balance of probabilities we accept Mark's evidence at 10,45, as stronger than the counter-evidence.

The above strong evidence persuades us that Jesus expected to become the vicarious victim of Satan.

G. Jesus as the Isaianic Suffering Servant.

Some scholars, such as Morna Hooker, deny that Jesus saw himself as the Suffering Servant. Thus, Hooker argues that the quotations from

Deutero-Isaiah in the Gospels do not imply an identification of Jesus with the Servant, but rather refer to the redemptive activity of God himself in that the signs of the prophesied New Era are being fulfilled at last in the person of Jesus. Further, if the Isaianic quotations do not suggest that Jesus thought of himself as the Servant, there is "no justification for assuming that individual words, even though they may be thought to derive from the Servant Songs, point to such an identification."[43] But surely Jesus does not need to quote from Isaiah to show his self-estimate as the Suffering Servant? The more times he describes his rôle in terms reminiscent of the Servant, then the more probable it is, in the light of his natural Jewish familiarity with Scripture, that he should be contemplating as model a figure there described whose career follows a similar pattern to that which he foresees to be the purpose of his own. And since Jesus had good reason to expect that as a prophet he would suffer, but believed that he would suffer vicariously by bearing the Messianic tribulation on behalf of sinful man, what Biblical model would more likely spring to his mind than the Isaianic Servant? V. Taylor regards it as "hyper-criticism" to doubt that Jesus has Isaiah 53 in mind at Mark 9,12b — ". . . he should suffer many things and be treated with contempt?",[44] and R. Otto considers these words only intelligible on this basis.[45] The connection with Isaiah 53 here, confirms for Taylor similar reference to the Servant at Mark 8,31, 9,31 and 10,33-4, and the quotation from Isaiah 53,12 at Luke 22,37 "confirms the view that Jesus had deeply pondered the description of the Suffering Servant and saw it as a foreshadowing of His own experience of suffering and death."[46]

We have argued above that Jesus intended, by accepting the pre-Messianic tribulation in the place of the many, to facilitate the arrival of the Kingdom and the consequent overthrow of Satan and the demons. It is clear from Isaiah 53 that it was God's will that the Servant should suffer for all. V.6 states, ". . . the Lord has laid on him the iniquity of us all." and v.10, "Yet it was the will of the Lord to bruise him;". However, it seems inconsistent with Jesus' loving relationship with God as *'Abba'* ('Dad') that Jesus should believe that God should want him to suffer as the Servant for all.[47] Yet although he is wounded, bruised and chastised and makes his grave with the wicked, his ultimate destiny is glory, for "he shall prolong his days" and shall "divide the spoil with the strong." Therefore, thinking of himself as the Servant, Jesus had reason to expect that he would 'rise' after his suffering and death; this also accorded with his Danielic view of the last things, namely that after his suffering in place of the many had brought in the Kingdom, he, as the Son of Man and in the company of the other righteous, would live the resurrected life in the Kingdom.[48]

We accordingly accept the evidence that Jesus considered himself to be the Suffering Servant.

H. The Suffering Servant as a Ransom to Satan.

The concept in Mark 10,45 of Jesus' death as a ransom does not conflict with the function of the Suffering Servant's death. As mentioned above, Isaiah 53,10 described the Servant's death as a sin offering, *asham*, This substitutional idea of sacrifice seems very similar to that of a ransom in that, as in a ransom, Jesus' life is accepted instead of, and as the equivalent of, the lives of all sinners. But who did Jesus think was receiving his life as a ransom or offering in place of sinners? The sacrificial offering concept in Isaiah 53 plainly indicates God, but there is reason to suppose that Jesus believed that it was Satan who received the ransom. For whoever does the punishing presumably receives the ransom as the consideration for freeing others from punishment. It seems that there was a belief in Jesus' day that God had delegated to Satan the punishment of sinners. At Enoch 53,1,3-5 we read, "There mine eyes saw a deep valley with open mouths . . . I saw all the angels of punishment abiding there and preparing the instruments of Satan. And I asked the angel of peace who went with me, 'For whom are they preparing these instruments? And he said unto me: 'They prepare those for the kings and the mighty of this earth that they may thereby be destroyed.'" This view of Satan as the bailiff or prison governor executing the judgments of the heavenly court springs naturally from the Book of Job, chapters 1-2, where he is not only the accuser of errant man before God but is also authorised by God to torment Job. Jesus himself expresses this view of Satan as not only accuser but punisher, in his words to Peter at Luke 22,31, "Simon, Simon, behold, Satan demanded to have you that he might sift you like wheat, but I have prayed for you that your faith may not fail; and when you have turned again, strengthen your brethren." We think that Jesus means here that Satan, anticipating Peter's thrice denial of Jesus, has demanded that Peter should be arraigned before God and punished by Satan, but that Jesus has interceded with God on the ground that Peter will retain his faith and repent of his wrongs to Jesus. We do not perceive any evidence countering Luke's evidence here from his special source ('L').

The probability of Jesus having believed that it was Satan who would administer the tribulation, is supported by later statements about Jesus' death in the NT. Paul writes at I Corinthians 2,8, "None of the rulers of this age (των ἀρχοντων του αἰωνος) understood this; for if they had, they would not have crucified the Lord of glory." By των ἀρχοντων του αἰωνος Paul almost certainly means the devil: John refers to ὁ ἀρχων του κοσμου at 12,31, 14,30 and 16,11 in connection with the coming judgment and Jesus' death, and he clearly means Satan. And at Revelation 2,10 we read of this function continuing, "Behold, the devil (ὁ διαβολος) is about to throw some of you into prison, that you may be tested, and for ten days you will have tribulation." (cf. 1 Cor. 5,5). Schweitzer had no doubt about Satan's rôle in the pre-Messianic tribulation; he wrote, "In the first period . . . He expected that He, with his Elect gathered about Him, would be delivered over for a time by God into the power of the 'Evil One' and have to endure 'temptation', that is, suffering and death."[49]

J. Jesus as Suffering Servant and Son of Man?

In answer to the High Priest's question at his trial, "Are you the Christ, the Son of the Blessed?", Jesus replies, "I am; and you will see the Son of Man sitting at the right hand of Power, and coming with the clouds of heaven." (Mark 14,61-2). Apart from the 'sitting' reference to Psalm 110,1, these words describe the Son of Man at Daniel 7,13. Scholars dispute over the authenticity of this reply and over other uses by Jesus of the term 'Son of Man' apparently in reference to himself (see Ch. VI), but if it is accepted that Jesus took his view of the End-time from Daniel and I Enoch, it is at least possible that he saw himself as suffering in place of the Saints in Daniel 7, 21 and 25. It is, therefore, similarly possible that he saw himself as also standing in the shoes of the Saints to receive the Kingdom (vv.22 and 27). The Saints of the Most High also receive the kingdom in v.18, but this verse is an explanation of vv.13-14 in which 'one like a son of man' comes with the clouds of heaven to the Ancient of Days who gives him 'dominion and glory and kingdom'. Thus, if there is to be the tribulation of an individual, Jesus, in place of the corporate suffering of the Saints, it would not be unreasonable for Jesus to identify himself with the individual, the Son of Man, who receives the Kingdom. That he did so identify himself is, we think, indicated by Luke 22,28-30 (probably 'Q' in the main, par. Matthew 19,28) where Jesus says to the disciples, "You are those who have continued with me in my trials; as my Father appointed a kingdom for me, so do I appoint for you that you may eat and drink at my table in my kingdom and sit on thrones judging the twelve tribes of Israel." We have no evidence to counter the Gospel evidence of these words, and find the order of ἐν τοις πειρασμοις μου ('in my trials') followed by the grant of the Kingdom to be mildly supportive of Jesus' self-estimate as the Danielic Son of Man.

Could Jesus, however, have modelled his function in eschatology on the rôles of *both* the Suffering Servant and the Son of Man? We see little difficulty since the rôles function consecutively rather than simultaneously, being played at different stages of the End-time programme. We suggest it was the Isaianic concept of the Suffering Servant which inspired Jesus to suffer vicariously to bring in the Kingdom, but that it was the Danielic concept which induced him to believe that, having suffered for the Saints, he would in their place, as the Son of Man, receive the Kingdom. Perhaps in the maelstrom of tension and emotion in Jesus' mind the two concepts became fused to some extent as appears to be the case at Mark 10,45 and 14,24; Taylor considered that Jesus had so far identified the two that "He can say of the Son of Man what, as far as the text of Scripture is concerned, is true only of the Servant."[50]

The elevation of Jesus to supernatural Son of Man after his death need not prejudice his human status while on earth. It has not been suggested that Enoch was other than human while on earth, yet in 2 Enoch, probably belonging to the start of the Christian era, Enoch is transformed after death into an angel, and in the Hebrew Book of Enoch he is identified with Metatron and *sits* in heaven on a throne "like the throne of glory."[51] His elevation is thus not greatly dissimilar from that of Christ as described at Romans 8,34 and Philippians 2,9-11. Artapanus in the first century B.C. presents Moses as a miracle-worker who becomes the teacher of Orpheus and is "deemed by the priests (of Egypt) to be honoured like a god. . . ".[52] Elijah also was human on earth, yet finally per 2 Kings 2,11 ascended to heaven by chariot of fire and whirlwind. That he will nevertheless return before the Day of the Lord, is announced at Malachi 4,5, and at Ben Sira 48,10 it is recorded that he is ready at the appointed time to calm the wrath of God and to restore the tribes of Jacob. In the Qumran fragment IIQ Melchisedek, Melchisedek who at Genesis 14,18 is the human king of Salem, is described as "the heavenly one", executes God's judgment on Belial and the demons, and, according to J.A. Fitzmyer,[53] is a figure above the angels to whom God delegates judgement at the end of time. There are thus good precedents for achievement by former humans of elevated supernatural rôles.

Nor do Jesus' functions as the Servant and the Son of Man create an inconsistency with his belief that the agent of his suffering and death would be Satan. Although in Isaiah 53 it is God who orders the substitutional suffering of the Servant, the authorities cited above show that Satan was God's appointed agent of punishment. And in the Danielic model, the horn who makes war with the Saints (7,21), was probably identified with Satan, perhaps even during Antiochus' lifetime!

III. CONCLUSION

The early Fathers knew who received Jesus' life as a ransom: MacQuarrie wrote, "With variations of emphasis the teaching of the

Fathers is that the meaning of the death of Christ for faith lies in the victory which he won at the Cross over the powers of darkness. He put to flight the demons, destroyed their dominion over man, and so rescued man from sin and death. This theory was elaborated, notably by St. Gregory of Nyssa, into the idea that the death of Christ was a ransom paid to the devil as the price of man's liberation . . . this theory of the meaning of Christ's death prevailed in the Church for about one thousand years, until St. Anselm rejected it. . . "[54] Accepting, as we do, the authenticity of Mark 10,45, however, and the evidence deduced above that Jesus believed that Satan would administer the tribulation, we feel that Gregory's elaboration had been anticipated by Jesus' own thought three hundred years and more earlier.

Thus, any presentation of not only the healing ministry of Jesus, but also the very purpose of his life and death, which does not give prominence to Satan and his minions, will offer a misleading impression, for his life was lived and his death was contemplated, in reaction to these adversaries. The writer of 1 John 3,8 puts it more succinctly, "The reason the Son of God appeared was to destroy devils."

NOTES

1. Similar negative evidence of our experience may be opposed to the existence of God, but the evidence for the existence of God comprises not only Biblical assertions but also the existence of the world whose creation, following Aquinas as mentioned in Ch. 1, must, we believe, have required some mover.
2. See Chs. 1 and 2 of D.J. West's **Psychical Research Today**, London, 1962.
3. E. Langton, **Good and Evil Spirits**. London, 1942, wrote at p.54, "So complete is the possession often believed to be that the subject is no longer regarded as responsible for his or her actions. Every word and deed is held to proceed solely from the invading spirit." See generally on demons his Chapter VI, also his **Essentials of Demonology** London, 1949.
4. Even in J. Riches' **Jesus and the Transformation of Judaism**, London, 1980, there are only two page-references to 'Satan' in the index. Satan holds the stage, however, in evangelical works such as Michael Green's **'I believe in Satan's Downfall'**, London, 1981.
5. 'Demonology and the Classic Idea of Atonement', **Exp.T.**, Vol. LXVIII, No. 1, pp.3-6 at p.3.
6. **TDNT**, Vol. VII, p.159.
7. **The Riddle of the NT**, London 1947³, pp. 173-4

8. **BDB,** in loc.
9. See also Lamentations 3,38 and Ezekiel 14,9.
10. See further thereon N. Smart, **The Religious Experience of Mankind,** London, 1971, pp.302-315.
11. **The OT in the Light of Anthropology,** London, 1935, p.77.
12. Cited in **Dictionary of the Bible,** ed. J. Hastings, Edinburgh, 1909, s.v. 'Magi'.
13. A.W.F. Blunt in **Israel. Social and Religious Development,** London, 1924, p.138.
14. Cited in **Dictionary of the Bible,** supra, s.v. 'Satan'.
15. **The Apocrypha and Pseudepigrapha of the OT in English,** ed. R.H. Charles, Oxford, 1913, Vol. II p.170.
16. **Op. cit.** p.6.
17. On the validity of this evidence see pp.8-11 supra.
18. **Op. cit.** pp.174-5.
719. Three manuscripts from Cave 5 at Qumran confirm the original of the Testament of Levi to be in Aramaic. However, in the Aramaic fragments there of 1 Enoch the Similitudes are replaced by a Book of Giants; J.T. Milik consequently thinks that the Similitudes were composed post-Qumran. See G. Vermes, **The Dead Sea Scrolls, Qumran in Perspective,** London, 1977, pp.210-11.
19A. Charles, **Op. cit.** Vol. II p.411 dates The Assumption between A.D. 7 and 30.
20. See also Jubilees 23,29.
21. It is cited by J.M. Robinson in **A New Quest of the Historical Jesus** London, 1959, p.70 as a typically authentic saying.
22. **The History of the Synoptic Tradition,** ET, Oxford, 1972, pp.231-2.
23. **Life of Apollonius** 4,20.
24. Philops. 31. Other examples of this popular belief appear in the NT. At Mark 9,38 John tells Jesus that he saw a man casting out demons in Jesus' name, and forbade him, and at Acts 19,13 there is a reference to "itinerant Jewish exorcists".
25. The same allegation is reported at Matthew 11,18 (par.) to have been made against John the Baptist.
26. In accord with convention we term them 'miracles', but we do not believe that they transcended 'natural laws'; on conflict between Gospel evidence and 'natural laws' see Chapter I supra.
27. Alexander of Abonuteichos is another Hellenistic example, and Enoch, Elijah and Moses from the Jewish tradition. See further pp.172-74 infra and **The Myth of God Incarnate,** ed. J. Hick, London, 1977, Ch.5.

28. Mark 2,3-12 is ambivalent in this connection; the main purpose of the healing was not to show Jesus as a divine healer, but to show his power to forgive sins—yet that, too, proclaims the θειος ἀνηρ!
29. **The Parables of the Kingdom**, London, 1935, p.15.
30. **The Mysticism of Paul the Apostle**, London, 1931, p.58.
31. 'A Future for Apocalyptic?' in Biblical Studies. **Essays in Honour of William Barclay**, ed. J.R. McKay and J.F. Millar, London, 1976, p.64.
32. Ibid.
33. Op. cit. p.58.
34. **TDNT**, Vol. VI, p.31.
35. Alexandrian, Western, Caesarean and Byzantine witnesses appear in the supporting texts, X¹CKADWθφ, although the inclusion could be due to scribal assimilation to Matthew.
36. E. Lohmeyer, **the Lord's Prayer**, ET, London, 1965, p.225.
37. God is shown as author of the suffering by Jesus' prayer to God to remove the cup but rather his will be done. (Luke 22,42).
38. **My Life and Thought**, London, 1933, p.52.
39. See e.g. Luke 7,39 (good example because Pharisaic polemic); 24,14 (after resurrection); Matthew 21,10-11; Mark 6,15; 11,32.
40. V. Taylor **The Gospel according to St. Mark**, p.555. The description in Rev. 20, 1-6 of a cosmic battle between an angel and Satan, shows how this expectation continued in the early Church.
40A. But T.W. Manson, **The Servant-Messiah**, Cambridge, 1961, pp.77-9 argues that Jesus left Galilee to continue in Judaea and Peraea the ministry he had begun in the North.
41. **NT Theology**, Vol. I, London, 1971, p.292.
42. Op. cit. pp.292-3.
43. **Jesus and the Servant**, London, 1959, p.149.
44. **Jesus and his Sacrifice**, London, 1937, p.97.
45. **The Kingdom of God and the Son of Man**, ET, London, 1938, pp.249-55.
46. Ibid.
47. But see the evidence at note 37 supra.
48. Per Daniel 7, 9-27.
49. Op. cit. p.58.
50. Op. cit. p.113.
51. See further hereon **The Myth of God Incarnate**, supra, pp.108-110.
52. Eusebius, **Praeparatio Evangelica**, 9,27.
53. 'Further Light on Melchisedek from Qumran Cave 11', **Journal of Biblical Literature**, Vol. 86 (1967), pp.24-31.
54. Op. cit. p.4.

CHAPTER III

Should Christians be 'kosher'?

Is the dietary freedom enjoyed by Christians justifiable in the face of the attitude of Jesus, their Lord and Master, towards the Jewish law as evidenced by (a) the Gospel assertions of Jesus' own words and deeds, and (b) the NT assertions of the post-resurrection words and deeds of the early disciples which, it seems reasonable to think, are likely to have been influenced by that attitude of Jesus?

I. INTRODUCTION

The attitude of Jesus towards the Jewish law of his day may be summarised by saying that:

1. He was generally observant of both the Pentateuchal law[1] and the interpretations and additions of the Scribes.[2]
2. He interpreted the Pentateuchal law in a radical way.[3]
3. He considered the ethical commands in the Pentateuch more important than the cultic,[4] but he generally observed both.[1]
4. He was critical of some scribal interpretations of the Pentateuch and additions to it.[5] (See Excursus III—Korban.)
5. He disregarded the scribal law if it obstructed his ministry to those he wished to help.[6]

Under the influence of Paul's teaching, Christians[7] have in modern times adopted an eclectic approach to the OT law by choosing to observe its ethical provisions, particularly the Decalogue, but treating the ritual precepts as superseded by the teaching of Jesus.[8] Many orthodox Jews acknowledge that the destruction of the Temple rendered most of the purity laws obsolete since (a) the main reason for purity was to ensure the ritual purity of persons, food and utensils connected with worship in the Temple,[9] and (b) most Jews are now ritually unclean since the ashes of the Red Heifer which are required for purification from corpse-impurity can no longer be prepared.[10] But the destruction of the Temple did not render the rules concerning prohibited diet and kosher food obsolete, and in this Chapter we will enquire whether these dietary laws and other cultic laws still capable of observance should be observed by all those who claim to be followers of Jesus.

Since Jesus himself generally supported the whole law, not just the ethical, it would be natural for him to expect his Jewish followers also to observe the whole. But what we have to enquire is whether Jesus would have required *Gentile* followers to observe the cultic law for we think that most Christians of to-day would claim to be followers of Jesus. We stress here that we speak throughout this Chapter of the historical Jesus of Nazareth: the communication of the will of the risen Christ, which Christians believe to take place through the operation of the Holy Spirit, cannot be verified by the historian—he can only report alleged instances of its operation. Thus, it may be argued that the Holy Spirit, in accord with man's development beyond primitive taboos, guided Christians not to observe the cultic law, but the mystical evidence supporting that argument is not evidence which the historian can sift. Moreover, few would claim that all the important actions taken by the Churches throughout the centuries in the name of the Holy Spirit have been so guided; often individual Churches each alleging the Spirit's guidance have been in conflict with each other! So it is difficult on an issue which is not straightforward and on which Christian practice has varied, to attribute the doctrine or behaviour which has ultimately triumphed, to the operation of the Holy Spirit. And where the historically dominant behaviour may be inconsistent with a known attitude of the Founder of the faith, it may have even less authority to claim its source in the Holy Spirit.

Yet, whether Jesus would have required Gentiles to observe the cultic law may itself be an illogical question if Jesus would not have accepted Gentile followers on the ground that his kerygma and teaching were intended exclusively for Jews. So we must ask—did Jesus intend that his message should be preached to Gentiles?"[11]

II. JESUS' INTENT REGARDING MISSION TO GENTILES

Some evidence indicates that Jesus did not intend his teaching to be extended to the Gentiles, but that he considered it to be limited geographically to Palestine, and to be directed to the Jews only. Thus, the commissioning of the disciples at Mark 3,13f. and 6,7f. does not indicate more than a regional mission, and Matthew's addition at 10,5b-6 to Mark's tradition in 6,7f. expressly confines the mission to the Jews—"Go nowhere among the Gentiles, and enter no town of the Samaritans, but go rather to the lost sheep of the house of Israel." Similar is the 'M' material at 10,23b, ". . . you will not have gone through all the towns of Israel, before the Son of man comes." Admittedly, this material may be the product of Matthew's Judaising tendency,[12] but even Luke, in the commissioning of the 70, only reports Jesus at 10,1 as sending the disciples into "every town and place where he himself was about to come", which, as we shall see, was mainly Jewish communities.

Again, in the healing of the daughter of the Syrophoenician at Mark 7,24f. (Canaanite at Matthew 15,22, but Gentile in either case) Jesus utters a strongly anti-Gentilic logion, "Let the children first be fed, for it is not right to take the children's bread and throw it to the dogs." (7,27).[13]

Yet some features of this pericope seem to indicate support for the Gentile mission: the πρωτον ('first') indicates that the Gentiles are to be be evangelised, although after the Jews, and it is significant that the Judaizing Matthew has left out Mark's 'Let the children first be fed'.[14] Moreover, Jesus strongly commends (7,29) the woman's reply that even the dogs may eat of the children's crumbs. In 'M' there are incidental phrases derogatory of Gentiles such as 18,17 (and his version of 'Q' at 5,47), but this is again Matthew's tendency. But in favour of a universal mission is the 'Q' material at Matthew 8,10-11 where Jesus commends the faith of the Roman centurion, and adds that many will come from east and west and sit at table with Abraham, Isaac and Jacob in the kingdom of heaven, while the sons of the kingdom will be cast forth (although Luke at 13,28-29 places these words in a different context). And although in the story of the Gadarene swine at Mark 5,1-20 Jesus refuses to accept the Gentile demoniac as a disciple, he does urge him to tell his friends of God's deeds and mercy. At Luke 4, 25-27 ('L') Jesus, lamenting the unbelief of his home-town, tells the people how Elijah was sent by God to a widow in Sidon, not Israel, and how in Elisha's time not an Israeli leper but Naaman, a Syrian leper, was cleansed. The absence of this reminder in Mark and Matthew's account of the visit to Nazareth does not in my opinion weaken Luke's report as evidence that on *some* occasion Jesus uttered this statement including Gentiles in God's care.[15] A similar contrast is made in 'Q' at Matthew 12,39-42 (par. Luke 11,29-31) where Jesus favourably compares the men of Nineveh who repented at Jonah's preaching and the Queen of Sheba who travelled far to hear Solomon's wisdom, with this 'evil and adulterous generation' which sought a sign. It seems unlikely that Jesus made a comparision between Jonah's three days and nights in the whale and a prophesy of his own sojourn in Hades for that time. In the terms of our forensic model Matthew's evidence that Jesus spoke these words is outweighed by the weighty, in our opinion, evidence of the unlikelihood that Jesus would even expect to spend that time 'in the heart of the earth', and by the lighter evidence that neither Mark or Luke contain this prophesy in a parallel passage or elsewhere.[16] But there seems no cause to doubt the historicity of Jesus' commendation of the Gentiles' faith in this passage. Yet Jesus' purpose in both these passages may have been to emphasize by comparison the lack of faith of his own countrymen rather than to indicate his concern for a Gentile mission.

In the apocalyptic discourse at Mark 13 Jesus states that before the End (το τελος) (v.7) the Gospel must first be preached to all nations (v.10). But against this assertion of Mark there is forceful counter-evidence.

Firstly, this alleged statement of Jesus is inconsistent with his well-attested belief that the Kingdom of Heaven (which would be established at the End) was very near; it is thus unlikely that Jesus would have thought there was time for the Gospel to be preached to all nations beforehand.[16A] Secondly, the statement is couched in words which Mark uses often in his Gospel;[17] this in itself need not indicate Marcan redaction since most authors tend to repeat a story in their own customary phraseology. However, it is unlikely that Jesus spoke of the content of his preaching as being the Aramaic equivalent of εὐαγγελιον (Gospel or Good News), which, in addition to being a Marcan word, seems more likely to be the verdict of the Church rather than how an eschatological preacher would himself describe his message of repentance. We think the counter-evidence is stronger than Mark's assertion in these verses.

At first sight, the parables of the Vineyard (Mark 12,1-11) and of the Marriage Feast (Matthew 22,1-10 par. Luke 14,16-24) seem to indicate the vineyard and the feast as the Kingdom of God being offered to the Gentiles after its rejection by the Jews. At Mark 12,9 we read that the owner of the vineyard will give it ἀλλοις ('to others' = Luke 20,16), and Matthew or his tradition have Jesus explain the parable as "the Kingdom of God will be taken away from you and given to a nation producing the fruit of it." (21,43). In the parable of the Marriage Feast the invited guests spurn the invitation, so the host bids his servants bring in all those they can find in the highways. But it seems likely that in the original form of the parables, the new tenants of the vineyard and the new guests at the feast symbolise not the Gentiles but the righteous poor of Israel,[18] so that the parables do not argue for an intended outreach of Jesus beyond the Jews.

It behoves us now to look not at what Jesus *said*, but at what he actually *did* as regards taking his message to Gentile territory. Mark's own lack of interest in geography render it likely that the place-names and itinerary of Jesus in that Gospel formed part of the tradition received by him.[19] It seems likely that Jesus ventured into the Hellenic Decapolis at Mark 5,1f., notwithstanding the difficulty of the most probable textual reading there, "the country of the Gerasenes".[20] Both Gerasa and Gadara (an alternative reading) are in the Decapolis, but far South-East of the Sea of Galilee into which the swine plunged (5,13). It seems very likely, however, that the inhabitants of the territory concerned were non-Jews for they keep pigs, and afterwards the demoniac proclaims Jesus' deeds in the Hellenic Decapolis. At 7,24 Jesus visits Tyre and Sidon, heathen towns of Phoenicia, and apparently his deeds were well known in these territories for "he could not be hid" (v.24). Nor was his fame confined to the Jews there for the Syropheonician hears of him. At 7,31 there is the strange report that Jesus returned from Tyre 'through Sidon to the Sea of Galilee, through the region of the Decapolis.' If Jesus did take this circuitous route to the Sea via the Decapolis, then he again visits Gentile territory, but the text does not disclose whether evangelism was the reason for the unusual journey. Thus, although we have evidence of Jesus travelling to Gentile territory, the only evidence of a concern to spread his message in that territory is his injunction to the Garasene demoniac to tell his friends of the Lord's goodness to him (Mark 5,19).[21] We think however, that this may have been a softening of the refusal to take the demoniac with him, rather than an indication of an evangelical purpose.

Our survey of Jesus' reported statements concerning the Gentiles and their relationship to his ministry, and of the geographical extent of his ministry, indicates to us that Jesus probably did confine his own mission to Jews, but that he did not exclude the possibility of his message being preached to Gentiles afterwards. For the evidence to this end of (inter alia) (1) Jesus' commendation of the Syrophoenician woman and of the faith of the Roman centurion and (2) Jesus' travel into Gentile territory, seem to us stronger than his words limiting his mission which were spoken at the start of his ministry when he was contemplating his immediate and primary duty to the Jews. It is now therefore appropriate for us to return to our first question and consider whether Jesus would have required Gentile followers to observe the cultic law.

III. JESUS' POSSIBLE ATTITUDE TO GENTILE LAW-OBSERVANCE

Although it has been said that "the state of a man's mind is as much a fact as the state of his digestion",[22] the construction of a man's probable viewpoint upon an hypothetical issue through consideration of his views on other matters more or less related, is a dangerous exercise which can only lead to the most tentative conclusions. However, the quest for the views of Jesus on this issue may be assisted by the following enquiries:-

1. What does the written law, primarily the Pentateuch, state concerning the observance of the law by non-Jews?
2. What do the Rabbinic tradition and the practice of the Jews in the time of Jesus stipulate concerning such observance?
3. What did those who directly received Jesus' teaching, namely the Apostles and other first Palestinian Jewish followers indicate by their own words and conduct the views of Jesus to have been?

A. Evidence of the Pentateuch.

We think it is justifiable to search the Pentateuch since, as mentioned earlier, Jesus generally supported the written law, and so may be thought to have been influenced in his own views by the extent to which the Pentateuch, as interpreted in his day, required observance of the laws by non-Jews.

The only non-Jew to whom the written law is in any respect expressed to apply, is the *ger* (Heb. *ha-ger*), the alien who resides permanently in Israel. The earliest reference to the *ger* is in the Book of the Covenant (8th Century B.C.) where we read at Exodus 22,21, "You shall not wrong a stranger *(ger)* or oppress him, for you were strangers in the land of Egypt." (cf.23,9).[23] At 23,12 the *ger* is to have the benefit of resting on the Sabbath. The RSV translates *ger* here as alien, and this seems the more fitting translation elsewhere since he is often not a stranger, particularly in relation to the family with whom he works; it is the fact that he is a non-Israelite which gives him a different status under the law. And the extent to which the *ger* is required to observe the law, increases with his gradual integration into the community. Thus, by the time of the Deuteronomic Code (early 7th Century B.C.) the *ger* is obliged to keep the great religious festivals; the *ger* (the sojourner—RSV) is included amongst those who are to rejoice at the feast of Weeks (16,11) and at the feast of Booths (16,14).[24] Significantly, at 29,11 the "sojourner who is in your camp, both he who hews your wood and he who draws your water" is included in the people of Israel who enter into the covenant with Yahweh in the land of Moab. The literary conception of the *ger* is changing from a man who enters the land from outside to one who enters the *religion* from outside.[25]

In the Priestly Code (6th Century B.C.) the integration of the *ger* into the religious community is taken further.[26] This is particularly illustrated in Numbers 15 in regard to worship. At v.15 we read, "For the assembly there shall be one statute for you and for the stranger who sojourns with you . . . as you are, so shall the sojourner be before the Lord". This identity of status is shown in the forgiveness of the Israelites and the stranger, after sacrifice, for a communal unwitting error (v.26), an individual's unwitting sin (v.29), and in the condemnation of the high-handed sinner, native or sojourner (v.30). Kuhn writes,[27] "Thus (*ger*) denotes the non—Israelite who is almost or (with the exception of circumcision) wholly accepted into the religious constitution of the Jewish people." This raises an important question—was the *ger* of the Pentateuch interpreted in the time of Jesus as a resident alien who had been circumcised? Kuhn writes that circumcision was expected, if not required, of the *ger* as an external sign of membership of the community. Yet in the older legislation it is contemplated that a *ger* might not be circumcised. At Exodus 12,48 it is provided that a *ger* can only keep the Passover *if* he is circumcised. This provision is preserved by literal translation in the Targumim Onkelos, Ps-Jonathan and Jerusalem Fragments. Thus, while the position is not free from doubt, it does appear likely that Palestinian Jews in the time of Jesus who heard the Hebrew Bible and the Aramaic versions, would understand the Pentateuchal references to the *ger* to intend a resident alien who was *not necessarily circumcised* (unless he wished to keep the Passover). In contrast, a Hellenistic Jew reading the LXX where *ger* is often translated by προσηλυτος which to such a Jew in Jesus' time meant a circumcised convert (as opposed to a σεβομενος or φοβουμενος (τον θεον), would probably consider the *ger* of the Pentateuch to be circumcised. The fact that the *ger* was required to sacrifice and worship in the Temple according to the Pentateuch probably did not require in early times that he be circumcised, since the halakhah that no Gentile could enter the Temple Rampart (Kelim I,8) and the Temple inscription warning the alien not to enter within the balustrade,[28] related to the Second Temple. Ezekiel shows at 44,6-9, that foreigners were admitted to, and even ministered in, the First Temple, and at 14,7 Ezekiel equates the *ger* with the Israelite in the duty to reject idols and worship Yahweh.

Certainly by the time of the Priestly Code many of the laws have been expressed to apply to the *ger*. These include the Sabbath laws and laws about worship in the assembly as previously mentioned, and laws concerning the Day of Atonement (Lev. 16,29), sacrificing only in the Temple (Lev. 17,8-9), compensation for injuries (Lev. 17,8; 20,2), blasphemy (Lev. 24,16), incest and other sexual misbehaviour (Lev. 18,26). Importantly for our enquiry into Christianity and the food laws, the prohibitions against eating blood, and the meat of a creature which has died of itself (Heb. *nebelah*) or been torn by beasts (Heb. *terefah*) are now applied to the *ger* (Lev. 17,12,15), whereas in the Deuteronomic Code (14,21) it was expressly permitted to give *nebelah* to the *ger* "that he may eat of it." These prohibitions and Deut. 12,21[29] gave rise to the practice of ritual slaughter whereby all the blood is drained from the animal, and none of its prescribed organs is injured. Food slaughtered not according to the correct procedure is to-day termed non-*kosher*(Heb.). Strangely, the laws in Lev. 11,1-23 concerning prohibited food (e.g. swine) are *not* expressed to apply to the *ger*: it seems anomalous, that, although forbidden to eat lawful meat not correctly slaughtered, the *ger* could, at least in theory, eat prohibited meat provided it was correctly slaughtered![30] The reason may be that the law on prohibited meats, like participation in Passover, is applicable only to the people redeemed by Yahweh, and hence holy, since Lev. 11,45 at the end of the passage on prohibited meats, states, "For I am the Lord who brought you up out of the land of Egypt to be your God; you shall therefore be holy, for I am holy."

The laws of purity were not expressed to apply to the *ger*, except for the impurity suffered by eating *nebelah* and *terefah* and the impurity sustained in preparing the ashes of the Red Heifer (Numbers 19,10). At first thought the reason might seem to be that purity was mainly required for entry even to the Court of Women[28] in the Temple, and the *ger*, being a Gentile, could not enter anyway,[30A] but this obstacle to Gentile entry probably did not apply in the First Temple, as discussed above. However, it is probably a mistake to expect uniform consistency in the practical application of a principle in primitive law (or even modern law!).[31] Notwithstanding these two instances involving *gerim* in susceptibility to purity, the general approach may have been that, since they were not incorporated into Israel by circumcision, they were still Gentiles, and thus impure per se, and so could not be made impure a second time: the uncleanness of Gentile land was acknowledged as early as the 8th century B.C. (Amos 3,6). Finally, a non-native Israelite could not inherit land (Lev. 25), marry a priest (Lev. 21), or eat holy food with a priest's family (Lev.22,10) and could be lent money on usury (Deut. 23,20).

To summarise the position of the *ger*, by the time of the Priestly Code the uncircumcised resident alien was generally obliged to observe the Torah, spiritual, ethical and cultic, and the principal exceptions to this were the purity laws and the laws affecting prohibited meat and participation in the Passover.

B. Evidence of Rabbinic Tradition.

We enquire now into Rabbinic tradition and Jewish practice concerning observance of the law by non-Jews because, although Jesus attacked some provisions of the traditional law (e.g. Korban at Mark 7,10-13 (see Excursus III)[32] and Sabbath at Mark 3,1-5), yet as a Jew in Palestine he would observe much of the tradition as part of the customs of daily life (e.g. purity for Temple worship; the benediction before food, Berakoth 6,1-8). And it is reported at Mark 11,16 that Jesus would not allow anyone to carry anything through the Temple, thus enforcing the Scribal rule at Berakoth 9,5. Scribal traditions regarding the legal obligations of non-Jews are, we believe, relevant to an enquiry into what laws Jesus would have imposed on Gentile followers, because of the likelihood, dependent on the nature of the ruling (see the summary on p.71 supra), of Jesus either following or reacting against it.

Development beyond the Pentateuchal laws in the position of the non-Jew 'joining' Judaism, came from the Jews in the Diaspora in Hellenistic times. For many Gentiles were attracted by the ethical principles and the monotheism of the Jews: those who were circumcised were known as προσηλυτοί (proselytes) and were as much subject to the laws as native Jews. Not surprisingly, however, in view of their remoteness from the Temple and its cult, greater importance was attached by many Jews in the Diaspora to the need to observe the ethical laws, and circumcision was treated as less essential. Thus, in De Migratione Abrahami, 89, Philo of Alexandria (c.B.C.20-c.A.D.50) writes of some Jews who "regarding laws in their literal sense (τους ῥητους νομους) in the light of symbols of matter belonging to the intellect, are over-punctilious about the latter, while treating the former with easy-going neglect. Such men I for my part should blame. . . ."[33] Philo then adds that although the Sabbath and the Festivals and circumcision illustrate spiritual teaching, yet the practical rules affecting them must be observed. Again, in the fourth book of the Sybilline Oracles written 79-90 A.D., the writer promises the Messianic kingdom to all who accept the True God, abandon idolatry, murder, theft, fornication and sodomy, generally lead a good life, and are *baptized*.[34] Even in Judaea there were differing opinions over the need for circumcision. At Yebamoth 46a R. Joshua b. Hananiah maintained towards the end of the 1st century A.D. that baptism without circumcision was sufficient for the admission of a proselyte, while R. Eliezer b. Hyrcanus argued in favour of circumcision without baptism.[35] However, the contrast with the generally stricter views prevailing in Palestine is shown by the conversion of Izates, King of Adiabene, in 45A.D. Ananias, a Jewish merchant from the Diaspora, urged him not to be circumcised, since this might give offence to his subjects, but told him that if he had fully decided to espouse the customs of the Jews (ζηλουν τα πατρια των Ἰουδαιων), that was more important than circumcision. However, Izates was later persuaded by the advice of a Galilean Jew, and was circumcised.[36]

Some other Gentiles who were not proselytes (circumcised converts) had a relationship with Judaism of which the Old Testament does not speak explicitly, but for whom scribal traditions and practice provided rules and a recognised status. These are the God-fearers (Heb. *yir'ey shamaim* in Rabbinic writings and σεβομενοι or φοβουμενοι τον θεον in Greek.)[37] They are Gentiles who worshipped the one God, Yahweh, and attended the synagogue, but chose not to be circumcised or observe the whole of the law. Josephus at Contra Apionem 2,282 wrote that there was not one city or nation to which the custom of abstention from work on the seventh day had not spread, and where the fasts and the lighting of lamps and many of the prohibitions in the matter of food were not observed. There are several references to God-fearers in the New Testament. The

Roman centurion whose servant Jesus cured at Luke 7,1-10, is a good example; Luke inserts in this 'Q' passage that the Jewish elders said to Jesus, "He is worthy to have you do this for him, for he loves our nation, and he built us our synagogue." (vv.4-5)

Although there were God-fearers in Palestine, like the centurion, naturally most of these Gentiles were in the Diaspora. Josephus (A.D.37-c.100), as recited above, Juvenal (fl.c.90 A.D.) and Tertullian (c.A.D.160-230)[38] all testify that it was observance particularly of the Sabbath and food laws which generally obtained in these circles. Juvenal writes of some Romans "who have had a father who reveres the Sabbath, worship nothing but the clouds and the divinity of the heavens, and see no difference between eating swine's flesh, from which their father abstained, and that of man; and in time they take to circumcision."[39] Although Juvenal and even Josephus post-date Jesus, there is no reason to think that the practice of God-fearers differed in Jesus' time, for the very fact of their distinct identity in the NT[40] indicates that they were not fully integrated Jews.

The Palestinian Jewish evidence indicates that God-fearers were expected to observe the Noahide laws. These are the six commands believed to have been given originally to Adam, and repeated after the flood with a seventh added, to Noah and his sons. Since Noah's sons were considered to be the ancestors of the whole human race, these commands were deemed by the Jews to be binding even on Gentiles, and so were thought appropriate for God-fearers.[41] Although there are varying versions of these commandments, the preponderance of Rabbinic evidence is that they comprise setting up courts of justice and prohibition of idolatry, blasphemy, fornication, bloodshed, robbery and eating flesh cut from a living animal (Tos. A.Z. 8,4; Sanhedrin 56a,b.; Gen.R.16,6). The last-mentioned prohibition represents Rabbinic interpretation of Genesis 9,4(P). In Creation God had ordained vegetation as the food of man (Gen. 1,29), but after the Flood 'every moving thing that liveth' was to be meat for man (Gen. 9,3).[42] But the injunction is then added, 'Only you shall not eat flesh with its life, that is,its blood.'(v.4). (Verses 5 and 6 then prohibit murder for the same reason that the life is in the blood.) This prohibition against eating blood is, as mentioned, the basis of the *kosher* laws; *nebelah* and *terefah* must not be eaten because the blood has not been drained out (*nebelah)* or has been drained out improperly (*terefah*).[43] Thus, at Leviticus 17,10-16 (Holiness Code) the same prohibition against eating blood is elaborated (vv.10-14), and is followed by the practical consequence that every person who eats what dies of itself (*nebelah*) or is torn by beasts (*terefah*), is unclean. However, in the Palestinian

Targum, a large part of which is assigned by some scholars to the end of the Second Temple period or earlier,[44] Genesis 9,4 is paraphrased as prohibiting the eating of flesh torn from a living beast. The LXX and the Targum Onkelos give a fairly literal translation of the Hebrew verse, and the Book of Jubilees (109-105B.C.)[45] which, having a strict Pharisaic provenance could well have originated the Rabbinic interpretation, surprisingly follows the natural meaning of Genesis, for Jub. 6,7-9 almost repeats Gen. 9,4-7, and the prohibition of eating flesh with the blood is emphasised at 6,10 and 7,28-31. (Admittedly, the syntax of Gen. 9,4 is enigmatic, and Eissfeldt[46] notes that a glossator has probably added 'with its blood', Heb. *b'naf'sho*.) Notwithstanding the natural meaning of Genesis, most of the Rabbinic evidence includes in the Noahide laws the proscription of flesh cut from a living animal, rather than the eating of flesh with the blood in it,[47] and in view of the Palestinian Targum in which the 'living animal' interpretation appears, this is likely to have been the dominant interpretation in the time of Jesus.

At what date the Rabbis first adopted the Noahide laws as the legal obligation of Gentiles, and hence God-fearers, is difficult to assess. At Jubilees 7,20 Noah makes laws for his sons, but they do not coincide with the Noahide laws discussed by the Rabbis, only fornication being clearly in the two sets. Thus, in view of the Pharisaic authorship of Jubilees, we may suppose that the Rabbinic version of the Noahide laws took shape at some time after Jubilees.

It seems likely, however, that from Hellenistic times the Rabbis in the Diaspora urged some minimum law observance upon the Gentiles attracted to the synagogues, so some version of the laws given to Noah was probably deemed appropriate for God-fearers in Jesus' time.

C. Evidence of first Palestinian Jewish followers.

We now look at what the Apostles and the first Palestinian Jewish disciples of Jesus considered to be the obligation of Gentile Christians towards the Jewish law, for their views should at least to some extent reflect the attitude of Jesus himself. The Acts of the Apostles and the Letters of Paul show that the dominant view of the Palestinian Jewish Christians was that Gentile followers of Jesus should become proselytes, i.e. be circumcised and observe the full Jewish law. At Galatians 6,12-13, Paul writes, "It is those who want to make a good showing in the flesh that would compel you to be circumcised. . . but they desire to have you circumcised that they may glory in your flesh." And at Philippians 3,2 he exclaims, "Look out for the dogs. . . look out for those who mutilate the flesh." Paul was fighting against the Palestinian Jewish Christian missionaries who were advocating circumcision and consequently observance of the whole law (Gal.5,3). At Colossians 2,16 he counters, "Therefore let no one pass judgment on you in questions of food and drink or with regard to a festival or a new moon or a sabbath."

Paul had the opposite view, as indicated by the above texts. He believed that Jew and Gentile should each live according to the station in which God had placed him, i.e. the Jew should be circumcised and observe the Jewish law,[48] the non-Jew should not. At 1 Corinthians 7,17-19 Paul writes, "Only let every one lead the life which the Lord has assigned to him, and in which God has called him. This is my rule in all the churches. Was any one at the time of his call already circumcised? Let him not seek uncircumcision. Was any one at the time of his call uncircumcised? Let him not seek circumcision. For neither circumcision counts for anything nor uncircumcision, but keeping the commandments of God."

But which of the commandments of God was the Gentile Christian at his initiation by baptism required to observe? This would clearly indicate the views of early Christians on law-observance. The baptism of Jewish Christians could not add to their law-observance since, by circumcision, they had accepted the whole law. Yet what happened when Gentiles were baptised by Jewish Christians, such as Peter and Philip? No promises regarding the law are recorded in the Acts of the Apostles, where baptism with water is associated with repentance and remission of sins and the gift of the Holy Spirit.[49] It would not be surprising if God-fearers, such as the Ethiopian eunuch (Acts 8,27)[50] and Cornelius (Acts 10,2f), had considered that their baptism confirmed, if not increased, their pre-existing obligation as God-fearers, to the law. For their Jewish Christian baptizers, Peter and Philip, like others at Jerusalem, still attended the Temple and were part of Judaism.[51] Christians baptised by Paul and his followers were baptised "into Christ Jesus" (Romans 6,3) or "into Christ" (Galatians 3,27) which probably required faith in him as Redeemer and Lord, rather than a specific allegiance to Jesus' view of the law.

Until his vision at Joppa (Acts 10,9-16) Peter probably observed the purity laws that effectively dissuaded Jews from associating with Gentiles, for at Acts 10,27 he mentions these laws, and even after the vision he ceased to eat with Gentiles when James' emissaries arrived at Antioch (Galatians 2,12). On the other hand, his speech at the Council of Jerusalem (Acts 15,6-11) argues that Gentiles should not be required to be circumcised and observe the whole law which is presumably the "yoke" mentioned at 15,10.[52]

An attempt to reconcile these conflicting viewpoints was made in the Decree referred to at Acts 15,20 and 29 and 21,25. The main difficulty affecting the authenticity of the reported Council of Jerusalem (49 A.D.)[63] is that Paul does not appear to mention it in his Letters, even though he is said to be there (15,12). For Paul's account at Galatians 2,1-10 of a meeting with James, Peter and John contains an entirely different conclusion, namely that Paul and Barnabas are free to evangelise the Gentiles on the sole condition that they are to remember the poor of Jerusalem (2,10). We think the most likely explanation is that Luke's report of the Council is authentic in substance, and that Paul does not mention the Decree, because although he initially accepted it, yet after the continuation of the Judaizers' demand for circumcision,[54] he feels free from obedience to the Decree, and preaches complete freedom from the law. And even if Luke's Council at Jerusalem is inauthentic, the evidence from the early Church and of continuing Christian observance of the food laws (to which we shall return at p.98f.), argues that the early Palestinian Jewish Church did issue a ruling on the extent to which Gentile Christians should observe the Jewish law. On the assumption that Luke's account of the Jerusalem Council is authentic,[55] we look more closely at its contents.

The Alexandrian text of the Decree in Acts containing the four prohibitions of pollutions of idols, fornication, what is strangled, and blood, seems to us more likely to be correct than the texts which omit fornication, or omit things strangled and add the Golden Rule,[55A] since it is unlikely that Christian copyists would add cultic prohibitions, but quite possible that they would omit them, and add moral rules.[56] With similar reasoning some scholars think that $\tau\eta s$ $\pi o \varrho \nu \varepsilon \iota a s$ ('fornication') is more likely to have translated the Hebrew or Aramaic for incest, i.e. marriage within the prohibited Levitical degrees (18,6-18), than for general fornication;[57] Klausner mentions that marriage with a deceased wife's sister was not uncommon in Greece.[58] Following the sexual imagery of the prophets in describing the relationship between God and his people, $\pi o \varrho \nu \varepsilon \iota a$ has also been used with the meaning of religious faithlessness.[59] If, however, as will be discussed below, the Council prohibitions are based on the prohibitions on the *ger* in Leviticus 17 and 18, then Chapter 17's detailed prohibition of sexual immorality may be intended.

The meaning possessed by $\pi o \varrho \nu$ — in Acts 15,20 and 29 and 21,25, and the true purpose of the Decree, may be affected by whether in v.20 $\tau\omega\nu$ $\dot{\alpha}\lambda\iota\sigma\gamma\eta\mu\alpha\tau\omega\nu$ (ritual pollutions) governs not only $\tau\omega\nu$ $\varepsilon\dot{\iota}\delta\omega\lambda\omega\nu$ and $\tau\eta s$ $\pi o \varrho \nu \varepsilon \iota a s$ (idols and fornication) but also $\pi\nu\iota\kappa\tau o\upsilon$ and $\tau o\upsilon$ $\alpha\dot{\iota}\mu\alpha\tau o s$ (what is strangled, and blood). For if $\tau\omega\nu$ $\varepsilon\dot{\iota}\delta\omega\lambda\omega\nu$ and $\tau\eta s$ $\pi o \varrho \nu \varepsilon \iota a s$ are linked in this way, then the promiscuity intended by $\pi o \varrho \nu \varepsilon \iota a s$ is likely to be more related to idolatry than general sexual vice, and if all four genitives are governed by τῶν ἀλισγηματων, then the reasoning behind the Decree probably originated in the ritual impurity of Gentiles. In fact, there seems to be no grammatical reason why they should not all be governed by ἀλισγηματων. The arthrous nature of τῆς πορνειας and του αἱματος contrasted with the anarthrous nature of πνικτου is not an obstacle.[60] Blass-Debrunner, para. 276(1) state that where two or more substantives are connected by και, the article can be carried over from the first to the other especially if the gender and number are the same, but also occasionally when the gender is different; on the other hand, there are cases where the repetition of the article with the same gender or number is necessary or more appropriate (2).

All four genitives can be treated as subjective; Bauer, s.v. ἀλισγημα translates "pollution by idols", and we would translate the whole phrase, "pollutions by idols and religious harlotry and strangled meat and blood".[61]

Admittedly, the verb ἀλισγειν (to pollute) is used in the LXX with reference to polluted food, but πορνειας is the only of the four genitives without a food connection, so that the slight extension to pollution by vice is not hard to accept. Moreover, discussion at the Council would presumably be in Aramaic, and the Decree itself framed originally in Aramaic or Hebrew, and then perhaps translated into Greek for issue to the non-Jews in Antioch, Syria and Cilicia (Acts 15,23). So the word in James's judgment translated by Luke or his source as ἀλισγηματων may represent a Hebrew or Aramaic word bearing a wider sense of defilement, such as the late Hebrew *ga'al* which in the LXX the verb ἀλισγειν translates at Malachi 1,7 (twice) and 12, and Daniel 1,8 (twice), all in connection with food: yet at Isaiah 59,3 the root *ga'al* is used for the defilement of hands, at Zephaniah 3,1 of Jerusalem, and at Isaiah 63,3 of raiment.

We accordingly think that the link between the four abstentions in the Decree at Acts 15,29 and 21,25 is the ritual pollution caused by them all, and that the reason for the omission of των ἀλισγηματων in the actual wording of the Decree (if, indeed, 15,20 does not more faithfully translate the original wording) is due to concern in the letter to the Gentiles not to give offence by stressing their personal impurity. We also think that the difficulties which have arisen over the understanding of πορνειας(ν) are partly due to the separation of it from εἰδωλοθυτων(ον) and to the omission of ἀλισγηματων at 15, 29 and 21, 25. For, linked to idolatry by ἀλισγηματων, πορνειας the more clearly is seen as harlotry in the sense of faithlessness. And this governing of all four genitives by ἀλισγηματων is supported by the fact that all the prohibited things *do* ritually defile.

Association with idols certainly defiled. It was so in the OT as Genesis 35,2, Jeremiah 2,23 and Ezekiel 23, 7 and 30 and 36,25 attest, and intertestamentally as in Jubilees 20,7; and it also defiled according to the scribes, vide A.Z.1,9.[62] Palestinian Jews at the time of the Council would therefore view idols thus, even though Paul's enlightened followers knew otherwise (1 Cor.8).

πορνεια also defiled. In its original meaning of sexual immorality it is stated to defile the participator and the land itself at Leviticus 18,24-5. When even marital intercourse ritually defiled, (Leviticus 15,18), it is not surprising that irregular coitus also had this effect! Sexual immorality still defiles at 2 Peter 2,10—τους ὀπισω σαρκος ἐν ἐπιθυμιᾳ μιασμου πορευομενους and Jude 8—οὗτοι ἐνυπνιαζομενοι σαρκα μεν μιαινουσιν—but ritual defilement ceased to be relevant (except for priests) after the fall of the Temple rendered worship there impossible, so it seems likely that roots like μιαιν—with a ritualistic connotation would tend to take on a metaphorical meaning of moral defilement in subsequent literature such as the above. But fornication is more often used in the OT in a metaphorical sense of the pursuit of religious harlotry with idols.[63] Only a small step was necessary from the literal sense to this transferred meaning because of the ritual prostitution which was practised in pagan religions such as the Canaanite.[64] The close assocation of the two sins is shown by phrases like Ezekiel 23,37, "with their idols they have committed adultery;". Fornication in this metaphorical sense of whoring after other gods attracts pollution through its very assocation with idols: at Jeremiah 13,27 we read, "I have seen your. . . adulteries. . . lewd harlotries on the hills in the field. Woe to you, O Jerusalem! How long will it be before you are made clean?" The Gentiles and the sins of idolatry and immorality seem to have been closely entwined in the minds of the Israelites: the Gentiles worshipped foreign gods, Israelites ensnared into such worship were faithless to their true Lover like a harlot, and it was the sexuality of the daughters of Gentiles, which was liable to ensnare Israelites into idolatry. The Palestinian Targum on Lev. 18,21 states, "And of thy offspring thou shalt not give up any to lie carnally with the daughters of the Gentiles to perform strange worship." The connection between foreign marriages and idolatry is also shown at Exodus 34,16; Deuteronomy 7,3-4 and Ezra 9-10.

πνικτον defiled since it means strangled meat, and almost certainly represents 'what dies of itself', the Hebrew *'nebelah'*, which, like *'terefah'* defiles the eater, according to Lev. 17,15.[65] The eating of αἱμα (blood) is strongly condemned in the Pentateuch, but neither in Lev. 17 nor elsewhere is the eating of it expressly stated to defile. However, in

Lev. 17, verses 10-14, the prohibition of blood because it is the life of the flesh, is set out, and is immediately followed by the provision at v.15 that, in effect, flesh with the blood in it defiles. It therefore seems reasonable to suppose that the consumer of blood by itself is defiled.[66] Moreover, the suggestion that πνικτου is a scribal gloss explaining αἵματος does not persuade, for πνικτου precedes αἵματος in Acts 15,20 and, in any case, blood defiled not only when eaten in strangled (i.e. non-*kosher*) meat.

It seems likely that the technical *shechitah* method of killing animals had evolved by A.D. 49 (the date of the Council).[67] We do not know whether Ezekiel uses *nebelah* in its developed sense of meat which has been incorrectly slaughtered according to the *shechitah* method when he cries, ''. . . I have never defiled myself; from my youth up till now I have never eaten *nebelah* or *terefah* (4,14). However, Philo (c. B.C.20-A.D.50) knows the *shechitah* method of slaughter since he speaks of the barbarians who "prepare meat for the altar by strangling and throttling the animals, and entomb in the carcase the blood which is the essence of the soul and should be allowed to run freely away."[68] And at Hullin 1-2 exact rules concerning the correct manner of slaughter are specified, including a ruling by the Houses of Shammai and Hillel on whether the use of a reaping-sickle is valid. There seems no reason to doubt this attribution, so that, placing the Houses' disputes at c. A.D.20-70,[69] it seems likely that the *shechitah* method had evolved by A.D.49; the general procedure would probably be customary 'law' before the Sages were required to adjudicate on disputed points of detail.[70] Further, the Palestinian Targum (see infra, p.87) makes early reference to a defect in ritual slaughter. Thus, πνικτου probably does represent in Acts 15 meat not slaughtered by the *shechitah* method rather than simply meat of an animal which had 'died of itself', i.e. been found dead.

The above considerations persuade us that it is their defiling effect which is the common quality binding together the above activities prohibited by the Council; it is the ritual pollution caused not only by idols but also by religious harlotry, strangled meat and blood, which is the Council's reason why the Gentiles should abstain from these four actions.

However, many scholars consider that the compromise reached at the Council between the circumcision party and the antinomian views of Paul, (although allegedly expressed there by Peter), was based on the obligations imposed in Leviticus 17 and 18 on the *ger,* the uncircumcised resident alien. For, in those chapters, the Israelite and the *ger* are firstly required, at 17,8-9 to bring their animals for slaughter to the Temple for sacrifice to the Lord, and not to "slay their sacrifices for satyrs after whom they play the harlot"(v.7). This prohibition on the *ger* would explain the injunction in the Decree to abstain from meat sacrificed to idols (εἰδωλοθυτων) and religious faithlessness (πορνειας) Next, verses 10-14 comprehensively prohibit the eating of blood, and vv. 10,12 and 14 expressly extend these provisions to the *ger.* Verse 15 then provides that the eater of *nebelah* or *terefah* is unclean, and, as mentioned above, *nebelah* corresponds to πνικτου (what is strangled) of Acts 15. Those who interpret πορνειας literally as sexual immorality rather than metaphorically, see its place in the Decree as deriving from the condemnation of incest, adultery, sodomy and bestiality in Leviticus 18 which ordinances are extended to the *ger* at v.26. Although the *ger* is included in all these proscriptions, we wonder why, on this Levitical view of the Decree's origin, the Council should have selected these laws from the many Pentateuchal laws which, as seen above, expressly included the *ger.* For such important laws as the Sabbath laws, the festival laws and the laws against blasphemy are hardly covered by the idolatry provision in the Decree. Admittedly, the sacrifical laws binding on the *gerim* were not so relevant to those as far from the Temple as Antioch and Cilicia, nor would civil rights under the Pentateuch have much importance in jurisdictions outside Palestine.

Nevertheless, support for the prohibitions in the Decree being derived from Leviticus comes from the Palestinian Targum[44] which states in its paraphrase of Lev. 17,15, 'And every man who eats flesh which is thrown away because of a defect in its ritual slaughtering[71] or the flesh is torn, whether native or *ger* shall. . . be unclean. This indicates that the interpretation of the Levitical *nebelah* as that which has been strangled, (i.e. incorrectly slaughtered) rather than as 'what dies of itself' (RSV) was known before the destruction of the Temple, and thus explains the meaning of πνικτου in the Decree, and supports the Levitical origin of the prohibitions at the Council. Further support for that origin comes from Acts 15,21 whose argument we interpret to be that Gentile converts, even though they are far from Jerusalem, should accept these Mosaic prohibitions because they know them well since from ancient times the law of Moses (which, of course, includes Leviticus) has been read every Sabbath in the synagogues of the Dispersion.

Other scholars believe the Council was applying to Gentile Christians the seven Noahide laws which Jews, as discussed above, considered to be the laws which Yahweh intended should be observed even by non-Jews. But even if we give the prohibitions in each list the interpretation most conducive to conformity to the other list, i.e. by understanding αἷμα (blood) in the Decree as bloodshed and πορνεια as meaning sexual immorality, the prohibition in the Noahide laws of blasphemy, robbery and eating flesh from a living animal,[72] and the requirement of courts of justice (or social justice) do not appear in the Decree; nor can the Council's ban on strangled meat be equated with a Noahide law. Maccoby[73] however, does see the decree as a version of the Noahide laws, and we can agree with him that the omission from the Decree of setting up courts is understandable, but we cannot accept that blasphemy is likely to have been subsumed under idolatry in the Decree; for, if the offences overlap, why were both mentioned in the Noahide list? Nor can we agree that robbery is covered by 'murder' which is a possible translation of $αἷμα$, blood, in the Decree; the one is directed at property, the other at life itself. Maccoby suggests alternatively that these absentees from the Decree may have been omitted by Christian editors who were unwilling to see the list as a version of the Noahide laws. "Indeed," he writes, "we find throughout chapter 15 a strong reluctance to interpret the commandments listed by James as Noahide commandments, for to do so would be to admit that, when James issued these commandments, he was in no way going beyond accepted Jewish thought."[74] But would it not have been strange if James, the devout Nazarene,[75] had stepped outside Jewish thought? Whether the source of the Decree were the Levitical or Noahide laws or Gentile pollution or popular demonology, it still derived from accepted Jewish thought. Indeed, it is difficult to conceive of a Decree containing prohibitions of idolatry and non-*kosher* meat which would not have that inspiration.

We think a further obstacle to the Noahide laws as the basis of the Decree is that the Noahide laws were intended for all non-Jews while the Gentile Christians whose obligations were considered by the Council, lay in a much closer position to Judaism than other Gentiles.

A different connecting link between the Decree's prohibitions was found by Karl Six[76] who argued from the Clementina that the connecting idea in the group was the danger of communion with demons. Demons were believed to be responsible for much evil in the world, as described in our Chapter II and Excursus. B.W.Bacon following Six, claimed that the food laws represented in the Decree by things sacrificed to idols, blood and things strangled are joined with fornication because "he who surrenders the protection of the food laws exposes himself to the same danger of "alienation from the life of God" as he who "makes his members the members of a harlot."[77] Demons frequent idols,[78] and feed on things strangled and blood. Demons are also attendant upon fornication,[79] which, unlike all other sins, involves not only the guilty man but all who eat or associate with him.[80] The connection of demons and thence impurity with improper eating and improper sex stems ultimately, according to Bacon, from a heathen mysticism which regards the transmission and maintenance of life as a special means of union with divine life.[81] Thus, the prohibitions are considered to be a consistent group of regulations necessary for the preservation of the purity of the people of the Lord that are under the law, in their intercourse with the new people of the Lord without the law.

This connection of demons with idolatry and improper sex and food is supported by Lev. 17,7, "So shall they no more slay their sacrifices for satyrs after whom they play the harlot." The Hebrew *'serim'* here translated 'satyrs' is of uncertain meaning, but BDB s.v. define *'sa'ir'* as "satyr, demon (with he-goat's form, or feet. . . hairy demons)" and state that in this verse it is used as a name for idols. The association of idols with demons is supported by the Targum Ps. Jonathan whose paraphrases of the verse reads, "Neither shall they offer any more their sacrifices unto idols which are like unto demons, after which they have wandered." Nevertheless, we think that the Levitical laws affecting *gerim* would have been more likely to have influenced the thinking of Jewish Christians, and especially James, than would demonology.

However, the interpretation of the Decree cannot be accurately assessed in isolation from the circumstances which caused it to be formulated. The reason for convening the Council[82] is expressed in Acts 15 in two ways. At v.1 Luke states that some Judaeans were teaching the Christians at Antioch that unless they were circumcised, they could not be 'saved' ($\sigma\omega\theta\eta\nu\alpha\iota$). At v.5 some Christian Pharisees claim that it is necessary that Gentile Christians be circumcised and charged to keep the law of Moses. V.1 stipulates circumcision as a condition of 'salvation'; verse 5 requires it as a condition of entry into Christianity. The distinction between 'salvation' and entry into Christianity should not be pressed, however,—the issue was essentially, 'Did Gentiles have to be circumcised, and keep the whole law of Moses?'. Peter at vv.7-11 argues that Gentiles do not need to keep the law, for, like the Jewish Christians, they will be 'saved' by grace. And the speeches of Barnabas and Paul (v.12) implicitly argue that God, by performing wonders amongst the Gentiles (through themselves) has shown that he does not require them to observe the law. James' argument from prophesy (vv.16-18) only shows God's intention that the Gentiles shall seek him, and does not indicate whether they should observe the law. And James' judgment at v.20, which is followed (almost entirely) by the Council at 15,29 and 21,25, hardly contains a comprehensive statement of the Mosaic laws which the Gentiles should observe even though at vv.19-20 James says that they should not trouble the Gentiles except for the four prohibitions: he mentions neither the Sabbath[83] nor prohibited food (i.e. swine etc.). While the judgment clearly dispenses with the need for circumcision, it is not in our view a comprehensive statement of the law-observance required of Gentiles, and is only intended to declare the minimum observance necessary to permit commensality. For there were the following impediments to Jewish and Gentile Christians celebrating the Eucharist together and the meal of which the Eucharist was then part,[84] and, indeed, eating together generally: —

1. The bodies of Gentiles were ritually impure in Jewish law, and it is interesting that their need for cleansing is implicitly admitted by Peter at the Council (although consistently with his approach it is a *spiritual* cleansing) in his words, "he made no distinction between us and them, but cleansed (καθαρισας) their hearts by faith." (15,9). Alon states that the ritual impurity of Gentiles is not decreed in Torah, but is of scribal origin.[85] It appears implicit, though, at Lev. 18,24-30 that the Canaanites became defiled through their immorality. At Genesis 35,2 the defiling effect of foreign gods is attested, and the impurity of Gentiles is attributed by of halakhoth also to their association with idols.[86] And the uncleanness of Gentiles is clear in the Prophets: at Isaiah 52,1 Yahweh, declaring the restoration of Zion, says, "there shall no more come in unto you the uncircumcised and unclean", and at 52,11 he bids the exiles on leaving Babylon, "touch no unclean thing."[87] This uncleanness is emphasised in the Book of Jubilees (109-105 B.C.) where the warning is given about Sodom and Gomorrah, "And walk not after their idols and their uncleannesses..." (20,7). Even Alon thinks that the 18 Decrees passed in A.D.51[88] only confirmed a Gentile impurity which had been embedded in the tradition from early times.[89] For this reason of their impurity, Yahweh tells the exiles at Ezekiel 36, 24-25, "For I will take you from the nations.... I will sprinkle clean water upon you, and you shall be clean from all your uncleannesses, and from all your idols I will cleanse you."

The impurity of the Gentile was derived not only from presumed association with idols, but from a linked immorality as indicated above. This link may have sprung from Exodus 32,6 where after Aaron had made the idolatrous golden calf, the people sacrificed to it, and then sat down to eat and drink, and rose up to 'play'.[90] Again, we have read above at Leviticus 17,7 after the command to bring sacrifices in the open field to the tent of meeting, "So shall they no more slay their sacrifices for satyrs, after whom they play the harlot." From the time of Hosea, the prophets portrayed idolatry as sexual betrayal of the Lord; although this is often metaphor, as discussed above, it is no doubt founded on the fact that the pagan cults, especially Canaanite, involved worship with sexual immorality.[64] Thus, Hosea 1,2, ". . . the land commits great harlotry by forsaking the Lord." Indeed, much of both Hosea and Ezekiel's prophesy is condemnation of Israel's idolatry which is symbolised as playing the harlot;[91] the root 'πορν—' is used generally to translate in the LXX the Hebrew root, *'zanah'* (to fornicate). This link is also shown in the NT: at 1 Thess. 4,3-5 the brethren are enjoined to "abstain from immorality. . . not in the passion of lust like heathen who do not know God." At Romans 1,24-25, Paul writes that ". . . God gave them up in the lusts of their hearts to impurity, to the dishonouring of their bodies among themselves because they. . . worshipped and served the creature rather than the Creator. . . " But this immorality which accompanied idolatry, also rendered the actor unclean ritually. At Leviticus 18,20 we read "And you shall not lie carnally with your neighbour's wife and defile yourself with her." Similarly, defilement arises from sodomy and bestiality (vv.22-23). As discussed above, this defilement from an idol-linked immorality supports in Acts 15,20 the governing of both εἰδώλων and πορνειας by ἀλισγηματων

Because of this Gentile impurity received from idols and immorality, many are the injunctions to Jews not to associate with Gentiles: at Jubilees 22,16 we read, ". . . separate thyself from the nations, and eat not with them, for their works are unclean and all their ways are a pollution and an abomination and an uncleanness." Thus, Peter correctly states the Jewish position at Acts 10,28, "You yourselves know how unlawful it is for a Jew to associate with or to visit any one of another nation; but God has shown me that I should not call any man common or unclean;" (κοινον ἢ ἀκαθαρτον). Thus, the Jews would not enter Pilate's praetorium so that they should not be prevented by defilement from eating the Passover (John 18,28). Perhaps it was his Gentile uncleanness which caused the centurion to tell Jesus at Matthew 8,8 (= Luke, 7,6) that he was not worthy that Jesus should enter his house.

Usually, suffering ritual impurity did not matter unless the sufferer wished to enter the Temple (or participate in the Passover), but sustaining impurity from a Gentile was to be avoided irrespective of Temple entry.[92] (Impurity could in any case be removed by immersion in a *miqveh,* but this would be unnecessary unless worship or Passover was contemplated.) In the Fathers according to Rabbi Nathan (Ch.8), it is told how a girl was ordered to immerse because she had been a captive among the Gentiles, and had eaten and drunk their food, and no intention to enter the Temple is mentioned.[93]

Thus, an attempt is made in the Decree to compromise over the contraction of impurity which would be suffered by Jewish Christians eating with Gentiles. Although the Gentiles are impure per se, they cannot sustain impurity from any other person or thing, for the laws of purity are only commanded to the Israelites (and in three exceptional cases, as we have seen, to the *gerim*), and the Gentiles are impure anyway. So the effect of the Council decree is that the Jews will tolerate and accept the innate impurity of the Gentiles and will associate and eat with them notwithstanding, provided that the Gentiles will avoid these principal practices which probably gave rise to their conclusively presumed uncleanness in the first place. A.W.F. Blunt [94] suggested that baptism and the gift of the Holy Spirit were accepted as a sufficient purification so that no defilement was contracted by associating with Gentile Christians. Perhaps Luke attributed this reasoning to Peter at the Council (Acts 15, 7-9). but in James' speech at vv.19-20 and in the Decree at vv.28-9, notwithstanding the Gentiles conversion (v.19) and the Holy Spirit's guidance of the Council, the Christian graces were not, in fact, accepted as superseding the Gentiles' need to avoid polluting their Jewish brethren.

2. The second impediment to commensality was that Gentiles did not slaughter the animals which they ate by draining all the blood out by the *shechitah* method, i.e. their meat was not *kosher.* As mentioned above, the eater of meat not so slaughtered *(nebelah),* or who otherwise ate blood in his food. was rendered unclean by it, and had to wash his clothes, immerse in a *miqveh* and remain unclean until evening (Lev. 17,15). Despite the subsequent strange interpretation in Sifra,[65] the natural meaning of 17,15, namely that such eating ritually defiled the eater, was clearly the original belief and is likely to have persisted into the 1st century A.D. Thus, Ezekiel 4,14 attests defilement by non-*kosher* food, ". . . I have never defiled myself; from my youth up till now I have never eaten what died of itself *(nebelah)* or was torn by beasts, nor has foul flesh (Heb. *pigul*) come into my mouth." According to the author of Daniel in the 2nd century B.C., it appears to have been the fear of eating non-*kosher* food which caused Daniel not to "defile himself (Heb. yithga'al) with the king's rich food", but to eat vegetables (1,8).[95] Similarly, in the Book of Tobit, written about 200 B.C., Tobit, when captive in Nineveh, would not eat the bread of the Gentiles, "because I remembered God with all my soul" (1,11-12). Judith, whose book was written c.160-140 B.C., ate the food she brought with her rather than eat the provisions of the Assyrian, Holofernes, (12,1-2). But the strongest evidence of the persistence into the 1st century of the natural meaning of Lev. 17,15 is the Palestinian Targum interpretation cited at p.87 supra. There is also evidence which is difficult to date, that meat slaughtered by a Gentile was presumed to be *nebelah*.[96] Defilement by *nebelah* or blood,

like defilement by a Gentile, was avoided by a Jew irrespective of pending Temple entry.[97]

3. The third social impediment was the commandment that "You shall not boil a kid in its mother's milk." (Ex. 23,19; 34,26; Deut. 14,21). While this practice may originally have been banned as pertaining to pagan worship,[98] it came to be interpreted by the Pharisees as prohibiting the eating of a mixture of meat and milk. The Targum of Onkelos[99] translates both the Exodus provisions as, "Thou shalt not eat flesh with milk."; Ps.-Jonathan translates 23,19 as "you are not permitted to dress or to eat of flesh and milk mingled together", and 34,26 as "You are not allowed to boil or to eat flesh and milk mixed together." (The Jerusalem Fragment on 34,26 is the same).[100] Such mixture is not expressed by Scripture or by the scribes to defile, but is prohibited, and the prohibition probably prevailed in the first century A.D. because very detailed regulations affecting it are set out at Hullin 8,1-5 of the Mishnah, whose compilation was finalised c.200 A.D.

4. It was prohibited by Lev. 7,23-25 to eat the fat of ox, sheep or goat, and this, too, probably applied at the time of the Jerusalem Council, for the stringency of the law concerning it is compared with that relating to blood, at Hullin 8,6. This also would deter Jewish Christians from eating with Gentiles, for who could be sure that all the fat had been removed from a meal? Again, although this food is prohibited, it is not expressed to defile. Similarly, the law preventing the eating of the sinew of the hip of an animal, which is recorded at Genesis 32,32 as being a custom "to this day", and, being JE material, is of ancient origin, was another hindrance prevailing at the time of the Council, and its parameters are described at Hullin 7,1-6.

5. Further, the Gentiles, being impure themselves, would pass their impurity to food handled by them. The intensity of the impurity of a Gentile is still debated,[101] but the better view seems to be that it is the impurity of a corpse,[102] which is the most intense, being a 'father of fathers'. Consequently, food touched by a Gentile, and made susceptible by water, would become a father of impurity, and the Jewish eater thereof would become a first-degree offspring of impurity. Even if the Gentile was only a father of impurity,[103] the touched food, made susceptible, would become first-degree offspring, and the eater would become second-degree impure according to the rulings at Zabim 5,12 which we think were made in Hananiah's upper room in A.D.51,[104] but which probably prevailed as custom earlier.[105] Unless the Jewish Christians were *haberim*,[106] the suffering of this impurity would not matter unless Temple worship was imminent.[107] In the circumstance of eating with a Gentile and therefore

probably in the Diaspora, imminent Temple worship would be unlikely, and in any case the impurity could be removed by immersion in a *miqveh*. The *haberim*, however, insisted on the purity of even their ordinary food (*hullin*), so a Jewish Christian who was a *haber*, would not eat with a Gentile for this, amongst other, reasons. We have, however, no reason to think that a substantial number of the Jewish Christians were *haberim* so that fear of ritual defilement by *contaminated* food of Gentile Christians was probably not a serious impediment to association.

6.   A further danger for a Jew in eating meat at a Gentile's table was that, if bought from a Gentile butcher, it might be the unused part of an animal which had been sacrificed at a heathen altar, since only part of the animal was burnt at the altar, the remainder being eaten by the priests or the offeror, or sold to a butcher for re-sale to the public.[108] The wine at a Gentile meal might be wine from which a heathen libation had been made.[109] For the Jew, to eat such food or to drink such wine was to acknowledge the heathen deity, and was therefore idolatrous. The fact that Gentile food was probably untithed did not matter (except to the *haber*), for, according to the Torah, only the producer had to tithe, and only the produce of Israel required tithing (Numbers 18).[110]

These legal obstacles to table-fellowship, and indeed to any social intercourse, would if enforced have physically separated Jewish from Gentile Christians, and have prevented any further attempts by observant Jewish Christians to convert Gentiles. The Jewish Christians were probably influenced by a desire for unity and a concern not to frustrate the spread of the Gospel, and the Decree of the Council appears to have been a compromise measure designed to lay down minimum law-observance by Gentiles which would permit commensality and social contact generally. The Jewish Christians must be willing to dine with Gentiles despite their personal impurity and the possibility that they might be served flesh mixed with milk, or meat containing the sinew of a thigh, or fat, provided that the Gentiles abstained from polluting themselves (and thereby, others) with idols (including idol-meat), immorality, non-*kosher* meat and blood. We think that the rationale behind the Decree is disclosed by ἀλισγηματων (pollutions) in the v.20 form if it is construed as governing πορνειας, πνικτου and αἵματος in addition to εἰδωλων. For we have seen that they all do cultically defile, and it was the defilement involved in association with Gentiles which caused the Jewish Christians to separate themselves (e.g. at Antioch, Gal. 2,12-13). But the complete removal of that danger by the circumcision of the Gentiles, (which, by making them Israelites, would remove their impurity) was not required by the Council —

they were prepared to ignore the prohibitions against associating with Gentiles, and against eating mixed meat and milk, thigh sinew and fat, provided that the Gentiles abstained from idolatry (which included food offered to idols) immorality, strangled meat and blood, for they all defiled.[110A] If the Gentiles continued to eat non-*kosher* meats themselves, they might have them on the table at meals with the Jews, and the Jews (although not the Gentiles) would be defiled. The defilement would not matter to the Jews because of the remedy of the *miqveh,* but the breach of the religious prohibitions would.

However, Maccoby[111] argues that the prohibitions in the Decree did not facilitate the sharing of meals since they did not forbid the eating by the Gentiles of pork and other 'unclean' meats which the Jews were not allowed to eat. But it was hardly necessary for the Decree to include such a provision for it is unlikely that Gentile Christians would be so insensitive as to bring to a common meal food which in common knowledge was abhorrent to Jews. It is noteworthy that ἀλισγηματων could not have governed 'forbidden food' as we believe it governed πνικτου and αἵματος, for while Lev. 11,24-8 provide that the toucher or carrier thereof is rendered unclean, and has to immerse, neither Leviticus nor Deuteronomy rule that the eater is rendered unclean. Admittedly, unless utensils are used, it is almost impossible to eat food without touching it. But Rashi writes on Lev. 11,24 that a defilement of the soul which cannot be removed by immersion is incurred by the eater of forbidden food, and such a sanction would perhaps not have evolved if eating of forbidden diet had produced ritual defilement. We should add here that even if, contrary to our view, the Decree was based on *gerim* laws, forbidden diet would not have been included since it is not forbidden to the *gerim.*

D. Review of Evidence and Conclusions.

The above survey of the possible sources of the hypothetical attitude of Jesus towards observance of the law by Gentile followers indicates that: —

1. The Pentateuch provided the legal obligations of the *gerim* as an analogy for Gentiles.
2. The Rabbinic views prevailing in Jesus' day provided the precedent of the Noachide laws which were considered binding upon all Gentiles, and particularly upon 'God-fearers'.
3. The views of Jesus' earliest disciples (who are the most likely to have been influenced by his own views) comprise: —
(a) a Jewish Palestinian insistence that Gentiles should be circumcised, and observe the whole law.
(b) the Pauline view that Gentile Christians are not bound by the Jewish

law; they should, however, obey the ethical commandments which are summed up in the commandment to love their neighbour as themselves (Romans 13,8-10).

(c) another Jewish Palestinian view, compromising with (a) and (b) above and expressed in the Decree in Acts 15, namely that, in order to permit association between Jews and Gentiles, and eating together in particular, the Gentiles should abstain from idolatry (including idol-food), immorality, strangled meat and blood.

It is possible, of course, that Jesus would not have been influenced by any of the above indicators, but would have done a 'new thing'[112] by making an entirely original decision on Gentile law-observance. We do not think Jesus would have espoused the Pauline view. However widespread may have been the view that the law ceases in the day of the Messiah,[113] Jesus generally observed the law, as we have previously discussed. The antinomy preached by Paul would have been quite foreign to one of Jesus' upbringing and customary worship in Temple and Synagogue. Nor do we think that Jesus would have been influenced by the scribal application of the Noahide laws to Gentiles, partly because of their arbitrary nature in, for example, including courts of justice but omitting the Sabbath, and partly because Jesus' followers would have a closer connection with Judaism than other Gentiles, even God-fearers.

We do believe, however, that Jesus would have been influenced by the Pentateuchal model of the *gerim* in deciding on the legal obligations of his Gentile followers.[114] For the *gerim* were in an analogous position to the Gentile Christians; the *gerim* were newcomers to the Israelite religion in the same way that the Gentile Christians were newcomers to the 'Jesus' movement within Judaism. Thus, we think that Jesus would have approved of the Council Decree because (a) it incorporated four of the most important laws which *gerim* had to observe according to the OT, and (b) it attempted to surmount the obstacle created by the impurity of Gentiles[115] and to preserve the desired unity of his followers (John 17, 11 and 20-23). For we doubt that Jesus would have supported the Palestinian Jewish insistence that his followers should be circumcised and observe the whole law, because that was not imposed by Moses on *gerim* unless they wished to become full Jews. Moreover, the Christian initiatory rite of baptism, which was also an initiatory rite for Jewish proselytes,[116] was a satisfactory substitute for circumcision.[116A] There does not seem in the legal position of the *gerim* to be anything which Jesus' radical view of the law would have caused him to alter in applying their laws to Gentile Christians. Jesus would have approved that the purity laws did not in general apply to *gerim*, for it seems clear from Mark 7,

1-23, that he did not consider those laws of prime importance. As regards the ethical laws of the Pentateuch, these were binding on the *gerim*,[117] and it is clear from Jesus' teaching in passages such as the advice to the Rich Young Man (Mark 10, 16-21) that Jesus intended that all his followers should observe them, subject to his radical interpretation illustrated there and in the Sermon on the Mount and in the teaching on divorce (Mark 10,2-12).

We accordingly think that Jesus would have required his Gentile followers to observe the laws which the Pentateuch applied to the *gerim*. We have noted that the number of laws which applied to them increased historically, but Jesus, like his contemporaries, would not view the Scriptures in the critical way of the modern scholar, but would treat them cumulatively as the word of God, so that in seeking the laws of the *gerim*, he would identify not only those in the earlier codes of Exodus and Deuteronomy but also the greater number in the Priestly Code. He would thus have thought the laws in the Decree, supplemented by the other *gerim* laws in the Pentateuch, so far as applicable to the Diaspora, to be appropriate for his Gentile followers. Other *gerim* laws so applicable would be, inter alia, the Sabbath laws, those affecting the Day of Atonement (apart from the Temple ritual) and blasphemy,[118] but the rules regarding Temple sacrifice and festivals would not be suitable since in Jesus' day, as discussed, the Gentile could not go beyond the rampart of the Temple; the civil laws, also, were hardly practicable for Gentiles living under other civil jurisdictions. Further, only a Gentile who, by circumcision, had wholly identified with the Jews could be of that nation who were redeemed in Egypt, and consequently celebrate the Passover. Probably, the Sabbath observance and participation in the assembly represented in the Diaspora by the synagogue, and the keeping of the *kosher* rules of the Decree, would have been the *gerim* laws with most impact on the daily life of the Gentile follower of Jesus. Conversely, because the laws on prohibited food (pork etc.) were not applied in Leviticus to the *gerim*, perhaps due to Lev. 11,45 (see pp.77-8 supra), we do not think Jesus would have imposed them on Gentiles. The Gentiles' freedom in this respect would not hinder eating with Jews because the Jews' inability to eat the unclean animals and fishes would be well known to Gentiles, and such food would in any case be usually recognisable on the common table.

We are supported in our view regarding Jesus' probable application of the *gerim* laws to Gentiles, not only by the possibly unconscious choice of certain *gerim* laws at the Jerusalem Council by the predominantly Palestinian Jewish "apostles and elders" (15,22), but also by the persistence of the *kosher* requirement in the Ebionite (Palestinian Jewish) Clementine Homilies and in its actual observance by sections of Gentile Christianity. For Jesus, too, was a Palestinian Jew whose attitude to observance of the law by those who wished to join his movement within Judaism, might well have been similar to those Palestinian disciples and his brother who determined at the Council the conditions for association with Gentiles. In the Homilies at 7,4 we read in Peter's address to the Gentile people of Tyre, "And the things which are well-pleasing to God are these: to pray to Him, to ask from Him . . . to abstain from the table of devils, not to taste dead flesh, not to touch blood; to be washed from all pollution ($\lambda\upsilon\mu\alpha\tau\text{os}$); and the rest in one word,—as the God-fearing Jews[119] have heard, do you also hear, and be of one mind in many bodies; let each man be minded to do to his neighbour those good things he wishes for himself."[120] The addition of the Golden Rule here recalls its inclusion in D, the Latin Version, Irenaeus (in Greek and Latin), Tertullian, Cyprian, and other Latin texts of Acts 15,29. At 7,8 in addressing the Gentile people of Sidon, Peter says, "And this is the service He has appointed: To worship him only . . . and to be baptized for the remission of sins . . . to abstain from the table of devils, that is, from food offered to idols, from dead carcasses, from animals which have been suffocated or caught by wild beasts, and from blood; not to live any longer impurely ($\dot{\alpha}\kappa\alpha\theta\alpha\varrho\tau\omega\text{s}$); to wash after intercourse; that the women on their part should keep the law of purification; that all should be soberminded . . . "[121]

At 8,19 an angel declares to the giant offspring from the union of angels with women, God's will for them as follows:— ". . . that you lord it over no man; that you trouble no one, unless any one of his own accord subject himself to you, worshipping you, and sacrificing and pouring libations, and partaking of your table, or accomplishing aught else that they ought not, or shedding blood, or tasting dead flesh, or filling themselves with that which is torn of beasts, or that which is cut, or that which is strangled, or aught else that is unclean ($\dot{\alpha}\kappa\alpha\theta\alpha\varrho\tau\text{ou}$) . . . But if any of those who worship me go astray, either committing adultery, or practising magic, or living impurely, or doing any other of the things which are not well-pleasing to me, then they will have to suffer . . . "[122] It is conspicuous that in each of these extracts from the Jewish Christian Homilies the dietary prohibitions imposed on non-Jews (the giants being a non-Jewish race of their own) coincide with the Council of Jerusalem.

Evidence from another document which probably contains Jewish Christian influence, is the injunction in the Didache at 6,2, "as regards diet keep the rules so far as you are able but keep strictly from idol sacrifice for it is the service of dead gods."[123] This at least indicates that the eating of meat offered to idols was not the only food regulation in the Christian community addressed.

Concerning observance of the law by Gentile Christian communities, there is evidence at Revelations 2,14 and 20, where the letters of John to the churches of Pergamum and Thyatira denounce φαγειν ειδωλοθυτα και πορνευσαι, (eating food sacrificed to idols, and fornication), but this does not indicate whether these communities observed the Levitical dietary laws. But Tertullian (c. A.D. 160-230) at Apology 9,13 bids the heathen blush before Christians who "do not eat the blood even of animals who also on that account abstain from things strangled and found dead lest we be defiled (contaminemur) by any blood at all secreted inside the internal organs."[124] The reference to defilement is very interesting as it indicates survival of the defiling effect of nebelah in Lev. 17,15 and supports αλισγηματων as the common root cause of the four prohibitions at Acts 15,20.

Eusebius (c.A.D. 264-340) records in Ecclesiastical History V. 1,21 that in the persecution at Lyons and Viennes (c.A.D. 161-180) Biblias challenged her persecutors, asking, "How could such as these devour children who considered it unlawful even to taste the blood of irrational animals?"[125] And in the Apostolic Constitutions (late 4th century) we find at Ecclesiastical Canon no. 63, "If any priest. . . eats flesh with the blood of its life, or that which is torn by beasts or died of itself, let him be deprived; for this the law itself has forbidden."[126] While this work is thought to have been produced by a Syrian writer, it is still surprising that the authority for the dietary law is the Torah rather than the Jerusalem Council. However, Clement of Alexandria (c. 150-220) attributed the Christian avoidance of things strangled to the Jerusalem Decree in two instances (Paedagogue 2,7; Stromata 4,15). Clearly, the observance of the kosher laws had, notwithstanding Paul, commanded substantial acceptance in the early churches, and the evidence closest to home is the Penitential of Archbishop Theodore of Canterbury wherein as late as A.D. 668-690 he wrote, "If without knowing it one eats what is polluted by blood or any unclean thing, it is nothing, but if he knows, he shall do penance according to the degree of pollution."[127] He also imposes a three weeks' fast on any woman who enters a church or takes Holy Communion during menstruation, so deep was the impress of ritual pollution in the current Christian mind.

It is the more surprising that this strict view of law-observance prevailed in parts of Western Christendom because it had to contend with the vehemently antinomian attitude of Paul discussed above.

We do not wonder, however, that the freedom from the law which Paul allowed to Gentile Christians was so contrary to the observance which we believe Jesus would have required. For the NT records do not disclose that Paul ever met Jesus, and Paul claimed to have received much of his information about Jesus by visionary revelation from the risen Christ:[128] information about the views of Jesus allegedly thus acquired cannot carry the same weight for the historian as the recorded statements and behaviour of those disciples who were taught by Jesus during his earthly life.

Nevertheless, Jesus would not have required from his followers a legal observance stricter than his own. Judaism in the time of Jesus was fluid, and there were several different attitudes to the law co-existing. The Pharisees, Sadducees, Essenes/Qumranians and the *'am-haarez'* (Heb. for 'people of the land') all differed in their approach, and there were different degrees of observance even within Pharisaism.[129] There is a clear trend in the Gospel reports of Jesus' teaching which suggests that he had a more radical approach to the law than many of his contemporaries. His teaching on the Sermon on the Mount, and about divorce and the Sabbath, evince a concern to extract the underlying purpose of the law.[3] Thus, notwithstanding Moses' provision for divorce, Jesus said that divorce was an accommodation for man's sins, and the real will of God was that marriage was an indissoluble union. A second feature of Jesus' attitude towards the law was that he attached a greater weight to the ethical laws than to the cultic.[130] This attitude places Jesus in the tradition of the prophets such as Amos, Hosea, Jeremiah and Isaiah, and this and his call to repentance before pending judgment[131] are, perhaps, two of the main reasons why many of his countrymen considered him to be a prophet.[132] We doubt, however, that the ethical influence of the prophets on Jesus would have caused him to relax the requirement of the *gerim* laws for Gentiles. For the prophets did not seek to abolish the cultic laws, they only insisted that the cult was not efficacious unless accompanied by right behaviour.[133] Thus at Isaiah 56,3-8, the foreigner and the eunuch (perhaps treated together because of their uncircumcision) are welcomed to the house of God provided they "keep my sabbaths' and "hold fast my covenant". It has been said that the prophets combined a universalism which welcomed all men to Zion with a particularism which regarded Israel as the special object of divine favour. But even if we accept universalism as the dominant attitude of the prophets, "The most we can positively say is that in Deutero—(and Trito-) Isaiah the Gentiles are to come to Israel's light (60,3), rather than that Israel is to carry the light to the Gentiles."[134] Thus, while the prophets welcomed the nations to Israel, the welcome is likely to have involved some obligation to the law, as indicated above: there seems no reason to think that Jesus' attitude would have differed.

IV. CONSEQUENCES FOR CHRISTIANS TO-DAY

If our conclusion that Jesus would have expected Gentile followers to observe the Mosaic laws affecting the *gerim,* and would thus have approved of the Jerusalem Decree, is correct, then Christians of to-day who look to Jesus, rather than Paul, as Lord and consequently as the arbiter of their behaviour, are confronted by the need for a decision as to whether they, too, should observe the dietary rules. For while the destruction of the Temple in A.D. 70 rendered obsolete the Jewish need for purity before Temple entry, defilement by non-*kosher* meat, by the sinew or by mixed meat and milk were, and are, to be avoided as religious prohibitions by Jews and *gerim* irrespective of Temple entry. As noted above, Scripture imposed on *gerim* the observance of other laws of which the Sabbath, in particular, is still capable of observance and is observed by Jews. Although Jesus, judged by Mark 2,23-28 and 3,1-6, did not support the strict Pharisaic interpretation of 'work' on the Sabbath, yet he does not in these passages deny the principle of the Sabbath commandment so that this, too, appears to be an obligation of the Gentile who to-day follows Jesus. For the Christian Sunday was not intended as a substitute for the Jewish Sabbath (the day of rest on a Saturday) although some early Christians such as Justin Martyr did condemn the Jewish Sabbath.[134A]. Far from being considered as the day of rest after creation, Sunday was celebrated eschatologically as the first day of the new creation and as the day of Jesus' resurrection. The early Christians after attending worship treated Sunday as an ordinary working day, and it was Constantine's edict of the 4th century which by making Sunday a holiday mistakenly turned it into a Christian Sabbath.[135]

A Christian's allegiance to Jesus rather than to Paul will pose other fundamental questions for him. For example, although many scholars would argue that Jesus did not claim divinity,[136] and that it is Paul who makes the first such claims for Jesus,[137] the credal formulas of most Churches still affirm Jesus' identity with God. Yet can the Jesus who recited the Shema as the most important commandment,[138] have intended thus to jeopardise the unity of the Godhead, or comprehended the sophistical explanations of Greek-thinking Trinitarians? Again, Jesus may, despite his expectation of the imminent Kingdom, have intended by his training of the disciples that his message should be spread by others, but is it likely that he who frequented the Temple and supported its priesthood,[139] should have intended to form another sacerdotal priesthood outside the Aaronic ordained by God? These questions are discussed in Chapters 5 and 6 infra.

In short, we believe that Jesus' qualified observance of the law, which, according to our conclusion, would have caused him to require that those early Gentile followers should observe the *kosher* laws, would also have caused him to restrain them from several other paths whither they were led by Paul, and should cause us to-day to probe the consequences of our devotion to Jesus—or is it really to Paul?[140]

NOTES

1. Mark 1, 44; 6,56; 14,12; Matthew 5,18 (par.Luke 16,17); 17,27; 23,23 (par.Luke 11,42). Jesus could presumably have spoken Peter's words at Acts 10,14 concerning prohibited diet.
2. Mark 11,16; cf. Berakoth 9,6, "He may not enter into the Temple Mount with his staff . . . nor may he make of it a short by-path;". Mark 6,41; cf. Berakoth 6,1-8. According to John 4,27 the disciples marvelled that Jesus was talking with a woman; cf. Aboth, 1,5.
3. Matthew 5; Mark 10,2-12; Codex D after Luke 6,4.
4. Mark 7,15; 12,33-4; Matthew 12,6-7.
5. Mark 7,9-12; Matthew 23,16-22.
6. Mark 3,1-5.
7. Disciples were first called Christians at Antioch (Acts 11,26) where there were both Jewish and Gentile followers (11,19-20), so 'Christian' presumably included both, although the Jewish Christians in Judaea were called Nazarenes. Here, however, we use 'Christian' to mean Gentile Christian.
8. For example, Article 7 of the Articles of Religion in the Anglican **Book of Common Prayer** states, " . . . Although the law given from God by Moses as touching Ceremonies and Rites do not bind Christian men, nor the Civil precepts thereof ought of necessity to be received in any commonwealth; yet notwithstanding, no Christian man whatsoever is free from the obedience of the Commandments which are called Moral."
9. **Maimonides' Code, Book X, Uncleanness,** E.T. Danby, New Haven, 1954, p.393.
10. Since there is no longer a High Priest to officiate in their preparation (see Numbers 19).
11. If the people amongst whom Jesus grew up, were largely of non-Jewish descent, this might have affected him with a concern for Gentiles. E.R. Bevan, **The House of Seleucus,** London, 1902, Vol.II at p.256 refers to the Galilee of the Gospels as inhabited by the Ituraeans who were

forcibly circumcised by Aristobulus (104-103B.C.), and notes there (n.10), "The population amongst which Christ worked, and from which perhaps most of the apostles were drawn, was largely of non-Jewish descent." S. Freyne, **Galilee from Alexander the Great to Hadrian**, Delaware and Indiana, 1980, writes, however, at pp. 43-4 that the Ituraeans were to the North West and while they may have infiltrated into Upper Galilee, there is little chance of them, being brigands, having taken over a whole territory.

12. See e.g. H. Hubner, **Das Gesetz in der synoptischen tradition**, Witten, 1973, p.9f.
13. Cf. John 4,22, ". . . salvation is of the Jews."
14. Cf. Taylor, **Mark**, p.350.
15. J.M. Creed, **Luke**, London, 1950, p.66, however, doubts the authenticity of the implied analogy between the Capernaumites and the heathen widow of Sarepta and Naaman, as being too remote.
16. See also the reasons given A.H. M'Neile, **Matthew**, London, 1915, p.182.
16A. S.G. Wilson, however, **The Gentiles and the Gentile Mission in Luke-Acts**, Cambridge, 1973, in loc., apparently considers Jesus' belief to be that the mission to the Gentiles would be 'outside history'; he writes that Jesus did not expect a mission to the Gentiles because he 'believed that this hope would be fulfilled in the apocalyptic events of the Endtime.'
17. Cf. Taylor, **Mark**, pp. 507-8.
18. See J. Jeremias, **Parables**, pp.70f. and 63f.
19. See W. Marxsen, **Mark**, pp.93-94.
20. Metzger, op. cit., p.84.
21. Some texts (including p45) have $\delta\iota\alpha\gamma\gamma\epsilon\iota\lambda\alpha\nu$ ('proclaim widely') instead of $\dot{\alpha}\pi\alpha\gamma\gamma\epsilon\iota\lambda\alpha\nu$ ('report') which supports a sort of missionary activity for the demoniac. But this is hardly a strong enough indication to support evangelism as the reason for the return at 7,31.
22. Per Bowen, L.J. in **Edgington v. Fitzmaurice** (1885) 29 Ch.D. 459 at 483.
23. Thus, *'ger'* did not at this stage connote any allegience to the host country's god.
24. Although at Lev. 23,40 only native Israelites are to dwell in booths.
25. See Moore, **Judaism**, Vol. 1, pp.328-329.
26. The increase of legal strictness upon the **ger** between Deuteronomy and the Priestly Code is well described by S.R. Driver in **Deuteronomy**, ICC, Edinburgh, 1902, pp.165-6. On the date of P see Booth, **Jesus**, pp. 144-5 and 238.

27. **TDNT** VI, 729.

28. The Temple Rampart or balustrade separated the Court of Gentiles from the Courts of Women, of Israel and of Priests, and from the Sanctuary. The Court of Women was so called because women could go no further. Men could advance to the Court of Israel, but general worship usually took place in the Court of Women of which the women occupied only a raised gallery.

29. The Rabbinic regulations affecting *shechitah* are given an origin at Sinai from the words, "you may kill. . . as I have commanded you" in this verse.

30. So, apparently, Lev. 17,14, ". . . you shall not eat the blood of any creature (Heb. *kol basar*)." The *ger's* freedom to eat prohibited meat was probably of small practical benefit; to acquire the abhorred meats would presumably be difficult, and to eat them, socially ostracising.

30A. On the slab of the Temple inscription discovered by Clermont-Ganneau the prohibition on entry affects the '$ἀλλογενης$' which literally means a person not of Jewish *birth*. Josephus at **Bellum** V, 194 describes the inscription as prohibiting the '$ἀλλοφυλον$', which literally means a person of another *race* i.e. not a Jew by birth *or conversion,* but this is only secondary evidence. However, J.M. Baumgarten in 'Exclusion from the Temple: Proselytes and Agrippa I', **JJS** XXXIII, p.216-225 reviews this and other evidence, and concludes that the inscription was not applied to proselytes.

31. "The life of the law has not been logic: it has been experience." wrote Mr. Justice Holmes, **The Common Law,** Boston, 1881, p.1. Concerning other forces, particularly custom, in the development of law, see Booth, **Jesus,** pp.146-150.

32. We suggest in that Excursus that Jesus was, in fact, mistaken concerning the practice of the scribes regarding Korban.

33. Loeb edn. Vol. IV, p.183, We cannot agree with K. Lake, **The Earlier Epistles of St. Paul,** London, 1930, p.24, that in this context $τους \ ῥητους \ νομους$ can mean *traditional* law.

34. See IV, 24-33 and 163-70. As Lake, **op.cit.** notes, circumcision and the Jewish law are not mentioned.

35. From Josephus, **Bellum** II, 454 concerning Metilius, it appears that at the time of the War or at the time of Josephus' writing it was possible to 'turn Jew' without being circumcised, ". . $και \ μεχρι \ περιτομης \ Ἰουδαισειν \ ὑποσχομενον$. . ."

36. Josephus, **Antiquities,** XX, 38-47.

37. A distinct class of such persons has admittedly been doubted by A.T. Kraabel, but T.M. Finn in 'The Godfearers Reconsidered' **CBQ** Vol.

47, No.1 pp.75-84, calls in aid Philo and Josephus to support the evidence in Acts of their separate identity.
38. **Ad Nationes** I,13.
39. **Satires** XIV, 96-99 transl. J. Klausner, in **From Jesus to Paul**, ET, London, 1942, p.38. And see K. Lake **Epistles**, pp.37-40.
40. E.g. Acts 10,2; 16,14.
41. See Moore, op. cit. Vol. 1, p. 274f.
42. C.R. North in **The OT Interpretation of History**, London, 1946, at p.111 writes, "Only in the first world-age were men and beasts not carnivorous. A later age looked forward to such a happy condition as the ideal (Isaiah 11,7), perhaps as a return to primeval blessedness, and the permission to eat flesh which marks P's second era looks like a concession to the unideal." To-day agricultural economists, dieticians and animal rights activists might well agree with the First Isaiah—eating flesh is an uneconomical way of consuming the fruits of the earth, red meat is bad for the diet, and obtaining it is cruelty to animals.
43. Eating without removing the blood was considered a sin by Saul and the people at 1 Sam. 14,33-34.
44. This dating to the end of the Second Temple period or earlier is supported by J. Heinemann at JJS 25 (1974) pp.114-122. Differing views are held by scholars concerning the date of the Targumim, but P. Kahle thinks that in the PT we have material largely from pre-Christian times.
45. So dated by Charles, **The Apocrypha and Pseudepigrapha of the OT** Vol. 2, Oxford, 1913, p.6.
46. **Biblia Hebraica**, Stuttgart, 1969.
47. Sed vide contra, Danby, **The Mishnah**, p.356, n.9.
48. It was alleged (not without justification in view of statements such as Romans 10,4) that Paul had taught that even Jewish Christians did not need to observe the law (Acts 21,21).
49. See W.F. Flemington, **The NT Doctrine of Baptism**, London, 1948, pp.49-50.
50. The narrative in vv. 27-38 is not inconsistent with his admission as a proselyte into Judaism, for immersion would be his mode of entry like a woman convert. Targum Ps-Jonathan on Deut. 21,21 states regarding a woman captive taken to wife, ". . . let her put off the dress of her captivity, and, dipping herself, become a proselyte in thy house. . . "
51. See e.g. Acts 2,46; 3,1.
52. However, M. Dibelius claims, at **Studies in the Acts of the Apostles**, ET, London, 1956, p.95, ". . . the words are not in the least appropriate to the Peter of the Antiochan dispute. . . ". They are more antinomian even than Paul!

53. Klausner, **op.cit.** p.365 thinks it took place c.47 A.D., and see his discussion at his n.12; W.G. Kummel, **Introduction to the NT**, ET, London, 1966, p.398, states 49 A.D.
54. As evidenced in later letters issuing from Paul or his followers such as Colossians 2,8, 11-13, 16, 20-21.
55. Although several scholars, such as Dibelius, op.cit. p.100, conclude that it is not. Dibelius concedes however, that there was an Apostolic Decree in the terms stated by Luke (pp. 99-100). I.H. Marshall believes that the Decree existed in some form, and considers Rev. 2,14,20 to contain references to it (**Luke: Historian and Theologian**. Exeter, 1970, p.184).
55A. 'Do not do to others what you would not wish to be done to yourselves.'
56. Thus, W. Sanday, 'The Text of the Apostolic Decree', **The Expositor**, Vol 6 (8th Series), pp.290-305 at pp.298-305; J. Klausner, **From Jesus to Paul**, ET, London, 1942, p.368, n.18; C.S.D. Williams, **Acts of the Apostles**, London, 1957, p.183; D.R. Catchpole, 'Paul, James and the Apostolic Decree', **NTS** 23 (1977), pp.428-44 at p.429. Contra K. Lake, op. cit. London, 1930, pp.48-60.
57. Thus, E. Haenchen, **Die Apostelgeschichte**, Göttingen, 1956, p.459; **TDNT VI**, 593; W.M. Ramsay, **St. Paul the Traveller and the Roman Citizen**, London, 1942[19], p. 169; contra Catchpole, op. cit. p.429.
58. Op. cit. p.42.
59. E.g. at LXX Hosea 4,11 and 12 and Jeremiah 3,2.
60. Indeed, there is textual support for τοῦ πνικτοῦ, and that reading is accepted by B.M. Metzger, **A Textual Commentary on the Greek NT**, London/New York 1971, p.434.
61. The RSV translates v.20, "but should write to them to abstain from the pollutions of idols and from unchastity and from what is strangled and from blood." We think this translation is incorrect becuse it treats the three genitives following ἀλισγηματων των εἰδωλων (pollutions of idols) as also governed by the ἀπ(ο) (from) of ἀπεχεσθαι (abstain) rather than by ἀλισγηματων itself.
62. See also **Maimonides' Code, Book X, Cleanness**, ET, H. Danby, Yale, 1954, p.273.
63. At Jeremiah 3,1-3 idolatrous fornication stops the spring rains!
64. See De Vaux, **Ancient Israel**, London, 1961, p.384.
65. This verse is interpreted in Sifra as meaning that only the eater of the carrion of a clean bird is defiled during the time that the carrion passes through his gullet. This surprising interpretation need not concern us,

however, since scholars date the material in Sifra to the second century AD or later, and stress the interpolations in it. See Booth, **Jesus**, pp.209 and 248.

66. At 1 Sam. 14,31-35 the Israelites who ate the captured animals with the blood are said to 'sin (Heb. *hata'im)* against the Lord', and there is no reference to their cultic defilement: defilement may have been a later development.

67. Bowman, **The Gospel of Mark,** Leiden, 1965, p.168, mentions that the priestly tradition about *shechitah* must have originated before the Samaritan schism (4th Cent. B.C.) since the Samaritan priestly *halakhah* knows it.

68. De Specialibus Legibus, IV, 122.

69. Although the majority view is that the two Schools persisted from c.A.D.20 to 100 (e.g. **Encyclopaedia Judaica** IV, 737), A, Guttman in **Rabbinic Judaism in the Making,** Detroit, 1970, pp.106-113, argues that the division ceased shortly after A.D. 70: it seems that most of the recorded disputes between the Houses stem from before A.D.70 (*Enc. Jud.* ibid; Moore, **Judaism,** I, p.80).

70. See Booth op.cit. p.149.

71. We have translated here since J.W. Etheridge, **The Targums,** London, 1865, is ambiguous with "strangled (or corrupted)".

72. Maccoby, **The Mythmaker,** London, 1986, pp.218-9, n.1, notes the plasticity of exegesis of Gen. 9,4 and cites Jubilees 7 and Tos. A.Z.8,6, but in none of the Rabbinic versions of the Noachide laws do the prohibitions of blood and strangled meat appear.

73. Op.cit. pp.140-143.

74. Op.cit. p.143.

75. See Eusebius, **Ecclesiastical History,** Book II, Ch.23.

76. **Das Aposteldekret (Act 15,28,29),** Innsbruck, 1912.

77. 'The Apostolic Decree against πορνεια', **The Expositor** Vol.7, 8th series, pp.40-61 at p.54.

78. This belief is demonstrated at Targum Ps-Jonathan on Lev. 17,7, "Neither shall they offer any more their sacrifices unto idols which are like unto demons after which they have wandered."; also at I Cor. 10,19-21, "No, I imply that what pagans sacrifice they offer to demons and not to God. I do not want you to be partners with demons. You cannot drink the cup of the Lord and the cup of demons. You cannot partake of the table of the Lord and the table of demons."

79. Cf. Testament of Simeon, 5,3, "Beware, therefore, of fornication. For fornication is mother of all evils, separating from God, and bringing near to Belial." But demons may also attend the marriage bed, Tobit 8, 1-3."

80. Bacon, 'Decree', p.60. Cf. I Cor. 5,11; Hebrews 12,6.
81. **Op.cit.** p.54. the power of demons was also, however, the subject of *popular* Jewish belief. See A. Deissmann. **Light, from the Ancient East**, London, 1927, pp.302f. and Foerster, **TDNT**, II, p.12.
82. "The apostles and elders were gathered together to consider this matter. . . " (Acts 15,6).
83. The prime importance of Sabbath observance as a condition of acceptance into Israel is clear from Isaiah 56, 3-7.
84. Paul's account of the Eucharist at 1 Cor. 11,17-34 shows that it was then celebrated as part of a common fellowship meal. Cf. Jude 12.
85. 'The Levitical Uncleanness of Gentiles' in **Jews, Judaism and the Classical World**, ET, Jerusalem, 1977, p.146.
86. Alon, **op.cit.** pp.148,172.
87. See also Hosea 1,2; 8,5; Amos 7,17; Ezekiel 4,13; 23,7,30.
88. Concerning these decrees and their date (which other writers place at 66-67 A.D.), see Booth, **Jesus**, pp.162-9.
89. **Op.cit.** pp.156-8.
90. Heb. *litsahek,* LXX παιζειν, to be construed as fornication, we think, in view of the dances (τους χοϱους) seen by Moses at Ex. 32,19. Cf. 1 Cor. 10,7-8.
91. E.g. Ezek. 23,36, "with their idols they have committed adultery."
92. Alon, 'Uncleanness', op.cit. p.148. Concerning the special need of the priest, the farmer and the fisherman for purity, see Booth, **Jesus**, pp. 155-6, and concerning the exceptional position of the *haber,* see pp. 93-4 supra.
93. See on this story, Alon 'The Bounds of the Laws of Levitical Uncleanness', in **Jews, Judaism**, p.225.
94. **The Acts of the Apostles**, Oxford, 1922, p.204.
95. See on the Daniel, Tobit and Judith instances, Montgomery, **Daniel**, pp.130-1.
96. Alon, 'Bounds', p.225 n.93.
97. **Aboth de Rabbi Nathan**, Ch. 8.
98. See Driver, **Deuteronomy**, p.166.
99. The date of this Targum is also much disputed (cf.n.44). This is a very literal Targum which majority opinion believes to have a Babylonian provenance, and to be dated about the 3rd century A.D., although it probably contains traditions from earlier times.
100. Admittedly, Philo (c.20B.C. to c.50A.D.) interprets the Exodus provision only as prohibiting the cruelty of boiling a dead lamb in its mother's milk which previously sustained its life. The Mekhilta (about same age as the Mishnah, see Booth, **Jesus**, p.248 n.10) thereon

(Kaspa c.5) prohibits the cooking of meat together with milk.
101. See the discussion at Alon, 'Uncleanness', pp. 168f.
102. This would strictly mean that a Gentile convert should be sprinkled with the ashes of the Red Heifer (Numbers 19), but in fact he is immersed: however, the Hillelites considered he should be sprinkled. Other views were that the Gentile was impure as a *zab* (a sufferer from gonorrhoea) or as one contacted by a reptile, and thus was less impure than one defiled by a corpse. See Alon, 'Gentiles', p.175f.
103. Like a *zab* mentioned immediately above.
104. See note 88.
105. Regarding the relationship between custom and law, see Booth, **Jesus**, p.146f.
106. Regarding the supererogatory standard of purity maintained by the *haberim*, see Booth, **Jesus**, Ch.5.
107. Or contact with holy persons (priests) or produce (tithes); see Booth, **Jesus**, pp.155-6.
108. See Robertson & Plummer, **1 Cor.** Edinburgh, 1911, p.166 and C.K. Barrett, **1 Cor.** London, 1968, pp.194-7.
109. An example is shown at Deissmann, **Light from the Ancient East**, ET, London, 1927⁴, p.351 n.2.
110. The scribes had extended the law to Babylonia, Egypt, Syria, Ammon and Moab, but Barrett's statement at his **1 Cor.** p.188 that Jews could not eat 'idol-food' because the heathen would not have paid tithe on it, is incorrect since (a) it was the producer's duty to pay the tithe and only the *haberim* separated the tithe again if there was 'doubt', and (b) tithe was not payable on produce of Corinth.
110A. Cf. Ramsay on the Decree, "To render possible a real unanimity of feeling, the Nations must accept the fundamental regulations of purity." (op.cit. p.168).
111. Op.cit. pp.141-2.
112. Cf. Isaiah 43,19.
113. See e.g. **The Mysticism of Paul the Apostle**, ET, London, 1931, pp.188f.; the new law, however, may only be more explanatory than the old (W.D. Davies, **Paul and Rabbinic Judaism**, London, 1948. pp.71-3.
114. See Bultmann, **Theology of the NT**, ET, London, 1952, Vol. I, p16.
115. Jesus did not consider external impurity as important as purity of heart (Mark 7,15; see Booth, **Jesus**, pp.69-71 and Ch.6), but he could hardly ignore Gentile uncleanness which had been embedded in Jewish culture since the 8th century prophets, Amos and Hosea.
116. See Flemington, **Baptism**, p.4.
116A. Cf. Blunt, **op.cit.** p.204 and R. Joshua (c.A.D.90) at Yeb. 46a.

117. See Lev. 18,26; 20,2; 24,16, and Driver, **Deuteronomy,** p.165.
118. Cf. Matthew 5,33-7.
119. Not to be confused with God-fearing Gentiles; another description of the Jews as God-fearing, in a Jewish inscription in the theatre at Miletus in Imperial times, is cited by Deissmann, **Light,** in Appendix VIII.
120. Transl. The Ante-Nicene Fathers, Vol. VIII, p.268.
121. Op.cit. p.269.
122. Op.cit. p.274.
123. Transl. Lake, **Epistles,** p.58.
124. Our translation. The stress on the strictness of the abstention is noteworthy.
125. Transl. C.F. Cruse, Bohn, London, 1874, p.161.
126. Transl. Anti-Nicene Christian Library, Vol. XVII, p.265.
127. See thereon M. Douglas, **Purity and Danger,** London, 1966, pp.60-61. Until 1500, meat was forbidden to the monks of the Stams monastery in the Austrian Tyrol, so the fish yield of the Piburger See, a lake given to the monks in 1282, was important!
128. See Galatians 1,11-17; 1 Cor. 11,23; 2 Cor.12,1-7 and Barrett, **2 Cor.** pp.308-9 thereon.
129. See Booth, **Jesus,** pp.201-2.
130. See Mark 7,1-23.
131. See e.g. Mark 1,15.
132. See Mark 6,15; 11,32; Matt. 14,5; 21,26; Luke 7,16; 7,39 (a good example because incidental to polemic); 13,33; 24,19 (a good example as post-resurrection); John 4,19; 9,17. See also Chapter 6 infra.
133. See e.g. Amos 5,21-4.
134. North, **Interpretation,** p.177 (60,2 amended to 60,3).
134A. Dialogue, 23,3; see also Epistle of Barnabas, 15.
135. See Dix, op.cit. pp.336-7 and pp. 14-15 supra.
136. Many would say that he was not conscious of being even the Messiah, see Bultmann, **Theology,** Vol. 1, pp.26-32. The attribution of divinity to Jesus has probably ever since the Arian controversy, excluded from the Church many who have accepted Jesus as the supreme revealer of God's will for man (see pp.194-5 infra). It also creates obstacles to fellowship between Christians and members of the world's other monotheistic religions. See John Hick, ed. **The Myth of God Incarnate,** London, 1977. pp180-4.
137. E.g. Philippians 2,6-11; Colossians 1, 15-20.
138. Mark 12,29.
139. See e.g. Mark 1,44.
140. J. Weiss, **Paul and Jesus,** ET, London, 1909, pp.2-3 quotes Wrede

with approval, ". . . the title, Jesus' disciple, is hardly applicable to Paul. . . He is far more widely removed from Jesus than Jesus himself is removed from the noblest forms of Jewish piety . . . The teaching of Jesus is directed entirely to the individual personality. Man is to submit his soul to God and to God's will wholly and without reserve. . The central point for Paul is . . . a complex of divine actions which open to mankind a salvation prepared for man. He who believes these divine acts—the incarnation, death and resurrection of a divine being—can obtain salvation."

CHAPTER IV.

The Last Supper—to be repeated?

Does the evidence of the NT assertions of Jesus' words and actions at the Last Supper support or oppose the practice of the Church in continually repeating the Last Supper?

Parish or Family Communion has largely displaced Mattins as the principal Sunday morning service of the Church of England, yet this recent Anglican development only gives the repetition of Jesus' words and actions over the bread and wine the primacy in Sunday worship which, through the Anaphora and the Canon of the Mass, they have occupied in the Orthodox and Roman Catholic Churches for many centuries.

The Scriptural warrant for the primacy of the rite of the Last Supper in Christian worship may not be so strong as is often assumed, and we intend in this Chapter to examine (A) what, according to the NT evidence, Jesus said and did in connection with the bread and wine at the Last Supper, (B) whether Jesus intended that those words and actions should be repeated after his death by his followers, and (C) the consequences which our conclusions on these two questions entail for worship by his followers to-day.

In this examination we will apply the legal method adopted in the previous Chapters, namely that the statements of the NT writers are evidence for the authenticity of what they state, and that in order to determine whether the writer has discharged his burden of proof of authenticity, his evidence is to be weighed against any counter-evidence.

I. THE NT EVIDENCE

A. Routes in Delivery of Tradition.

Reports of Jesus' words and actions in connection with the bread and wine at the Last Supper are contained in each of the Synoptic Gospels[1] and in Paul's First Letter to the Corinthians (in this Chapter called a Gospel). However, the strength of the statements of an Evangelist (we treat Paul as such in this context) as evidence will vary according to the extent to which they appear to have originated with an eye-witness (including an ear-witness i.e. first hearer) who is independent in the sense of being a different person from the original reporter of other Gospel reports of the same incident. The weight of a Gospel statement as evidence will also be affected by the extent to which it has been handed down by tradents (i.e. persons who have verbally passed on the story) who are similarly independent in the sense that they have not handed down the other Gospel reports of the incident. Clearly, the Evangelist's report would have the greatest weight if he had witnessed the event or words himself; the next best would be if the Evangelist had received his report direct from an eye-witness, like the reports which Mark is thought to have received from Peter. Much of the Gospel evidence was probably received more remotely from the eye-witness, and for the purpose of illustration we set out below some of the routes whereby reports may have reached the Evangelist:-

1. Reports may have originally been given by more than one independent eye-witness as defined above, and the reports may have been passed down to the Evangelists by a series of tradents entirely separate from the tradents who passed down the other reports. It is difficult to know whether this is so, for the only clues to the route taken by a tradition (story) which reached a Gospel are the comparisons of content and language with the same story in the other Gospels.

The routes taken by these reports which are independent in origin and in delivery are easily shown:

Here the evidence of Ev. A will be admissible for or against the authenticity of the report of Ev. B, and vice versa.

2. The Gospel report may originally have been given by an eye-witness whose story has been passed down to more than one Evangelist by entirely different lines of tradents. Again, it will be difficult to prove that these are the routes taken by the reports in the Gospels, but such a situation may be indicated where the content of the stories in the Gospel reports is similar, but the translation Greek is substantially different. However, variations in the wording of similar reports may only indicate different tradents at the Greek translation stage; the story or speech may have passed in Aramaic down one line of tradents until passed by one tradent to two others who, passing it on in Greek, used different Greek words for the same Aramaic word.[2]

The routes here are:

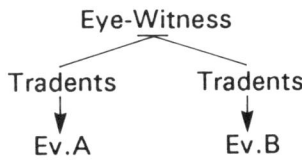

Here the evidence of Ev. A will not be admissible for or against the authenticity of the report of Ev. B that e.g. Jesus said certain things, since the two reports stem from the one eye-witness. The report in the one Gospel can only corroborate the evidence constituted by the report in the other Gospel, to the effect that *the eye-witness related* that e.g. Jesus said certain things.

3. The Gospel report may have originated with the same eye-witness as the reports in the other Gospels, or from a different eye-witness, but in each case the report has been handed down in only part of its journey by different tradents. Here are four examples of such routes involving a common tradent at some stage:

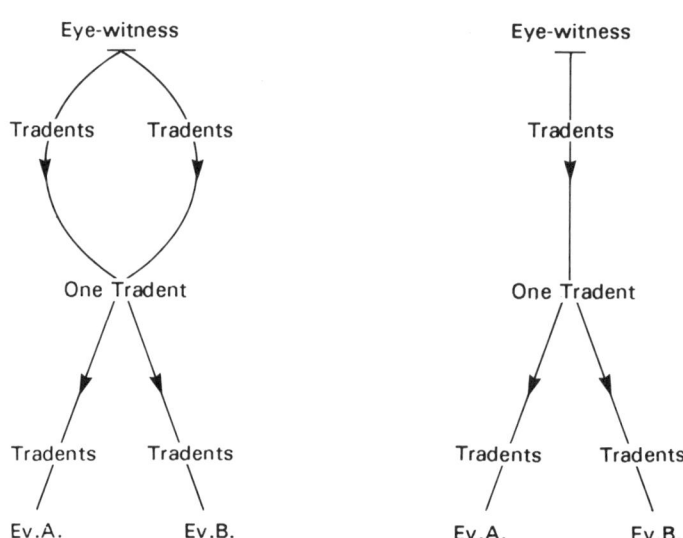

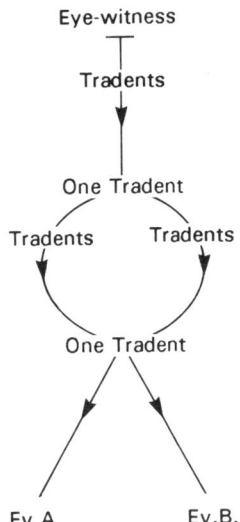 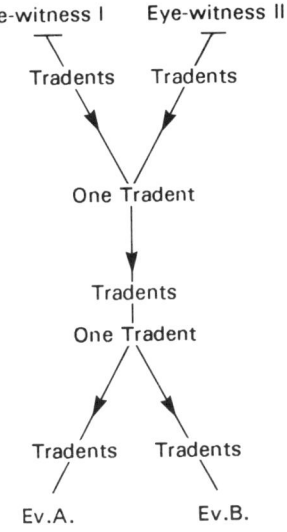

In all four cases the reports recorded by the two Evangelists have at some stage passed through one tradent who, when passing on the second report, has probably to some extent combined or conflated it with the first report he received. Where the tradent passed on the report which appears in Gospel A, before he received the second report which appears in Gospel B, then separate lines of tradition are maintained, and the two reports will support the authenticity of each other. However, where both reports were received by the tradent before he passed either on, then that mingling of the traditions in his memory probably results in the reduction of the witnesses from two to one; in that event, each Gospel report can only provide supporting evidence of the content of the one united tradition related by the common tradent. In fact, it is not possible to know whether two traditions were combined by one tradent or whether he received and passed on one tradition before the other. Indeed, it is difficult to elucidate by what route a tradition has reached the Evangelist, but the above permutations do illustrate the wide range of possibilities. Some stories such as the feedings of the thousands have probably been reported by hundreds of eye-witnesses, and the lines of tradition may have criss-crossed through scores of tradents before reaching the Evangelist.
4. The Evangelist may have copied his report from the written Gospel of another Evangelist. Here the one Gospel is not additional evidence to

the other Gospel. Again, it is difficult to assess whether a Gospel report is simply a copy of a report in another Gospel which the copying Evangelist has revised to express his theological viewpoint, or whether the reports in the two Gospels have at some stage of their delivery passed through a common tradent as described above.

The above illustrations provide a glimpse into the complex variety of routes whereby a Gospel story may have travelled from the original witness to its final form on the Gospel page. During its travel the story will have been subjected to the vagaries of the tradents' hearing and memory, and to their inclination to omit whatever seems irrelevant, insert whatever suits their religious or personal purpose, and generally to embroider. The difficulty of assessing the strength of the Gospel evidence which has been exposed to this risk of distortion during its delivery can readily be appreciated. Nevertheless, the Evangelists' assertions in their Gospels constitute evidence, and the historian must not shrink from the task of weighing that evidence.

We now consider by what routes the NT reports of the Last Supper reached the Evangelists. Matthew, on the general assumption that Mark is the earliest Gospel, has clearly copied Mark,[3] for Matthew's account at 26,26-29, repeats Mark's account at 14,22-25 with unimportant variations, and thus does not add to the strength of Mark's evidence. Paul claims at 1 Corinthians 11,23 that he 'received from the Lord' the account of the Last Supper which he passes on to the Corinthians, but since Paul was not a disciple of Jesus during Jesus' lifetime, and since in any case there was no available time for Jesus to speak to Paul about the Last Supper before the Crucifixion, Paul probably means either that (1) he received the report from the 'risen' Christ, perhaps as part of the Gospel to which he refers at Galations 1,12-13, or (2) that he received it not directly from Jesus, but through tradents who reported an eye-witness account.[4] Whatever be the manner of its delivery to Paul, we can reasonably treat his account as evidence of an independent witness; as it was written prior to the Gospels, his evidence is not copied therefrom. Consequently, evidence which is common to Mark's and Paul's accounts of the Supper, is strong, and we will now seek to identify it.

B. Evidence common to Mark and Paul.

There are important differences between the content of Mark's report and that of Paul's. At Mark 14,22 Jesus says over the bread, 'This is my body', whereas Paul by adding 'which is for you' to the saying, attaches the idea of vicarious suffering (1 Cor. 11,24). By contrast, at Mark 14,24 Jesus refers to his blood as 'poured out for many', whereas in Paul Jesus does not include vicarious words in the wine-saying (11,25). Thus, we cannot include the vicarious idea in the common evidence which we now seek, because the Evangelists put it in different places and, let it be added, in different terms.

After both the bread and wine sayings Paul adds Jesus' command to repeat the action in remembrance of him, whereas Mark has neither command. In the Marcan saying over the wine Jesus says, 'This is my blood of the covenant. . . ' whereas in Paul Jesus says, 'This cup is the new covenant in my blood.' Whether these two sayings are sufficiently similar to demonstrate a common content, is difficult to assess; Jeremias argues that their meaning is the same—"This (wine) (is) my blood (shed for the concluding of) the covenant."[5] We agree that both 'this' in Mark and 'this cup' in Paul refer to the wine, but the description of the covenant as 'new' only appears in Paul so is not a common element. However, although the link between the blood and the covenant is not expressed by Mark and Paul in the same words, its substance is expressed in both texts, and in view of the vicissitudes of the oral tradition, it is only the substance of Jesus' speech which we can hope to discover.[6] We think (with Jeremias)[7] that Mark's formulation of the wine saying is the older; Paul's formula is awkward, and may represent an attempt to avoid blood-drinking notions.

A minor difference is Mark's use of 'blessed' ($εὐλογησας$) after taking the bread (though not the cup), whereas Paul has 'given thanks' ($εὐχαριστησας$); 'blessed' in the sense of 'praised God for' is correct both for bread and wine, since the Jewish blessing, very probably used by Jesus, commences in both cases, 'Blessed art thou, our Father in heaven, who . . . '[8] A more important difference is the absence in Paul of the eschatological words after the wine at Mark 14,25, 'Truly I say to you, I shall not drink again of the fruit of the vine until that day when I drink it new in the kingdom of God.'

The variation in the 'for you' and 'for many' and their positioning, and the difference in the formulation of the wine saying could, we think, easily have arisen in the passing on of the same tradition by different series of tradents, and the 'anamnesis' command could well have been added by later tradents under the influence of Church practice. But the Marcan words over the wine which look forward to the Messianic feast, introduce a theme of the Supper of which Paul's account bears no trace, and which persuades us that the two reports have not only in the later stages been handed on by separate tradents, but are stories told by separate eyewitnesses. Admittedly, Paul writes at 1 Cor. 11,26 (immediately following his account), 'For as often as you eat this bread and drink this cup, you proclaim ($καταγγελλετε$) the Lord's death until he comes.', meaning, we think, that when the disciples eat and drink in remembrance of Jesus' death, they announce to the world the benefits achieved by that death until Jesus comes in the Kingdom. Although in Apostolic Constitutions VIII,[9] 12,16 these words are reported as spoken by Jesus in the first person, in Paul's account they are clearly Paul's commentary on the command to repeat. But even if they were Jesus' words, their eschatological thought is so unlike Mark's verse as to indicate separate origins for their traditions; for in Mark Jesus expects the immediate arrival of the Kingdom, whereas in Paul continued celebration of the Eucharist is contemplated.

Treating the two reports as separate witnesses, their common content is consequently well attested, and may be related as follows:
1. **Regarding the bread, Jesus took it, said the blessing, broke it, and said, 'This is my body.'**
2. **Regarding the wine, Jesus took the cup, said the blessing, and said, 'This is my blood of the covenant.'**

We will now consider what counter-evidence is to be weighed in the balance against this combined evidence of Mark and Paul.
C. Evidence opposed to Mark and Paul.
Luke.

Contrary evidence is contained in Luke's report of the Supper, at his Ch.22, but we must first examine which textual version of his report is the original one, since there is a Longer and a Shorter. We append below the Shorter version in capitals and the additional words of the Longer version are placed in small letters:

14. AND WHEN THE HOUR CAME, HE SAT AT TABLE, AND THE APOSTLES WITH HIM.
15. AND HE SAID TO THEM, "I HAVE EARNESTLY DESIRED TO EAT THIS PASSOVER WITH YOU BEFORE I SUFFER;
16. FOR I TELL YOU I SHALL NOT EAT IT UNTIL IT IS FULFILLED IN THE KINGDOM OF GOD."
17. AND HE TOOK A CUP, AND WHEN HE HAD GIVEN THANKS HE SAID, "TAKE THIS, AND DIVIDE IT AMONG YOURSELVES;
18. FOR I TELL YOU THAT FROM NOW ON I SHALL NOT DRINK OF THE FRUIT OF THE VINE UNTIL THE KINGDOM OF GOD COMES."
19. (a) AND HE TOOK BREAD, AND WHEN HE HAD GIVEN THANKS HE BROKE IT AND GAVE IT TO THEM, SAYING, THIS IS MY BODY (b) which is given for you. Do this in remembrance of me.
20. And likewise the cup after supper, saying, "This cup which is poured out for you is the new covenant in my blood."

The Longer version is read by all Greek manuscripts except D and by most of the ancient versions and Fathers. The Shorter or Western text which, as shown above, gives the sequence cup-bread rather than cup-bread-cup, is read by the Greek manuscript D and the Old Latin versions a,d,ff2,i and 1. The Old Latin versions b and e contain the Shorter version, but secure the bread-cup order by placing v.19a before vv.17 and 18. Some Syriac versions omit the second cup and place the bread first but contain additions from 1 Cor.[10] The textual evidence for the Longer version is thus much stronger, but we will now consider the evidence offered by the probable sources and manner of composition of the above Lucan verses.

Verses 15 and 16 are, we think, from Luke's special source ('L') for they are both peculiar to Luke's account, and it appears that he has drawn them from tradition.[11] In v.15 the ἐπιθυμιᾳ ἐπεθυμησα ('I have earnestly desired') follows the formula used in the LXX for translating the Hebraic infinitive absolute with finite verb.[12] Luke could simply be following this LXX usage himself in order to express intensity, but we think it is more likely to be the result of Greek translation of a Palestinian tradition.[13] Nor do we think that Luke has created the vow in v.16 over the Passover as a parallel to the wine-vow; at least where parallelisms appear in Mark, J.M. Creed[14] notes that Luke is inclined to remove them.

At first glance the content of v.17 is similar to Mark 14,23 in that the actions of taking, blessing and giving to the disciples to drink are present in both Gospels, but the 'divide it among yourselves' (διαμερισατε εἰς ἑαυτους) in Luke which indicates that the disciples are to drink it all, leads naturally to Jesus' vow that *he* will not drink until the Kingdom comes; this emphasis is not surprisingly absent in Mark who follows the disciples' drinking[15] not with Jesus' vow (which follows later) but with the words of interpretation over the wine. Since in his v.17 Luke thus differs from Mark not merely in language used but in emphasis, and since in his next verse not interpretative words but the vow is contained, we think Luke's verses stem not merely from different tradents but from a different source. Admittedly, Mark's wording of the vow at v.25, following the interpretative words, is similar to Luke's in that both contain οὐ μη πιω ('I will certainly not drink'), του γενηματος της ἀμπελου ('of the fruit of the vine') and ἡ βασιλεια του θεου ('the kingdom of God'), but further indication that Luke is using a separate source may lie in his not using Mark's wording for the limit of the vow, i.e. 'until that day when I drink it new in the kingdom of God.' Luke might have preferred Mark's formula with the LXX expression της ἡμερας ἐκεινης ('that Day')[16] but has remained loyal to his own source, perhaps because Mark's 'until. . . I *drink it new* (καινον) in the Kingdom. . . ' hints that Jesus drank himself at the Supper, whereas Luke's v.17 indicates not.

Nor does the similarity of Luke's v.19a to Mark's and Paul's actions and saying over the bread suggest that Luke has relied on either Evangelist; probably by the time the Evangelists received the traditions they were all fairly standardised in the actions and saying over the bread, apart from the vicarious addition. Mark's, Paul's and Luke's versions here differ slightly, but this is to be expected, due either to different tradents or redaction, and no argument can be drawn therefrom, we think. Moreover, it is recognised that Luke used his sources in blocks,[17] and it is unlikely that he switched from his own 'L' source to Mark just for the actions and saying over the bread in v.19a, when the following v.21 (in the Shorter Version) continues with the betrayal announcement which we deduce from its variations from Mark's 14,18-21, to be also from Luke's own source.[18]

The Longer version adds the words το ὑπερ ὑμων διδομενον ('which is given for you') to the saying over the bread in the Shorter Version. This amplifies the το ὑπερ ὑμων ('which is for you') in Paul's bread saying, and the additional wording of the Longer version containing vv.19b and 20 so closely follows 1 Cor.11,24b (from το ὑπερ) to 25a (ἐμῳ αἱματι) in general that we are persuaded that a scribe has made the addition to conform Luke's version to the Pauline account with its emphasis on Jesus' sacrifice and his remembrance (which account became dominant in the Church of the 2nd century). We do not think that Luke copied the additions from 1 Cor. because there is no other indication that he knew that Letter, and it seems strange that he should in mid-story, indeed in mid-sentence, change in v.19 from following his private source to following an unwritten or liturgical tradition. Admittedly, it also seems strange that the scribe did not also insert into Luke, 1 Cor. 11,25b (the command to repeat the action over the wine in remembrance). Perhaps the scribe, wishing to interpolate no more that necessary, considered that the command to repeat over the bread would suffice to ensure the continuance of the rite.

The ordering of the wine before the bread does not seem to have been a creation of Luke. At 1 Cor. 10,16-17 Paul refers to the 'cup of blessing which we bless' before he mentions the 'bread which we break'. Similarly, the Didache whose regulations "reflect the life of a primitive Christian community somewhere in Syria (or possibly Egypt) towards the close of the first century",[19] contains thanksgivings first over the chalice and then over the particles of bread (Ch.9). Nor does the order of cup-bread conflict with the ritual of the Passover meal, since at Pesah 10,2 we learn that over the first cup of wine the host said a Benediction (Heb. *berakah*) and that only after the drinking of a second cup of wine did the host say the Benediction over the unleavened bread.

We thus see no difficulty over Luke's cup-bread order, and judge that the evidence that the additions of the Longer version, including the second cup, were added to produce conformity with the Pauline account, outweighs the textual evidence in favour of the Longer version.

Having concluded, therefore, that Luke's evidence consists of the statements in the Shorter Version, we now weigh that evidence in relation to the common evidence of Mark and Paul:—

1. We think that the common evidence of the bread-cup order outweighs Luke's counter-evidence and its limited support as mentioned above.
2. Luke's independent report of the words and actions over the bread at v.19a constitute supporting evidence for the common evidence.
3. Although for the reason explained below (p. 123), we are reluctant to admit evidence e silentio, yet the interpretative words over the wine are so integral to the Supper that Luke's omission of them must be allowed as counter-evidence. That counter-evidence, however, which by its nature can hardly be cogent, is in our view outweighed by the common evidence.

Luke's counter-evidence accordingly does not affect our conclusion above (p. 118) on the common tradition. There is other counter-evidence to the inclusion of the reference to 'the covenant' in the common wine-saying, but that is more appropriately considered when we have investigated whether the other traditions add to the form of that saying.

We must stress at this point that the common evidence, supported as it is by two separate traditions, has a greater claim to authenticity than the evidence arising from only one tradition; its probability is a stronger probability.

D. **Gospel Traditions other than common Mark and Paul.**

Mark.

Looking now at Mark's additional tradition, small differences regarding the bread which may appear pedantic, but which we treat as significant later (p. 138-9) are that at Mark 14,22 Jesus on a strict construction of the text appears to say 'This is my body' while *distributing* the bread, but at I Corinthians 11,24 he appears to say those words while *breaking* it. This is indicated in Mark by the two italicised phrases following: 'And as they were eating, he took bread, and blessed, and broke it, *and gave it to them, and said,* "Take; this is my body."'[20] (και ἐδωκεν αὐτοις και εἰπεν, λαβετε). We place in italics the words to be contrasted in Paul: ". . . took bread, and when he had given thanks, he *broke it, and said,* "This is my body which is for you. . . " ἐκλασεν και εἰπεν). We think that

Paul's evidence is stronger than Mark's here since Jesus probably meant that the bread was like his body because his body was to be broken like the bread; Jesus' principal concern at this solemn moment would be, that he should be understood, and if the words were said while he *broke* the bread, then there would be little danger.[21] But if he said them while *giving* the bread, the disciples might have thought they were to treat the bread as his flesh, and consequently been offended (as John at 6.66 indicates that some disciples were, although we think they mistook Jesus' intent). Otto writes that Jesus "does not liken himself to bread in a general way, in the sense that as bread is food for the body, so am I food for the soul. He compared himself rather to the broken bread."[21A]

The same differences re-appear over the wine. In Mark, Jesus appears to say 'This is my blood' *after* he has given them the cup and while they were drinking (ἔπιον, imperfect tense) from it. Mark 14,23 reads, 'And he took a cup, and when he had given thanks, he gave it to them and they all drank ('were drinking' is more correct, we think) of it. And he said to them, "This is my blood. . . ". At 1 Cor 11,25 we read, 'In the same way also the cup (inferring, 'he took') after supper, saying, "This cup is the new covenant in my blood. . . ". Thus Paul describes the words with which Jesus likens the wine to his blood, as being said over the cup *before* Jesus hands it to the disciples. Here again we prefer Paul's evidence; Jesus probably intended to show the disciples that his blood was to be poured out like the wine had been, and therefore he would say the words *before* he passed the cup to them. If he spoke the words while they were drinking, the disciples would, similarly to the bread, think that he was asking them to drink his blood, and they, as good Jews, might have been revolted, the drinking of blood being an oft-repeated Levitical prohibition.[22]

We thus prefer Paul's evidence that Jesus spoke the bread-words while breaking the bread, and the wine-words over the cup before passing it. Mark states that Jesus gave the bread (14,22) and the cup (14,23) to the disciples; Paul does not mention the 'giving', but it is implicit in his account from the circumstances. To express Mark's tradition here but Paul's sequence we will add after Jesus' respective symbolic words to the disciples, the following: — '**He then gave the bread to them.**' and '**He then gave the cup to them**'.

Mark's tradition also states (14,24) that Jesus added, 'which is poured out for many' (το ἐγχυννομενον ὑπερ πολλων) after 'This is my blood of the covenant'. This additional phrase is absent from Paul's version of the *wine*-words (11,25), but the same note of vicarious or atoning suffering is recorded by Paul in Jesus' words over the *bread*.[23] The authenticity of this Marcan addition is supported by the procedure affecting the wine. The wine was mixed (with water) before it was placed at the side of the host,[24] so that Jesus, to avoid the horrific impression that by his words, 'This is my blood', he was inviting them to drink blood contrary to the serious prohibition of the Law, says 'This is my blood poured out for many.' Thus, Jesus explains that just as the wine is poured out, so his blood will be poured out at his death: but Jesus needed to add the 'poured out' because he was not pouring the wine himself—it had previously been poured into the cup which lay on the table.[24] Conversely, Jesus did not need to say over the bread 'broken for you', because he broke the bread at the same time as or immediately after he said 'This is my body', so the simultaneous breaking would show, without Jesus saying 'broken for you', that his body like the bread was to be broken at death. Strictly, the present participle ἐγχυννομενον is used, as in Hebrew and Aramaic, with a future sense, i.e. *to be* poured out'.

Mark's 'for many' might give the impression of being Church reflection on Jesus' death, for both the 'poured out' and the 'for many' recall the death of the Isaianic Suffering Servant: at 53,12 we read, '. . . because he poured out (Heb. *he'ereh)* his soul to death. . . yet he bore the sins of many (Heb. *nasa rabim heta).* But Jesus also, we believe, saw his death in the model of the Suffering Servant, so this reflection may equally have been expressed by his own words. The use of 'many' is semitic, meaning 'all except one',[25] and the thought of vicarious suffering accords with what we think was Jesus' purpose, namely that in order to bring in the Kingdom of heaven, he was to accept the pre-Messianic suffering which would otherwise be the fate of all men.[26] Admittedly, Mark's evidence of the 'for many' phrase over the wine is not corroborated directly by another tradition. Paul omits the phrase, but has a similar phrase 'for you' over the bread, while John at 6,51 connects vicarious suffering with the bread but nowhere with the wine. Justin omits the concept both over bread and wine but very little weight can be attached to his evidence.[27] However, we would not normally count the omission of words in one tradition as opposing evidence to the evidence of their inclusion in another, since we would be reluctant to treat any Gospel report as containing *all* the words that Jesus said on a particular occasion, even on a tense one like the Last Supper where Jesus' specific words might have made more of an impression on the disciples' minds than usually.

We would hesitate before allowing other considerations to over-rule Mark's evidence of the 'for many' phrase, since Paul's evidence regarding the bread-words suggests that the vicarious aspect of the suffering was expressed at the Supper. We note Jeremias'observations[28] that words which 'move around' are suspect, but their movement may simply illustrate the fallibility of human memory and oral delivery. The difficulty of reaching a decision on this 'for many' phrase is accentuated by the precarious chance, as discussed above, of the exact words of anybody remaining intact and without distortion in transmission for forty years or so from their utterance. Nevertheless, we have to judge on the evidence available to us, and we think that Mark's evidence for the phrase supported by the evidence of Jesus' view of his suffering as substitutional, and the evidence of similar thought in Paul's and John's words concerning the bread, are weightier than the negative evidence arising from the omission by Paul and John of the vicarious idea in connection with the wine.

Jesus' further sentence over the wine (the vow) at Mark 14,25 does not appear in Paul, but the same content appears in Luke in Jesus' second sentence over the wine at 22,18. Both traditions have the emphatic negative οὐ μη, re-inforced in Mark with οὐκετι ('no more') and in Luke with ἀπο του νυν ('from now'). Jeremias notes that this wording is 'in the form of a careful declaration of intent, almost an oath.'[29] The only important difference of wording between the Marcan and Lucan forms is that the oath in Mark is not to drink any more from the fruit of the vine 'until that day when I drink it new in the kingdom of God', whereas in Luke it is 'until the kingdom of God comes.' While it is possible that Luke may merely have abbreviated the Marcan form which lay before him, we incline to think, as explained above (p. 119), that Luke who would from a literary viewpoint probably have preferred the Biblical 'that day when I drink it new', has retained the plainer phrase 'the kingdom of God comes' because that was in his separate tradition comprising the whole account of the Last Supper, namely verses 14-19a, according to our conclusion above (p. 121). While Luke's oath over the wine is not so different from Mark's that it could not be due to distortion by separate tradents, we think that it comes from a separate witness of the Last Supper because it forms part of the said separate tradition in vv. 14-19a of which vv. 15-17 are largely unparalleled in Mark, and must have emanated from a separate witness.

Thus, the oath over the wine is found to be attested by the separate traditions evidenced by Mark and Luke which constitute strong evidence because they emanate, in our view, from separate witnesses of the Supper. We see no opposing evidence, since we do not treat the silence of Paul and John as such; indeed, Paul's own comment following his account of the Supper, that by eating the bread and drinking the cup 'you proclaim the Lord's death till he comes', gives some support to this eschatological theme.

The additional tradition thus established here by Mark's evidence is the addition to the wine-saying of the following words emphasized in black:

'This is my blood of the covenant, **which is poured out for many. Truly, I say to you, I shall not drink again of the fruit of the vine until that day when I drink it new in the kingdom of God.**'

Paul.

Turning to Paul's account apart from that common to Mark, the first addition to be noticed is the 'which is for you' after 'This is my body' in v.24. The only contrary evidence is the silence of Mark and Luke, but John at 6,51, as mentioned above, supports the vicarious thought regarding the bread. Jesus' reference at Mark 14,24 to the wine as 'poured out for many' introduces the same thought, however, and since this purpose of his death may well have been present to Jesus' mind for the reasons discussed respecting the Marcan phrase, Paul's evidence is, in our view, stronger than the evidence of the silence in Mark and Luke.

An addition by Paul to the wine-words common to his and Mark's evidence is the description of the covenant as 'new'. We accept Paul's evidence here since (1) although Mark does not expressly so describe it, the covenant to be solemnised by Jesus' blood must logically be a new one, and (2) the covenant was likely to have been connected in the minds of both Jesus and his disciples with Jeremiah's prophesy of a new covenant at 31, 31-34.

Very important in Paul's tradition are Jesus' words over the bread at 1 Cor. 11,24, 'Do this in remembrance of me', and his similar words over the cup at 11,25, 'Do this, as often as you drink it, in remembrance of me.' The authenticity of these words vitally affects whether Jesus intended at the Last Supper to establish a cultic rite to be repeated by his followers. Paul's is the only evidence for these words in the NT accounts of the Supper, since we have classified Luke's Long Version as secondary. (Justin includes virtually the same remembrance words in connection with the bread at Apol. 63,30.) As mentioned above, the silence of the other accounts concerning these words of remembrance is not counter-evidence since the accounts can hardly claim to be exclusive. The counter-evidence which may exist is the unlikelihood of Jesus having commanded the repetition of the acts concerned. Therefore, in evaluating this possibility, we must first ask—what was Jesus commanding to be repeated?

We have established that Jesus took bread, blessed it, broke it and said, 'This is my body which is for you.' According to Paul, Jesus adds, τουτο ποιειτε εἰs την ἐμην ἀναμνησιν ('Do this for the recall of me', or per Jeremias, 'that God may remember me').[30] As G. Dix has pointed out,[31] Jesus could not have been commanding the disciples to bless and break and distribute bread at the start of a meal, since "this is precisely what they will in any case all of them do. . . every time they sit down to supper on any evening with any other jew in Israel." Nor do we think it likely that Jesus was commanding them to repeat *his* words every time they broke bread. It seems uncharacteristically severe and formal for Jesus to have imposed a rule that every time the disciples ate, the leader should not only before breaking the bread bless the Lord in accordance with scribal law for his goodness in providing it, but should also when breaking it recall the death of Jesus. It is also arguable that if Jesus had intended to command the repetition of the interpretative words over the bread, his command would have been, 'say' this, rather than 'do' (ποιειτε) this, in remembrance of me; it is possible, however, that this ambiguity has arisen from the Graecizing of the Aramaic or Hebrew words of Jesus. Notwithstanding a Jewish Christian practice,[32] it seems unlikely that Jesus meant 'remember me at the breaking of bread at every Passover', since the words over the wine are 'as often as you shall drink it'.

Regarding the command over the wine, we have established that Jesus took the cup, said the blessing, and added, 'This is my blood which is poured out for many.' Although Jesus continues (according to our view of Luke's evidence at p.130), 'Take this and divide it among yourselves. . . ', Paul would add before those words, 'Do this, as often as you drink it, in remembrance of me.' This appears to be a command to remember Jesus whenever they drink wine. As Jeremias explains,[33] wine was only drunk on festive occasions including the meals at the beginning and end of the Sabbath (although, presumably, the rich indulged more frequently). Thus, the remembrance of Jesus over the bread would take place much more frequently than the remembrance of him over the wine, unless the frequency of wine drinking was to be increased. But what are the disciples commanded to do regarding the wine in remembrance of Jesus? Jesus has taken the wine, said the blessing, and likened the wine to his blood; since his followers would recite the Jewish blessing anyway, the only new feature which could be perpetuated would be the comparison of the wine to his blood. But even though the Jewish blessing over the bread was recited before it was broken, and the blessing over the wine recited before the cup was passed round, we think it unlikely that Jesus commanded the saying of interpretative words during the breaking of the bread and over the wine, because by their closeness to the Jewish blessings, those words would constantly detract from the concentration of thought upon those blessings; it was important that the necessary intention accompanied prayer.³⁴ Perhaps Paul's tradition had originated in a Gentile community where they probably would not recite the Jewish blessings over bread and wine, so that the repetition of Jesus' words would not interfere with concentration on the blessings.

Paul's evidence of Jesus' commands may be thought to be supported by the practice of Christians as recorded by Justin onwards, which is to eat and drink in assembly bread and wine over which Jesus' interpretative words have been recited. However, this practice cannot be regarded as independently *corroborating* Paul's evidence, since the Church's ritual has been *based upon* Paul's evidence. Moreover, the sayings over bread and wine have been perpetuated by a Gentile Church unaware of the difficulty which would be caused for Jewish Christians by their inconvenient propinquity to the Jewish blessings. For the speaking of words of interpretation of the bread and wine on an unique occasion after the Jewish blessings at passover is quite different from the commanding of their conventional repetition after those blessings.

We think that the unlikelihood of Jesus having commanded the repetition of these solemn interpretative sayings immediately after the respective Jewish blessings outweighs the evidence of Paul.

The additional tradition thus established by Paul's evidence is the addition of **'which is for you'** to Jesus' saying over the bread, 'This is my body'.

Luke.

We have already considered (pp. 118-121) Luke's *counter-evidence* to the common tradition of Mark and Paul; now we are to seek in Luke's Shorter Account any independent tradition which *adds* to that common tradition. Jesus' words at Luke 22,15, 'I have earnestly desired to eat this passover with you before I suffer;' are not evidenced elsewhere, but there is no counter-evidence against Luke's. The thought behind Luke's words is so different from anything in the other traditions that we think the tradition has not only been passed down by separate tradents, but has been originated by a separate witness at the Supper. As mentioned earlier, the use of the verb and the dative noun in ἐπιθυμιᾳ ἐπεθυμησα is translation Greek for the semitic verb and infinitive absolute expressing intensity ('I have earnestly desired') which perhaps indicates an early origin for the tradition.

Luke 22,16 contains in vow-like wording Jesus' declaration that he will not eat the passover until it is fulfilled in the kingdom of God, and the meaning here, that Jesus will not eat the passover until its 'type' is accomplished in the Messianic feast, is similar to the meaning at Mark

14,25 (and at Luke 22,18) that Jesus will not drink again till he drinks at the Messianic feast. However, the wording of the two concepts is (as suggested above, p. 118) sufficiently dissimilar to indicate that Luke has not modelled a saying about the passover food to be parallel to the saying about the wine, but has received a separate tradition. Whether v.16 forms part of the same tradition as v.15 is, however, affected by whether the two logically link together. Firstly, it seems contrary for Jesus to say, 'I have desired to *eat* this passover before I suffer (v.15) because I will *not eat* it until. . . ' (v.16). This conflict between the desire to eat and yet the vow not to eat, is alleviated if, with Creed,[35] we infer the ἀπο του νυν (from now) from the wine-vow of v.18; then the meaning is 'I have desired to eat this passover, for I will not eat it from now (i.e. again) until. . . ' But there are two objections to this solution: it is not logical to insert words into one verse because they appear in similar thought in a later verse (there is manuscript evidence for οὐκετι in v.16 but Metzger[36] excludes it since it is absent from important mss. such as p75, A and B). Secondly, even with such an insertion, the two verses still present a non-sequitur—why should Jesus desire to eat the passover because he will not eat it again until. . . ? Thus, we cannot see justification for inserting or inferring either οὐκετι or ἀπο του νυν.

We think the inconsistency is resolved by understanding the desire to 'eat the passover' (φαγειν το πασχα) as meaning to *celebrate* the passover, rather than literally to eat it. To 'eat' (φαγειν) the passover is used in this sense of celebrating it at Mark 14,12 (followed by Matthew at 26,17) and at Mark 14,14 where Matthew at 26,18 uses ποιω, but where Luke at 22.11 follows Mark. Jesus in our view neither eats the food of the Passover nor drinks the wine.[37] At v.16 Jesus emphatically declares that he will not eat the passover, and at v.17 after taking the cup and giving thanks, he gives it to the disciples telling them to *divide it amongst themselves;* it was the custom for the host to drink first,[38] but these words coupled with the declaration that from now on he will not drink, preclude the drinking by Jesus first.

Jesus means, we think, at v.15 that he has greatly desired to 'celebrate' this passover because he has anticipated that the authorities will take the opportunity to seize him when he comes to Jerusalem for the festival, and that thus the pre-Messianic tribulation will commence. For Jesus is frustrated by waiting for the suffering to start. He expresses this same impatience at Luke 12,50 (also 'L' material), 'I have a baptism to be baptised with; and how I am constrained (συνεχομαι) until it is accomplished!' The literal meaning of συνεχεσθαι is 'held together' so that 'reined in' or 'tense' or 'pent-up' is probably the broader meaning intended here (cf. Bauer s.v.).

The οὐ μη in both v.16 and v.18 is so emphatic a denial that it may indicate an oath or vow, and Jeremias[39] notes that a vow of abstinence, as here, could be used to support petitionary prayer; the petitioner almost attempts to *will* God to grant the petition by drastic refusal of some vital need such as food or drink until the petition is granted. In other words, the petitioner showed his overwhelming desire for the thing sought by vowing some rash abstinence until it was granted; at Acts 23,12 for example, the Jews bound themselves by an oath not to eat or drink until they had killed Paul.[40] In that the vow of abstinence constitutes an attempt to obtain a favourable answer to prayer by forcing God's hand, it seems unlikely that Jesus' relationship with his heavenly Father would permit him to 'threaten' the Father by a vow of this sort; it savours of the same unloving action towards God as relying on God for preservation when invited to throw oneself from a high tower—such temptation of God was not countenanced by Jesus (Matt. 4,5-7; par. Luke 4,9-12) whose obedience to the Father is a central theme of the Gospel records. On the other hand, the vow at the Supper could be regarded as simply a demonstration of Jesus' confidence of the nearness of the onset of the Kingdom, and in that light it seems no closer to 'forcing God's hand' than his belief that his rôle was to bring in the Kingdom by suffering in place of the people, since their expected tribulation had not taken place.

We are persuaded by this latter view. Jesus has been beseeching God to bring in the Kingdom from early days; he prayed 'thy Kingdom come', and he told the disciples it would arrive before they had gone through the towns of Israel (Matt. 10,23). Jesus is now so confident of the almost immediate arrival of the Kingdom that he feels able to vow that he will not eat until he celebrates the Messianic passover.

Thus, the apparent internal conflict between these two verses is resolved, we think, if Jesus is understood to mean, 'I could hardly wait for the celebration of this passover with you to arrive, so that I could actually get started on the challenge of the suffering, and now the suffering is starting, the Kingdom is so close that I will not eat the passover until I celebrate it in the Kingdom of God!' Consequently, there is no evidence of internal conflict to oppose Luke's evidence of Jesus' words in these two verses, and we accordingly adjudge them both to have lain in Luke's separate tradition.

Regarding Jesus' taking of the cup at Luke 22,17 we decided above that Luke's evidence of the cup-bread order was overwhelmed by the combined evidence of Mark and Paul to the contrary, but Jesus' command, 'Take this and divide it amongst yourselves', coheres with his vow not to drink until the Kingdom comes as expressed in the following v.18. Both these verses are from Luke's separate tradition, and while the drink-vow in v.18 supports Mark's evidence thereof at 14,25 which we have already incorporated into our established content of the Supper account, there is no evidence in Mark or Paul to gainsay the distribution words of v.17 which, as mentioned, are consistent with the vow. We accordingly treat them as authentic and, further, are persuaded by the consistency between Jesus' command to the disciples to share the wine amongst themselves and the ensuing vow not to drink until the Kingdom comes, that Luke's version of the drink-vow is more likely than Mark's to be the original one. Regarding v.19a which ends the Shorter Version, we have already mentioned that, being also taken from Luke's separate tradition, this supports Mark's version of the saying over the bread.

The additional tradition thus established by Luke's evidence is the desire and vow concerning the passover, the words of delivery to the disciples of the wine, and the vow concerning the wine (respecting which we find Luke's evidence of its form more persuasive than Mark's) as follows:

'Jesus said, 'I have earnestly desired to eat this passover with you before I suffer; for I tell you I shall not eat it until it is fulfilled in the kingdom of God. . . Take this and divide it among yourselves; for I tell you that from now I shall not drink of the fruit of the vine until the kingdom of God comes.'

E. Evidence opposing the 'Covenant' reference in the Tradition.

As mentioned earlier (p. 121), we must finally consider some counter-evidence to the words over the wine which the evidence hitherto adduced has established as 'This is my blood of the new covenant which is poured out for many.' The counter evidence arises primarily not from any internal inconsistency of this statement but rather from its complicated nature. For, compressed into this one short sentence are the ideas that Jesus will die through his blood being poured out, that he is dying in place of men generally, and that the blood poured out at his death will seal or solemnise God's covenant with man. Although not contained in the same sentence, we have seen that another theme of the Last Supper was the expectation of the imminent Kingdom. Now three of these themes are easily integrated in Jesus' information to the disciples at the Last Supper that his blood like the wine is to be shed, and for their benefit, and that his death will bring in the Kingdom; the disciples have been prepared for this information by previous teaching attested in the Gospels. But there is no other reference by Jesus in the Gospels to the concept of *covenant*, except for the saying of Jesus at Luke 22,29 ('L' material) that 'I have arranged (or disposed— διατιθεμαι) for you as my Father has arranged a Kingdom for me, that you may eat and drink at my table in my Kingdom.' (our translation).

Creed[41] thinks that διατιθεμαι in this verse is meant to recall the Biblical covenant and to be a substitute in Luke for the reference to ἡ διαθηκη (the covenant) in the omitted words over the wine, but surely the meanings of ἡ διαθηκη in the wine saying, and in the verbal form διατιθεμαι in this verse, are different. In the wine saying it is express in Paul and implicit in Mark that the covenant is a new one, and is therefore being compared with the old one made at Sinai which involved expressions of will by two parties, God and the people; Moses told the people the words of the Lord, and the people replied that they would do those words (Ex.24,3 and 7.) The bilateral covenant at Sinai was solemnised with the blood of oxen (Ex. 4-6,8); the new bilateral covenant is to be solemnised with the blood of Jesus.[42] But as J. Behm has pointed out,[43] ἡ διαθηκη can mean an unilateral declaration or ordinance of God, which, of course, is consistent with its use elsewhere as last will and testament. And this unilateral meaning is clearly the use at Luke 22,29 where God has unilaterally arranged a kingdom for Jesus just as Jesus has arranged or disposed for them to dine with him in the Kingdom. Thus, a bilateral use of ἡ διαθηκη in the wine saying would be the only reference by Jesus in the Gospels to the bilateral covenant. Although probably only a small part of Jesus' teaching is contained in the Gospels, the absence of any other reported reference by him to the bilateral concept of covenant constitutes in our view evidence of unlikelihood that he would introduce it into the condensed explanatory words over the wine.

The probability that Jesus saw himself in the rôle of the suffering Servant of Isaiah 49 and 53, and of the Danielic and Enochic Son of Man, is discussed and approved in our Chapters 2 and 6, but neither the Son of Man nor the Suffering Servant are closely linked to the inauguration of a new covenant. Otto writes that the Servant was expressly given by Yahweh as 'a covenant to the people' at Isaiah 42,6 and 49,8.[44] At 42,6 Yahweh says of the Servant, 'I have given you as a covenant to the people, as a light to the nations', and at 49,8 'I have kept and given you as a covenant to the people. . . ' But this is an unilateral act of God's favour, an assurance of salvation to the prisoners, the blind etc;, it is not a 'type' for the making of a new covenant 'twixt God and people which Jesus is expressed to solemnise in the wine saying.

In Daniel 7,13 we read that '. . . with the clouds of heaven there came one like a son of man. . ' and Jesus refers almost certainly to himself in these terms at his trial before the High Priest (Mark 14,62), but while dominion, glory and kingdom are give to the Son by the Ancient of Days (7,14), such a grant is of the nature of unilateral disposition and probably the 'type' of Jesus' words at Luke 22,29, and it gives no hint of a consensual covenant between God and man. Nor is the inauguration of a new Sinai-type covenant mentioned in connection with the Son of Man in the Book of Enoch, whose thought is largely a development of the Danielic vision respecting the Son.

Jeremias[45] cites the Qumran documents as showing 'how vital the promise of the new covenant (Jer. 31,31-4) was in the days of Jesus.' Certainly the Qumran Community believed themselves to be the faithful remnant with whom God had entered into the New Covenant prophesied by Jeremiah. The covenant was the basic premise of the Community; at Community Rule I, we read, 'All those who embrace the Community Rule shall enter into the Covenant before God to obey all his commandments. . .',[46] and at Damascus Rule VI, 'But God remembered the Covenant with the forefathers, and he raised from Aaron men of discernment, and from Israel men of wisdom, and he caused them to hear. And they dug the Well. . . None of those brought into the Covenant shall enter the Temple to light his Altar in vain. .'[47] Nevertheless, there is no evidence in the Gospels that Jesus and his circle saw themselves as "the sole beneficiaries of a new Covenant in the final age", as Vermes claims.[48]

As mentioned, the only explicit reference in Jesus' recorded teaching to the new covenant is at the Last Supper (Mark 14,24). However, the kernel of Jesus' preaching is the eschatological proclamation of the Kingdom of God, and God's rule is the subject-matter of that new covenant between man and God. At Jeremiah 31,33 God describes the content of the new covenant as 'I will put my law within them and I will write it upon their hearts; and I will be their God, and they shall be my people.' Behm writes, "The $\kappa\alpha\iota\nu\eta\ \delta\iota\alpha\theta\eta\kappa\eta$ (new covenant) is a correlative of the $\beta\alpha\sigma\iota\lambda\epsilon\iota\alpha\ \tau o\upsilon\ \theta\epsilon o\upsilon$ (Kingdom of God). While the latter portrays God as the absolute Lord of the age of salvation, the former seeks to express the overruling divine will which sets the goal. One and the same goal of fulfilment is indicated by both the thought that God reigns and the thought that the new divine order is valid, i.e. the order which finally determines the relation of God to man."[49] Thus in Jesus' proclamation of the Kingdom he may have intended implicit reference by association to the new covenant.

Yet there does seem to have been a tendency for words to be added to the tradition in the course of time. In Matthew's version of the words over the wine at 26,28 the words 'for the forgiveness of sins' have probably been added by him to Mark's account which he was following. It is possible that as new ideas about the significance of Jesus' death were gleaned from Scripture, they were introduced into the tradition, and perhaps the reference to the new covenant was thus inserted into these interpretative words.

Lastly, it can be argued that there is an internal inconsistency in the mixing of the atoning blood and the solemnizing blood in the words over the wine: can Jesus' blood both be poured out for the benefit of others like the Suffering Servant's and ritually ratify the making of a new covenant between God and Man?

The question of the authenticity of Jesus' reference to the covenant represents a challenge to the proper use of legal methodology.[50] The counter-evidence to that of Mark and Paul, constituted primarily by lack of recorded teaching by Jesus about a new bilateral covenant and the unlikely encapsulation of almost conflicting concepts into a short sentence, strikes us as strong. On the other hand, we have the apparently separate traditions attesting the covenant reference which we think are probably derived from separate witnesses, recorded by Mark and Paul. Our methodology need not insist, however, that Jesus connected the wine with his blood, and his blood with his death for others and with the covenant-blood, all in one sentence as asserted by the Evangelists. Otto writes,[51] "Christ said more on that evening than is contained in the brief records of the ancient pericope. It was not important that it should go into detail, for its only aim was to supply a short document to authorise the rite which was already observed and which, with all its associated meanings was known and practised in the church. In a succinct hieroglyph, using only the significant words, it said just what was necessary for the purpose."

The principal thrust, however, of our methodology is that due weight must be given to the evidence of the Evangelists, and its due weight is heavy where there appear to be two separate strands of tradition, and particularly heavy where the two strands appear to emanate from separate witnesses of the occasion recorded.[52] As mentioned, the compressed nature of the sentence over the wine seems to be strong evidence against these witnesses to the covenant reference, but our treatment of the Evangelists' statements as evidence does not require that we treat them only as evidence that Jesus spoke the words recorded in the sentence recorded. We are enquiring into what Jesus said and did in connection with the bread and wine at the Last Supper, and we are not debarred from interpreting Mark and Paul's evidence of the wine-words, together with the counter-evidence of the unlikely compression therein of differing concepts, as proving that Jesus did connect the wine with his blood, and his blood with his dying for others and with the sealing of a new covenant, but in different sentences. It is not essential that the linking of his death with the new covenant should have been uttered contemporaneously with the other wine-words; the timing of the words here is not important evidentially, as it can be in some issues, such as whether the instruction by the accused to the colleague with a gun to shoot the policeman is given before or after the gun is fired. (R v. Bentley).[53]

Consequently, considering that:
(a) the weight which must be given to the evidence of Mark and Paul, originating in separate witnesses, is heavy,
(b) in view of the importance of the new covenant in Deutero-Isaiah, Jeremiah and Ezekiel and its topicality as shown by the Dead Sea Scrolls, Jesus may well have referred to it in his unrecorded teaching, and
(c) since we are only seeking proof that **sometime** at the Supper Jesus linked his blood with the inauguration of a new covenant, the improbable linking of that concept with two others in one Gospel sentence is not a difficulty,
we find the evidence of Mark and Paul, interpreted as asserting that at some time during the Supper Jesus spoke of his blood in connection with the new covenant, to be stronger than the counter-evidence.

Obviously, we do not know the words used by Jesus when connecting his blood with the covenant, nor at what point during the Supper he spoke them, but we think that the substance of his words can be expressed in a formula such as, **'My blood will solemnise the new covenant.'** In order to indicate our conclusion that this connection was expressed separately, we will place the above formula after the other words interpreting the wine.

F. Conclusion on words and actions at Last Supper.

Thus, our enquiry into the evidence of the Gospels and Paul establishes that on a balance of probabilities the authentic words and actions of Jesus over the bread and wine at the Last Supper were as follows:—
1. Jesus said to his disciples, 'I have earnestly desired to eat this passover with you before I suffer; for I tell you I shall not eat it until it is fulfilled in the kingdom of God.'
2. And he took bread, said the blessing, broke it, and said, 'This is my body which is for you.' He then gave the bread to them.
3. And he took the cup, said the blessing, and said, 'This is my blood which is poured out for many. My blood will solemnise the new covenant. Take this and divide it among yourselves; for I tell you that from now on

I shall not drink of the fruit of the vine until the kingdom of God comes.' He then gave the cup to them.

II. JESUS' INTENTION FOR THE FUTURE

Although we have found the express command to repeat, as reported by Paul, to be inauthentic, this does not exclude the possibility that Jesus might nevertheless have intended that his followers should repeat in some way or to some extent his words and actions at the Last Supper. The Church's Eucharistic practice, continuous through the centuries, demands that the possibility be at least considered.

Much depends on the purpose of Jesus' words and actions. If Jesus was intending by his words and actions simply to communicate important information in a memorable way, then there seems to be no reason why he should have intended his followers regularly to repeat the symbolic communication. If, however, Jesus intended (1) that his disciples at the last supper should receive spiritual benefit by the consumption of bread and wine which he gave to them after comparing them to his body and blood, and (2) that future followers should receive spiritual benefit by the consumption of bread and wine according to a similar procedure, then he clearly did intend the repetition of his words and actions. The following factors suggest to us that Jesus did not intend their repetition.

A. The Theme of the Supper.

Those words and actions must be interpreted in the light of the circumstances surrounding the Last Supper, as recorded by the Evangelists. Jesus had predicted his suffering and death since Peter's confession at Caesarea Philippi (Mark 8,29f. and par.), and in his vow not to eat the passover until the Kingdom, he shows his awareness that his suffering is about to commence. Indeed, in Mark before the bread and wine (14,18) and in Luke immediately afterwards (22,21), Jesus announced his impending betrayal.

Following that prediction of his suffering and the Kingdom, Jesus breaks the bread, saying, 'This is my body which is for you'. He thereby demonstrates by a parable that his body is to be broken in death for others. Then over the cup he declares that, like the wine, his blood is to be poured out, and for the sake of many; he thus again expresses the manner and purpose of his death. Finally, by his vow affecting the wine Jesus repeats his assurance that the Kingdom is to arrive very soon.

Thus, the theme of Jesus' discourse is eschatology—the pre-Messianic suffering and the breaking-in of the Kingdom. When this is to happen so soon, what point is there in commanding his disciples to repeat a dining ritual? Shortly they will be with him sitting on thrones in the Kingdom and judging the tribes of Israel (Luke 22,30)! It may be argued that this is just another example of the paradox affecting eschatological prophets as noticed by Otto[54] —that,like Zoroaster and Mohammed, they predict the imminent end of the world, but they also give ethical and other instruction to their followers which appears unaffected by a foreshortened time scale. The difference here, however, is that Jesus' reported instruction regarding the bread and wine relates to things to be said and done *after his death,* whereas Jesus' other teaching, such as the Sermon on the Mount, and the teaching of Zoroaster and Mohammed, inculcate present behaviour without reference to the death of the teacher.

B. The disciples' dining customs.

The unlikelihood of Jesus having intended the repetition, as a rite, of his words over the bread and wine is also indicated by the dining customs of the disciples after his death.

At Acts 1,14 we read that the disciples 'with one accord devoted themselves to prayer. . . ', and at Acts 2,42 that the newly baptized 'devoted themselves to the apostles' teaching and fellowship, to the breaking of bread and to the prayers.' Jeremias, although he maintains that the first meals of the early Church were not repetitions of the Last Supper but of the table fellowship (i.e. ordinary meals) which the disciples had enjoyed with Jesus,[55] nevertheless argues that the breaking of bread at 2,42 refers to the Eucharist, and that 'the breaking of bread' is never used as the name for the whole meal.[56] Dalman, however, considers that it could be so used,[57] and it seems to us unlikely that the breaking of bread refers to the Eucharist in the neighbouring verse 46 which reads (our translation), 'and daily spending much time in the Temple together and breaking bread in their homes, they shared their food with joy and simplicity of heart, praising God and having favour with the whole people.' Surely the natural meaning here is that they had fellowship meals together in their homes and shared their food.

J. Behm states correctly in our view, "The technical use of $\kappa\lambda\alpha\nu$ $\accentset{\,\prime}{\alpha}\varrho\tau o\nu$ and $\kappa\lambda\alpha\sigma\iota\varsigma$ $\tau o\upsilon$ $\accentset{\,\prime}{\alpha}\varrho\tau o\upsilon$ for the common meals of primitive Christianity is to be construed as the description of a common meal in terms of the opening action, the breaking of bread. Hence the phrase is used for the ordinary table fellowship of members of the first community each day in their homes (Acts 2,42,46), and also for the common meals of the Gentile Christian communities (Acts 20,7;cf.1 Cor. 10,16). In the former, table fellowship is one of the forms in which the early Christian sense of fellowship finds expression. It has no liturgical character, but is full of religious content because of the recollection of the table fellowship which Jesus had with his followers during his earthly ministry. . . "[58] It is, indeed, unlikely that the disciples should soon after Jesus' death repeat his words about his body over their breaking of bread (they would not often have wine)[59] since, as discussed in Chapter I, their attitude was one of intense expectation that Jesus was to arrive as Danielic Son of Man at any moment. For this reason they shared their food with 'joy and simplicity of heart', and praised God. Because Jesus had promised the disciples that they would eat and drink at his table in the Kingdom, and because at the Last Supper he had promised that he would not drink again until he drank anew ('with them' adds Matthew at 26,29, correctly, we think, according to the tenor), the disciples probably believed that Jesus would return as Messiah at one of their communal meals such as they had enjoyed with him.[60] Sayings of Jesus such as at Luke 12,37 may have been recalled by the disciples at this time. There, in a parable (vv. 35-8, cf. Mark 13,33-7) showing the need for readiness for the coming of the Son of Man, Jesus says, "Blessed are those servants whom the master finds awake when he comes; truly, I say to you, he will gird himself and have them sit at table, and he will come and serve them.

It was only much later, we think, when they realised that Jesus' parousia was not to be as immediate as they had hoped, that Gentile Christians, perhaps influenced by the Hellenistic Mystery religions, developed the rite of remembering Jesus' death in his words and actions over the bread and wine, and treated the bread and wine as being his body and blood for spiritual sustenance.

Probably the most characteristic feature which the disciples remembered about Jesus in their table fellowship, was his breaking and giving of the bread as their leader at the start of the meal; that is mentioned in both the miraculous feedings,[61] and it is the feature by which the disciples recognised Jesus in his resurrection appearances at Luke 24,30-31 and 35 (cf. John 21,12-13).

After Jesus' death, these fellowship meals which re-created the joy at table which the disciples had experienced with him, and in which they looked forward to his triumphant return, would still start with the breaking of bread, but would not normally involve wine, because of their impoverished state as during his life.[62] Hence the meals could naturally be called 'the breaking of bread', and we have early records of such joyful meals partaken with thanksgiving and anticipation, in the Didache and Tertullian.[63] In 1893 F. Spitta[64] distinguished between these joyful agapés or love-feasts in which the remembrance of Jesus' death was subservient to the element of thanksgiving, and the Pauline Eucharist in which his death was remembered over the bread and wine in accordance with his supposed instructions. In 1926 H. Lietzmann,[65] pursuing this distinction, traced back the thankful 'breaking of bread' through the

Egyptian liturgy of Sarapion (4th century) and the Didache (c.150 A.D.) to Acts 2,42-47. This 'Jerusalem' type of Eucharist Lietzmann contrasted with the third- century Roman liturgy of Hippolytus which was descended from an Eucharist largely created by Paul as a memorial of Christ's death, and based on Jesus' words over the bread and wine at the Last Supper.

Although the compilation of the Didache can, as mentioned, probably only be roughly dated at about 150 A.D., yet its Church regulations, as quoted above, "reflect the life of a primitive Christian community somewhere in Syria (or possibly in Egypt) towards the close of the first century. . . "[66] It is consequently very relevant that the prayers in the Didache over the chalice and the bread give thanks for the life and knowledge made known to the worshippers through Jesus, and possess an eschatological theme both in the prayer that the Church may be brought from the ends of the earth to the Kingdom, and in the Aramaic prayer 'Marana tha' ('Lord, come quickly!').

It seems that the Didache is describing a Jerusalem-type breaking of bread because the commanded words over the bread and wine are missing: it also seems to be an agapé because of the rubric, 'when all have partaken sufficiently, give thanks in these words:'. It thus appears unlikely that the church of the Didache believed that Jesus had commanded the repetition of his words over the bread and wine.

It appears from Paul's rebukes to the Corinthians for their greed and irreverence at 1 Cor. 11, and from his careful recitation to them of the words of Jesus over the bread and wine, that up to that time (A.D. 54/55), they were not remembering the death of Jesus over the bread and wine, but were enjoying an (excessively!) festive meal[67] (cf. Jude 12). 'The cup of blessing which we bless' and 'the bread which we break' mentioned by Paul at 1 Cor. 10,16 may relate not to Jesus' commanded words, we think, but to the customary Jewish thanksgivings, even though Paul is there urging the Corinthians to treat the bread and wine as a sharing in the body and blood of Christ. Paul's injunctions and recitation of the institution in Ch. 11 probably do, however, mark the first step in the separation of the ritual over bread and wine from the meal, in that from that time they may well have both been placed together at the end of the meal.

Reaching back to even earlier evidence of breaking bread, at the post-Resurrection meal at Emmaus, recorded by Luke at 24,30-31, Jesus took, blessed (εὐλογησεν) and broke bread with the two disciples, but there is no indication that the blessing was other than the usual Jewish blessing over bread: Jesus did not apparently call to remembrance his death over it. Similarly, in the meal on the beach at John 21, 9-14 Jesus took the bread (and fish) and gave it to the disciples, but there is no suggestion that he recalled the words concerning his death—in each case they recognised the giver as Jesus because of his oft-repeated giving of the bread to them in the past.[68]

A.J.B. Higgins, however, denies the reality of a Jerusalem breaking of bread, unaffected by the remembrance of Jesus' death in the commanded words. He argues (inter alia) that Paul did not originate the rite in memory of Jesus' death, because the command to repeat over the bread belonged to a tradition he claims to have received; this remembrance of Jesus' death was not due to the influence of Hellenistic memorial feasts but to the primitive Palestinian church repeating the Last Supper which, being a passover meal, contained a central element of remembrance even before Jesus' additions. He writes, "It seems then, that the antithesis 'primitive-Palestinian breaking of bread in Acts' and 'Hellenistic-Pauline Eucharist' is false, and that the element of remembrance of Christ's death was just as probably present in the former as in the latter."[69]

Our above understanding of the 'breaking of bread' in Acts 2 as a name for the common meal persuades us, however, that the disciples in Jerusalem were not repeating the Last Supper, but were rather eating in each other's homes the same kind of communal meals as they had enjoyed with Jesus. No doubt, despite the predominant mood of thanks and expectancy of his return (cf. $\dot{\alpha}\gamma\alpha\lambda\lambda\iota\alpha\sigma\epsilon\iota$ $\varkappa\alpha\iota$ $\dot{\alpha}\phi\epsilon\lambda\acute{o}\tau\eta\tau\iota$ $\varkappa\alpha\varrho\delta\iota\alpha$s, Acts 2,47), the disciples cannot fail to have reflected on his cruel death, but it is a big step from that admission to the belief that they constantly as a rite repeated his words at the Last Supper; those words, after all, were only forewarning them of the nature and purpose of the death which he anticipated, but which was glorified by his resurrection.[70] The same note of thanks and expectancy prevails in the Didache; thought of his death may well have been present, but they clearly felt no need to repeat his prophesy of his death and its purpose every time they had bread and/or wine together.

J.M. Creed identifies the true nature of the Last Supper, when he writes of Luke's description of it, "Luke could scarcely have described the Supper as he does, if he had thought of the Eucharist on Pauline lines as a proclamation of the death of Christ according to a rite instituted by Jesus at the Last Supper. And there are other indications that he did not do so: the disciples at Emmaus (c.XXIV) had not been at the Last Supper, yet they recognise Jesus in 'the breaking of the bread'. The action was presumably characteristic and followed a familiar form. It is this custom which is perpetuated in the early Church as pictured in Acts (ii.42,46). The Last Supper falls into place with the other occasions of 'breaking bread', but it does not originate the rite."

C. **The influence of the Mystery Religions.**

We think that Paul, in order to compete with the attractions to Gentiles of the Mystery religions, transformed Jesus' teaching at the Supper concerning the nature, time and purpose of his death, into a sacramental meal. For it was Hellenistic Christianity that provided fallow ground for the sacramental development of Jesus' words over the bread and wine. The Gentile Christians were probably influenced by the devotees of the Mystery religions, who united themselves with, and received strength from, their divine heroes by eating their flesh and drinking their blood in a sacramental meal.[71] These Christians literalised Jesus' words and treated the bread and wine at their fellowship meals as if they were converted into the body and blood of Jesus. Early signs of this approach are Pauls words at 1 Cor. 10,16, 'The cup of blessing which we bless, is it not a participation ($\kappa o\iota\nu\omega\nu\iota\alpha$) in the blood of Christ? The bread which we break, is it not a participation in the body of Christ?'. The developed form of this sacramental treatment is illustrated at John 6,53-56 and particularly v.56, 'He who eats my flesh and drinks my blood, abides in me and I in him.' Similarly, baptism, which to John the Baptist was a 'baptism of repentance for the remission of sins' (Mark 1,4), has under the probable influence of the Mysteries, become for Paul the death of the old life and a resurrection to new life; he writes, 'We were buried therefore with him by baptism into death, so that as Christ was raised from the dead by the glory of the Father, we too might walk in newness of life.' (Rom. 6,4 cf. Col. 2,12). Similarly, John reports Jesus as saying, '. . . unless one is born anew, he cannot see the kingdom of God.' (3,3).

The similarities between aspects of the Mystery religions and Christianity are numerous. The former arose out of the worship of vegetation deities and consequently their annual death and resurrection are solemnised. In the cults of Cybele and Attis from Phrygia the initiate is re-born, his sins are remitted, and he is brought into communion with the Godhead; in the Attis cult the fiction of new birth was maintained for a while afterwards by feeding the convert on milk like a baby.[72] The Mystery cults also involved a sacramental meal, and the meal in Mithraism seems to possess most associations with the Last Supper. It ritually commemorates the banquet which Mithras, then a mortal, celebrated with the Sun before Mithras ascended to heaven, and the devotees achieve communion with Mithras by the consumption of bread, wine and water.[73] Explanatory of Paul's injunction to the Corinthians not to partake of the cup or the table of demons (I Cor. 10,21) are the invitations to dine at the table of 'the Lord Serapis' at Nos. 110⁷⁴ and 523 of the Oxyrhynchus Papyri; the Egyptian cult of Serapis based in Alexandria, was widely spread through the Hellenistic world. The benefits conferred by these religions resembled those of Christianity and were expressed in similar language. They imparted salvation (σωτηρια) and the deity was called 'saviour' (σωτηρ). Salvation included protection from sickness and misfortune but primarily incorruptibility of the soul (ἀφθαρσια cf. 1 Cor. 15,42,50,53) and immortality (ἀθανασια cf. 1 Cor. 15,53,54).⁷⁵ With this common background of concepts it is not surprising that, as K. Lake wrote, ". . . many of the Greeks must have regarded Christianity as a superior form of "Mystery Religion". (That) is . . . of enormous importance in considering the course of development of Christian doctrine from the belief that the Messiah was Jesus, and that he was speedily coming to set up the Kingdom of God, to the creed in which the original meaning of the word "Messiah" or "Christ" was almost wholly forgotten, Jesus was regarded as a Redeemer-God, and the Sacraments became the real centre of Christianity."⁷⁶

D. The Symbolism of the Bread and Wine.

As explained above (p.122) we accept Paul's evidence that Jesus spoke the interpretative words while breaking the bread, and over the cup before passing it round. The purpose of Jesus' words was to tell the disciples that his body was to be broken just as the bread was being broken, and that his blood would be poured out just as the wine had been poured out. The symbolism, we believe, then ceased, for the notion that Jesus, the Jew, should invite his disciples to drink blood or eat human flesh, even symbolically, is unthinkable. Consequently, the bread and wine did not continue to be like his body and blood so as to be spiritual food and drink for the disciples. Indeed, the magical connotations of such an idea seem alien to mainstream Jewish thought. The Israelites treated the lambs at the Exodus and at subsequent passover festivals as bodily, not spiritual, food; similarly the manna in the wilderness, although given by God, was nevertheless considered purely physical food. (Exodus 12,4;16,3).

The erroneous impressions that Jesus said, 'This is my body . . . ' at the moment of giving the bread to the disciples, rather than when breaking it, and said 'This is my blood . . . ' at the time of passing the cup to them, rather than previously, are responsible for the belief of many Christians today that Jesus intended the bread and wine to be eaten and drunk for spiritual benefit *as if they were his body and blood*. This misunderstanding has been perpetuated through the centuries by the Church's liturgies which still provide for the repetition by the celebrant of similar words identifying the bread and wine with Jesus' body and blood at the time of delivery of the morsel and the cup to each communicant.

It accordingly does not seem justifiable to deduce from Jesus' procedure at the Supper an intention that the bread and wine when consumed by the disciples should be treated as his body and blood, and it is consequently difficult to accept that Jesus intended the elements as spiritual food then or for the future.

E. Conclusion.

We are persuaded by the above factors that, notwithstanding the Church's ancient practice, Jesus did not intend the ritualistic repetition of his words and actions at the Last Supper, and that the Church's Eucharistic rite probably originated with Paul and Gentile Christians, who were influenced by the Mystery religions.

III. THE CONSEQUENCES FOR WORSHIP TO-DAY

We have concluded that Jesus did not intend that his words and actions respecting the bread and wine should be repeated and thus become part of a religious rite, but only intended thereby to explain symbolically to his disciples the manner and purpose of his death. It therefore does not seem logical that those words and actions should occupy the dominant position in the worship of his followers. We must now consider what form of worship Jesus may have wanted his disciples to continue. Since Jesus expected that his disciples were very shortly to be eating and drinking at his table in the Kingdom and judging Israel, he is very unlikely to have considered how they were to worship in his absence. We therefore have to consider what Jesus would have intended, had the situation been present to his mind. Notwithstanding the difficulty of hypothesis thus involved, it seems to us likely that he would have wanted his followers to continue to worship in the way which he had observed, and had taught his disciples to observe while he was with them.

We read in the Gospels that Jesus—

A. Attended the Temple at the festivals (e.g. Mark 11,11,15).
B. Attended the synagogue (e.g. Mark 1,39).
C. Shared with his disciples meals of thanksgiving to God and fellowship with each other (e.g. Mark 2,15; 3,19-20; 6,41-42; 8,6-8; cf. 1,19; Luke 24,30-31; John 21,12-13).
D. Prayed privately (e.g. Mark 1, 35).

A and B. Attendance at Temple and Synagogue.

Attendance at the Temple has been impossible since its destruction in A.D.70, but Jesus' followers of to-day can still attend synagogues. They would not be able adequately to express their love for him there, however; readings from the NT, Christian hymns and prayer would, understandably, not be allowed since Judaism does not accept Jesus as Messiah. But it seems reasonable to suggest that Jesus would have wanted his disciples to continue a synagogal form of worship of God, but with the necessary adaptation to permit expression of their conception and love of himself. Let us enquire, therefore, how Christian worship today (apart from repetition of the Last Supper) compares with the worship in the synagogue of Jesus' day. Provided worship of God remains 'in spirit and in truth' (John 4,23-4), there seems no reason why its Christian development from the synagogal form of his own day should not be acceptable to Jesus. At least, we can find in the early liturgy of the synagogue the elements of worship which Jesus would know and probably revere.

For we know that Jesus customarily attended the synagogue on the Sabbaths (e.g. Mark 1,21; Luke 4,16f., 6,6); probably he attended on other days also for Mark 1,39 relates that Jesus "went throughout all Galilee, preaching in their synagogues and casting out demons." But did the first followers continue Jesus' practice of attendance? The evidence indicates that they did. At Acts 1,12-14 Luke reports that the disciples returned to Jerusalem after the Ascension, went to the upper room where they were staying, and 'all these with one accord devoted themselves to prayer. . . '; τῃ προσευχῃ, translated here as 'prayer' can also mean a place of prayer, i.e. a synagogue, and is used to mean a synagogue by Luke at Acts 16,13.[77] The disciples, excluding women who were not counted, no doubt exceeded the quorum (probably ten)[78] necessary for constituting 'a synagogue' to say the prayers. However, whether or not the earliest Christians formed their own synagogue or attended an established one, it seems clear that prayer together ('common' prayer) was an important feature of their life. Acts 2,46 also mentions the newly baptized attending the Temple, and at 3,1 Peter and John are going up to the Temple at the hour of prayer, the ninth hour; thus may we assume that the prayers of Jesus' first followers were those of the Temple and the synagogue. We also note that it was in a synagogue or synagogues that Stephen disputed with his opponents (Acts 6,9), and that it was to the synagogues at Damascus that Paul was travelling to find followers of the Way (Acts 9,2). It was also to the synagogues of a town that Paul first went in search of converts on his missionary journeys (Acts 13,14; 17,10; 19,8). The form of worship adopted by the first Christians can only have been that of the synagogue because that was the only form which most of them will have known (apart from the Temple).

We must accordingly enquire into the nature of the synagogue services in the first half of the first century A.D., and compare those services with the present forms of Christian worship. The synagogue had three daily services, morning, afternoon and evening. The morning and evening services probably originated in the practice whereby the worshippers of the district whose priestly course was sacrificing in the Temple, conducted prayers in the local synagogue at the same times.[79] When the Herodian Temple altered the evening sacrifice to afternoon, the evening service was retained in the synagogue additionally to the afternoon one, because the saying of the *Shema* in the morning and evening, publicly or privately, had long been a traditional observance.[80] The morning and evening services consisted of the *Shema* and its blessings, and the *Tefillah* (prayer) or *Amidah* which developed into the *Shemoneh Esreh* (18 benedictions) with their congregational responses. The afternoon service contained the *Tefillah* alone.[81] The modern version of the *Shema* consists of three passages, Deut. 6,4-9 ('Hear, O Israel. . .'), 9,13-21 and Num. 15,37-41, and it is fairly certain that at least the first passage was recited in the time of Jesus. This passage is the closest statement the Jews had to a creed until Maimonides' Thirteen Principles of the Faith. The accompanying blessings principally concerned the time of day. It is probable that the Decalogue was also read in these services in Jesus' day.[82]

Regarding the *Tefillah,* not all the 18 benedictions were prayed in the time of Jesus, and C.W. Dugmore states that the first three and the last three are the oldest. The individual worshippers offered their private petitions, which were summed up by a Reader, and it is thought that the benedictions developed out of the Reader's summarising prayer.[83]

There were readings from the Law on Sabbath mornings and afternoons, Mondays and Thursday afternoons, holy days and certain other occasions. In at least one of the Sabbath services there was a reading from the prophets.[84] It seems that in Jesus' day there was probably opportunity for commentary or homily after each reading from Scripture.[85] Thus, at Luke 4,16-21 we hear how Jesus was asked to read the *haftorah*, (the reading from the prophets), and comment on it afterwards. The *Hallel* psalms (113-118) were sung on 19 festival days in the year, and other psalms may have been sung on other occasions.[86] Thus the principal elements in the synagogue worship were credal statement, prayer, scripture, homily and psalm.

Because the synagogue services containing these elements constituted the only forms of worship known to most early Christians (apart from the Temple), these elements naturally passed into the specifically Christian forms of worship when, due partly to the introduction of the curse on the heretics and Nazarenes in the daily 'benedictions', the Christian Jews were dissuaded from participation in the synagogues.[87] These services influenced both the pro-Anaphora of the Eastern Church and the

Canon of the Mass (or Ministry of the Word of the Holy Communion) of the Western Church.

For the synaxis ('meeting for worship') before the Eucharist is described by Dix as "simply a continuation of the jewish synagogue service of our Lord's time, which was carried straight over into the christian church by its jewish nucleus in the decade after the passion."[88] The synaxis could be held separately from the Eucharist, and it was only later that they became inseparable. Pliny in his letter to Trajan (c. A.D. 90) recounts a synaxis held apart from the Eucharist, which was celebrated later in the day. He had elicited from arrested Christians the rather abbreviated report that they assembled before daylight on a fixed day and sung, each in turn, a hymn to Christ as a god, and then swore not to commit theft, robbery or adultery, nor to break their word or deny a deposit;[89] these promises sound like a distorted reference to the Decalogue. The surprising omissions are prayer and scripture reading, but as Pliny was making judicial enquiries, no doubt a minimum of information would be proffered to him. Justin Martyr describes a synaxis which is followed by the Eucharist. He writes that on Sunday at a meeting of all, the memoirs of the apostles or the writings of the prophets are read. Then the president gives his admonition and exhortation, and then they all offer prayers.[90] Even though this is describing Roman practice, the Jewish framework of scripture, comment, and prayer is followed: perhaps it is too early for credal statements, and the *Shema* might have been unacceptable through its overtly Jewish liturgical link.

Paul, writing to the Ephesians and the Colossians in the fifties, urges the singing of psalms and hymns and spiritual songs with thankfulness to God,[91] and at 1 Timothy 2,1 the author urges that supplications, prayers, intercessions and thanksgivings be offered for all men. Evidence for scripture and other readings in the non-Eucharistic part of early worship may lie in Paul's plea at 2 Tim. 4,13 for his books and parchments to be brought.

Thus, the synaxis part of the Eucharistic service preserved the elements of prayer, scripture, homily and psalmody which, with the addition of the *Shema*, were the main elements of the service which Jesus knew in the synagogue.

With regard to worship unconnected with the Eucharist, it is likely, and supported by Acts 2,42, that the Jewish Christians who were accustomed to pray in the Temple or synagogue, or privately, in the morning, afternoon and evening when possible, will have continued a Christianised form of such observance when they were no longer able to worship in the Temple or synagogue. Tertullian[92] supports the custom of prayers which without any reminder are due at the beginning of the day and night.', and Hippolytus[93] mentions eight times for daily personal prayer. It is not clear whether the morning and evening prayers were said in groups, and this may well have varied from time to time and place to place. Acts 2,42 indicates common prayer, but later, Hippolytus admits private prayer in the morning as a substitute for attendance at a meeting for instruction.[94] In the continued observance of the morning and evening Jewish prayers probably lies the seed from which developed the Canonical Hours.

The next stage of the Hours' development arrived with the rise of the monastic movement. Dix[95] points out that in the fourth century the synaxis and Eucharist remained for a while the whole of corporate worship in the secular churches. But the increasing numbers of hermits and later, cenobites, having all the day to fill with worship, magnified the content of the then system of private prayer and edification. In the desert the psalms were regularly recited in order, and took the conspicuous position they have since held in Christian worship. The later corporate worship of the monasteries in scripture reading, prayer and psalmody was extended to the secular churches, initially through devout laymen at Antioch meeting in church for nocturnal prayer, and through Cyril's organisation at some time prior to Etheria's pilgrimage in A.D. 385, of a regular round of Canonical Hours in the church at Jerusalem.[96] These Hours were adopted as its Divine Office by the Roman Church under Pope S. Damasus c. A.D. 382, and of them, Lauds and Vespers of which the morning and evening service of the synagogue were the influence,[97] became nearly 1200 years later the kernel of the Morning and Evening Prayer of the Anglican Book of Common Prayer. Thus did the non-Eucharistic worship, certainly of Western Christendom, spring from those elements of prayer, scripture and psalm found in the synagogue. We may assume that Jesus would approve the continuation of worship so derived.

In the Protestant Churches the synagogal elements of prayer, scripture and psalm are continued in both the Ministry of the Word part of the Eucharist and in Morning and Evening Prayer, but since the latter are self-contained services, it seems that they are the more suitable for continuation to-day as the main diet of worship. Clearly, the church's occasional re-enactment of the Last Supper (including the consumption of bread and wine by the worshippers) as a means of recalling dramatically the nature and purpose of Jesus' death, is right and proper, but the repeated consumption of bread and wine as if it were the body and blood of Jesus for the purpose of receiving spiritual nourishment therefrom, appears to use as previously discussed, to have no justification in the acceptable evidence of Jesus' words and actions.

C. Common Meals.

We think that Jesus would have wanted his followers to continue the common meals which he used to eat with his disciples. From the time that the disciples realised that Jesus was God's anointed one ('Messiah') for the purpose of bringing in the Kingdom by his suffering, and of then returning as Son of Man,[98] those meals will have been imbued with the excitement of anticipation of the Messianic banquet.[99] The request of James and John to sit at Jesus' right and left in his glory (Mark 10,35-37), Jesus' fasting at the Last Supper till he eats and drinks in the Kingdom (Luke 22,16-18), and his promise at the Supper that his disciples will eat and drink at his table in the Kingdom (Luke 22,29-30), all show the heightened anticipation as the crisis of the Kingdom drew near, but it must have been present previously in a less intense form. Paul's Letters to the Thessalonians (1, chs.4 and 5 and 2,ch.2) show the intensity in the fifties of the expectation of Jesus' return, and a hundred years' later Justin at Trypho 51,2 quotes as Jesus' preaching, that he will come again to Jerusalem, and eat and drink anew with his disciples.

Those common meals were continued after Jesus' death by his Jewish disciples, and were later called in Greek 'agapé' meals, i.e. meals of love towards God and fellow-Christians. We noticed above (p. 136) that these meals were characterised by joy and simplicity of heart and praise of God. It seems logical that Jesus' followers to-day should continue those meals of fellowship in the same spirit of joyful expectation of the Messianic banquet of the Kingdom, and of praise to God for the extent to which God already reigns in men's hearts through the life and work of Jesus (cf. Didache, 9 and 10).

The thanksgiving could be particularly expressed in the Jewish benedictions over bread at the start of the meal and over wine at the end, which would assist fellowship with God, while the meal itself would assist the joyful fellowship of the Christians amongst themselves.

John records at 13,2-18, how at the Last Supper Jesus washed and dried the disciples' feet; this was a symbolic act of service and humility, for such a task was carried out in a Jewish household by the lowest servant. Although this incident is not mentioned in the Synoptics,[99A] John's evidence is not opposed by any counter-evidence in our view, and it accords with Jesus' teaching on service and humility at Mark 10,42-45.[100] Indeed, it is noteworthy that Luke places his version of that teaching at the Last Supper. Jesus' intention that this feet-washing should be repeated by his disciples is very clearly shown at John 13,14-15, "If I then, your Lord and Teacher, have washed your feet, you also ought to wash one another's feet. For I have given you an example, that you also should do as I have done to you." This beautifully symbolic act of Jesus, which seems to reproduce in nuce so much of his life and teaching, could most suitably be re-enacted occasionally at Christian agapés as a summary of that love for his disciples which his followers can aim to return to Jesus and to each other.

The practical organisation and victualling of these agapés to-day would limit their frequency probably to fortnightly or monthly, but they would have the potential of being true feasts of Christian love,[101] rather than the formal ritualistic occasions which the celebration of the Eucharistic bread and wine can so easily become.

D. Private Prayer.

Jesus would certainly have wanted his followers to continue the private prayer which he practised, often retiring alone,[102] and which he taught his disciples to pursue.[103] This practice has, indeed, been preserved by Christians from the beginning, as discussed above.

E. Conclusion.

The Christian observance of Common Prayer in the Morning and Evening involving prayer, Scripture, psalmody and creed, compares well with the kind of service which Jesus attended in the synagogue, and the restoration of the fellowship meal would preserve the particular contribution of Jesus to Christian worship. Thus, the synagogue-like services, the fellowship meal and the private prayers are the forms of worship which we think Jesus would have wished his followers to continue if he had known that God's Kingdom was not to come in its fulness immediately.

NOTES

1. John's Gospel contains in Chapter 13 an account of Jesus' washing of the feet of the disciples at the Last Supper, and John reports in that Chapter and Chapters 14-17 much teaching of Jesus at the Supper, but his Gospel does not mention the bread and wine at the Supper, (although there is teaching about Jesus' flesh and blood in Chapter 6,32-58).

2. J. Jeremias, **The Parables of Jesus**, London, 1972, pp.25-6.

3. Marcan priority should not, indeed, be accepted unquestioningly but only after reference to the Gospel versions of the particular pericope. O.L. Cope in **Matthew. A Scribe trained for the Kingdom of Heaven**, Washington D.C., 1976, writes, "The rules of transmission of the tradition may indicate that first one then another of the gospels preserves the earlier

tradition." (p.5). He notes there, with E.P. Sanders, that R. Bultmann in **The History of the Synoptic Tradition,** E.T. Oxford, 1963, favours in at least 14 instances Matthew or Luke or their common tradition as more original than the Marcan form of a passage.
4. See C.K. Barrett, **The First Epistle to the Corinthians,** London, 1971² pp.265-6.
5. **The Eucharistic Words of Jesus,** E.T., London 1966,³ p.169.
6. Cf. R.P. Booth, **Jesus and the Laws of Purity,** Sheffield, 1986, p.19.
7. Op. cit. pp.170-1.
8. See G. Dalman, **Jesus-Jeshua,** E.T., London, 1929, p.135.
9. Ante-Nicene Christian Library, Edinburgh, 1870, Vol.XVII, p.232. Generally considered a work of the late 4th century. See J.A. Jungmann, **The Early Liturgy,** E.T. London, 1960, p.5.
10. For a table of the various texts see B.M. Metzger, **A Textual Commentary on the Greek NT,** London and New York, 1971, p.175.
11. The introductory v.14, 'And when the hour came, he sat at table and the apostles with him', is also different in formulation from Mark's 14,17, and marks, we think, the start of Luke's separate tradition.
12. Jeremias, op.cit. p.208 compares Luke's use of $ἐπιθυμειν$ with the infinitive here to his use of it at 15,16; 16,21; 17,22, and argues that, as in those cases, it expresses here also an unfulfilled wish, 'I would very gladly have eaten this passover lamb with you before my death.' That, however, would require a following $ἀλλα$, not the Lucan $γαρ$, so as to read naturally 'but (not 'for') I tell you I shall not eat it until it is fulfilled. . . ' Moreover, the other Lucan instances cited are not uses of $ἐπιθυμειν$ with the dative noun which is an imitation of the Hebrew infinitive absolute, and emphasises the verbal idea (B-D, para. 196(6); GK, p.342(n). We think this emphasised desire to eat the passover cannot easily contain in addition the idea of its *un*fulfilment. Cf. Dalman, op.cit. pp.126-130. C.F.D. Moule in **An Idiom-Book of NT Greek,** Cambridge, 1963, notes at p.177 that this Hebrew construction is rarely used in pure Aramaic. Its use here is very allusive to its use at LXX, Genesis 31,30, "you have longed greatly for your father's house".
13. Jeremias, op.cit. p.197 includes the phrase as evidence for the Eucharistic words being spoken in Hebrew rather than Palestinian Aramaic, but at n.1 he cites Dalman who admits that the construction is found in the Palestinian Aramaic of the Targums.
14. **The Gospel according to St. Luke,** London, 1930, p.lviiif.
15. Interestingly, in Mark they all drink, whereas in Luke they are to drink all of it (share amongst themselves).
16. The expression 'that Day' in the sense of the eschatological 'Day of

the Lord' is used e.g. at Jer. 4,9; 5,18.
17. Creed, **op.cit**. p.lxv.
18. Luke's different source is indicated by his placing the betrayal announcement **after** the bread saying whereas Mark places it **before** the bread actions; also in Luke the traitor's hand is with Jesus' on the table whereas in Mark it is dipping bread in the same dish. Indeed, the whole structure of the betrayal passage differs in the two Gospels.
19. M. Staniforth, **Early Christian Writings**, London, 1968, p.226.
20. Matthew apparently understands Mark as meaning that Jesus spoke after breaking and while giving, for he writes, "$και$ $ευλογησας$ $εκλασεν$ $και$ $δους$ $τοις$ $μαθηταις$ $ειπεν$" (26,26).
21. Dalman, **op.cit**. pp.140-1 thinks that the interpretation words were said during the distribution of the bread, since he claims a custom (without quoting authority) that each piece was separately broken and distributed. But the simile of the broken body would be lost unless the words were said during the breaking, and Jesus' manner of breaking may have been idiosyncratic rather than customary since the disciples appear to have recognised him by his familiar practice (Luke 24,30 and 35).
21A. R. Otto, **The Kingdom of God and the Son of Man**, E.T. London, 1938, p.296.
22. E.g. Lev. 17,10-16.
23. John emphasises the vicarious nature of Jesus' suffering at 6,51, 'and the bread which I shall give for the life of the world is my flesh.'
24. Berakoth 8,1-2.
25. The Hebraic *rabim*, and see V. Taylor, **The Gospel according to St. Mark**, London, 1952, p.546.
26. Concerning Jesus' purpose see Chapter II supra.
27. At Apology 63,26f. Justin claims to quote from the Gospels—"$εν$ $τοις$ $γενομενοις$ $υπ'αυτων$ $απομνημονευμασιν$ $α$ $καλειται$ $ευαγγελια$", but this confirms the secondary nature of his evidence.
28. **Op.cit**. pp.195-6.
29. **Op.cit**. p.209.
30. **Op.cit**. p.252.
31. **The Shape of the Liturgy**, London, 1945, p.59.
32. Jewish Christians (Ebionites) observed the Eucharist as an annual feast, like the Jewish passover, in memory of Christ's death (see A.J.B. Higgins, **The Lord's Supper in the NT**, London, 1952, p.55 n.2).
33. **Op.cit**. p.50f.
34. Berakoth 2,1; 5,1; 46a.
35. **Op.cit**. p.265 in loc.
36. **Op.cit**. p.173.

37. So also Jeremias, **op.cit.** pp.211-212.
38. See Dalman, **op.cit.** p.153.
39. **Op.cit.** pp.214-215.
40. Cf. 1 Sam. 14,24 where Saul's warriors swear not to eat till victory is won.
41. **Op.cit.** p.269.1
42. Thus, J. Behm **TDNT**, 1, 174, "As the old divine order of Sinai was sealed and inaugurated by blood. . . so the new with its gifts is established and set in force by the blood of Jesus.' Cf. Jeremias, **op.cit.** p.169.
43. **TDNT** II, 126f.
44. R.Otto, **The Kingdom of God and the Son of Man**, E.T., London, 1938, p.293.
45. **Op.cit.** p.195.
46. G. Vermes, **The Dead Sea Scrolls in English**, London, 1962, p.72.
47. **Op.cit.** pp.102-103.
48. G. Vermes, **The Dead Sea Scrolls. Qumran in Perspective**, 1977, p.214.
49. **TDNT, II, 134.**
50. Particularly regarding the weight and literal interpretation of the Gospel statements as evidence.
51. **Op.cit.** p.290.
52. See pp.110-11 supra.
53. (1953) C.L.Y. 830 (English criminal case). Similarly, in a much older English civil case exclamations of viewers while looking at a picture were admitted as evidence to show that the figures portrayed were meant to represent the defendant's sister and brother-in-law (Du Bost v. Beresford (1810) 2 Camp. 511).
54. **Op.cit.** p.60.
55. **Op.cit.** pp.66,115, cf.237.
56. **Op.cit.** pp.19-121.
57. **Op.cit.** p.136.
58. **TDNT, III, 729-30.**
59. See p.123 supra.
60. So A. Schweitzer, **The Kingdom of God and Primitive Christianity**, E.T., London, 1968, pp.148-150. Sayings such as Luke 12,37 will also have encouraged this belief.
61. Mark 6,41 and 8,6.
62. Jeremias, **op.cit.** p.115.
63. **Didache, 9 and 10**; Tertullian, **Apology,** I,39. Tertullian lived from about A.D.160 to about A.D. 230 in N. Africa. Hippolytus has a fuller account of an agapé in his **Apostolic Traditions,** at xxv, xxvi, 1-13 and xxvii.

He wrote about 250 A.D.
64. **Zur Geschichte und Litteratur des Urchristentums,** I, 1893, pp.289f.
65. **Messe und Herrenmahl,** 1926, pp.250-55.
66. M. Staniforth, **Early Christian Writings,** London, 1968, p.226. And see Ch.V infra.
67. See J. Weiss, **Earliest Christianity,** Vol.I, New York, 1959, pp.59-60.
68. Cf. J. Weiss, op.cit. p.57.
69. **Op.cit. p.59.**
70. J. Weiss, op.cit. p.59 writes "There is nothing in the narratives of the Book of Acts to suggest that the death of Jesus was central to the thought and feeling expressed in them. When we read. . . that they broke bread. . . 'with gladness and singleness of heart', we get the impression that the thanksgiving referred generally to God's acts of mercy, and that the rejoicing was over the certainty of the coming salvation, rather than specifically the thought of the death of Jesus. And if we are correct in assuming. . . that the earliest disciples did not look upon his death as their Lord's chief saving act of love, but that on the contrary they believed in him **despite** his death, it remains very improbable that they looked upon this breaking of the bread as 'showing forth the Lord's death' as Paul later expressed it."
71. Cf. J. Enoch Powell, **No Easy Answers,** London, 1973, pp. 2 and 5.
72. See J. Frazer, **Adonis Attis Osiris. Studies in the History of Oriental Religion,** London, 1906, Bk.II, chs. 1 and 2.
73. See E.O. James, **Sacrifice and Sacrament,** London, 1962, pp.196-98.
74. This is in the form, 'Chairemon invites thee to a meal at the table of the Lord Serapis in the Serapeum, to-morrow, the 15th, from 9 o'clock onwards.' A. Schweitzer, **The Mysticism of Paul the Apostle,** E.T., London, 1953^2 denies that in the Egyptian cult-feasts as here, or in the temple of Isis, the diners expected to enter into real fellowship or union with the deity. But does not the venue indicate such an intent?
75. See further, R. Bultmann, **Primitive Christianity,** E.T., London, 1956, pp.185-192.
76. **The Earlier Epistles of St. Paul,** London, 1930, pp.44-5.
77. See H. Greeven, **TDNT,** II,808. C.S.C. Williams, **The Acts of the Apostles,** London, 1957, however, at pp.57-8 expresses the article, translating as 'the prayer' denoting "a liturgical form of prayer based probably on that of Temple or synagogue worship."
78. Megillah I,3; 4,3.

79. See C.W. Dugmore, **The Influence of the Synagogue upon the Divine Office**, Oxford, 1944, pp.15-16. However, K. Kohler, **The Origins of the Synagogue and the Church**, New York, 1929, attributes the times of prayer and the prayers themselves to the Hasidim (p.66).
80. The Karaites ultimately settled on only two obligatory prayer times corresponding to the pre-Herodian Temple sacrifices; see further, P. Selvin Goldberg, **Karaite Liturgy**, Manchester, 1957.
81. Dugmore, **op.cit.** pp.12-13. The Ten Commandments and the Shema were recited daily in the Temple (Tamid 5,1)
82. **Op.cit.** pp.16-22 and 104-5. See also Kohler, **op.cit.** Ch.xii, who considers the *Shema* also to be a Hasidean institution.
83. **Op.cit.** pp.22-23.
84. At Megillah 4,1 it is stated, "On a Monday and a Thursday and on the afternoon of a Sabbath the Law is read by three. . . they do not close with a reading from the Prophets", and at 4,2 "On a Festival-day (the law) is read by five, on the Day of Atonement by six, and on the Sabbath by seven. . . they close with a reading from the Prophets." We cannot be sure that this was entirely the position in Jesus' time, since the Mishnah was finally compiled c. A.D.200, and we do not know the date of these lemmas.
85. See hereon Moore, **op.cit.** Vol.I. pp.305-7.
86. Dugmore, **op.cit.** pp.14-5. Kohler, **op.cit.** pp.90-1 connects the Hallel with 19 festal days, and cites authority (late) for the fifth book of Psalms being recited daily by the *Hasidim.*
87. The Malediction was probably included in the Benedictions c. A.D.90, and the last Bishop of Jerusalem to be a 'believing Hebrew' died c. A.D.135. See Dugmore, **op.cit.** pp.4-5, but contra, H. Maccoby **The Mythmaker**, London, 1986, pp.179 and 219, n.10.
88. **Op.cit.** p.36.
89. **Epistolae,** X. 96-7.
90. **Apology,** I, 66-7.
91. Eph. 5,19; Col. 3,16.
92. **De Oratione,** xxv.
92A. These are hours of the Jewish day which was calculated from 6am to 6pm.
93. **Apostolic Tradition,** xxxv.
94. **Op.cit.** xxxv,2-xxxvi,1.
95. **Op.cit.** p.326.
96. **Op.cit.** pp.326-7.
97. Dugmore, **op.cit.** p.51 mentions Etheria's report that, while only the monks and virgins attended the other services, at Lauds and Vespers the

laity and the bishop attended. Dugmore comments, "The special importance attached to [Lauds and Vespers] is best explained on the hypothesis that they represent the tradition of the primitive church at Jerusalem derived directly from Synagogue practice and continued throughout that obscure period of which we have few, if any, records, until they became incorporated in the monastic Hours of Prayer sometime in the fourth century." Dix, **op.cit**. p.330-1 notes two other Jewish influences on Lauds and Vespers. He refers to the general daily use of Pss. 148-150 at the end of Lauds, and notes that the private recitation of these psalms was customary with pious Jews in the first century. (Cf. the singing of canticles, the set psalm and psalms 95 and 100 at Anglican Morning Prayer.) He also traces the blessing of the evening lamp at public Vespers to the Jewish domestic custom.

98. Probably from the time of Peter's confession of Jesus' Messiahship at Mark 8,29, for at 8,31 Jesus 'began to teach them that the Son of Man must suffer many things. . . '

99. See Jeremias, **op.cit**. p.205.

99A. Although Creed, **op.cit**. suggests that Luke 12,37 may be the source of John's story (p.176).

100. Scholars may point to the influence of the early Church on Mark 10,45b, but the theme of service to others as opposed to pursuit of worldly power seems clearly consistent with the spirit of Jesus' ministry and teaching; indeed, on the basis of our conclusion in Chapter 2 that Jesus intended to bear the pre-Messianic tribulation for others, there is no cause to see a retrospective insertion by the early church at 10,45b. Thus we find no counter-evidence against Mark's assertion that Jesus said this.

101. The following unkind epitaph awarded them by A. Wright, **A Synopsis of the Gospels,** London, 1906, p.141, would then deserve a smile—"The agapé happily was soon abolished, and churches ceased to be hotels."!

102. E.g. Mark 1,35.

103. Matthew 6,5-13; Luke 11,1-4.

CHAPTER V.

Why Priests?

Gospel assertions, we think, receive insufficient weight as evidence not only from some radical but also from some ecclesiastical commentators. An example arose in the controversy over the ordination of women to be priests in the Church of England when little attention was given to the propriety of a Christian Church appointing *anybody* to be a priest. The distinguishing feature of Christianity amongst monotheistic religions is, as its name suggests, its devotion to Jesus, who did not appoint any priests. In this Chapter we examine the evidence of the Gospels and of Church tradition in an attempt to discover Jesus' possible intentions regarding the exercise of priestly and other ministry among his followers.

I. JESUS AND PRIESTHOOD

At Mark 3,13-19 Jesus appointed twelve of his followers to accompany him, and to be sent out to preach and expel demons, but there was no mention of sacrificial or other priestly duties, nor at Mark 6,7-13 when Jesus sent out the twelve two by two; they preached that men should repent, they expelled many demons and healed many sick.

Jesus did not authorise his apostles to offer sacrifices or do other priestly things because since the reforms of King Josiah following the discovery of the Deuteronomic book in 621 B.C., sacrifices were only lawful in the one Temple at Jerusalem (Deuteronomy 12,2-14), and neither Jesus nor his disciples were priests of that Temple. Although Jesus seems to have adopted the prophetic approach of preferring mercy to sacrifice (Matthew 12,2; Hosea 6,6), his desire to prevent abuses at the Temple (Mark 11,15-17) and his sending a leper to a priest to have his cure announced at the Temple (Mark 1,44) indicate a respect for the holy place and its officers. His attitude to worship, though, is perhaps summarised at John 4,24, 'God is spirit, and those who worship him, must worship in spirit and truth'; it thus seems unlikely that, in contrast to the rest of Jewry, he would have desired the animal sacrifices or other priestly duties to be continued after the destruction of the Temple — by his followers or anybody else.

So why are there *any* priests in the Christian Church when Jesus appointed twelve laymen as his assistants? A reason posited for priests arises from Christian theory concerning the death of Jesus. One 'atonement' theory is that Jesus sacrificed his life to God in order that God would accept his death instead of requiring the death of all other human beings as punishment for their sins. Protestants claim that there is no further sacrificial work to be done by Christians, since Jesus on the Cross made a perfect and sufficient sacrifice for the sins of the whole world (see e.g. the consecratory prayer and Article of Religion 31 in Anglican Book of Common Prayer; cf. Hebrews 10,12-14, 18). But the Orthodox and Roman Catholic Churches continue to sacrifice to God through their priests in that they offer the bread and wine to remind God of Jesus' offering of his broken body and outpoured blood, and to induce God thereby to overlook man's sin. Thus in the Eucharistic prayer of Hippolytus' *Apostolic Tradition* it is stated, "Memores igitur mortis et resurrectionis eius offerimus tibi panem et calicem gratias tibi agentes quia nos dignis habuisti adstare coram te et tibi ministrare."

The Gospel assertions of Jesus' words over the bread and wine (discussed at Ch. IV) and of Jesus' 'ransom' saying at Mark 10,45 do provide evidence that Jesus contemplated that he would suffer vicariously for others, and that his blood would be the sacrificial blood of a new covenant with God, but there is no Gospel evidence that he thought his sufferings should be sacramentally re-enacted by priests, or anybody, to bring them repeatedly to God's mind and mercy after his death. For, as discussed in Ch. II, in our opinion the Gospel evidence shows that Jesus believed that, because the pre-Messianic suffering did not fall upon people generally, it was God's will that he should suffer on their behalf and thereby enable the Kingdom of God to arrive. In view of this belief in the imminence of the Kingdom, it seems unlikely that Jesus would have desired that his suffering should be symbolically repeated after his death.

Sacrifice and priesthood are clearly linked. Since there is no evidence in the Gospels to justify continued offering of the sacrifice of Jesus' body and blood, appeal can only be made to the Church as the guardian of unwritten tradition passed down the ages from the time of the Apostles. The Church's tradition, then, can presumably be cited as the source of the pronouncements of the Council of Trent which declared in 1562, that the sacrificial offering of the mass was propitiatory and impetratory, and anathematised any who said it was only a memorial meal, and should not be offered for the living and the dead, for sins and punishments; it was a sacrifice having the power of atonement and petition, offered by Christ himself at the Last Supper and committed to the Apostles and their successors for all time.

Vincent of Lerinum writing about A.D.434, justified the rôle of Church tradition as one of the two foundations of the Church's faith by explaining that the other, Holy Scripture, could not be understood without the guidance of the tradition which shows what has been believed everywhere, always and by all.² Origen went further—'That alone ought to be believed to be truth which differs in no respect from the ecclesiastical and apostolic tradition.'³

It cannot be denied that the Church's 'tradition' of treating the bread and wine as an offering or sacrifice to God has an early pedigree. Hippolytus' *Apostolic Tradition* which we cited above, dates from about A.D.250, but it was only 96 A.D. when Clement wrote, also at Rome, that the bishop's office is to 'offer the gifts' (προσφερειν τα δωρα) of the Church (1 Clement 44). And Justin also writing at Rome about 160 A.D. explains the 'pure offering' mentioned at Malachi 1,11 as 'The sacrifices which are offered (προσφερομενων) to God by us Gentiles, that is the bread of the eucharist and cup likewise of the eucharist.' (Dialogue 41). The same interpretation of the Malachi 'pure offering' is given in the Syrian Didache where at section 14 proposed communicants in the Eucharist are urged to be reconciled 'so as to avoid any profanation of your sacrifice. For this is the sacrifice of which the Lord has said 'Everywhere and always bring me a sacrifice that is undefiled...' Thus in the Eastern church also, the bread and wine are considered a sacrifice by about 100 A.D., although the Eucharist described in the Didache (9 and 10) resembles more a thanksgiving agapé. Other early Syrian evidence is afforded by Ignatius of Antioch writing about A.D. 115 to the Ephesians; he there describes the Eucharistic assembly as 'the place of sacrifice' (θυσιαστηριον), and 'he who is not within it is deprived of the bread.'⁴

But the evidence of a Church tradition is only cogent if it does not conflict with the words or intent of Jesus as evidenced by Gospel assertions. Here, the evidence of tradition does so conflict because Jesus by his words and actions at the Last Supper showed his disciples that he was to suffer in place of them and in order to initiate a new covenant between God and man, whereas the Church's repeated offering to God of Jesus' broken body and blood in the symbols of bread and wine is alien to that intent. We noted in chapter IV the connection between the new covenant and the Kingdom of God. A feature of the new covenant (and thus of the Kingdom) is stated at Jeremiah 31,34 to be that all men shall know God for 'I will forgive their iniquity and their sins shall be no more.' In the Kingdom of God which Jesus believed his suffering would inaugurate, man's past sin was to be forgiven, and there would be no future sin for God's law would be written on men's hearts. Given Jesus' familiarity with Jeremiah and therefore with these features of the new covenant, how can he have intended that his body and blood should be repeatedly offered for the release of future sin? Apart from the situation under the new covenant, Jesus' parable of the Prodigal Son (Luke 15, 11-32) shows his belief that God's loving willingness to forgive is solely dependent upon man's sincere repentance (cf. the Lord's Prayer).[5]

Since the evidence of Gospel assertions which shows that Jesus did not suggest any priestly duties to his disciples, and did not intend that any sacrifice should be offered in addition to his own suffering and death, outweighs the evidence of church tradition, showing early treatment by Christians of the Eucharist as a sacrifice, we judge that Jesus did not authorise the repeated sacrifice or the Christian priesthood.

II. MINISTERIAL EXCLUSIVITY
A. The Functions.

The principal functions which Christian priests have reserved for their exclusive performance are the celebration of the Mass or the Lord's Supper, the hearing of confessions and the granting of absolution, privately or publicly. By the time of Ignatius' Letter to the Smyrneans (c. A.D.110) the right to preside at the Eucharist had been reserved to the Bishop or his appointee.[6] Admittedly, when education was reserved to a privileged minority, as in ancient and some modern times, tasks like the recital of the liturgy, requiring religious sensitivity and clear enunciation, were best carried out by priests who were members of that educated minority. But a time arrives through the spread of education when ordinary people are equipped to do things for themselves. Historically, both priests and lawyers (and the two have often been one) have, for the preservation of their own privileged status, striven to keep to themselves the means to propitiate the gods, and to effect legal transactions, respectively. But just as lawyers in England have recently surrendered their conveyancing monopoly because others are able to do the work, so should priests surrender their residual monopolies since other Christians are now educated and able to do the work.[7] And if priests make this surrender, there will be no further practical cause for a caste of priests, so that they will be able to exercise more fully to the benefit of the Christian community their particular abilities without being pre-occupied (unless their gifts there lie) with the sacerdotal function.

For at 1 Corinthians 12,4-5 Paul writes that there are varieties of service, but it is the same God who inspires them all in every one. Now as then, the Church needs preachers, pastors, administrators, general leaders and leaders of worship, but it does not have a function for priests to perform. Some priests may conduct the Mass in a manner more conducive to communion with Jesus than a competent lay man or woman would, and some may not, depending on the particular gifts of the individual. But it is very probable that the abilities of some present priests equip them to be more effective church leaders, pastors or preachers, than celebrants of the Mass or mediators of confession and forgiveness.

Whether it is proper stewardship of money for the Church to have a paid full-time worker or workers in a particular parish may depend upon the other Christian resources in the area, but it must be wasteful to have a priest rushing round several churches on a Sunday in an area of competent lay Christians, because of a dogma that only a priest can officiate at the Mass. The mechanical 'ex opere operato' view that the bread and wine will only vouchsafe communion with Jesus if a priest, not a lay person, has recited the consecratory prayer and invoked the Holy Spirit, is a residual aspect of primitive religion or magic from which Christians should be liberated. The concepts that procedure in sacrifice or worship is of vital importance, and that error therein is a sin (Lev. 4), and that God is angered if ritual is not performed by a caste of priests (witness Korah, Dathan and Abiram at Numbers 16) may belong to the formal, external part of religion that Jesus deprecated at Mark 7,15, 'the things outside a man do not defile him as much as the things that come from within him.'

B. The Defence of Exclusivity—the Apostolic Succession.

The priestly privileges are defended by the doctrine of apostolic succession for which early evidence is found in a Letter of St. Clement of Rome to the Church at Corinth which had deposed some presbyters appointed by persons authorised by the Apostles, and had itself appointed some new presbyters. He wrote about 96 A.D. in this Letter that the Apostles, foreseeing the jealousies which should arise about ministerial office, did not only constitute bishops and deacons, but afterwards also made provision, in case of their decease, for a continuous succession of ministerial office. He consequently claimed that those who had once been duly constituted ministers, either by Apostles, or by other faithful men after them, with the consent of the whole Church, could never justly be deposed from the ministry which they had so long and blamelessly exercised.[8] R.C. Moberly comments, "it would be difficult to find a stronger assertion than this, of the principle that ministerial office is . . . dependent for its validity upon transmission, continuous and authorized, from the Apostles, whose own commission was direct from Jesus Christ."[9]

But where is the Gospel evidence that Jesus intended that only the Twelve or persons authorised by them, should exercise ministry in his Church? This cannot be logically deduced from his sending out the Twelve on missions as mentioned above; indeed, according to Luke 10, 1 and 17 Jesus appointed seventy (or seventy-two according to some texts) and they expelled demons, and were given by Jesus authority over serpents, scorpions and all the power of Satan (vv.17-18). Although Jesus gave powers to his disciples, he did not intend those powers to be exclusive. Thus at Mark 9,39 Jesus tells the disciples not to forbid a man who has been casting out demons in Jesus' name but without his authority.[10] In fact, Jesus never expected that his disciples would conduct an earthly ministry for he believed that after his pre-Messianic suffering, he would bring in the Kingdom as the Son of Man and he and the disciples would sit on thrones judging the twelve tribes of Israel (Matthew 19,28; Luke 22,30).[11]

In addition to the unlikelihood of Jesus having intended to restrict ministry to the Apostles and those succeeding to them, a further objection to the doctrine of apostolic succession to priestly powers is the quite different nature of Jesus' commission to the Apostles.

Jesus' authority to the Apostles to minister.

We noted above that the disciples were sent out by Jesus to preach repentance, to expel demons and to heal the sick. There are texts, however, which are alleged to confer general authority on Peter and the Apostles over other Christians, and these we will now consider.

Matthew testifies at 16,17-18 that Jesus said to Peter, after Peter had confessed Jesus as the Christ, 'Blessed are you, Simon Bar-Jona! For flesh and blood has not revealed this to you, but my Father who is in heaven (v.17). And I tell you, you are Peter, and on this rock I will build my church, and the gates of Hades shall not prevail against it.' (v.18). Against this evidence of Matthew in v.18 there is substantial counter-evidence. Firstly, this is one of only two uses in the NT of the word 'church' ($\dot{\varepsilon}\varkappa\varkappa\lambda\eta\sigma\iota\alpha$); it is unlikely that Jesus used the word on either occasion since, as mentioned, he expected the Kingdom of God to arrive almost immediately which would, of course, supersede human organisations. If Jesus did utter v.18, it is unlikely that he meant that Peter was to be the head of the body of followers since, if he had meant that, the later discussions at Matthew 18,1-4 and 20,20-23 concerning who was to be the greatest in the Kingdom, would hardly have taken place. More probably, Jesus meant that the foundation ('rock') of the fellowship of his disciples would be faith in himself as the Messiah.

Jesus next says to Peter at Matthew 16,19, 'I will give you the keys of the kingdom of heaven, and whatever you bind on earth shall be bound in heaven, and whatever you loose on earth shall be loosed in heaven.' 'The keys' are often interpreted as the right to exclude from the kingdom, but possession of the keys more naturally marks the office of a chief steward, who only holds the keys on behalf of the Lord. But Matthew's evidence of this promise of the keys is overborne in our view by the counter evidence of its incongruity both with the discussions about primacy at Matthew 18 and 20, and also with the nature of the kingdom explained by Jesus in those discussions. The power to bind and loose represents the Rabbinic power to legislate by declaring what is permitted and what is forbidden.[12] The evidence of the Gospel assertion seems overborne here also; at Matthew 18,18 power to exclude from the Christian community is given to all the disciples in similar terms, but more cogently, Jesus would hardly appoint anybody else as arbiter of entry to the Kingdom or his earthly fellowship when he expected the immediate incursion of the imminent Kingdom and that, as Son of Man, he himself would judge entry thereto. It is equally unlikely that Jesus, expecting the Kingdom, should have laid down a procedure for regulating entry to the society of his earthly followers. Further counter-evidence to the Matthean evidence that Jesus granted to Peter a special ministry of leadership is the ambiguous position which Peter held in the early church: although in the early chapters of Acts he seems to be the foremost disciple, speaking, for example, at the appointment of Matthias (1,15f.) and at Pentecost (2,14f.) and to the Sanhedrin (4,8f.) and Ananias and Sapphirah (5,3f.;8f.), yet by Chapter 11 he has to justify his conduct to the circumcision party (1,2f.), Paul condemns him at Antioch (Galations 2,11f.), and by the time of the Council of Jerusalem James is clearly leader of the Palestinian Church (Acts, 15,19). We accordingly think that the Matthean evidence for special powers for Peter in Chapter 16 is over-ridden by the counter-evidence, and we are inclined, with T.W. Manson, to see Matthew 16 as an attempt in Palestinian tradition to elevate the importance of Peter as a counter-balance to that of Paul.[13]

Support for the pastoral authority of Peter is contained in the 'Feed my sheep' injunctions to Peter at John 21, 15-17. We do not count as contrary evidence to John's assertions the fact that they are contained in an appendix to the Gospel for it was clearly an early appendix[12] and constitutes Gospel assertions by its author, but the fact that these words are recorded as spoken by Jesus after his death, constitutes stronger counter-evidence (see pp.24-5) than the evidence of John's uncorroborated report.[14] The same counter-evidence predominates in our view over John's evidence at 20,23 that the risen Jesus there authorised the disciples to forgive and retain sins. Still further counter-evidence that Jesus gave either Peter (Matthew 16) or the disciples (Matthew 18 and John 20) power to bind and loose in the sense of forgiving sins, is that only God has power to forgive sins against God (Mark 11,25), as we acknowledge in the Lord's Prayer. Interpretation of Jesus' apparent claim to forgive sins at Mark 2,10 is much disputed,[15] but that verse can hardly mean that men in general can forgive them.

We consequently conclude that the Gospel evidence does not establish that the Apostles, or Peter alone, received a wider authority beyond the mission charges to preach repentance, to expel demons and to heal the sick. Having considered the first link in the Apostolic succession, namely the commission from Jesus to the Apostles, we turn to the second link, namely the authorizing by the Apostles of their successors.

Jesus' authority to the Apostles to delegate.

What evidence is there that Jesus authorized the Apostles to authorize others to preach, exorcise and heal? Bearing in mind again the cogent point that Jesus expected the imminent arrival of the Kingdom, it would be remarkable, indeed, if Jesus did grant a power to delegate. Indeed, there is evidence that the Apostles did not exercise or claim to exercise in some churches a power to authorize others. A Harnack argued that in the earliest period there co-existed an universal ministry of Apostles, prophets and teachers and a local ministry of presbyter-bishops and deacons. The former could operate within the whole Church and derived its authority from the Holy Spirit, whereas the latter were appointed by the local Christians to work in their local church.[16] B.H. Streeter showed that the evolution of ministry was more diverse and dynamic in the different churches than Harnack had allowed, but except at Jerusalem where church order was influenced by the model of the synagogue, it seems that a development at different speeds in different churches from a dominance of the itinerant ministry of Apostles, prophets and teachers to the resident one of bishops and deacons, was the usual course.[17] It thus is unlikely that in the case of all churches the first link in the alleged Apostolic succession was ever made, since in some churches the local ministry would probably not evolve in time for an active Apostle to lay hands on their bishop; indeed, Harnack had good evidence to support his claim that the bishops and deacons were elected by the local church, rather than appointed by an Apostle.

For the Didache is thought to represent the practice of a church in Syria at about 100 A.D.; Streeter suggested that this scroll of teaching was sent from a large, settled church like that at Antioch to less developed churches in Syria.[18] In the church of the Didache, Apostles, prophets and teachers were still the first rank of ministry, but bishops and deacons had been appointed. At Didache 15 the authors tell the recipient churches that they must *choose for themselves* bishops and deacons; they must be men who are humble and worthy 'for they are carrying out the ministry of the prophets and teachers for you'. The recipients are told how to recognise a genuine prophet, and that such are entitled to the first fruits of their produce and flocks for 'it is they who are your 'High Priests'.

Since it is the prophets, men inspired by the Holy Spirit, who, after the Apostles, are pre-eminent in the earliest church, it seems unlikely that the Apostles should have by-passed them, and authorised instead local bishops to exercise the Apostles' powers, particularly since the evidence of the Didache is that at least in some Syrian churches the churches chose their own bishops and deacons. Thus, although Clement of Rome might have been able to show that the local ministers within his jurisdiction could trace their laying-on of hands back to Peter, his implicit suggestion that apostolic succession accorded with the history of the appointment of bishops and deacons in all the churches,[19] was almost certainly an exaggeration.

In further regard to the second link, namely the granting by Jesus of power to the Apostles to authorise others to their ministry, it is noteworthy that the Apostles, where we have records of appointments by them, do not empower their appointees to carry on the ministry of preaching repentance, exorcising and healing, which Jesus instructed themselves to conduct. For example, at Acts 1,15-26 Matthias was chosen 'to become with us a witness to his [Jesus'] resurrection' which, while it no doubt involves preaching, need not involve the preaching of repentance, and is not connected with exorcism or healing. Again, at Acts 6,1-6 where the Apostles have not time both for the ministry of the word and the distribution to the Hellenist widows, they do not appoint others to their own ministry (which still included healing and exorcism, Acts 5,16), but appoint the Seven to carry out the distribution (vv 2-4). Admittedly, we read that, of the Seven, Stephen (Acts 6,8) and Philip (8,4-7) widened their ministry, but this appears to have been done without apostolic authorisation.

However, against the evidence of the NT and the Didache tending to deny a doctrine of apostolic succession, ecclesiastical commentators such as Moberly, would proffer the evidence of 'dogmatic theology'. Moberly writes, '. . . it is a somewhat characteristic temptation of careful textual interpreters to try to work what are called the historical or exegetical methods, as if it were possible that they should yield their best results apart from the light of the truths of dogmatic theology.' And speaking of F.J.A. Hort's book 'Christian Ecclesia', he writes that the author appears to 'interpret the history as if the narrative detail of historical passages could yield their fullest meaning apart from the doctrinal verities which underlie. . . This comes most clearly into view when he draws negative conclusions from his text, and offers by them, to correct traditional belief. If, for example, by this method, he claims to show that the Apostles received from our Lord no authority to govern in the Church . . . is he not, so far, misunderstanding the scope of his own method, and carrying it into exactly the kind of conclusions which it is inherently unable to bear?'[20]

Thus is dogmatic theology and Church tradition ('traditional belief') accepted by some not only as counter-evidence, but as counter-evidence over-riding NT assertions. We do not demur at the acceptance of such evidence, but it should not be allowed to over-ride NT evidence.[21] For dogmatic theology may be defined as the systematic statement of Christian beliefs and such beliefs can only be derived from NT evidence or Church tradition. Insofar as the beliefs arise from NT evidence, they can hardly, be opposed to NT evidence! Insofar as the beliefs arise from Church tradition, then the successive oral deliveries of the tradition through the centuries make it inferior to NT evidence committed to writing in the first century.

That the Apostles received authority to govern from Jesus, or a power to sub-delegate to infinity the powers they did receive, is denied by the Gospel evidence, so that the evidence of Church tradition in favour of such an Apostolic succession is in our judgment overborne.

III. CONCLUSIONS

We accordingly conclude that: —

1. The assertions of Church traditions are by reason of their susceptibility to distortion weaker evidence than Gospel assertions. Consequently, the assertions of dogmatic theology cannot effectively oppose Gospel assertions.

2. The evidence of Gospel assertions proves that: —

(A) Jesus did not in the missionary training of the disciples or at the Last Supper or at any other time request or authorise the Twelve to offer sacrifice, forgive sins, or perform any other priestly duty.

(B) Jesus did not intend that any sacrifice should be offered to God after his own expected suffering and death because he believed they would be immediately followed by the arrival of God's Kingdom.

(C) Jesus did authorise the disciples to preach, exorcise and heal, but he did not authorise them to delegate those powers to others because, again, he expected the imminent arrival of the Kingdom.

But the Kingdom in the sense expected by Jesus did not arrive, nor did Jesus as Son of Man to judge. What Jesus would have intended in the changed situation can only be speculated, but it seems reasonable to assume that he would have wished his followers through the ages to preach the obedient love of God and self-forgetful service of man, which he taught and practised. That must involve some form of human organisation for the purposes, at least, of training the preachers and arranging corporate worship. So, as mentioned above, preachers, pastors, administrators and leaders are needed, and those who are presently priests, are no doubt ideally suited to one or more of these services.

We only submit that there is no need for them as priests, primarily because communion with Jesus in the remembrance of the Last Supper does not involve further sacrifice to God. J.B. Lightfoot wrote that sacerdotal phraseology was used "to imply a substantial identity of character with the Jewish priesthood i.e. to designate the Christian minister as one who offers sacrifice and makes atonement", but "Above all, it [the kingdom of Christ] has no sacerdotal system. It interposes no sacrifical tribe or class between God and man, by whose intervention alone God is reconciled and man forgiven."[22]

NOTES

1. Although H.W. Robinson, **The Religious Ideas of the OT**, London, 1913, p.143, notes that originally it was open to any Israelite to perform the sacrifice, and the priest is not even mentioned in the Book of the Covenant. See hereon E.O. James, **Sacrifice and Sacrament**, London, 1962, p.226.

2. **Adversus profanas omnium novitates haereticorum Commonitorium**, cited in J.F. Bethune-Baker, **An Introduction to the Early History of Christian Doctrine**, London, 1903, p.59.

3. **De Principiis**, Proem I, cited by Bethune-Baker, **op.cit.** p.58.

4. Ephesians, 5.

5. Cf. J. Weiss, **Paul and Jesus**, E.T. London, 1909, p.10.

6. Smyrna 8.

7. And just as barristers are to surrender their monopoly in representing man in the High Court, so should priests release their exclusivity in representing man before a Higher Court!

8. 1 Clement 44.

9. **Ministerial Priesthood**, London, 1919^2, p.115.

10. Jesus' refusal to allow the ex-demoniac, Legion, to join his band of followers (Mark 5,18-19), is hardly a contrary instance.

11. So, also, E. Schillebeeckx, **Ministry—a case for Change**, London, E.T., 1981, p.5.

12. The binding and loosing cannot relate to **persons** being excommunicated or forgiven by the Church because the subject of the binding and loosing is the neuter ὃ ἐαν (whatever).

13. **The Sayings of Jesus,** London, 1949, pp.203-4.
14. See B. Lindars, **The Gospel of John,** London, 1972, pp.618f.
15. See pp.182-4 infra.
16. **The Constitution and Law of the Church in the First Two Centuries,** E.T., London, 1910. And see Schillebeeckx, **op.cit.** p.15.
17. **The Primitive Church,** London, 1929, pp.71-2 and passim.
18. **Op.cit.** pp.144-5.
19. 1 Clement 42-44.
20. **Op.cit.** pp.xliv-xlv.
21. We discussed in Chapter IV the inferiority of evidence of Church tradition when opposed by Gospel evidence.
22. Quoted from Lightfoot's 'Dissertation on the Christian Ministry' by Moberly, **op.cit.** p.240.

CHAPTER VI.

Is Jesus God?

Gospel assertions as at John 8,58 that Jesus is God, are opposed by the counter-evidence of the experience of modern man that no human being whom he has met, was God. But, as discussed in Chapter I, the evidence of experience may be over-ridden by Gospel or other evidence which is strong and consistent.[1]

To this question, 'Is Jesus God?', — traditional Christianity replies unwaveringly 'Yes' and expresses her developed view in the Creed of Nicaea, '. . . And in one Lord Jesus Christ, the Son of God, begotten of the Father, only-begotten, that is, of the substance of the Father, God of God, Light of Light, true God of true God, begotten not made, of one substance with the Father, through whom all things were made . . . '[2] But in an attempt to investigate the question critically and historically, we must examine what titles and qualities were attributed to Jesus by those who knew him on earth, or by Jesus himself, and whether those titles and qualities constitute identity with God as God is understood in the Judaeo-Christian tradition.

But D.M. Baillie argues that to ask 'Is Jesus God?' is inappropriate, and he cites Dean Inge, "The controversy about the Divinity of Christ has been habitually conducted on wrong lines. We assume that we know what the attributes of God are, and we collect them from any source rather than the revelation of God in Christ . . . But surely Christ came to earth to reveal to us not that he was like God, but that God was like himself."[3] Yet although in the Gospels, by parable and saying, Jesus taught about the Father and his Kingdom, e.g. that the Father was merciful and forgave those who forgave others, he did not claim the qualities of the Father for himself. Apart from John's Gospel, it would be difficult to find a saying of Jesus which suggests that he is like God, or that God is like him. Moreover, the subject of Jesus' divinity must surely be considered in the light not only of what Jesus told us about the Father, but also in the light of the Old Testament understanding of God, and the views of theistic philosophers. We feel that we must fashion our mould of God in the shape of the full Judaeo-Christian tradition, and then enquire whether Jesus fits the relevant contours of that mould.

H.P. Owen defines theism as "belief in one God, the Creator, who is infinite, self-existent, incorporeal, eternal, immutable, impassible, simple, perfect, omniscient."[4] He states that all these divine properties are implied in the Bible, but that the expression and amplification of them were due to the influence of Greek philosophy. It should not be expected that Jesus, if God, would display all these properties while subject to the limitations of human existence. We might reasonably expect, however, if Jesus were God, to find NT evidence that, if not perfect, omniscient and omnipotent, he possessed proximity to moral perfection, unusual knowledge and powers, and that his contemporaries (and himself) assigned to him existence before the creation of the world, and a connection with that creation.

We now enquire into the status of Jesus by studying firstly, the titles applied to him during his lifetime, secondly, the signs of status disclosed by his teaching and other ministry, and thirdly, the estimates of Jesus held by his early followers after his death.

I. THE TITLES OF JESUS
A. Prophet.

Perhaps the strongest evidence from the Gospels concerning Jesus' rôle supports the estimate of him as prophet. That the 'ordinary people' (the *am-haarez*—people of the land) viewed Jesus in this light, receives strong support at Luke 7,39 because it is alluded to by a Pharisee who is clearly opposed to that view. After a 'sinful' woman has poured ointment over Jesus, Simon, a Pharisee, says, 'If this man were a prophet, he would have known who and what sort of woman this is . . . '. Luke, by omitting Mark's story at 14,3f. of the anointing at Bethany before the passover, suggests that he regards his own story at 7,36f. ('L' material) as recording the same incident. But only Luke's account contains conversation with the Pharisee and the Pharisee's reference to Jesus as a prophet. Whether or not that saying of the Pharisee is authentic, Luke's tradition is early evidence that Jesus was popularly regarded as a prophet.

At 6,14f. Mark records assessments of Jesus after the preaching and healing by him and his disciples had become known: some said he was Elijah (the greatest of the prophets), some that he was a prophet like the prophets of old, but Herod agreed with those who considered Jesus to be John the Baptist, risen from the dead, and John, of course, was considered a prophet (Matthew 14,5). These assessments are, we think, authentic, since the early Christians, who considered Jesus to be more than a prophet, had no motivation to invent them. They are repeated at Caesarea Philippi by the disciples (Mark 8,28). That Jesus was a prophet, like John, is a view very likely to have been held. Jesus was probably a follower of John, for he only began his own ministry after John had been arrested (Mark 1,14), and his calling of men to repentance in the face of the coming judgment must have been sufficiently reminiscent of John for

Herod and others to have believed he was John resurrected. Nor had the early church any reason to invent Mark's report at 14,65 that at Jesus' trial some (probably his guards) covered his face, struck him, and then told him to *prophesy* (presumably as to who had hit him—Luke 22,64; Matthew 26,65).

Popular acclamation of Jesus as prophet is also evidenced by Matthew at 21,10-11 ('M' material) where the crowd, asked who is entering Jerusalem, reply, 'This is the prophet Jesus from Nazareth of Galilee.' Only Matthew adds this acclamation of the crowd to the account of the entry into Jerusalem. The artificial structure of the colloquy is indicated by 'all the city' asking the question and 'the crowds' replying, but this does not invalidate Matthew's evidence that the people thought of Jesus as a prophet. Similarly, at Luke 7,16 we have no cause to doubt the evidence of Luke's 'L' source that Jesus' revivifying of the widow of Nain caused the people to describe him as a great prophet. The description of the risen Jesus by the two disciples on the road to Emmaus as 'a prophet mighty in deed and word' at Luke 24,19 is again only attested in Luke's own source ('L'), and while there are evidentiary difficulties over Jesus' resurrection appearances, Luke's source is again admissible evidence for the estimate of Jesus as a prophet.

Although most critics would attribute much of John's Gospel to meditation on Jesus' life and death, many would probably agree with C.H. Dodd that "behind the Fourth Gospel lies an ancient tradition independent of the other Gospels, and meriting serious consideration as a contribution to our knowledge of the historical facts concerning Jesus Christ."[5] Good examples of this tradition are the stories concerning Jesus' conversation with the woman of Samaria at John 4,6-26 and the healing of the man blind at birth at 9,1-34. The words of Jesus to the Samaritan woman and his healing of the blind man cause each of them to acknowledge him as a prophet.

We must here note the difference between *a* prophet and *the* prophet. *The* prophet was the one who was to come at the end of time as a fore-runner of the Messiah: this belief was founded on sayings such as Moses' prediction at Deuteronomy 18,15, 'The Lord will raise up for you a prophet like me from among you . . . '. The context indicates that this prophet is not an eschatological one, since he is to be 'just as you desired of the Lord your God at Horeb on the day of assembly'—and the Israelites were hardly then asking for a leader to bring in the last days! However, by the time of Jesus this prophet was believed to be the herald of repentance before God's direct rule; on the strength of this verse the Samaritans awaited the coming of the Teacher who is clearly Moses redivivus—he was also called *Ta'eb,* the Restorer.[6] *The* prophet who was to be the forerunner, was also identified as Elijah in reliance on Malachi 4,5, 'Behold, I will send you Elijah the prophet before the great and terrible day of the Lord comes.' Similarly, the Qumran sect expected the Prophet to arrive along with the Messiahs of Aaron and Israel.[7]

In contrast are the other prophets, typified in the Gospels by '*a* prophet' who, though the teaching of most of them was eschatological in that they warned of a pending judgment on the Day of the Lord,[8] yet laid no claim to be the herald of that Day.

The description of Jesus in the Gospels as prophet means in some places *the* final prophet; in other places he is called prophet because his authoritative teaching and healing miracles recall the words and deeds of the biblical prophets. We cannot agree with Cullmann's perception that in most of the passages Jesus appears as *the* eschatological prophet rather than as *a* prophet.[9] Clearly, Simon the Pharisee was not thinking of a final prophet at Luke 7,39. At Mark 6,14-16 and 8,27-28 the various popular views of Jesus as John the Baptist, Elijah or one of the prophets, embrace Jesus both as the final prophet before the end-time, *and* as a biblical prophet. John's message was that men should repent of their sins, and be baptised as a sign of their forgiveness since 'the axe is laid to the root of the tree'. Jesus' central message was similarly eschatological, namely that men should repent since the Kingdom of heaven was at hand. Thus, the view of Jesus as John returned to life, which is highly credible because of the nature of Jesus' teaching, entails a belief that Jesus was *the* final prophet—as does also the belief that he was Elijah come back to life, since that was to happen at the End-time. But the view of Jesus as 'one of the prophets' does not support that view—it only indicates that his healing miracles and powerful words placed him in the mould of the prophets of old. The description of Jesus as a great prophet at Luke 7,16 is because his revival of the widow's son recalls Elijah's and Elisha's similar works, and the crowd's acclamation at Matthew 21,10-11 of 'the prophet Jesus from Nazareth' contains no hint (apart from the definite article) of *the* eschatological prophet; nor does the disciples' description at Emmaus of 'a prophet mighty in word and deed' at Luke 24,19.

Jesus is similarly assessed as '*a* prophet', meaning 'one of the prophets' by the Samaritan at John 4,19 and the blind man at John 9,17. But at John 6,14 after the feeding of the multitude, the people said, 'This is indeed the prophet who is to come into the world!' This is acknowledged by commentators to be a reference to the Messianic prophet following Moses at Deuteronomy 18,15.[10] Jesus is also identified as *the* prophet at John 7,40, and it is clear from vv.40-1 that the eschatological Mosaic prophet is not to be confused with the Messiah appointed by God to bring in the Kingdom, because whereas some said, 'This is really the prophet', others said, 'This is the Christ', thus marking a popular distinction between the two. The view that Jesus might be the Mosaic prophet is also reflected in John's enquiry from prison, 'Are you *he who is to come,* or shall we look for another?' (Matthew 11,3 par. Luke 7,19).

To summarise, the evidence seems unopposed that some of Jesus' contemporaries considered Jesus to be the final prophet who was to come before God's direct rule supervened, and that others believed him to be simply a prophet in the long line of prophets.

We now turn to the evidence for Jesus' self-estimate as a prophet. This is stronger than for any other self-estimate except, perhaps, as Son of Man. At his rejection by the people of his own neighbourhood Jesus said, 'A prophet is not without honour, except in his own country, and among his own kin, and in his own house.' (Mark 6,4). Since this was probably a common proverb, perhaps we should not place too much weight upon the implicit reference to himself as a prophet. This pericope's claim to authenticity is increased by the negative statement in the following verse where Mark records that Jesus could do no mighty work there except the healing of a few sick people.[11] A clear reference by Jesus to himself as a prophet is evidenced by Luke alone at 13,33 where, following a warning from the Pharisees about Herod, Jesus says that he must be on his way 'for it cannot be that a prophet should perish away from Jerusalem.' This, too, has the ring of a proverb, but it seems less likely that Jesus would apply this proverb to himself unless he thought of himself as a prophet.

There is, however, good evidence that Jesus did *not* consider himself to be the final prophet, for at Mark 9,13 in response to the disciples' comment on the scribal prediction that Elijah must come first (i.e. before the Messiah), Jesus says that Elijah has come 'and they did to him whatever they pleased, as it is written of him.' Matthew adds at 17,12 that the disciples understood Jesus to be referring to John the Baptist, and while only Matthew contains this comment, it does seem a natural assumption for the disciples to make. Matthew also adds to the 'Q' saying at 11,13 (par. Luke 16,16), which reads, 'For all the prophets and the law prophesied until John;', the further words, 'and if you are willing to accept it, he is Elijah who is to come.' Since neither Mark nor Luke have these references to John, Matthew's evidence is not unopposed. Evidence from silence is weak, however, and since the addition might arise not from his redaction but from his own source ('M') or from the version of 'Q' received by him, we accept his evidence on a balance of probability.

We are persuaded by the above evidence that Jesus saw himself as a prophet but not as *the* final prophet. According to Vermes, Jesus was a charismatic prophet in the style of Hanina Ben Dosa; Hanina, too, was able to cure at a distance, placed absolute reliance on God, and was deemed by his contemporaries to be another Elijah.[12] The difference, though, between Jesus and the charismatic prophets was that the charismatics in their teaching seem to have placed little emphasis on the last days. Vermes argues that for Jesus to be classed as a prophet, it is unnecessary that he should be *the* final prophet. With this we can agree, but not with Vermes' styling of Jesus as a non-eschatological prophet in the mould of Hanina, for there is good evidence that the kernel of Jesus' message was 'repent for the kingdom of heaven is at hand', and so much of his teaching concerned the nature of that kingdom and the qualities required for entry.

Cullmann argues that even the concept of Jesus as *the* eschatological prophet is an insufficient estimate of Jesus' earthly work since that prophet does not forgive sins, or die an atoning death.[13] However, we hope to show below that Jesus only pronounced the result of the sinner's faith, rather than personally forgave his sins, and that the Gospel evidence that Jesus considered his death to atone for the sins of others, is ambiguous.

Our conclusions that (1) Jesus was considered by some of his contemporaries to be a prophet in the line of biblical prophets, and so considered himself, and (2) other contemporaries considered him *the* final prophet, constitute evidence that Jesus was not God, for it has never been suggested that any of the prophets were divine, not even *the* final prophet.

B. Teacher.

With this title we also consider 'Rabbi' ('my Master') since the two are almost synonymous as forms of address; at John 1,38 the term 'Rabbi' is explained for the reader as 'Teacher'. There are many references in Mark's Gospel both to the teaching activity of Jesus and to his being addressed as 'Teacher'.

Mark stresses the importance of the teaching early in his Gospel: at 1,21 Jesus enters the synagogue and teaches, 'And they were astonished at his teaching for he taught them as one having authority, and not as the scribes.' (v.22). At 6,2 Jesus teaches in a synagogue, and at 6,6 Mark summarises, 'And he went about among the villages teaching.', and at 10,1, 'and again, as his custom was, he taught them.'

Jesus is addressed as Teacher many times and by all sections of the population—the disciples (Mark 4,38; 12,1), Sadducees (12,19), a scribe (12,32), Pharisees and Herodians (12,14), ordinary people (9,17; 10,17,20); indeed, at 10,17 he is called, 'Good Teacher', and Jesus by his express rejection of the epithet 'Good', implicitly accepts the description as Teacher.[14] There is no cause to question Mark's evidence in these instances; there is no evidence to the contrary, and Mark's evidence is supported by the many examples of Jesus' teaching in the other sources, 'Q','L' and 'M'.

However, neither the activity of teaching nor the title of Teacher predicates divinity! Admittedly, Jesus has been likened to the Teacher of Righteousness of the Qumran community.[15] That Teacher was certainly accorded special qualities in the literature of the community—God had made known to him all the mysteries of the prophets, he was the priest whom God had enabled to interpret all the words of the prophets, and the Teacher had made known to recent generations what God would do to the last generation, the congregation of traitors.[16] But it can hardly be argued that these special favours from God bestowed any pre-existence or involvement in creation, and in any case, few would accept an identification of Jesus as the Teacher of Qumran.

C. Lord

The Greek *'kurios'* (lord) means the same as the Hebrew *'adonai'* (strictly, my lord) and the Aramaic *'mar'*. By the first century before Christ the Jews had replaced the biblical name for God—*yahweh*—by the word *adonai* in their synagogue worship.[16] The translators of the Hebrew bible into Greek (the Septuagint) no doubt influenced by the practice in the Hebrew synagogue liturgy, translated *yahweh* as *kurios.* It is generally accepted that Jesus and his disciples spoke Aramaic,[17] so the Gospel uses of *kurios* (except when quoting the OT) are probably translating the Aramaic *mar.* Since both *adon* and *kurios* originally meant a lord or master, and only later acquired the meaning of *the* Lord and Master, it seems likely that *mar* and *mari* (my lord) underwent this same transition. When Christians referred to Jesus after the Resurrection by the term *kurios,* they no doubt did mean the Lord in the sense of God; thus at Philippians 2,9-11 the hymn proclaims that God has bestowed on Jesus the name which is above every name, that at the name of Jesus every knee should bow, and every tongue confess that Jesus Christ is *kurios.* However, because the Resurrection (in whatever form it took) clearly had a cataclysmic effect on the estimation of Jesus in the minds of his contemporaries, we think we should consider the post-Resurrection estimation separately in a subsequent part of this essay.

We therefore turn to whether the pre-Crucifixion uses of *kurios (mar)* in the Gospels were absolute, meaning **the** Lord (i.e. God), or general in the sense of Master as resulting from the close teacher/student relation. In all uses of *kurios* in Jesus' lifetime, the word seems to be used in the general sense of Master or Teacher, or as a respectful form of address to Jesus as Master or Teacher. An example of the use of the word in the general sense of 'Master' without any Christological connotation is at Mark 2,27-28 where Jesus says, 'The sabbath was made for man . . . so the Son of man (meaning here simply 'man') is *'kurios'* even of the sabbath.'; *kurios* here means master or controller in that man uses the sabbath as his conscience dictates.

Similarly, at Mark 11,2-3 Jesus instructs his disciples that if anyone asks them why they are taking a colt from a village, they are to reply that the lord *(kurios)* has need of it. Here also *kurios* is used in the secular sense of the disciples' Master or Teacher, since the description is to be given to anyone, follower or not, who enquires. At 12,35-37 Mark uses *kurios* with both the absolute and general designations. Although scholars dispute Jesus' intent here, the most obvious meaning is that Jesus is challenging the view that the Messiah must be the son of David and is thereby suggesting that the Messiah must have a more elevated status (although not necessarily superhuman as some commentators think.).[18] Jesus quotes Ps.110,1 as 'The Lord (*kurios*—Mark omits the definite article) said to my Lord (*kurios*), Sit at my right hand, till I put thy enemies under thy feet.', and then enquires how the Messiah could be David's son when David there calls him 'my Lord'; thus we have firstly the use of *kurios* in the LXX sense of God, and next its use simply as David's Master or superior. Another use of *kurios* as God, but not meaning Jesus thereby, is at Mark 13,20 where Jesus says that if the Lord (*kurios*) had not shortened the days of the tribulation (pre-Messianic), no human being would be saved.

There are many instances of Jesus being addressed as *'kurie'* (the vocative of *kurios*). Jesus acknowledges popular use of this title for him when he says at Matthew 7,21, 'Not every one who says to me, Lord, Lord, (*kurie, kurie*) shall enter the kingdom of heaven' (also v.22). This form of address is used by a leper at Matthew 8,2, a centurion at 8,5 and by disciples at Luke 11,1 and 10,40 (Martha).[19] But in none of these pre-Crucifixion uses is there any suggestion that Jesus is called *kurios* with a meaning involving more than the respect accorded to a revered Teacher or Rabbi.

D. **Son of God**

We consider this title in conjunction with other titles such as 'the

Holy One of God', which describe a close connection between Jesus and God. It is important to note that Jesus never expressly used such titles regarding himself; they were only employed by others.

Although the Evangelists sometimes depict the demoniac as recognising the connection between Jesus and God, Jesus addresses the demon within, thus indicating his belief that it is the demon which recognises him. At Mark 1,24 the man with an unclean spirit calls Jesus 'the Holy One of God', and at 5,7 the Gerasene demoniac calls him 'Jesus, Son of the Most High God', but at 3,11 it is the unclean spirits themselves which call him 'Son of God'. Since Mark's evidence, implicit or express, of the existence of incorporeal demons, and of their speech, is outweighed in our judgment by the experiential evidence denying their existence, we will treat his statements as evidence that the demoniacs themselves recognised Jesus in this way. Strikingly, the Roman centurion at the cross also describes Jesus as the Son of God (Mark 15,39).

We must next consider what was understood by 'Son of God' when spoken in the Gospels. In the mouth of a Palestinian Jew the term probably meant someone appointed by God to perform a task; kings, for example, are so described.[20] God says to David, 'I will be his father, and he shall be my son' at 2 Samuel 7,14, and again, presumably to David, at Psalm 2,7, 'You are my son. To-day I have begotten you.' Similarly, angels seem to be attending on God to receive their tasks when at Job 1,6 and 2,1 the 'sons of God' and Satan present themselves before the Lord. An angel is commissioned as a Son of God in Daniel 3 where at v,25 a fourth man 'like a son of the gods' is seen in the fire and at v,28 Nebuchadnezzar blesses the God who 'has sent his angel and delivered his servants.' It is perhaps in this sense of the person appointed by God for an important task that Jesus hears God saying to him at his baptism, 'Thou art my beloved Son; with thee I am well pleased' (Mark 1,11), and the disciples may well have understood in the same sense God's description of Jesus at the Transfiguration, 'This is my beloved Son; listen to him' (Mark 9,7). On the other hand, it may have been Jesus' closeness to God that induced the appellation of Son, for the heavenly voice (*bath kol*) also called the charismatic Rabbi Hanina ben Dosa, and the learned Rabbi Meir, 'my son', according to the Talmud.[21] Although this evidence in the Gospels and Talmud is outweighed in our opinion by the experiential evidence that God does not speak publicly with a human voice, yet these reports can be accepted as evidence that in the Jewish tradition persons considered close to God were called Son of God without any ascription of divinity.

Amongst the Hellenes[22] also, the title 'Son of God' was used by kings. The Ptolemaic kings of Egypt were portrayed as sons of the sun-god Helios, and from the time of Augustus the Emperors of Rome bore the title 'divi filius'; the titles in these cases were meant to convey that the royal persons were themselves divine. The title 'Son of God' was also sometimes applied to the 'θειος ἀνηρ', the divine man, who effected miracles of healing and otherwise.[22A]

In Origen's Ad Celsum, written c.A.D. 248, Celsus cites many prophets in Palestine who said they were gods or sons of gods or divine spirits. A contemporary of Celsus in the second century A.D. was Lucian of Samosata who wrote about Peregrinus, a real person, who was a confidence trickster and, while living in Palestine with Christians, was revered by them as god 'next after that other they still worship, the man crucified in Palestine. . . ' Lucian regarded Christians as very gullible—'If any charlatan or trickster. . . comes upon them, he quickly acquires wealth by imposing upon simple folk.'

Philostratus early in the third century A.D. wrote a Life of Apollonius, a typical 'divine man' and a Pythagorean philosopher, based on actual letters of Apollonius and other documents. Apollonius was believed by some to have been conceived by Proteus, a god of Egypt, and by others, by Zeus. Philostratus calls him both demon and god. Apollonius continued to teach after his death, and appeared to a doubter to convince him that the soul is immortal, and that he himself was alive. Another imposter described by Lucian was Alexander of Abonuteichos whose tame snake with a false human head was believed to be the incarnation of Asclepius, the healer, for it uttered prophesies, and effected healings. This oracle pronounced that Alexander himself was born out of the 'mind of God who had sent him to assist harassed men of virtue, and then return to God.'

It seems to us possible that Gentile Christian belief in Jesus' divinity, particularly in the sense that he came to earth from God and returned to God, may have arisen from their familiarity with 'divine man' characters like the above, even though those cited above lived after Jesus, for the ancient world had a remarkable cultural continuity—Augustine felt he belonged to the same world and cultural heritage as Plato. And there were such divinely connected figures long before the time of Jesus. The report that Plato himself was the child of Zeus is attested by, amongst other ancients, Speusippus, Plato's nephew. Aristotle reports that Pythagoras was the son of Apollos, and that he returned after his departure to heaven, to heal men. Empedocles lived about 444 B.C., and he was worshipped and prayed to as a god because of his healing, rain-making and other magical feats. Plutarch, who also reports Plato's divine birth, says that he does not find it strange that a god alters mortal nature by an other than physical approach, and makes it pregnant with a more divine offspring.

Other divine births pre-dating Jesus are those of Alexander the Great (ob.331B.C.) who, according to Plutarch, was descended from Hercules on his father's side and from mythical Trojan heroes on the distaff side. The Roman historian, Livy, in about 25 B.C. records how Romulus and Remus, the founders of Rome, were born following the rape of a Vestal Virgin by Mars, the god of war. Livy and Plutarch both relate the earthly departure of Romulus in a sudden storm and thick cloud. Livy adds, 'All with one accord hailed Romulus as a god and a god's son . . . '. Romulus is later reported to have returned to earth to declare the will of heaven that Rome should be the capital of the world.

In the light of these precedents it is not difficult to see how witnesses or subsequent tradents of Jesus' healing works, if possessing a Hellenistic background, might well see Jesus as a 'divine man' type of Son of God. Thus, after Paul had healed a cripple at Lystra, the crowds acclaimed him as Hermes, and Barnabas as Zeus (Acts 14,8-12).

We have yet to look at the cases in which Jesus implicitly described himself as a Son of God in that he calls God, 'Father' or *'Abba'* (Aramaic for 'Father'). In these cases Jesus is not claiming to be *the* Son of God, only *a* son as he urges his disciples to pray to God as Father (Luke 11,2 par. Matthew 6,9). Thus, at Mark 14,36 Jesus appeals at Gethsemane to *'Abba,* Father'. Similarly, at Luke 23,34 Jesus says, 'Father, forgive them; for they know not what they do.'. But calling God his Father was only a sign of the closeness and love he felt towards God, and does not indicate any claim to divinity on his own part; indeed, this custom was not peculiar to Jesus, for the ancient *hasidim* are reported to have spent an hour before prayer in directing their hearts to their 'Father in heaven'.[23]

At Mark 13,32 Jesus does refer to *the* Son in a context which persuades most commentators that he is referring to himself; he first says at v.26 that after the tribulation 'they will see the Son of Man coming in clouds with great power and glory', and at v.29, 'when you see these things taking place, you know that he is near, at the very gates.' Then at v.32 he says, 'But of that day and of that hour no one knows, not even the angels in heaven, nor the Son, but only the Father.' The evidence for the authenticity of this latter saying is strong, for Mark's evidence is supported by the unlikelihood of the early church having invented a saying thus limiting Jesus' fore-knowledge. But we think that Jesus was not there referring to himself as the Son of God, but as the heavenly Son of Man. We are influenced to this view by the uniqueness of this reference by Jesus to himself as the Son of God (if it were so), and by the references to the Son of Man in v.26 expressly and in v.29 by the pronoun. Moreover, at v.30 Jesus says that the people then living will not pass away before 'all these things' (the tribulation and the coming of the Son of Man) take place, and then after stressing the truth of his words (v.31), Jesus stresses at v.32 that not even the angels in heaven, nor the Son, but only the Father know the actual day or hour of the End-time. It seems natural in this context and immediately following 'angels in heaven' that 'the Son' in v.32 should mean the heavenly Son of Man.

At Matthew 27,43 Jesus is alleged to have claimed to be the Son of God. The chief priests, scribes and elders say to Jesus on the cross, 'He trusts in God; let God deliver him now if he desires him; for he said, 'I am the Son of God.' This jibe is added by by Matthew to Mark's account which at 15,32 has 'Let the Christ, the King of Israel, come down now from the cross . . . '; in the same context Luke at 23,35 has 'the Christ of God, his Chosen One'. We deem the 'M' evidence of Jesus' self-designation here to be overborne by the counter-evidence of Mark and Luke and the paucity of the evidence that Jesus ever so styled himself. The evidence of the 'Q' source (Matthew 4,3-4 par. Luke 4, 3 and 9) is that Satan prefaced two of Jesus' temptations with the condition, 'If you are the Son of God . . . ' We have accepted at pp.51-2 supra the 'Q' tradition of the temptations as evidence that Jesus believed that Satan had tempted him in those general ways, but its evidence of the language used by Satan is outweighed by the experiential evidence denying that an incorporeal being speaks to persons on earth with a human voice.

To summarise, the evidence, in our opinion, is insufficient to prove that Jesus considered himself to be *the* Son of God, but does prove that others addressed him thus. The evidence of the Jewish and Hellenistic cultural backgrounds shows that the Palestinian Jews who so addressed Jesus, believed him to be either commissioned by God as a Davidic Messiah or to have a close relationship with God, or if the speakers were Gentiles or Jews influenced by Hellenism, then they were persuaded by his miracles of healing that he was a divine man. But the Palestinian Jewish interpretations do not ascribe divinity to a Son of God, and while the Hellenistic interpretation does ascribe it, the nature of the men described as gods or sons of gods or divine men, shows them to be impostors in those rôles, and the interpretation consequently to be invalid.

E. **The Servant of the Lord.**

Passages in Deutero—Isaiah called 'the Servant Songs' (42,1-4; 49, 1-7; 50,4-11; 52,13-53,12) speak of God's servant who is bruised and afflicted and slaughtered for the sins of others, but by that suffering makes many others righteous before God. Most subsequent Jewish writers have not seen the Messiah in this mould,[24] but many commentators believe that Jesus modelled his career on this Servant. They point to sayings of Jesus such as 'For the Son of Man also came not to be served but to serve, and to give his life as a ransom for many.' (Mark 10,45).

Similarly, in Chapter IV we accepted the evidence of I Corinthians 11,25 and Mark 14,24, that at the Last Supper Jesus treated his death as a covenant solemnised by his blood, and the Marcan and Matthean accounts treat his blood as shed for many. These interpretations of his death compare well with the rôle of the Servant as a 'covenant to the people' (Isaiah 42,6) and with the Servant 'pouring out his soul to death yet bearing the sins of many' (Isaiah 53,12; cf. 53,4-6,10-11). Jesus' casting himself in the part of the Suffering Servant is also suggested by his saying at Mark 10,42-44 that, unlike Gentile rulers, whoever would be great among his disciples should be their minister, and whoever would be first, should be their servant; at Luke 22,27 Jesus adds the question who is greater, he that sitteth at meat or he who serves, while classing himself as one who serves. At Mark 9,33-35 after the disciples have been arguing as to who is the greatest among them, Jesus here also stresses that whoever would be first, must be last of all and servant of all. In John's Gospel at 13,2-16 Jesus dramatically demonstrates his function as servant by washing the disciples' feet; he then urges that since he, their Teacher and Lord has washed their feet, so ought they to wash each other's feet.[25] Cullman suggests that Jesus' predictions of his suffering and death at and after Caesarea Philippi (Mark 8,31; 9,31;10,33f.; cf.12,1f.;14,8) form a link with the Suffering Servant,[26] but there is no indication in these texts that the suffering is for others, which is the distinction of the Servant's suffering.

In only one Gospel instance did Jesus expressly apply to himself a Servant text from Isaiah; at Luke 22,35-36 ('L' material) Jesus advises his disciples to prepare for the coming disaster and adds (v.37), 'For I tell you that this scripture must be fulfilled in me, 'And he was reckoned with transgressors'; for what is written about me has its fulfilment.' Against Luke's evidence that Jesus spoke v.37, there is the counter-evidence of the double expression of the fulfilment of Scripture which suggests the involvement in the verse of the early Christians who searched the Scriptures for texts to prove that Jesus' actions had been foreshadowed by the prophets and others. Supporting Luke's evidence, however, is the appositeness of the Isaianic citation—Jesus anticipates arrest on charges of being a transgressor or rebel (Hebrew *psh'im* at Isaiah 53,12), and the disciples have to use swords to avoid arrest. We find the evidence supporting Jesus' citation of Isaiah here to be preponderant.

Further, R. Otto is convinced that at Mark 9,12 Jesus was "concretely aware of himself as the expiatory suffering Servant of God in Isaiah liii."[27] In response to a question from the disciples as to why the scribes say that Elijah must first come, Jesus says at 9,12, 'Elijah does come first to restore all things; and how is it written of the Son of man, that he should suffer many things and be treated with contempt? But I tell you that Elijah has come, and they did to him whatever they pleased, as it is written of him.' The reference in v.12b to the Son of man and his suffering appears to fit awkwardly with the rest of the reply; without that reference, Jesus is credibly explaining that the scribes are right—Elijah does come first to restore all things (hearts of fathers to sons as at Malachi 4,5), but Elijah (i.e. John the Baptist per Matthew 17,13) has already been, and they did to him what they pleased. However, these verses do make sense together if, with Wellhausen and Torrey,[28] we read v.12a as a question in reply—'Does Elijah come first to restore all things? Then how is it written of the Son of man that he should suffer and be treated with contempt?' Understood thus, there is a logical flow in Jesus' reply; he asks, 'How can the prophesy that Elijah will come first to restore things be reconciled with the prediction of the Son of Man's suffering, apparently notwithstanding Elijah putting things right?[28A] Anyway, Elijah has come, and, in fact, he didn't restore things because he was killed.'

Otto stresses the link between the several kinds of suffering at Isaiah 53, 2-4 and the 'suffer many things' at Mark 9,12b, and that the Greek ἐξουδενήθη in Mark ('was treated with contempt' or literally, 'was set at naught') is a translation of the Hebrew *lo hashab'nuhu* (literally 'we did not count him')[29] at 53,3. With Mark's v12a punctuated as a question, the awkwardness disappears, and we see no counter-evidence to Mark's evidence that Jesus made this reply. Moreover, Jesus says he is quoting, and the reference to the Suffering Servant at Isaiah 53 seems well identified except that Jesus speaks of the *Son of man,* not the *Servant,* suffering and being treated with contempt; this may be an instance where, as discussed below, 'the servant' was originally in the tradition, and early Christians, identifying Jesus as the Servant, have inserted 'Son of Man' knowing that Jesus did give himself that title sometimes when speaking of the future Kingdom.

By the above one explicit and one implicit reference to himself as the Servant and by the evidence in the Gospels that Jesus expected to suffer, and saw his rôle as a servant of others, we are persuaded that Jesus felt himself to be following the course of the Isaianic Servant. But it can hardly be shown that the Servant partook of the Godhead—he is promised long life (Isaiah 53,10), and a portion with the great (53,12) and exaltation (53,13), but these benefits do not betoken divinity.

F. **The Christ/Messiah.**

'Christ' is the Greek translation of the Hebrew 'Messiah' which means 'the anointed one'. An Israelite was anointed by way of appointment to an important task, but the Jews of Jesus' day and for some time past had understood 'the Messiah' to mean the one who would be appointed by God to act as his agent for the introduction of his kingly rule.

At Mark 8,29 when Jesus asks the disciples who they (as opposed to people generally) think he is, Peter replies, 'You are the Christ.' In v.30 Jesus instructs the disciples not to tell anybody about him, although many scholars claim that this instruction is an expression of Mark's 'Messianic secret' idea.[30] Although Jesus does not expressly deny the title of Messiah here, he adds in reply that the Son of Man must suffer, using, we think, the term 'Son of Man' simply as a modest circumlocution for 'I': the popular view did not connect the Messiah with suffering, as is indicated by Peter's rebuke to Jesus at v.32. Jesus' fierce reply to Peter at v.33 is strong evidence that he was unwilling to accept the title of Messiah — he says, 'Get behind me, Satan! For you are not on the side of God, but of men.' Jesus' charge that Peter was on the side of men, indicates that Jesus' reluctance to be called Messiah was because in popular belief the Messiah would be a victorious warrior in arms, crushing the Romans and other foes of Israel. Jesus also rejected this form of Messiahship when during his temptation he spurned the devil's offer of the kingdoms of the world with 'Begone, Satan!' and a quotation of Deuteronomy 6,13, 'You shall worship the Lord your God and him only shall you serve.'(Matthew 4,11 par. Luke 4,8).

Two other occasions when Jesus might be thought to have admitted his Messiahship, arose at his trials. Firstly, at Mark 14,61 the High Priest asks Jesus, 'Are you the Christ, the Son of the Blessed?', and Jesus replies, according to most Greek manuscripts, 'I am'. Matthew at 26,64 has, 'You have said so.', and Luke at 22,67-70 splits the question into two, and in response to 'the Christ' part Jesus says, 'If I tell you, you will not believe; and if I ask you, you will not answer.' In each Gospel, however, Jesus continues with a reference to the Son of Man sitting at the right hand of power, and (in the case of Mark and Matthew) coming with the clouds of heaven (cf. Daniel 7,13).

We are inclined to accept Mark's evidence of the High Priest's question and Jesus' reply on the basis that Matthew and Luke's versions are here revisions of Mark's tradition which is earlier and closer to the oral stage of the tradition. We think that Matthew and Luke softened Mark's unambiguous 'I am' into a more equivocal reply followed (as in Mark) by the Son of Man reference, to emphasise that Jesus was not an earthly warrior type of Messiah, but rather the heavenly Messiah. It is noteworthy that in a few codices of Mark's Gospel, Jesus replies 'You say that I am', similarly to Matthew 26,64 (and Luke 22,70), but we think these are attempts to harmonise Mark more closely to the other Gospels. But even the clear admission that he is the Messiah according to the Marcan textual evidence which we accept, has to be interpreted in the light of the following words about the Son of Man, which show that although he is the Messiah, his is not the kind of Messiahship about which the High Priest asks.

The second occasion concerns the trial before Pilate. At Mark 15,1 Pilate asks, "are you the King of the Jews?", and Jesus replies, "You have said so." 'The King of the Jews' was the Roman way of referring to the Jewish warlike, political Messiah, and Jesus' reply has the inference, 'You, not I, have said so.', for, again, he would not wish to admit that kind of Messiahship: yet if he had openly replied in the negative, he would also have denied his belief that he would after the tribulation return as the Son of Man-type Messiah.

We therefore conclude that Jesus' reply at Caesarea Philippi to Peter and his replies at his trials to the High Priest and Pilate, all indicate that Jesus believed himself to be the Messiah, but according to the 'Son of Man' interpretation of that rôle, not the popular one. Moreover, Jesus did not believe that he was already on earth that supernatural Messiah, but rather that he would become that figure after, by suffering, he had enabled the Kingdom of God to arrive.

This conclusion accords with Jesus' challenge to the scribal view that the Messiah (Christ) was the son of David. It appears that Jesus was sometimes addressed as 'Son of David' (e.g. Mark 10,47), and Jesus' objection to the title was probably because the idea that the Messiah would be of David's lineage was connected with the popular expectation of a Messiah who would be warlike and political, like David had been. Whether the Son of Man-type of Messiah was divine, we consider below, p.192.

G. Son of Man.

This is the title that Jesus, according to the Gospel evidence, most frequently applied to himself, and it is noteworthy that it is used by Jesus only, not by his disciples or others. The difficulty in understanding what Jesus means when he uses the term regarding himself is that the Greek in the Gospels for 'the Son of man' (ὁ υἱὸς τοῦ ἀνθρώπου) translates the Aramaic *bar nasha* which can mean (1) 'man' in general, or (2) the exalted Son of Man, or (3) by way of circumlocution, 'I', the speaker.

An alleged example of the first meaning is at Mark 2,27-8 where Jesus, in defence of the plucking of grain by his disciples on the Sabbath, says to the Pharisees, "the sabbath was made for man, not man for the sabbath (v.27); so the Son of man is lord even of the sabbath (v.28);". However, there are difficulties in the way of interpreting Son of man as 'man' here. Rawlinson has pointed out the unlikelihood of Jesus saying that 'man' was master of the sabbath when the sabbath had been created by God.[31] It is also strange for Jesus to say that man is the lord of other things, as the 'even' (καί) implies. Further, if man in general is intended in v.28 as well as in v.27, why has Mark or a tradent translated the presumably identical Aramaic word with ἄνθρωπος (man) in v.27 and υἱὸς τοῦ ἀνθρώπου (son of man) in v.28? To interpret 'son of man' in v.28 as the heavenly Son of man seems no more satisfactory since v.28 is not then a natural corollary to v.27 as the 'so' (ὥστε) suggests it to be; indeed, there seems to be no logical link between the sabbath being made for man, and the Son of man (whether it here means Jesus or not) being lord of the sabbath. This evidence of the unlikelihood of Jesus having said that the Son of man is lord of the sabbath, however that term is to be interpreted, is in our opinion stronger than the evidence of Mark's assertion, and we conclude that the statement in v.28 is a Christian insertion into the tradition.

The other instance where the first meaning of 'Son of man' has been alleged, is at Matthew 12,32 (par. Luke 12,10) where Jesus says that whoever says a word against the Son of man will be forgiven, but whoever speaks a word against the Holy Spirit will not be forgiven "either in this age or in the age to come." This seems to be a version from the 'Q' collection of a saying of which Mark gives another version at 3,28-29, "Truly, I say to you, all sins will be forgiven to the sons of men (τοῖς υἱοῖς τῶν ἀνθρώπων), and whatever blasphemies they utter; but whoever blasphemes against the Holy Spirit never has forgiveness, but is guilty of an eternal sin". Matthew virtually repeats at 12,31 Mark's 3,28-9, whereas Luke omits it, and then Matthew adds his above 'Q' version of the saying. Mark, followed by Matthew, places these verses at the end of Jesus' speech in the Beelzebul debate, but we think that they were spoken by Jesus on another occasion since Mark has to tell the reader why they are relevant to the Beelzebul charge against Jesus by adding at v.30 in parenthesis, "for they had said, "He has an unclean spirit." 'Sons of men' at Mark 3,28 clearly does mean man in general, but we think that in the 'Q' version it has been amended to the singular 'Son of man' by a Christian tradent who on receiving in Greek the version which Mark reproduces, has confused the reference to sins being forgiven *to the sons of men,* with sins *against the Son of man* being forgiven. We think the Marcan contrast between sins against the Holy Spirit and other sins, is more credible than the 'Q' contrast between words against the Son of man (whether or not Jesus be intended) and words against the Holy Spirit. We accordingly judge that the assertions of Matthew and Luke that Jesus referred to the Son of man in this saying, are weaker evidence than Mark's assertion and the intrinsic unlikelihood of the 'Q' version. Thus, in our view the singular 'Son of man' is not used in the NT to mean man in general.

There is much Gospel evidence of Jesus using the term 'Son of man' with the second meaning of the exalted Son of man. In some instances Jesus does not appear to be thinking specifically of himself as that Son of man. Thus in 'M', the source exclusive to Matthew, Jesus tells the disciples at 10,23 that they will not have gone through all the cities of Israel on their mission, before the Son of man arrives. Here Jesus clearly means the exalted Son who will inaugurate the Kingdom, but it is doubtful whether at that early stage of his ministry he thought of himself as that future Son. In Luke's separate source, 'L'. at 17,22,24 and 30 Jesus refers to the day of the Son of Man, and in another apocalyptic saying at 21,36 Jesus urges prayer so that the disciples may stand before the Son of Man; there is no indication that Jesus is in these verses contemplating himself in that rôle.

But in other instances Jesus does, we think, refer to himself as the Son of man. We have discussed above Jesus' reply to the High Priest at his trial where according to all the Synoptists he mentions the Son of man sitting at the right hand of power, and clearly means himself. We think, however, that Jesus refers to himself as the Son of man only where he means the already exalted Son or where, in reference to his coming Messianic suffering, he means proleptically the 'about-to-be exalted' Son. The latter use arises from Jesus' belief that immediately after his suffering he would bring in the Kingdom as Son of man. Thus, in explaining at Caesarea what kind of Messiah he is to be, he taught that the Son must suffer, be rejected and be killed (Mark 8,31); he similarly predicts the Son's suffering at Mark 9,31 and 10,33-34.

We consequently cannot agree that Jesus used the title 'Son of man' with the third meaning, i.e. by way of circumlocution for 'I', the speaker, since in the cases just mentioned where he is using the title for 'I', he intends a special, descriptive meaning, not simply a circumlocution or substitute for 'I'. There are, however, verses in the Gospels where Jesus is expressed to refer to himself as the Son of man and where the context gives the title no special connotation. For example, at Luke 7,34 (par. Matthew 9,19) Jesus says, "The Son of man has come eating and drinking; and you say, 'Behold a glutton and a drunkard. . . '"; he means here 'I, Jesus here on earth', not the heavenly Son. Similarly, at Luke 9,58 (par. Matthew 8,20) Jesus says, "Foxes have holes, and the birds of the air have nests; but the Son of man has nowhere to lay his head." In regard to verses such as these, we are influenced by Otto's view, and believe that because Jesus did, as discussed above, sometimes mean himself when referring to the Son of man in the Son's exalted or about-to-be exalted state, early tradents noticing this and believing that he *was* the Son of man, substituted that designation in stories where Jesus had only said 'I' or 'me'.[32] That substitution has been made, we think, in both the above examples, but better evidence of the reality of these substitutions is produced by Synoptic comparison. For at Luke 6,22 where Jesus tells the disciples that they are blessed when men shall hate them for the Son of man's sake, Matthew in his parallel at 5,11 writes, "for my sake." Although this saying is from the 'Q' source on which both Evangelists drew, we think that in the version of 'Q' available to Luke, "for the Son of man's sake" has been substituted for "for my sake". Otto cites a stronger case at Mark 8,27 where Jesus asks, "Who do men say that I am?", and this pronoun is repeated by Luke, but Matthew, who is also following Mark, has changed the question to, "Who do men say that the Son of man is?". Jesus almost certainly said 'I' in that question for the further reason that after the disciples' reply stating the opinions of others, Jesus, according to all the Synoptists, asks, "But who do you say that I am?"[33]

These substitutions give the impression that Jesus already thought of himself as Son of man in connection with his *earthly* ministry. That impression is usually considered to be mistaken, but there is a saying of Jesus in which, on the face of it, Jesus does claim to perform a judicial function of the Son of man during his earthly ministry, namely the forgiveness of sins. At Mark 2,5 Jesus says to the paralytic, 'My son, your sins are forgiven.' Some scribes are offended because only God can forgive sins, and Jesus says, 'Why do you question thus in your hearts? Which is easier to say to the paralytic, 'Your sins are forgiven,' or to say, 'Rise, take up your pallet and walk'? But that you may know that the Son of man has authority on earth to forgive sins' — he said to the paralytic — 'I say to you, rise, take up your pallet and go home.'

It is noteworthy that both here and at the only other recorded instance of Jesus declaring sins forgiven, namely Luke 7,48, Jesus states in the passive tense, 'your sins are forgiven.' Taylor has pointed out the similarity to the words of Nathan to David, 'The Lord hath put away thy sin' (2 Samuel 12,13).[34] It is also noteworthy that in many of his healings Jesus declares the cure to be the result of the invalid's faith in Jesus' healing powers; to the woman with a haemorrhage who believed she would be cured simply by touching Jesus' garments, he said, 'Daughter, your faith has made you well; go in peace, and be healed of your disease.' (Mark 5,28,34). To the blind man who cried out to Jesus, and said, 'Master, let me receive my sight.' Jesus replied, 'Go your way; your faith has made you well.' (Mark 10,51,52; cf. 6,6; 7,29; 9,23). Our conclusion from these two points is that at Mark 2,5 and Luke 7,48 Jesus is not himself forgiving sins, but rather declaring that the invalids' sins are forgiven *by God* because of their faith. This interpretation whereby Jesus only declares a forgiveness already given by God, is strengthened if at Mark 2,5 and 9, we read $\dot{\alpha}\phi\varepsilon\omega\nu\tau\alpha\iota$ which, as confirmed by Winer,[35] is the perfect passive tense, and would give the sense, 'Your sins have already been forgiven.' That reading is supported by strong textual witness and by Luke's parallels at 5,20 and 23 and 7,48. This interpretation is also consistent with Jesus' assumption elsewhere in his teaching that it is God who forgives sins (e.g. Matthew 6.12-15 (par. Luke 9,2-4); Luke 18,9-14).

Some scholars doubt the authenticity of this debate between Jesus and the scribes at Mark 2,6-10a.[36] It does seem unlikely that in the press and turmoil of the crowd necessitating the paralytic to be let down from the roof, Jesus should be able to sense the apparently unspoken (2,6) objections of the scribes. However, we can accept Mark's assertions as evidence that a debate with the scribes on these lines took place at some time; for although the Jews of that time did believe that illness was the result of sin or demons, and that the presence of demons might itself be due to sin,[37] the scribes are unlikely to have believed that mere faith in Jesus as healer could result in God forgiving their sins. And Jesus on this occasion (though not always, see John, 9,3; Luke 13,2) implicitly accepts the Jews' connection of illness with sin, but argues that once the invalid has faith, then his sins are forgiven and his illness cured so that it matters not whether he announces the cure to the invalid by saying 'your sins are forgiven' or 'rise. . . and walk'.

But verse 10 seems to be an interpolation. Against Mark's evidence that Jesus claimed there that the Son of man had authority to forgive sins, is the following counter-evidence of the unlikelihood of Jesus making such a claim concerning the Son of man. 'The Son of man' cannot here mean man generally, for it is unthinkable that a man could forgive sins against God. It is even unlikely that the title is a synonym for 'I', since Jesus was most reserved about his earthly position. We have concluded above that Jesus did claim that he would be the heavenly Son of man after his tribulation and death, but the claim to an earthly function as Son of man would be unique on his part. Further counter-evidence lies in the awkward way in which this verse fits into the composition of vv.8-12; at v.9 Jesus explains to the scribes that it is immaterial whether he tells the invalid his sins are forgiven, or tells him to rise and walk (because it is his faith which has caused his sins to be forgiven and consequently his body to be healed). At v.10 Jesus continues his words to the scribes in the form of a purpose clause, 'But that you may know that the Son of man has authority on earth to forgive sins', but then switches his address to the paralytic, telling him to rise and go home. The instruction to the paralytic is prefaced by an editorial parenthesis 'he said to the paralytic'. The purpose clause (10a) concerning the Son of man seems to break into the narrative which would otherwise flow naturally in vv.9,10b and 11 — 'Which is easier, to say the paralytic, 'Your sins are forgiven,' or to say, 'Rise, take up your pallet and walk? He said to the paralytic, 'I say to you, rise, take up your pallet and go home.' We accordingly judge that Mark's evidence at 2,10a that Jesus claimed power as the Son of man on earth to forgive sins, is outweighed by the evidence of the intrinsic unlikelihood of the claim and by the evidence of the stylistic awkwardness of the clause, which indicates that it was an insertion by Mark or a tradent into a written source of the tradition; the complexity of the syntax of vv.10-11 renders it unlikely to have been an insertion into oral tradition whose syntax must presumably have been fairly simple for the purpose of memorisation. We think that the early Christians invented Jesus' claim to forgive sins on earth as Son of man as a consequence of their belief that he was divine.

We do, however, accept the evidence that in some sayings in which Jesus referred to the Son of Man in his exalted state or in his condition of suffering prior to being exalted, he intended himself. We discuss below at p. 192 the attributes of divinity possessed by the exalted Son of Man.

II. SIGNS OF JESUS' STATUS IN HIS MINISTRY

Since the titles used by Jesus' contemporaries and by himself do not show that Jesus laid claim to divinity while on earth, we must now enquire whether features of his teaching or other ministry of themselves indicated his divinity.

The authoritative nature of Jesus' preaching impressed the people.

Mark records that when Jesus taught in the synagogue at Capernaum, the congregation 'were astonished at his teaching, for he taught them as one who had authority, and not as the scribes.' (1,22). Thus, in the Sermon on the Mount Jesus in several instances recites the Mosaic law, then adds, 'But I say to you. . . . ' (Matthew 5,21-48). Since the Jews believed that the law in their Bible was given by God through Moses, a claim to supersede that law might be thought a blasphemous claim to divinity, but in fact, quite drastically differing views on the interpretation of the law were allowed without any such charge.[38] And while the people marvelled at his teaching, the Gospel evidence does not suggest that he was considered divine because of it. At Matthew 12, 41-42 (par. Luke 11,31-32) where Jesus says, "something greater than Jonah/Solomon is here", he at first sight appears to claim an elevated status for himself, but the neuter Greek adjective is rightly translated 'some*thing* greater' (than Jonah and Solomon), so that Jesus is referring not to himself, but to the Kingdom or the preaching of it.

An aspect of Jesus' ministry which most people would say implied a claim to the Godhead, was Jesus' supposed forgiveness of sins; we have previously decided, however, that in the two instances reported, Jesus was only announcing what God had already done.

We imagine that the most popular argument for Jesus' divinity relates to his resurrection. For the reasons explained in Chapter I, we cannot accept the Gospel evidence for a bodily resurrection, but even if Jesus had risen bodily to the heavens, why should that indicate divinity? Enoch and Elijah had risen to heaven, but they were not considered divine (nor were Lazarus or the widow's son raised by Elijah), and since Jesus promised that his followers would rise, too, are they all to be considered divine? G.W.H. Lampe has pointed out that if a deceased friend appeared to us after his death, we would not for that reason believe he was divine.

Some statements of Jesus in John's Gospel make high claims: at 8,58 Jesus claims pre-existence in his saying, 'before Abraham was, I am.' Another example is at 14,6 where Jesus says, 'I am the way, and the truth, and the life; no one comes to the Father, but by me.' We think that John's evidence that Jesus made such statements as these, is outweighed by the internal evidence of the long discourses or conversations in which they are contained—they are too complex to have been passed on by tradents orally, and more likely represent the results of John's meditation on traditions of Jesus' teaching.

To summarise, the evidence of Jesus' divinity in the Gospel records of his teaching and other ministry is outweighed, in our view, by the counter-evidence. Supporting this conclusion there is evidence in his teaching that Jesus saw himself as quite different in *nature* from the Father, not simply different in *person* for that would be consistent with the position ultimately embodied in the theory of the Trinity. For example, at Mark 10,17 the rich young man addresses Jesus as 'Good Teacher', and Jesus replies, 'Why do you call me good? No one is good but God alone.' (v.18). Indeed, Jesus sees even the heavenly Son of man as possessing less prescience than the Father at Mark 13,32 where he says, 'But of that day or that hour no one knows, not even the angels in heaven, nor the Son, but only the Father.' Mark's evidence that Jesus said these things is strong, because the early Christians had no motivation to invent sayings showing Jesus' separation from the Godhead.

III. ESTIMATES OF JESUS HELD AFTER HIS DEATH

We now turn to the estimates of Jesus held by his early followers after his death, for we consider evidence of their views to be forensically relevant in that it may render more or less probable the matter in issue, namely Jesus' divinity. We decided in Chapter I, on the Gospel and other evidence, that (1) although Jesus appeared to the disciples after his death, he did not rise from the dead with an externally recognisable body, and (2) that the appearances experienced by the disciples were visions. But the Gospel evidence also shows that the disciples *believed* that he had actually risen with an externally recognisable body. Although their estimation of Jesus was thus influenced by a belief about him which, in our opinion, was mistaken, this does not preclude us from accepting, as evidence of Jesus' status, the reports of their estimates of him. For, although it cannot forensically be proved to be so, it is possible that truth (including a correct estimate of Jesus) may be vouchsafed by vision. We remind ourselves, however, that as discussed above in connection with Elijah and Enoch, resurrection of itself does not indicate divinity.[38A]

After Jesus' resurrection appearances the first Palestinian Christians believed him to be alive in heaven, and their estimates of him in relation to his earthly work were not necessarily relevant to his position in heaven. Thus, of the titles considered above, those of Teacher, Prophet and Suffering Servant could not adequately describe whatever rôle he had now assumed. But the Son of man title was now more relevant than it had previously been, since Jesus had taught that after his suffering and death, he would appear as that figure. Since he had suffered on the Cross, and God by raising him from the dead had approved his work and teaching on earth, the disciples naturally expected that Jesus would, as taught, return as that Son.

The Son of God title also was still relevant to these Christians, since the raising of Jesus by God was proof of Jesus' closeness to God. Cullmann sees the disciples' belief in Jesus as Son of God as belief that he was the only Son of God in a divine sense,[39] but initially, before the impact of Hellenistic views, their use of the title may, as during his lifetime, only have signified their belief in his special relationship to God. The title of Messiah/Christ was still relevant in that Jesus was now the Son of man-type Messiah which, since Caesarea Philippi, he had stressed he would be. Similarly, the title of Lord (*kurios*) was still used to signify 'revered Master',[40] the more revered because of his raising by God, but we do not think it connoted 'God' until it was used in that sense by Hellenistic Jews of the Diaspora, influenced by the use of *kurios* in the LXX to translate *y'hyah* (Yahweh) in the Hebrew Bible.

However, we think that the predominant thought of those first Palestinian Christians concerned Jesus' return as Son of man; as discussed in Chapter IV, this event was expected to take place at one of their common meals. Strangely, only Stephen in his vision at Acts 7,56 is recorded as speaking of the Son of man in relation (implicitly) to the risen Jesus; he says, 'Behold, I see the heavens opened, and the Son of man standing at the right hand of God.' The similarity of these words to those of Jesus at Mark 14,62 does not appear to us as strong evidence against Stephen having said them, and we accept Luke's report. Yet although we have no other evidence of early Christians calling Jesus 'Son of man', we do have evidence that they expected him to return to perform the principal function of that figure, namely, to judge all men.

There is strong evidence that the early Christians expected Jesus to return very soon, certainly during the lifetime of those living at Jesus' death. Paul wrote c.50 A.D.[41] to the Thessalonians to re-assure them concerning Christians who had died already, and he says, 'For this we declare to you by the word of the Lord, that we who are alive, who are left until the coming of the Lord, shall not precede those who have fallen asleep.' (1 Thessalonians 4,15). And by this time the brethren were already worried at the delay in Jesus' return, for Paul has to stress that nobody knew exactly when Jesus would return—he writes, 'But as to the times and the seasons, brethren, you have no need to have anything written to you. For you yourselves know well that the day of the Lord will come like a thief in the night.' (5,1-2). In the second Letter (written shortly after the first)[42] Paul has to dissuade them from thinking that the day of judgment had already arrived; he writes, "Now concerning the coming of our Lord Jesus Christ and our assembling to meet him, we beg you, brethren, not to be quickly shaken in mind or excited, either by spirit or by word... to the effect that the day of the Lord has come."(2,1-2).

The continuous expectation of Jesus' return to earth (parousia) is shown by the liturgical phrase *'marana tha'* which is found both in Paul's first Letter to the Corinthians (16,22) and in the Jewish Christian Didache (10,6), and means 'Our Lord, come!'. This Aramaic phrase is thought to have originated in the earliest Palestinian Christianity and to have been used at the Eucharist.[43]

Christians had good reason to expect an early parousia. Jesus had been expecting the arrival of the Son of man (though not himself in that rôle) during his disciples' first mission, for at Matthew 10,23 he says, ". . . you will not have gone through all the towns of Israel, before the Son of man comes." As stated previously, we accept this saying as authentic, since the church would hardly have invented a saying almost immediately shown to be false. The same may be said of Jesus' prophesy at Mark 13,30 concerning the pre-Messianic tribulation, "Truly, I say to you, this generation will not pass away before all these things take place." When warning of the unexpected coming of the Son of man at Luke 12,40 (par. Matthew 24,44), Jesus is probably not thinking of himself, but at 11,35 (par. Matthew 23,39) Jesus does refer to himself when after the woes over Jerusalem he concludes, "For I tell you, you will not see me again until you say, 'Blessed is he who comes in the name of the Lord.' And his imminent return as Son of man is surely implicit in his reply at Mark 14,62 to the High Priest's question whether he was the Messiah, "I am, and you will see the Son of man sitting at the right hand of Power and coming with the clouds of heaven." The argument that this saying is inauthentic because it combines a reference from Psalm 110,1 to sitting at the right hand of God with a reference from Daniel 7,13 to coming like a Son of man with the clouds of heaven, is in our view weak counter-evidence against Mark's assertion. Nor do we find strong counter-evidence in the argument that since in Daniel 7,13 the Son of man 'came' to the Ancient of Days, Jesus is not referring to his 'coming' to earth. For since Jesus envisages the Son as already at the right hand of God, there is hardly space for him to *come* to God; Jesus means we think that the High Priest on earth will physically see the Son coming to earth from the clouds. And if Jesus had meant that the Son was going to God and not coming to earth, it is difficult to explain convincingly the church's rapt expectation.

The belief that Jesus was coming to judge men sprang from current concepts of the function of the Son of man (see below), re-inforced by Jesus' own words. Thus, at Matthew 25,31-32 Jesus speaks of the Son of man coming in glory and sitting on his throne, and "before him will be gathered all the nations, and he will separate them one from another as a shepherd separates the sheep from the goats,";[43A] he then tells a parable about judgment. There is no cause to doubt the evidence provided by this 'M' material.

If, as the Christians expected, Jesus was, having suffered his pre-Messianic tribulation, soon to return as Son of man to judge,[44] then he would, according to the literature upon which the 1st-century concepts of the Son of man were based, possess in that capacity several of the attributes of divinity which we discussed at the start of this Chapter. Thus, as the Son, Jesus would justifiably be considered as God-like if not God. For at Daniel 7 it is said of the Son of man that to him, 'was given dominion and glory and kingdom, that all peoples, nations, and languages should serve him; his dominion is an everlasting dominion which shall not pass away. . . . ' (7,14). The Parables of Enoch, generally dated about 50 B.C., contain more information about the Son of man, and although this portion of 1 Enoch does not appear in the fragments found at Qumran, most scholars would still affirm that it is a pre-Christian Jewish work.[45] It is said there that before the sun and the signs were created, the Son of man's name was named before the Lord of Spirits; he was chosen before the creation of the world and for evermore (48,3,6). He is linked with the Messiah, for he is the Anointed of the Lord of Spirits (48,10). Most significantly in relation to early Christian belief, judgment of sinners on earth (69,27) and of sinning angels (55,4) is given to 'Mine Elect One', another title for the Son of man. Other divine attributes of the Son in Enoch are his moral perfection (49,2) and omniscience (46,3).

However, notwithstanding these expectations, Jesus did not make the promised early return to earth as Son of man or at all. Jesus may be the Son of man in heaven sitting at the right hand of God, but the only evidence assessable by the historian is (1) the Gospel assertions of Jesus' prediction that he would *soon* return to earth as Son, and (2) the fact that he did not do so. The millenialists may claim that Jesus will yet return as Son in the future,[46] but his promise was to come soon. The evidence that he did not return soon as Son, is relevant, and therefore admissible, evidence not against the Gospel assertion that Jesus predicted his return as Son of man, but against the accuracy of his prediction that he would become the Son, because it renders the accuracy of that prediction less probable. We find this counter-evidence of failure to return to be stronger than the evidence constituted by Jesus' prediction that he would become the Son of man, and we conclude that he did not attain that position.

Consequent upon Jesus' ever-increasing delay in returning as Son of man, some Christians concluded that Jesus had assumed a different rôle in the heavenly hierarchy. For had not God shown his approval of Jesus' earthly work by raising him from the dead? The Hellenistic-Jewish Christians of the Diaspora believed that Jesus was dwelling on high as *Christos* (Messiah) and *kurios* (Lord) which latter title, as mentioned, carried attributes of deity The Gentile Christians, similarly pondering the problem of this delay, were conscious of the resemblance between Jesus and the Hellenistic 'divine men' discussed above, so they recognised Jesus as a Redeemer-God who descended from the heavens, delivered man from demons, fate and death, and then returned on high. We can see this evaluation of Jesus in the early Christian hymn at Philippians 2,5-11 where Jesus, though "in the form of God", took the form of a servant, and became obedient unto death so that God highly exalted him. It was a short step from this to acknowledge Jesus' pre-existence and involvement in creation (1 Corinthians 8,6; Colossians 1,15-19).

Both these Hellenistic-Jewish and Gentile assessments of Jesus' status confessed him as God, yet we cannot admit them as evidence that he *was* God. In favour of Jesus' status as Son of man there was the Gospel evidence of his predictions that he would return as the Son, and that evidence was supported by the evidence of the expectation of his disciples after his death. But the evaluations of Jesus as divine in these other rôles, made partly in re-action to his inexplicable failure to return as Son of man, are not seemingly based upon any evidence from Jesus' words or deeds on earth that he would fill a rôle in heaven as Messiah, Lord or Redeemer-God, nor upon estimates by others made during his lifetime;[47] they are the intellectual constructions of his followers and are inadmissible as evidence of his status after death because they do not render it more or less probable that he achieved any of those positions.

The revised estimates which bestowed deity upon Jesus were not uniformly accepted. Of the Palestinian Jews, the Ebionites asserted that Jesus was only human, but that as Christ he would rule over the world to come, while the Nazarenes denied Jesus' pre-existence as God but called him the Son of God.[48]

IV. CONCLUSIONS

We summarise our thinking as follows: —

1. Against the NT assertions that Jesus is God, there is the counter-evidence of experience to the effect that no human being has possessed the creative and other qualities which the Judaeo-Christian tradition assigns to God. However, that experiential evidence may be outweighed by strong and consistent evidence to the contrary.

2. None of the estimates of Jesus' rôle made during his lifetime implied that he was divine. The title 'Son of man' was only used by Jesus himself, and then only to indicate his activity after death, or, proleptically, in the

context of his pre-Messianic suffering to come.
3. Jesus did not himself in his teaching or other ministry lay claim to divinity.
4. The earliest estimate of Jesus after his resurrection was as Son of man. This title did connote God-like attributes, but the evidence of Jesus' failure to return soon as Son to judge, disproves the accuracy of his claims to be, and of Christian belief that he was, the Son.
5. Jesus' delay in returning as Son led Christians in the Diaspora to form new estimates of Jesus' post-Resurrection status. They considered him to be God, but these estimates are not admissible evidence that he is God, since they are intellectual constructs not based upon evidence of divinity from Jesus' words and deeds nor from the estimates of others during his lifetime.
6. The evidence of our experience denying deity to a person who was a human being, is not opposed by strong and consistent evidence to the contrary (see 1 above).
7. Consequently, Jesus is not God.

Postscript. It is unfortunate, we think, that Jesus' equality with God became a pillar of Christian orthodoxy, for this, like the bodily resurrection mentioned in the Chapter II postscript, has probably become a stumbling-block for many who were attracted by Jesus' life and teaching. The first Christians were Jews and, as such, believed that God had revealed himself and his will for men in the Law and the Prophets. Many of them regarded Jesus as a prophet, and it seems reasonable for his followers today to regard him as the greatest in the line of prophets in that God has revealed himself to a much greater extent in Jesus: whether God, possessing infinite qualities, has revealed himself fully in Jesus, is impossible for finite man to know. Jesus revealed God during his life and death as a human being upon earth, but why, after his death, should he for this reason be estimated divine? He 'appeared' to the disciples after death, according to the Gospels, but that does not render him divine. In order for Jesus' life of obedience to God's will even unto death, to be accepted as God's revelation of how man should live, it is not necessary that Jesus should be regarded as God.

This belief in Jesus as God was a cause of Christianity's rupture with Judaism. Notwithstanding ingenious attempts to disguise the breach of the monotheism at the heart of Jewish faith, by adoption in the Trinity of the Greek philosophers' distinction between substance and forms,[48A] belief in the Son as God and in the Father as God is, without the intervention of sophistry, belief in two Gods. J.F. Bethune-Baker writes, "inherited from Judaism and the Old Testament was the fundamental principle, with which Christians started, of the existence of God, His unity and distinction from the world. As a second fundamental doctrine of their own they had the revelation of this God in Jesus Christ—the Incarnation and the Resurrection. They had an instinctive conviction that the fulness of the Lord was more than human. . . "[49] Much difficulty for would-be followers of Jesus has been created by this unwillingness to accept that just as God may unexpectedly use the heathen Cyrus[50] or Assyrians[51] to effect his purpose for the chosen people, so he may unexpectedly use a human being to reveal himself to man.

NOTES

1. On the evidence of experience and of natural laws, see Chapter I.
2. Translation taken from H. Bettenson, **Documents of the Christian Church**, Oxford, 1963², p.25.
3. **God was in Christ**, London, 1961, p.66.
4. **Concepts of Deity**, London, 1971, p.1.
5. **Historical Tradition in the Fourth Gospel**, Cambridge, 1963, p.423.
6. O. Cullmann, **The Christology of the NT**, E.T., London, 1959, p.19.
7. See G. Vermes, **The Dead Sea Scrolls: Qumran in Perspective**, London, 1977, pp.185-6.
8. See e.g. Amos 5,18; Isaiah 2,12; Jeremiah 4.
9. **Op.cit.** p.13.
10. E.g. B. Lindars, **The Gospel of John**, London, 1972, pp.190-191. Cf. John 1,21.
11. See thereon V. Taylor, **The Gospel according to St Mark**, London, 1953, p.301 ad.loc.
12. G. Vermes, **Jesus the Jew**, London, 1973, pp.89-90.
13. **Op.cit.** p.45.
14. Jesus also implicitly accepts the title of Teacher at John, 13,13. That rôle was emphasised by Justin Martyr who calls him Revealer of Truth (**Dialogue**, C.2).
15. See A. Dupont-Sommer, **The Essene Writings from Qumran**, Oxford, 1961, pp.370-372.
16. Vermes, **Qumran**, p.168.
17. See J. Barr, 'Which Language did Jesus speak?', **Bulletin of John Rylands Library** 53 (1970-71) pp.9-29 at p.17.
18. See e.g. Taylor, **op.cit.** pp.492-3.
19. At John 13,13 Jesus acknowledges to the disciples that he is both

their Teacher and their Lord.

20. See further Cullmann, **op.cit.** pp.272-5.

21. See Vermes, **Jesus,** pp.206-7.

22. For the following Hellenistic evidence the author acknowledges his indebtedness to Frances Young's essay, 'Two Roots or a Tangled Mass?' being Ch.5 in **The Myth of God Incarnate,** ed. John Hick, London, 1977. But see also concerning the deification of Alexander and the Diadochi, G. Murray, **Five Stages of Greek Religion,** London, 1935, p.153f.

22A. "If a man was found to have gifts and powers that were out of the ordinary, and seemed supernatural, the Greeks saw no reason not to describe him as a 'god', or as 'divine', even if there was no cult in his honour." (A.E. Harvey, **Jesus and the Constraints of History,** London, 1982, p.156).

23. See Vermes, **Jesus** p.211.

24. See M.D. Hooker, **Jesus and the Servant,** London, 1959, Ch.3.

25. This report in John constitutes strong evidence, we think, for it is not material which the early Christians, possessing a high Christology, would naturally invent.

26. **Op.cit.** pp.63-4.

27. **The Kingdom of God and the Son of Man,** E.T., London, 1938, p.250.

28. See Taylor **op.cit.** pp.394-5.

28A. We think 'putting things right' is an alternative translation of ἀποκαθιστανει in this context, since as a medical term it means 'to cure' (Bauer, s.v.).

29. **Op.cit.** pp.250-1. Liddell and Scott, **Greek-English Lexicon,** 8th edn. Oxford, 1901, note at p.1090 οὐδενοω as derived from οὐδεν and meaning 'to bring to nought'.

30. Perceived by W. Wrede in **Das Messiasgeheimnis in den Evangelien,** Göttingen, 1913.

31. A.E.J. Rawlinson, **St. Mark,** London, 1925, p.34.

32. See R. Otto, **op.cit.** Book 2, Ch.VIII. Cf. R.H. Fuller, **The Foundations of NT Christology,** London, 1965, pp.147-8.

33. Fuller, **op.cit.** p.150, cites Mark 10,45a as another example.

34. **Op.cit.** p.201.

35. **A Grammer of NT Diction,** E.T., Edinburgh, 1866,[5] p.93.

36. E.g. B.H. Branscomb, **The Gospel of Mark,** London, 1937, p.44; E.J. Pryke, **Redactional Style in the Marcan Gospel,** Cambridge, 1978, pp.48-9.

37. See Chapter 2.

38. Philo, an Alexandrian Jew (lived c. B.C.20 to A.D.50), interpreted the ritual Levitical law ethically by means of allegory, and the freedom of

thought permissible in the first century A.D. is shown by Rabbi Johanan b. Zakkai's comment on the basis of purity, 'It is not the corpse that defiles nor the water that purifies! The Holy One, blessed be He, merely says, I have laid down a statute, I have issued a decree. You are not allowed to transgress my decree. (Numbers R.19,8).

38A. H. Maccoby, **Revolution in Judea,** London, 1973, p.231, writes, "But Jesus's resurrection did not mean that he was divine; it only meant that Jesus joined the select band of human beings, including Enoch, Elijah (and in later legend King Arthur, Charlemagne, Frederick Barbarossa and others) whose protective rôle rendered them superior to death in the eyes of their devoted followers."

39. Op.cit. p.290.

40. E.g. Acts 1,6,24.

41. Per W.G. Kümmel, **Introduction to the NT,** E.T., London, 1966, pp.182-3. He also writes, "there can be no justifiable doubt that all of 1 Thessalonians is of Pauline origin."

42. See Kümmel, op.cit. pp.189-90, who also deems it to be authentic (p.190).

43. Fuller, op.cit. pp.156-158. At James 5,8-9 we read, "You also be patient. Establish your hearts, for the coming of the Lord is at hand....behold, the Judge is standing at the doors." This shows continuing expectation of Jesus' early return as Judge probably amongst Hellenistic Jews towards the end of the first century (See Kümmel, op.cit. p.291).

43A. Cf. Luke 22,19-30.

44. Acts 10,42 is further evidence of the early Christian belief that Jesus was the one 'ordained by God to be judge of the living and the dead."

45. See e.g. D.S. Russell, **The Jews from Alexander to Herod,** Oxford, 1967, pp.244-5.

46. Indeed, the whole Church proclaims in the Apostles' Creed and the Te Deum that Christ will come from the right hand of God to judge the quick and the dead.

47. See pp.165f. supra.

48. J.A. Fitzmyer, **Essays on the Semitic Background of the NT,** London, 1971, pp.441-443. H. Maccoby, **The Mythmaker,** London, 1986, pp.175-6, considers that 'Ebionites' ('poor men') was a later derogatory nickname for the Nazarenes, and writes of their beliefs that Jesus was a human being born by natural process, was given prophetic powers by God, was an observant Jew, and that his message had been distorted by Paul, whose visions were deluded, and who had falsely represented Jesus as having abrogated the Torah. Cf. Justin, **Dialogue,** XLVIII, 4.

48A. A.R.W. Livingstone, **The Greek Genius and its Meaning to Us**, Oxford, 1924, p.11, writes, "After Paul, the Church which was was born to protest against Hellenism, translated its dogmas into the language of Greek thought, and finally crystallised them in the philosophy of Aristotle."
49. **Op.cit.** p.157.
50. Isaiah 45,1-7.
51. Isaiah 10,5-6.

CHAPTER VII.

Reprise

Our assessment of the evidence for and against NT assertions, following the methodology described in Chapter I, has indicated that on a balance of probability: —

1. The reported resurrection 'appearances' of Jesus were the result of hallucinations.
2. The battle between Satan and his demons, and the Kingdom of God, was a central element of the life and death of Jesus.
3. Jesus would have expected his Gentile followers to observe the laws affecting the *gerim,* and hence the dietary rules and the Sabbath.
4. Jesus did not intend that his words over the bread and wine at the Last Supper should be repeated, and thus become part of a religious rite.
5. Jesus did not intend that there should be a caste of priests amongst his followers, or that further sacrifice should be offered to God after his death.
6. Jesus did not consider himself to be God, nor was he considered so by others during his lifetime. Jesus believed that after his death he would quickly return as Son of Man in the Kingdom of God, but that expectation was not fulfilled. Hence, Jesus is not God or supernatural.

Our conclusions concerning the resurrection appearances and Jesus' divinity (Numbers 1 and 6 above) and our discussion about demons in Chapter 2 were much influenced by our treatment of any inconsistency with the laws of nature or our experience as counter-evidence which would outweigh Gospel assertions, unless those assertions were strong and consistent. This treatment emphasises the fact that we have aproached the evidence as an historian and a lawyer (whose approaches, we have argued, should be basically the same). A theologian may give less weight to the evidence of inconsistency with natural laws on the ground that God is omnipotent, and can therefore cause events to happen whether or not they accord with the scientific laws he has previously instituted. The historian looks at the data of natural evil such as earthquakes and floods and the genetic randomness resulting in blind and malformed babies, and may decide that the evidence that God does not interfere with the operation of scientific laws is stronger than the Gospel evidence of breaches of those laws.

However, in the case of conflict between Gospel evidence and Church tradition, we decided in Chapter 5 concerning Jesus and priests that the Gospel evidence must prevail since the Church tradition has been exposed to much more risk of distortion in its delivery, through its fragmentary and chance committal to writing long after the writing down of the Gospel traditions. We similarly treat dogmatic theology as inferior to the Gospel evidence: if that system is not built on Gospel evidence, then it lacks sound foundations.

The serious consequence of the above six conclusions (if they be correct) regarding Jesus' status and teaching, drawn from the evidence of the Gospels, is that the beliefs and practice of Christians over the centuries have run counter to that evidence since: —

1. The ancient creeds and most modern belief stipulate the bodily resurrection of Jesus.
2. The centrality of Jesus' belief in a perceived battle with Satan and demons is not generally appreciated, we think, by modern Christians, in contrast to the early Christians. Given the modern age of scientific enquiry it is understandable that Christians do not see life as a battle with Satan, but a translation of Jesus' belief into current thought-forms might well suggest a view of life as a struggle with the forces of evil or the power of self. There seems to be little evidence that Christians to-day do have this adapted cosmic vision.
3. Comparatively few Gentile Christians have observed the Levitical dietary laws since the seventh century. The number of vegetarians increases, but we doubt whether many Christian vegetarians abstain from meat because of a desire to avoid non-*kosher* meat. Further, many Gentile Christians work on the Jewish Sabbath.
4. Christians have continually repeated Jesus' words over the bread and wine at the Last Supper, as a religious rite.
5. The Orthodox, Roman Catholic and Anglican churches have priests who repeatedly offer to God the symbolic body and blood of Jesus by way of further sacrifice.
6. As shown by the ancient creeds, Christians have traditionally believed Jesus to be God.

Since the disregard of dietary rules, the repetition of the Last Supper and the belief in Jesus as God (3, 4 and 6 above) are connected with the teaching of Paul rather than of Jesus, would not Christians more correctly be called Paulinists?

EXCURSUS I

Mark on Washing—ignorant or malicious?

In 'Jesus and the Laws of Purity' we concluded that Mark's tradition was correct at 7,5 in recording a question to Jesus as to why his disciples did not wash their hands before they ate; but the tradition was incorrect in attributing the question to the Pharisees and some scribes from Jerusalem (v.1) since we determined that, amongst laymen, only the *haberim* and some other pietists washed their hands before *hullin* (ordinary, non-holy food), treating it almost as *terumah* (priestly food).[1] Moreover, Mark's own insertion into the question, that the disciples' failure to wash contravened the tradition of the elders, was incorrect in our opinion, since the traditional law did not require those who, like the disciples, had not voluntarily undertaken the obligations of the *haberim*, to wash before *hullin*; indeed, in Jesus' day it was probably only custom, rather than scribal ruling, which required the *haberim* themselves to do so.[2]

We wish in this study to investigate (1) by historico-legal criticism of Mark's commentary on Jewish lustration practices in 7,3 and 4, whether his statements there are correct in law, and if they are not, (2) by redaction criticism whether their inaccuracy stems from ignorance or anti-Jewish malice on the part of Mark.

Verse 3.

οἱ γαρ φαρισαιοι και παντες οἱ Ἰουδαιοι ἐαν μη πυγμη νιψωνται τας χειρας οὐκ ἐσθιουσιν, κρατουντες την παραδοσιν των πρεσβυτερων,

"For the Pharisees, and all the Jews, do not eat unless they wash their hands observing the tradition of the elders;" (RSV, which concerning πυγμη contains the marginal note—"One Greek word is of uncertain meaning and is not translated."!)

It follows from our observations above that Mark is incorrect in his reference to 'all the Jews' washing their hands before eating, due to traditional law, την παραδοσιν των πρεσβυτερων. Even if we do not press the absoluteness of παντες (all) and translate 'most', the practice is clearly over-stated to the extent that Mark must have known it to be exaggerated. In that Mark knew the practice to be mis-stated grossly, we detect a hint not simply of polemic, but of malice towards the Jews.

The word πυγμη deserves careful consideration notwithstanding, since the very difficulty of interpretation which it has presented, indicates that it is probably a technical term affecting handwashing which, if correctly employed by Mark, testifies to his accuracy concerning the nature of the practice, even if he drastically over-stated its prevalence. We therefore examine this word in detail.

πυγμη

The first meaning mentioned by Liddell & Scott[3] is 'a fist', and two citations very relevant to us are the LXX of Exodus 21,18, παταξωσι... λιθῳ ἡ πυγμῃ ('strike...with a stone or fist'), and Isaiah 58,4, τυπτετε πυγμαις ταπεινον ('you beat the lowly man with fists'). Under this meaning they mention our verse, but say that πυγμη is interpreted as 'diligently', or 'often'. The second main meaning mentioned is a measure of length, the distance from the elbow to the knuckles which is about 13½ inches. The authority quoted for this, Julius Pollux, is interesting, for he flourished about 180 A.D., was a grammarian, and his Onomasticon, which explains the meaning of Greek words, gives this meaning at 2,147 and 158: but the meaning of a word can change in much less than the 110 years after the date of Mark's Gospel! Bauer s.v. πυγμη also defines it as the fist, and mentions the connected meaning of a fist-fight, as do Liddell and Scott.

M. Hengel[4] points out how the variants in the Greek text of 7,3 and the translations indicate that by the second century πυγμη was not understood any more in the washing context and had to be interpreted. He stresses that, nevertheless, a clear majority of the Greek uncial texts and practically all the miniscule texts have preserved the reading. Huck-Lietzmann's Synopsis[4A] cites witnesses from all textual traditions—A.B.D.θ,λ,φ et alia—whereas there is only limited authority for πυκνα ('often'), and still less for omitting the word altogether. It seems reasonably clear, therefore, that πυγμη is the correct reading, and that πυκνα was a textual attempt to interpret that difficult reading.[5] We accordingly consider the different ways in which πυγμη has been translated.

Hengel [5A] mentions that Theophylact in his commentary on Mark in the 11th century wrote with reference to πυγμη "For it is not written in the law to wash πυγμη, that is, up to the elbow (for πυγμη means the part from the elbow to the tips of the fingers)." Apart from the difference between the knuckles and the tips of the fingers, Theophylact follows Julius Pollux, and C.H. Turner[6] attempted to support this meaning by a story from the Historia Lausiaca by Palladius (consecrated Bishop in 400 A.D.) which recounts how a young man after a long hot journey plunged his hands and feet into a washbowl, νιψασθαι τους χειρας και τους ποδας πυγμη ὑδατι ψυχροτατῳ. An old ascetic took offence at this washing πυγμη for never in her sixty years had water touched her body, apart from the fingertips. Hengel rightly doubts whether the use of the word supports Theophylact, but it is an independent use of the word, which argues that Mark was using a phrase that was presumably understood in the context of handwashing in the early 5th century, and so may well have been correctly used by him in the 1st century. Even if, as Hengel suggests, the use of the word by Palladius was suggested by Mark 7,3, it must be presumed that Palladius understood Mark's use of the word in the same context, for an author is not likely to employ a word unintelligible to him! On the other hand if πυγμη was intelligible to a 5th century writer, why was it not so to those early scribes who altered it to πυκνα or translated it *pugillo?*

In the 16th and 17th centuries Th. Beza [7] and others opined that πυγμη was used in the instrumental sense of 'with the fist', and to explain this, they referred to an alleged Jewish custom whereby the clenched fist was rubbed in the palm of the hand. The objection to this interpretation is that there is no trace of such a custom in the Jewish writings.

John Lightfoot,[8] referring to the ruling at Yadaim 2,3 on purifying the hands, states that they are unclean up to the knuckles (Heb. *ath ha-pereq)*. However, both Danby and Blackman translate *ath ha-pereq* in Yadaim 2,3 as "up to the wrist". Jastrow defines *pereq* in this context as link, limb or joint[9] so that, as Hullin 106a indicates, the word can mean the joint of the hand (i.e. the wrist) or a joint in or above the fingers (i.e. knuckles) according to the context. We do not know whether 'to the wrist' washing applied in Mark's day, and J. Neusner[10] (*Purities* 19,194) assigns the formulation of the law at Yadaim 2 and 3 to Usha. But Mark's use of πυγμη in a handwashing context may be evidence of a similar rule in his time (and, perhaps, the time of Jesus).

J. Wettstein[11] saw in πυγμη an elliptical expression for πυγμη ὑδατος meaning 'with a handful of water' which approximately corresponds with the measure of a quarter log (about 90ccm.) required according to Yadaim 1,1 for the simplest washing ritual. Hengel notes the objection that πυγμη generally means the clenched fist or a measure of length as previously discussed, but never 'a handful'. Nevertheless, Hengel himself opts for this meaning, and identifies πυγμη as a Latinism. For Hengel[12] points out that the Old Latin version translates the conditional clause in v.3 as *"nisi pugillo laverint"* in which *pugillo,* meaning 'as much as one can hold in the fist, a handful' is used to translate πυγμη. He cites Isaiah 40,12, Leviticus 2,1f. I Kings 17,12 and Ezra 13,19 to show that *pugillus* was used to translate the LXX δραξ = a handful. But this argument tends to defeat itself, for if pugillus translates δραξ meaning a handful, why was the much clearer δρακι not used by Mark at 7,3? He attributes Mark's use of πυγμη to "a kind of translation of the Latin word-meaning to the similar sounding Greek idea". He counters the argument that there are no other literary uses of πυγμη in this sense by replying that the idiom was probably restricted to the simple Greek-speaking population of Rome, since literary Greek resisted foreign influence.

Like Wettstein, Hengel notes that the 'handful' corresponds to the ¼ log of Yadaim I,1, and he explains the prohibition at Yad. 1,2 of a man pouring water over his fellow's hands out of his own cupped hands, by the suggestion that there had previously been such a practice which had provoked the prohibition. The awkwardness of Hengel's proposed translation is that 'handful of water' still remains an unlikely descriptive detail. For the ¼ log was the minimum volume of water to be used, and the average Pharisee 'placing a fence around the law' (see below) would presumably use more; indeed, Shabbath 62b indicates the use of more. S.M. Reynolds[13] opposes to Hengel's interpretation, that in the provision at Yad. 1,2, prohibiting what Hengel believes was a previous practice (of a man pouring water over another's hands from his own cupped hands), Hengel has wrongly translated the Hebrew dual *b'hophn'ain* as "mit der hohlen Hand", since the correct translation of that Hebrew word (meaning 'from his cupped hands') into Greek would be πυγμαις, not πυγμη. Incidentally to this point, πυγμη is unlikely to mean literally 'with a hand full of water' as this Yad I,2 insists that the water can only be poured from a vessel. This was probably the rule in Jesus' day in view of the 20-30 gallon jars of water for purification mentioned at John, 2,6. This water could hardly be carried from the jars by hand, yet must have been used for hand washing, since the *miqveh* in which persons and vessels were purified, was required to be a natural pool, and this rule probably developed before Jesus' time (Eduyoth I,3).

But neither is the translation of πυγμη as a measure of length, from the fingers or knuckles to the elbow which has support from Pollux, Theophylact and Turner, convincing, for that conflicts with Yad. 2,3 which requires washing only *ath ha-pereq*. *pereq* seems unlikely here to mean a joint of the arm, i.e. elbow; Jastrow does not even cite its use for that joint. And even if Yad. 2,3 did not apply in Jesus' day, the area to be washed is hardly likely to have been more extensive in his day, in view of the generally intensifying nature of the purity laws (perhaps arising from the scribal desire to 'place a fence around the law'). In connection with *pereq* Jastrow[9] mentions Hullin 106a-b which contain the following baraitha, "Our Rabbis taught: the washing of the hands for common food (must reach) up to the joint; for terumah (it must reach) up to the joint; the sanctification of the hands and feet for Temple service (must reach) up to the joint." The word *pereq* is used for "joint" in each case, but S. Cashdan[14] notes thereon that for common food only the tips of the fingers to the second joint need be washed, for *terumah* up to the third joint (i.e. to the main knuckles of the hand), and for *kodashim* to the joint of the wrist. Thus, a rule requiring washing as far as the elbow is unlikely in Jesus' time.

C.C. Torrey[16] has suggested that an original Aramaic *l-g-m-r* producing the sense 'the Jews do not eat *at all* without washing their hands' has been misread by Mark as *l-g-m-d* meaning 'with the fist', but Black[16] notes that the alleged Aramaic root *'gumda'* for 'fist' is found in none of the lexica. We would add that πυγμη precedes and qualifies νιψωνται not οὐκ ἐσθιουσιν so that to translate 'not eat at all' is to misplace it. The variant πυκνα has little to commend it. Philo[17] uses the word with reference to the stars possessing πυκνη ἁρμονια — 'close' harmony'. πυκνα and the neuter πυκνον are used by Homer as an adverb in the sense of 'much, frequently'.[18] But the principal objection against this reading is the weakness of the textual evidence for it (only X,W, the Old Latin versions and the Peshitta).

Reynolds[19] proposed the translation 'cupping the hand' on the ground that Jews today, like the Jews of NT times, hold their hands for the ceremonial washing before the Seder "with fingers flexed or cupped, so that they (are) neither tightly clenched fists nor open or spread wide. The purpose of not clenching the fist is to allow the water to pass between the fingers so as to touch all parts of the hand. The reason for cupping the hands is to provide for the washing of the whole hand with as small a quantity of poured water as possible. The metaphor Mark used to describe this position is "fist"; we , however, would use the metaphor of "cup". "We find this suggestion attractive, for the hand held with the fingers half-way towards the clenched position, does bear resemblance to a cup. What deters us from accepting this view, is that there is no Talmudic authority for holding the hands in that position. The Talmud surely requires that the hands are held upwards as in a praying position. Edersheim[20] writes, "The hands were lifted up, so as to make the water run to the wrist."

We think that the rendering of πυγμη, most likely to be correct is 'with the fist' for the following reasons: (a) 'fist' is the best attested meaning of πυγμη, and the instrumental dative without ἐν is quite possible,[21] (b) when hands are washed in an ordinary non-cultic way to-day, the fingers and knuckles of the one hand are naturally rubbed in the palm of the other. Although Edersheim[20] translates 'to the wrist', he writes on the procedure, ". . . similarly, each hand was rubbed with the other (the fist), provided the hand that rubbed had been affused; otherwise the rubbing might be done against the head or even against a wall." This is a paraphrase of part of Yad. 2,3 although 'the fist' does not appear in the

Hebrew, (c) Since the *haberim* treated their *hullin* almost as *terumah*, they would probably wash up to the main knuckles of the hand if Hullin 106a-b then prevailed, so that the rubbing of the backs of the fingers, and the main knuckles, against the fingers of the inside of the other hand, could properly be described as washing 'with the fist'. It is possible, however, that Hullin 106a-b did not prevail in Tannaitic times (unless Yad. 2,3 is referring to the washing of hands by the priest before touching *kodashim*), since *ath ha-pereq* at Yad. 2,3 clearly means 'up to the wrist'; the second sentence there speaks of the water being poured beyond the wrist *(huts la-pereq)* and the water flowing back to the hand *(v'haz'ru l'yad)*[22] This would not necessarily exclude the meaning of 'with the fist' for πυγμη in Mark's v.3 since an energetic manner of rubbing the fist in the other hand for hygienic cleansing or drying purposes would then be described by Mark; the difficulty there is that hygienic cleansing is unlikely to be required by την παραδοσιν των πρεσβυτερων.

The above various possibilities of meaning do attest that πυγμη was a term of art describing some detailed feature of the ritual washing of the hands. It is not the generalising kind of remark wherein we have seen Mark to exaggerate previously. We think its use by Mark argues his competence in this area.

Since the question of whether the washing practices are required by the traditional law is an issue in both verses 3 and 4 we will consider κατα την παραδοσιν των πρεσβυτερων in v.3 along with αλλα πολλα εστιν α παρελαβον κρατειν at the end of our treatment of v.4.

Verse 4.

και απ'αγορας εαν μη βαπτισωνται ουκ εσθιουσιν, και αλλα πολλα εστιν α παρελαβον κρατειν, βαπτισμους ποτηριων και ξεστων και χαλκιων και κλινων "and when they come from the market place, they do not eat unless they purify themselves; and there are many other traditions which they observe, the washing of cups and pots and vessels of bronze and beds."

These assertions by Mark on matters of purity law must now be tested for accuracy in general, and contemporaneity with Jesus in particular.

<u>απ' αγορας εαν μη βαπτισωνται ουχ εσθιουσιν</u>

απ' αγορας is usually translated in a pregnant sense, 'after the return from market' (B.D. 209(4),[23] to produce the meaning that upon return from market they do not eat without first immersing themselves. An alternative translation is, 'anything from the market', producing the meaning that they do not eat anything from the market without first immersing it. This, however, involves the use of the middle or passive mood of βαπτιζω in a transitive sense, for which we cannot find any precedent. The comprehensive concept of *anything* from the market being immersed is also hard to equate with even the solicitude of the *haberim*, and we accordingly adopt the former translation. In fact, D(W) and a few Old Latin versions have ὅταν ἔλθωσιν after ἀπ' ἀγορᾶς, but this is probably a solution of the difficulty rather than original witness.

We prefer βαπτισωνται to the variant ῥαντισωνται. βαπτισωνται is contained in A D W θ fi (f13) and most of the Latin tradition, and means 'immerse themselves' (middle). ῥαντισωνται is supported by the Codex Siniaticus and B and some Sahidic codices, and means 'sprinkle themselves'. 'Sprinkling' must refer to sprinkling with the ashes of the Red Heifer, which was the only means of purification from corpse-uncleanness. But it hardly seems practicable that every time even *haberim* returned from market, they should sprinkle themselves with ashes of the Red Heifer. Admittedly, the market at Tiberias was built over a cemetery, and there is evidence that some Pharisees considered all the land of the Gentiles to be unclean with corpse-uncleanness, and that the *haberim* considered the male *am-haarez* ('a.h.') to be corpse-unclean.[24] Yet the ashes with which water had to be mixed for the purifying Sin-offering water, were distributed, according to Parah 3,11, between the Temple, the Mount of Olives and the divisions of the priests. This inconvenience combined with the requirement that cleanness is only restored after sprinkling on the third and seventh days after defilement (Numbers 19,12 and 19) makes it very unlikely that ῥαντισωνται is the correct reading; otherwise, the Pharisees who frequented the market would regularly not eat for six days![25] Immersion in the *miqveh* was the means of purification for other defilement of the whole body, and would much more easily be effected at or near home on return from market.[26] We believe this to be the form of purification intended by βαπτισωνται.

We therefore have to consider whether at any stage in the development of the purity law or practice some Pharisees immersed in a *miqveh* on return from market. In that the immersion is expressed as routine, it was on account of a presumed defilement, as a person would not be *actually* defiled every time he went to market.

ἀπ' ἀγορᾶς is no doubt specified by Mark not because of the buying and selling at the market, but because it was a place where people assembled; indeed, one meaning of the word is 'a place of assembly'.[27] Most presumptions involve an element of fiction, and we have seen (supra, p.201) that the *haberim* employed a fiction regarding the religious status of their food by treating it almost as *terumah*. We are inclined to think that the Pharisees involved in this immersion practice were the *haberim* and that the presumption related to the impurity of the *a.h.* to whom the *haberim* would be in close proximity in the market-place.

Hagigah 2,7 reads, "For Pharisees *(l'perushin)* the clothes of an *am-haarez* count as suffering *midras*-uncleanness."[28] *Midras*-uncleanness originates in the Priestly Code for it is provided in Leviticus 15 that in the case of the *zab* (man with a sexual discharge 15,2), the *niddah* (menstruant 15,19), and the *zabah* (woman with a sexual discharge 15,25), the bed on which they lie and the thing on which they sit, shall be unclean. Also by Lev.15 the toucher of the bed or thing sat upon, is defiled, as are his clothes. The traditional law included the new mother in the class of persons defiling thus, and extended the modes of pressure which transmitted the defilement (Zabim 2, 4).

Since the bed or chair of these classes of persons is declared impure in the Priestly Code, it is a father of impurity, and the toucher of it is impure in the first degree. Thus, the toucher of the clothes of the *a.h.* is likewise unclean in the first degree. This remained the law at Yavneh, except that R. Joshua imposed at Zab.5,1 as a general principle *(k'lal)* a more severe impurity on the toucher while actually touching, for the toucher then defiles food and drink in the first degree, and to that extent is a father of uncleanness: but when the toucher has ceased contact, the general principle is that he only defiled food and hands in the second degree (i.e. he is himself an offspring of impurity in the first degree).

Thus, a person who believes that the clothes of the *a.h.* suffer *midras*-uncleanness, will consider himself unclean in the first degree if he touches them, and will be obliged, following Leviticus 15, to purify himself by immersing his body and washing his clothes. Moreover, since the clothes of the *a.h.* being a Biblical source of impurity, are a father of impurity, they can defile even the clothes of another person by contacting them. This is illustrated at T.Tohoroth 8,13, "(If) one was dressed in a shirt and wrapped in a cloak, and he said "My concern was for the shirt, and my concern was not for the cloak"—the shirt is clean and the cloak is unclean." Clearly the concern is lest the *midras*-unclean clothes of the *a.h.* should touch the clothes of the Pharisee, and defile them.

The reason why this presumption arose concerning the clothes of the *a.h.*, appears from the tractate Tohoroth in the Mishnah and Tosefta, and particularly from passages such as M. Toh. 8, 1 and 2, to be that the wife of an *a.h.* is presumed, while menstruating, not to be careful what she touches, sits on, or puts other pressure on, so that she is presumed to have passed *midras*-uncleanness to the clothes of her husband, in addition, of course, to being unclean herself. Moreover, as mentioned above, her husband was considered to possess corpse-impurity, although contact with him did not apparently necessitate sprinkling with the water for impurity.

We are convinced that it was the *haberim* or other persons of similar supererogatory piety, who thus treated the clothes of the *a.h.* For we see at T. Demai 2,12 that the maintenance of the purity of garments was considered in the era of the Houses to be a condition of membership of an *haburah* (a purity club for *haberim*).

Having thus ascertained that at *some* stage in the history of purity practices, the *haberim* immersed themselves to remove impurity which they presumed they had contacted from being in proximity to an *a.h.*, we must now enquire whether this practice prevailed in the time of Jesus. We think it is legitimate to assume that, since the practice prevailed at *some* stage, we can accept Mark's statement at 7,4 as sufficient proof that the practice prevailed when he wrote; it is possible that Mark invented, for polemic, a pedantic practice which, by chance, the Pharisees adopted later, but the possibility is so less likely than the alternative, that we reject it.

Strictly in accordance with our forensic model we must treat Mark's statement as evidence that the practice did prevail in the time of Jesus, for though it is editorial comment, and not narrative, it is clearly intended to explain general Pharisaic scrupulosity in the time of Jesus. However, we treat Mark's witness on prevalence at that time as outweighed by the counter-evidence of his undoubted exaggeration that the practices in these verses affected 'all the Jews', and of his error that the practices were required by the tradition of the elders.

But there is both Mishnaic evidence and evidence from the Gospels that this practice of immersion prevailed in the time of Jesus. We have determined elsewhere[29] that the attribution to the Houses of the discussion at T. Demai 2,12 over the length of the periods during which the novice *haber* must keep his liquids and garments pure, was correct. If so detailed a point as the qualifying period for these purities was discussed in the era of the Houses (c.20-70 A.D.),[30] it is reasonable to suppose that the preservation of pure garments and the consequent immersions had been adopted by the *haberim* by A.D. 30, if not before.

And in the Gospels we see at Mark 2,16 the objection of the Pharisees to Jesus eating with the ἁμαρτωλοι and tax collectors. It is likely in our view that these Pharisees were *haberim,* and that the reason for their objection arose from the fact that Jesus was allowing himself to be defiled by (1) the ἁμαρτωλοι who erred in their neglect of the purity laws, i.e. were the *a.h.*, and (2) the tax collectors who sustained impurity through their necessary dealings with the *a.h.* and with Gentiles. The *haberim* may also have been concerned that Jesus would eat untithed food. S. Westerholm, however, claims that 'sinners' in a passage such as this and Luke 19,7 does not mean the *a.h.* generally, but refers rather to notorious sinners or those in trades connected with dishonesty or immorality.[31] He points out that, as Jesus was not an *haber,* there was no reason why he should not associate with persons who would involve him, according only to the *haberim,* in ritual impurity. But in such passages the attitude of the *haberim* is surely that of enthusiastic idealists who consider that other religious people should conform to their standards of purity. The fact that in both verses the complaint is that Jesus *eats* with publicans and/or sinners may be further indication that ritual purity is involved. Thus, in these two Gospel verses, we have further evidence of a concern of the *haberim* to avoid defilement by the *a.h.,* and this fear entails the need to immerse if the defilement is presumed to have taken place, as in a crowded market.

At Luke 11,38 a Pharisee is astonished that Jesus did not immerse himself before dinner. While this appears to be evidence for the immersion of the body in the time of Luke, we must consider the ἐβαπτισατο ('immersed himself') of Luke or of the tradition which he received. For here again the Pharisee was probably an *haber* and expressed mock surprise at Jesus' failure to immerse since, having invited Jesus when he was with the crowds (11,29), he assumed Jesus was defiled by the *a.h.* in the first degree. This Pharisee (with a similarly enthusiastic recruiting motive) encouraged Jesus to immerse according to his own practice as an *haber.* But if the *haber* was dining with Jesus before sunset, he would expect Jesus to immerse and then to wash his hands as a *tebul yom* (a person who had immersed himself the same day).[32] The detail that the Pharisee was surprised that Jesus did not also wash his hands, is probably too technical and unnecessary an addition to have been preserved in the oral tradition. If the Pharisee did not know that Jesus had been with the crowds (for 'Εν δε τῳ λαλησαι in v.37 may be editorial), then an *haber* would more probably encourage Jesus to wash his hands before *hullin,* than immerse himself. However, since on every occasion after association with the *a.h.* the haber would immerse in a *miqveh,* and if he wished to eat his *hullin* before sunset, would wash his hands also, we think that the reference to immersion there is correct, and is further evidence according to our forensic model for the prevalence of this practice of the *haberim* in the time of Jesus.

We accordingly consider that there is sufficient evidence outside Mark 7,4 to prove the accuracy of a practice of the *haberim* in the time of Jesus whereby they immersed their body in a *miqveh* after being in a place (but particularly a crowded public place such as a market) where they might have been touched by the clothes of an *a.h.* Thus we think that this statement at v.4 supports Mark's reliability on technical matters.

βαπτισμους ποτηριων και ξεστων και χαλκιων και κλινων

Mark next mentions in v.4 that there are many other traditions which the Pharisees and all the Jews observe, and he cites the dipping of cups and pots and vessels of bronze. The RSV translates βαπτισμους as 'washing', as does Bauer s.v. This, we think, is misleading for it implies a rinsing (νιπτομαι), as of the hands. In fact, a βαπτισμος is a dipping or immersion of the vessel in a *miqveh* which is a different ritual from the pouring of water over the hands from a vessel (Yadaim I,2); indeed, if vessels were rinsed in that water, it becomes invalid (I,4). The more correct translation is 'the dipping (or immersion)'.

The addition of και κλινων after χαλκιων is supported by A,D,W,θ,φ and most Latin texts, while the omission of those words is supported by an uncertain reading in P45, by Codices Vaticanus and Sinaiticus, and a few Bohairic versions. Metzger[33] notes the difficulty of deciding whether copyists added these words under the influence of Leviticus 15,4,20,24 and 26 or whether they were omitted through homoteleuton, or the seeming incongruity of washing or sprinkling beds. Although there are strong witnesses both for inclusion and omission, we are impressed by the fact that the Western witness D and most Latin texts include the words, for it is less likely that Lev.15 would be immediately present to the mind of Western copyists. We are further persuaded to include και κλινων in the verse by contextual considerations. For we have concluded that the cause of the *haberim* immersing after market was the *midras*-impurity of the clothes of the *a.h.* Now Leviticus 15,4,20,24 and 26 all provide that the bed on which persons suffering from a sexual discharge lie, is unclean, and that uncleanness was termed in the traditional law, *midras*-uncleanness. Although 15,12 provides that every vessel of wood which a *zab* touches shall be rinsed (*yishateph*) in water, (and the bed legs and frame would probably be wood),[34] Lev. 11,32 provides that any unclean utensil shall be put into water (*damaim yuba*) which indicates immersion. These Biblical provisions were interpreted as ordaining immersion for unclean beds; Kelim 19,1 refers to a man taking a bed to peices to immerse it (*l'ha-t'bilah*). Thus, the immersion of beds (on account of *midras*-impurity) would be a natural comment to follow Mark's references to the other immersions by the *haberim*. As the need to immerse defiled beds is implicitly indicated by the Priestly Code at the one end of our historical spectrum and by the Mishnah at the other, it is probable that this was a legal requirement in the time of Jesus.

We pass to the immersion of ποτηριων και ξεστων και χαλκιων. Bauer s.v. ποτηριον defines it as a cup or drinking vessel (cf. Matthew's reference to Jesus at the Last Supper, λαβων ποτηριον, 26,27). ξεστης, according to Bauer s.v., is thought to have meant originally a liquid measure of about half a litre, and to be a Rabbinic loanword from the Latin sextarius, but by the time of Mark it had come to mean simply a jug. χαλκιον is defined by Bauer s.v. as a copper vessel or kettle, and the use of the word here is its sole use in the NT.

We know from Lev. 11,32 mentioned above that non-earthenware vessels were immersed to remove impurity, for it reads, "And anything upon which any of them (unclean creeping things) falls when they are dead shall be unclean, whether it is an article of wood or a garment, or a skin or a sack, anything that is used for any purpose, it must be put into water, and it shall be unclean until evening. Then it shall be clean." By contrast, an earthenware vessel could only be cleansed by being broken (11,33). In the omnibus reference to *kol-k'li asher yeaseh m'laakah,* v.32 includes every utensil (except earthenware) within its ambit. Although on its terms v.32 only stipulates immersion where the defilement is caused by an unclean creeping thing, this form of purification was established as the remedy for the defilement of such utensils howsoever caused.

Despite the comprehensive words of v.32, which provides for the immersion of any non-earthenware utensil defiled as there mentioned, metalware and glassware were apparently not considered susceptible to impurity in normal circumstances until a later date. For Simeon b. Shetah (c.80 B.C.) either by himself (Shabbath 14b and 15a) or with Judah b. Tabbai (y. Shabbath 1,4 and y. Ketuboth 8,11) decreed uncleanness on metalware in the sense of holding it to be susceptible to impurity. Admittedly, at Numbers 31,21-3 Eleazar, the priest, proclaims a statute commanded by Yahweh to Moses concerning the booty taken from the defeated Midianites, namely that 'the gold, the silver, the bronze, the iron, the tin, and the lead, everything that can stand the fire' shall be cleansed by being passed through the fire. But in addition to the fire they must also be purified not by immersion but by sprinkling with the water for impurity. Clearly these are especially strict provisions applying only to the spoils of war: thus every garment taken has to be purified and 'every article of skin, all work of goats' hair, and every article of wood.' And as Neusner comments, the use of fire for purification is not extended or developed in the later law.

We wonder why metalware was not considered susceptible previously. Similarly, glassware was apparently not considered susceptible until Yose b. Yo'ezer (c.160 B.C.) and Yose b. Yohanan decreed to that effect, according to the same Talmudic passages. Neusner (Purities 22,79) suggests that impurity should be viewed as a gas of heavy viscosity which will flow until contained in a receptacle. Applying this notion to the kind of receptacle to which it would attach, it may have been thought that, even though it was 'sticky', impurity could not grip and remain on a smooth surface such as that of fashioned metal or glass.[35] However, a more likely reason for the decrees is that cups, jugs and other vessels for the table were not made from metal or glass until the respective generations of these Masters.[36]

Thus Mark's statement that among the traditions which the Pharisees observed, was the immersion of χαλκιων, is correct, since a copper vessel is metalware, and every utensil, except an earthenware one, was purified by immersion. Whether he is correct regarding ποτηριων and ξεστωξ depends on whether or not they were generally made of earthenware. Since metal and glass were valuable in ancient times, it seems likely that tableware of these materals would be possessed only by the rich; hence the ποτηριον and ξεστης used by a Pharisee would probably be made of pottery in most cases,[37] for the Pharisees were the plebeian party in comparison with the Sadducees.[38] Mark is probably incorrect, therefore, when he refers without qualification to the immersion of cups and jugs by the Pharisees, since earthenware cups and jugs would be broken when defiled. However, Mark may have intended only non-earthenware vessels.

κρατουντες την παραδοσιν των πρεσβυτερων

Having studied the lustration practices in these verses, we must lastly consider whether Mark is correct in (1) saying that in handwashing (v.3 cf. v.5) and in self-immersion (v.4) the Jews are κρατουντες την παραδοσιν των πρεσβυτερων, and (2) including in v.4 the washing of articles as examples of ἀλλα πολλα (ἐστιν) ἁ παρελαβον κρατειν. The two expressions are synonymous — what the Pharisees have received to observe, is the tradition of the elders, namely the scribes (hakamim).

The rinsing of the hands as the means of purifying them from defilement is ordained at Lev. 15,11 where the reference is to the hands of the zab, but the need to rinse the hands regularly before eating is probably in the time of Jesus only a custom of those who have undertaken to become haberim. The custom probably was incorporated into the traditional law by scribal adjudication on some aspect thereof not later than A.D. 70.[39]

The immersion of the body after the contraction of impurity is also decreed by Scripture (e.g. Lev.15 passim), but its regular immersion after being in a crowded place, such as a market, was again probably only a custom in the time of Jesus and was incorporated later into the traditional law affecting *haberim*.

The purification of articles by immersion is prescribed by Leviticus 11,32, but probably, because purity was only needed for Temple entry and for separating tithes etc., only the *haberim* amongst laymen in the time of Jesus would, following their custom, undertake such washings.

General Conclusions

1. Our enquiry into the legal history of the lustration practices described by Mark in 7,3 and 4, although affected by the ever-present difficulty of dating Rabbinic sources, indicates that:

a. 'All the Jews' did not wash their hands for ritual reasons before eating, and were not required by 'the tradition of the elders' so to do. Among 'the Pharisees' only the *haberim* did so in Jesus and Mark's day, and in Jesus' day it was probably only custom rather than scribal adjudication which they followed in so washing.

b. Whatever be the exact connotation of $πυγμη$, it indicates a detail of the rinsing procedure, related to 'the fist' in some way. The fingers and knuckles are so involved both with the extent of the hand to be rinsed, and with the manner of rubbing the hands, that we think Mark's familiarity with this detail as shown by his use of $πυγμη$ exhibits a competence in the ritual of handwashing.

c. Regarding the practice of immersing on return from market, alleged in v.4, Mark is again wrong in attributing this to 'all the Jews', but it appears that the *haberim* probably immersed in the time of Jesus after being in a crowded public place where they might have been touched by the clothes of an *a.h.*

d. Regarding the immersion of utensils and beds in v.4, it seems that 'all the Jews' is wrong here also. While beds are rendered unclean by persons with a sexual discharge lying on them, probably only the priest and the *haberim*, anxious to preserve the purity of their respective foods, would regularly immerse: there would be no need for other laymen to immerse their beds because they would immerse themselves before worship at the Temple, or before separating their tithes (if they were farmers), so that it would not matter if they had been defiled by their beds. Mark is, however, correct in describing the means of purification as being immersion.

For the same reason, it would only be the priests and *haberim* who would have cause to immerse the utensils mentioned. Immersion was, however, the correct form of purification for the $χαλκιων$, the copper vessels, but Mark was inaccurate over the $ποτηριων$ and $ξεστων$ since, except in the homes of the wealthy, cups and jugs were more likely to be earthenware articles, which were not immersed but broken, when defiled.

e. Mark wrongly attributes to the traditional law practices which originate in Scripture and are undertaken by *haberim* following their customs. For although the concepts of the purification of the hands by rinsing and of the body and non-earthenware articles by immersion originated in Leviticus, regular self-immersion after market by the *haberim* and their regular immersion of articles were probably not in the time of Jesus incorporated into the scribal law applying to them. These practices may have been so incorporated at the time of Mark's writing (A.D.65-67).[39A]

II. The deductions to be drawn by redaction criticism from our above conclusions on Mark's accuracy regarding lustration practice and law in the time of Jesus are, we think, the following:

a. Mark's attribution to παντες οἱ Ἰουδαιοι (even if translated favourably as 'most of the Jews') of the ritual lustration practices in vv. 3 and 4, all of which were pursued only by *haberim,* is clearly a gross exaggeration. Admittedly, it could be argued that Mark does not allege that the washings of the utensils are undertaken by all. Literally he states, 'there are many other things which they have received to hold fast to, the washings of cups and jugs and copper vessels and beds': this could be understood as meaning that 'all the Jews' received the tradition of these practices for observance, not by all, but by some of them. This strikes us, however, as rather a strained interpretation, and we cannot accept it.

b. We have concluded that Mark is probably correct in saying that hands are washed πυγμῃ. He is also correct in his understanding that beds and copper vessels are purified by immersion. It is also right that some cups and jugs are purified by immersion, although earthenware articles are broken, but Mark may have intended only non-earthenware vessels.

From this knowledge which Mark displays concerning the detail of handwashing and of the articles which are purified by immersion, we deduce that Mark had a good knowledge of lustration practices—certainly of those which prevailed in his day. We are supported in this view by the awareness which we find shown by Mark at 7,1-23 of the different defiling effects of contaminated food,[40] non-*kosher* food and prohibited food—another aspect of purity law.

c. Since the washing practices of these verses may well have been incorporated into the traditional law by A.D.65-7 when Mark was writing, we think that, despite his competent knowledge of the practices, he may well have been genuinely mistaken in thinking that they had been embodied into the traditional law for *haberim* by the time of Jesus. For there would be no reason why a non-Pharisee like Mark, probably living in Rome, should be interested, or able, to find out whether traditional law practices of his own day had only been customs unpronounced upon by the *hakamim* in Jesus' day.

d. However, in view of Mark's knowledge of the detail of handwashing and of the other purificatory practices mentioned in these verses, we consider that his gross exaggeration there of the prevalence of the lustration practices was not occasioned by ignorance, but by malice towards the Jews whose traditional law he wished to ridicule. This desire is further indicated by his maximising of the traditional practices in the ἀλλα πολλα clause of v.4, and of unjust rules in his και παρομοια clause, also redactional,[41] at v.13.

We believe that Mark's dislike of the Jews arose from his Pauline objection to the continuing attempts of the 'Judaizers' to impose the whole law on Gentile Christians, notwithstanding the Council of Jerusalem:[42] for animosity towards the 'Judaizers' continued to rage until at least the end of the 1st century as we see from Titus 1,10 and 14.

NOTES
1. See further on these conclusions, Booth, **Jesus and the Laws of Purity,** Sheffield, 1986, pp.202-3.
2. Ibid.
3. **A Greek-English Lexicon,** 8th edn. Oxford, 1901.
4. 'Mc 7 3 πυγμη: etc.' ZNW 60 (1969), pp.182-98 at p.183.
4A. E.T., F.L. Cross, Tübingen[9], 1936, in loc.
5. **A Textual Commentary on the Greek NT,** London and New York, 1971, p.93.
5B. Op.cit. p.186f.
6. 'The Lausiac History of Palladius' JTS 6 (1904-5), pp.321-55 at pp. 353-4.
7. **Novum Testamentum,** p.161.
8. **Horae Hebraicae et Talmudicae,** Leipzig, 1684, pp.618f.
9. **A Dictionary of the Targumim etc.,** New York, 1975.
10. **A History of the Mishnaic Law of Purities,** 22 Vols., Leiden, 1973. (herein called 'Purities' and followed by Vol. and page no.).
11. NT Graecum, 1752 (Graz, 1962), I, p.585.
12. Op.Cit. pp.191f.
13. 'A Note on Dr. Hengel's Interpretation of πυγμη in Mark 7,3', ZNW (1971), pp.295-6.
14. Soncino, **The Talmud, Hullin,** p.590.
15. **The Four Gospels: A New Translation,** New York, 1933, in loc.
16. **An Aramaic Approach to the Gospels and Acts,** Oxford, 1946, p.8.
17. **De Somniis,** Loeb edn., I,22; Vol V, p.306.
18. See **Liddell & Scott,** s.v. B.II.

19. *'PUGMEI* (Mark 7,3) as "Cupped Hand", JBL 85 (1966), pp.87-88.
20. **The Life and Times of Jesus, the Messiah**, London, 1900, II, p.11.
21. Although Bauer, **Lexicon**, $195, notes that in the genuinely instrumental sense the use of the dative has been sharply curtailed in the NT by the employment of ἐν. We are, however, much impressed by the cited LXX uses of πυγμῃ alone in this sense.
22. This may be an exceptional case where early Jewish law has historically grown more lenient.
23. **Grammar**, see p.111 supra.
24. E.g. **T.Toh.** 8,9.
25. See also on the difficulties of ῥαντισωνται in this context, A. Büchler, 'The law of Purification in Mark VII 1-23', Exp.T., Vol.XXL, pp.34-40 at p.38.
26. Many valid *miqve'oth* lay near Jerusalem for the pilgrims, and points concerning their validity sometimes came for decision to the Court called the Chamber of Hewn Stone, (Eduyoth 7,4).
27. Liddell & Scott, **op.cit.** s.v.
28. This sensitivity concerning the impurity of the clothes of a person observing a lower standard of purity probably prevailed pre-70 A.D. See Booth, **op.cit.** p.97.
29. **Op.cit.** pp.196-7.
30. **Op.cit.** p.246 n.33.
31. **Jesus and Scribal Authority**, Lund, 1978, p.70, following Jeremias, **NT Theology**, E.T. London, 1971, Vol. I, pp.109-12.
32. Since a *tebul yom* otherwise defiles *terumah,* per Zab. 5,12 which contains this and other purity rules forming part of the 'Hananiah' decrees which we think were made c,51 A.D.; see Booth, **op.cit.** pp.164 and 173.
33. **Op.cit.** pp.93-4.
34. Cf. Kelim XVIII, 4-7.
35. Thus glass utensils that are flat, are not susceptible to uncleanness (Kelim 2,1), although metal ones, strangely, are (11,1).
36. Although Pliny, **Natural History**, 36,191 credits the Pheonicians of the 1st century B.C. with the development of the art of glass blowing.
37. See L. Goppelt, **TDNT**, VI, 148.
38. See L. Finkelstein, **The Pharisees**, 2 Vols. Philadelphia, 1966, pp.74-5, 264-5.
39. See Booth, **op.cit.** p.198.
39A. See Booth, **op.cit.** p.150.
40. See Booth, **op.cit.** pp.220-1.
41. See V. Taylor, **The Gospel according to St. Mark**, London, 1952, p.341.
42. See pp.80-81 supra.

EXCURSUS II.

Why are some spirits described in the Synoptic Gospels as unclean?

As we have discussed in Chapter II, the Synoptic Gospels testify that the casting out by Jesus of unclean spirits from possessed persons was one of the main features of his ministry.[1] Thus, Mark summarises at 1,39, "And he went throughout all Galilee, preaching in their synagogues and casting out demons."[2]

Since in some Gospel pericopae Jesus is stated to expel an unclean spirit (πνευμα ἀκαθαρτον), and in others a demon (δαιμονιον), we must consider, for the purpose of our enquiry into their uncleanness, whether the terms are synonymous. In 'Q' there is evidence from Luke 11,24 (par. Matthew 12,43), where an unclean spirit is referred to, and from Luke 7,33 (par. Matthew 11,18) where John the Baptist is said to have a demon, that the two terms were considered similar by the collector of the 'Q' traditions, but since the references are not in the same passage, this evidence of the collector's view is not strong.

However, Mark clearly treats the two terms as the same. For the Gerasene demonaic is ἐν πνευματι ἀκαθαρτῳ at 5,2;[3] while at 5,15 he is τον δαιμονιζομενον.[4] Similarly, in the commissioning at 6,7 Jesus gives the disciples authority over the *unclean spirits,* following which, at v.13, they cast out many *demons.*[5] The source exclusive to Matthew ('M') refers to 'demons' at 7,22 and 10,8 but does not mention unclean spirits anywhere. Luke's source ('L') probably does equate demons and unclean spirits, for at 10,17 the seventy report that the *demons* are subject to them, and Jesus in reply (v.20) urges them not to rejoice that the *spirits* are subject to them; in that demons are here equated to spirits, and 'L' elsewhere only refers to evil (πονηρος) spirits or a spirit of infirmity (ἀσθεναιας), we can reasonably conclude that Luke or his tradents equated demons with ethically unclean spirits in the pericope 10,17-20.

Matthew shows by his emendation of Mark that he considers demons and unclean spirits to be the same. Thus, at 8,16 he largely follows Mark's account of the healing at even (1,32-34), yet he alters Mark's 'demons' to 'spirits'. His retention of 'unclean spirit' in 'Q' at 12,43 (par. Luke 11,24) is support for assuming that by 'spirits' he means 'unclean spirits'. There is also ground for thinking that Luke treated the two terms as equivalent. At 4,33 he alters Mark's reference at 1,23 to an 'unclean spirit' to 'spirit of an unclean demon' (or an 'unclean demon', D and pc), and at v.35 alters Mark's reference to 'the unclean spirit' to 'the demon'.[6]

In general, it is difficult to assess whether different Greek terms used in parallel Gospel sources possessed the same meaning for the tradents, since the terms translated by different Greek words in the Gospels may represent the same or different words in the original Aramaic version of the sources.[6A] Even apart from this caveat, it seems uncertain whether the tradents of 'Q' and 'M' treat demons as unclean spirits: but the three evangelists and 'L' apparently do, and since Matthew is traditionally regarded as impregnated with Jewish culture, and Luke with Greek culture, we think it safe to proceed on the basis that an idea prevailed generally in the first century A.D. that both demons and some spirits were unclean. We will accordingly treat demons and unclean spirits as synonymous in the Synoptics.[7]

The purpose of this study is to consider why in the Synoptics some spirits were considered unclean, and whether the nature of their uncleanness was ritual or ethical.[8] Clearly, these two issues are inter-related, and we propose to consider them together.

The Synoptics use ἀκάθαρτος to describe a spirit which is unclean,[9] but this little indicates the nature of the uncleanness attaching to the demon.[9A] In the LXX ἀκάθαρτος is used primarily to signify cultic uncleanness,[10] yet it is used occasionally in the sense of unholy or morally impure;[11] the positive καθαρος is also generally used in a cultic sense, but occasionally in an ethical sense.[12] In the NT ἀκάθαρτος is used most frequently with πνευμα, but is otherwise used both in the cultic sense (frequently)[13] and in the ethical (sometimes).[14] Since the root, καθαρ—, is thus shown to be capable of bearing either a cultic or an ethical meaning in both the LXX and the NT, the greater frequency of the cultic use hardly argues for a cultic meaning in any particular case, e.g. when ἀκάθαρτος is used with πνευμα.

We are, however, assisted by the 'Q' source's description of spirits and demons as πονηρος, for there they are undoubtedly ethically defective. Matthew uses πονηρος many times in his Gospel, but the only time he describes a spirit as πονηρος (rather than the devil as ὁ πονηρος), is in a 'Q' passage at 12,45 (par. Luke 11,26), where its use strikingly indicates that the tradents of 'Q', or Matthew himself, interpreted πνευμα ἀκάθαρτον as πονηρον: at v.43 (par. Luke 11,24) the πνευμα is described as ἀκάθαρτον and at v.45 that spirit is said to bring seven other spirits more πονηρον than himself.

In Mark a spirit or demon is never described as πονηρος nor expressly in 'M', but in 'L' or its redaction they are so termed at Luke 7,21 and 8,2 and in Acts at 19,12-16 in connection with healing miracles by Paul.

Thus, since the devil (presumably the arch-demon)[16] is described as ὁ πονηρος at Matthew 13,19 (par. Luke 8,12), and the unclean spirit is defined as πονηρος in 'Q' as mentioned, it seems likely that the ethical aspect of the spirit's uncleanness was recognised in the time of Jesus, if we date the compilation of the 'Q' tradition to about A.D.50.[16] This likelihood may be affirmed by Gospel passages where the causing of illness by moral sin is assumed by Jesus or his collocutors. Thus, at Mark 2,5 Jesus heals the paralytic, saying "your sins are forgiven": at John 5,14 and 9,2 the same causation is implicit. While there is in these pericopae no mention that the illness or the sin are demon-connected, the link between the sin and illness would encourage a view that where an illness was caused by possession by an unclean spirit, its impurity was of an ethical nature. In view of the increased attribution of πονηρος to the spirit in 'L' and Acts, it seems possible that the ethical aspect of its impurity gradually became dominant during the course of the first century A.D. The NT evidence does not, however, render the nature of a spirit's uncleanness free from doubt, and we will turn to the history of unclean spirits in Biblical literature for further assistance.

In the LXX there are several references to spirits as πονηρος[17] which translates the Hebrew root *ra* meaning ethically bad. But only at Zechariah 13,2 is a πνευμα ἀκαθαρτον mentioned, and ἀκαθαρτον there translates the Hebrew *tum'ah* whose root *t-m-a* can mean ethically *or* cultically unclean. There the Lord says that on the Day of Judgment he will cut off the names of the idols so that they will be remembered no more, and he will remove from the land the prophets and το πνευμα το ἀκαθαρτον. The quality of the impurity must be considered ambiguous, for while the preceding verse's reference to a fountain for cleansing from sin and menstrual uncleanness (*niddah*) may indicate a cultic meaning for *tum'ah* and hence ἀκαθαρτον, the linking of the unclean spirit with prophets in v.2 tends towards the unethical 'lying spirit' (*ruah sheqer*) of 1 Kings 22,23 which the LXX translates as πνευμα ψευδες.

However, perhaps not later than 170B.C., a story which may support the cultic uncleanness of the spirits had been founded upon Genesis 6,1-4, where it is recorded that the sons of God (the holy Watchers) had intercourse with the daughters of men and their offspring were giants. Thus, at Enoch 6 and 7[18] it is related how the angels lusted after the daughters of men, and chose themselves wives. The angels 'defiled themselves' with their wives who became pregnant, and bore giants as offspring. The giants "who are produced from the spirits and flesh, shall be called evil spirits upon the earth... Evil spirits have proceeded from their bodies;"[19] (presumably, after their death). These spirits oppress, and work destruction on the earth. It seems likely that one reason why some spirits were considered unclean, is that these fallen angels "united themselves with women so as to have defiled themselves with them in all their uncleanness".[20] Although living the eternal life, they defiled themselves with the blood of women.[21]

That these spirits also had a morally evil nature, is indicated by Azazel's teaching of humans (inter alia) to make implements of war and to beautify the eyelids.[22] Thus, "there arose much godlessness. . . and (men) became corrupt in all their ways."[23] Indeed, at 10,8 the works of the fallen angels are seen as the cause of all sin.

The union between the angels of God and the daughters of men is also related in the Book of Jubilees,[24] which Charles dates to 109-105 B.C.[25] Yet, although it is stated at 4,22 that the Watchers were defiled with the daughters of men, only once (10,1) are the demons referred to as unclean. The link between these demons and the demons portrayed in the Gospels is, however, suggested by 10,2 which refers to the demons leading astray and blinding and slaying Noah's progeny. Indeed, the ethical deficiency of the spirits is much more frequently mentioned in Jubilees than their cultic unfitness.[26]

Turning next to the Dead Sea Scrolls, the only mention of deficient spirits there is a reference to evil spirits in the Genesis Apocryphon;[27] there is, of course, repeated mention of the Spirits of Truth and Falsehood in the Scrolls, but the Spirit of Falsehood appears to have little connection with unclean spirits. In the Apocryphon (XX) God sends an evil spirit to scourge Pharoah. Egyptian healers are unable to cure Pharoah, but Abraham says, "I prayed (for him) . . . and I laid my hands on his head; and the scourge departed from him and the evil (spirit) was expelled (from him), and he lived."[28] Here the spirit appears to suffer from ethical impurity: the preceding prayer and laying on of hands bear a striking resemblance to Jesus' manner of healing.

In Philo (c. B.C.20-A.D.50)[29] references to cultic uncleanness are generally allegorised,[30] so it is not surprising that he treats demons as ethically impure spirits. Josephus, writing his Bellum Judaicum in Greek in A.D.75-9,[31] is apparently of the same opinion, for he states at VII,185, concerning the Baaras root, that "τα γαρ καλουμενα δαιμονια, ταυτα δε πονηρων ἐστιν ἀνθρωπων πνευματα", and when entering the living, are expelled by the root.

With the publication of the Mishnah, we advance to about 200 A.D., although it contains traditional material from as early as the second century B.C.[32] It contains only two references to an 'evil spirit', and none to an unclean spirit. The evil spirits at Shab.2,5 and Erubin 4,1 is *ruah ra'ah* and the contexts do not suggest cultic uncleanness. In the succeeding Rabbinic writings the existence of demons on a large scale is still acknowledged, and they are feared. In the Palestinian Talmud the place of abode of the demons is said to be the cemetery, while in the Babylonian, one reason for not entering a ruin is said to be that demons reside there. This belief existed in Mark's tradition, for at 5,3 we are told that the Gerasene demoniac lived among the tombs.

It appears from this brief historical review that ethical impurity was ascribed to demons from early times, and that this view of their impurity continued into Talmudic times. Alongside this view, there also seems to have flourished from about 170 B.C. or earlier the impression that demons were cultically unclean. This historical co-existence of the two views of the demon's impurity and the use of both πονηρος and ἀκαθαρτος in the Synoptics render it likely, in our view, that both kinds of impurity were thought to attach to demons in the time of Jesus.

Admittedly, the idea of the ethical impurity of demons seems to have predominated throughout our historical survey, but their cultic impurity survived into the NT and beyond in the following aspects:

1. The corpse is a prime source of ritual uncleanness,[33] and the Gerasene demoniac, as mentioned earlier, is reported to live among the tombs.[34]

2. De Vaux, writing of the archaic procedure in Leviticus 14,2-9 for cleansing leprosy, states, "skin diseases... are caused by a demon and this demon must be chased away."[35] It is accordingly noteworthy that leprosy, thus caused by a demon, renders the victim ritually unclean.[36] In the tannaitic period other sickness is attributed to demons; for example, in a baraitha at A.Z. 12b Shabriri is called the prince of blindness, although not all illnesses are attributed to demons. This approach is close to that in the Synoptic Gospels: at Mark 5.2f. madness is caused by an unclean spirit, at Mark 9,17-26 deafness, dumbness and epilepsy, at Matthew 12,22 blindness and dumbness, epilepsy again at Luke 9,38f. and dumbness again at Luke 11,14. It is arguable that (1) since the skin diseases caused by a demon render the sufferer impure cultically, so do the other bodily defects caused by a demon impart cultic impurity,[37] and (2) if demons thus render the objects of their attack cultically unclean, demons themselves must be cultically unclean. Two points, however, illustrate the lack of consistency in the NT evidence concerning the cultic impurity of demons. Firstly, although the leper was denied entry to the Temple consonantly with his cultically unclean status, there is no evidence that the deaf, dumb, blind or epileptic were denied entry which might be expected if they were possessed by a cultically unclean spirit.[38]

Secondly, as mentioned above, Jesus' words to the paralytics at Mark 2,5 and John 5,14 suggest that their disability was the direct result of *moral* sin,[39] and at John 9,2 the question of the disciples probably implies a popular belief that blindness resulted from moral sin.

Moreover, we should note that in the Gospels, as in the Rabbinic writings, demons are not thought to cause all illnesses: thus, at Mark 6,13 the disciples ἤλειφον ἐλαίῳ πολλούς ἀρρώστους καὶ ἐθεράπευον. Again, in the healing of the woman with a flow at Mark 5,25-34, there is no suggestion that she was demon-possessed; she had been to physicians, and Jesus referred to τῆς μάστιγός σου (v.34).

To summarise, the answer to the question at the head of this Excursus is that spirits are described in the Gospels as unclean whenever the term 'unclean spirit' is used as a synonym for 'demon', for demons were connected with both ethical and cultic impurity.

NOTES

1. John's Gospel does not report such expulsions, but accepts demon-possession; vide 7,20, 8,48-52, 10,20-21.
2. Cf. 3,14-15; 6,7; Acts 10,38.
3. Cf. 5,8 and 13.
4. Cf. 5,16 and 18.
5. Again, in 7,24-30 the daughter has an unclean spirit at v.25, but a demon at vv.26,29 and 30.
6. If 'unclean demon' is the correct reading at 4,33, Luke's alteration may indicate his unwillingness to link πνευμα with ἀκάθαρτον because of the centrality of the Ἅγιον πνευμα in his Gospel.
6A. Vide supra, pp.111-3
7. With T.W. Manson, **The Sayings of Jesus,** London, 1949, p.87 and J. Jeremias, **The Parables of Jesus,** London, 1954, p.197. At Tobit 6,8, however, δαιμόνιον and πνευμα πονηρόν are expressed as alternatives.
8. The contexts seem to exclude hygienic uncleanness.
9. Vide supra.
9A. F. Haugh at **TDNT** III, 428 considers that πνευμα ἀκάθαρτον means a cultically impure demon.
10. E.g. Leviticus 5,3; 15,4.
11. E.g. Isaiah 6,5.
12. E.g. Genesis 44,10; Psalm 24,4.
13. E.g. Acts 10,14,28.
14. E.g. Ephes. 5,5; I Cor. 7,14; Rev.17,4.
15. Vide Mark 3,22.
16. With A.M. Hunter, **The Work and Words of Jesus,** London, 1950,

p.131. W.G. Kümmel, **Introduction to NT**, London, 1966, p.56 estimates 50-70 A.D.
17. E.g. Judges 9,23; 1 Samuel 16,14f.; 18,10; 19,9.
18. R.H. Charles, **Apocrypha and Pseudepigrapha**, Vol. II, p.170, places the terminus ad quem of chapters 6-36 at 170B.C.
19. 15,8-9.
20. 10,11. Cf. 9,8; 12,4 and 15,4. At 19,1 they are said to be defiling mankind.
21. 15,4. The idea of their heavenly origin survives at Mark 1,24; 3,11 and 5,7 in their recognition of Jesus as on the same plane. Cf. W. Foerster, **TDNT**, II,19.
22. 8,1-4.
23. 8,2.
24. 5,1-2.
25. **Op.cit.** Vol.II, p.6.
26. E.g. 10,3,11 and 13. Contrast Tobit 3,8 and 17, and 8,3 where the involvement of Asmodeus with the marriage bed connotes his cultic, rather than moral, uncleanness.
27. A. Dupont-Sommer, **The Essene Writings from Qumran**, Oxford, 1961, dates this Apocryphon in the first century B.C.
28. G.Vermes, **The Dead Sea Scrolls in English**, London, 1962, p.220.
29. Vide Philo, Vol.I, p.ix, Loeb edition.
30. Thus, at **Leges Allegoricae**, III, 94, he interprets those ἀκάθαρτοι at LXX Numbers 9,6 as *morally* impure men, even though they had touched a corpse.
31. Vide Josephus, Vol.I, p.xi, Loeb edition.
32. Vide H. Danby, **The Mishnah**, Oxford, 1933, p.xiii.
33. Numbers 19,11.
34. Mark 5,3. The PT gemara on Terumoth I, 1 notes that demons dwell in the cemetery. Cf. Berakoth 6a.
35. R. De Vaux, **Ancient Israel. Its Life and Institutions**, London, 1961, p.463.
36. Leviticus 13, 45-46.
37. A. Oepke, **TDNT**, IV, 1092, states that in primitive Oriental and Greek thinking, sickness and impurity are closely connected under the master concept, miasma, and the one always causes the other.
38. Vide G. Dalman, **Sacred Sites and Ways**, London, 1935, pp.291-2. Cf. J. Jeremias, **Jerusalem in the Time of Jesus**, London, 1969, pp.117-8. However, no *priest* who had a 'blemish' or was blind or lame etc. could minister at the alter (Leviticus 21,16f.).
39. Cf. Mark 2,5.

EXCURSUS III.

Authenticity of the Korban pericope: an historico-legal view.

The Korban pericope (Mark 7,9-13) is judged by some critics to be authentic Jesus-material, by others to be the creation of early Christians.[1] Two factors which should affect its attribution to Jesus, are (1) whether the scribal practice condemned there prevailed in the time of Jesus, and (2) whether it is credible that Jesus condemned such a practice. In this study we will examine these two issues.

1. Prevalence of the scribal practice.

In this pericope Jesus charges the Pharisees and scribes that they abandon the command of God in order to observe their tradition. In proof of this charge, he cites that whereas Moses commanded the honour of parents, they, if a man says to his parents, "Korban' is whatever you would have been entitled to from me'", will no longer permit him to do anything for his parents.

The Greek κορβαν is a transliteration of the Hebrew *'qar'ban'* which means an offering, and 'to the Lord' is, in the Biblical use of the term, either expressed (e.g. Numbers 9,7,13) or implicit from the context (e.g. Leviticus 1, passim). By the time of Mark, at the latest, the word had developed into an encapsulated vow whereby a thing declared to be 'Korban' was treated as vowed to the Temple.

Mark's following editorial comment ὅ ἐστιν δωρον repeats the LXX translation of *qar'ban,* which is also explained by δωρον in Josephus.[1A] However, Hubner[2] rightly argues against Haenchen[3] that the property which was the subject of the vow, was not actually given to the Temple,[4] but that any benefit from it was denied merely to the person to whom the vow was addressed.[4A] The property was, vis-a-vis the addressee, *as if* it was dedicated to the Temple, but the owner still owned it, and apart from allowing any benefit to the addressee, could alienate it or otherwise deal with it. At Nedarim 3,2 a man sees others eating his figs, and says, "May they be Korban to you *(harey aleykem qar'ban'')*. Some of the thieves turn out to be his father and brothers, and the issue is whether the vow is binding, in view of the mistake regarding the relatives. The School of Shammai say that the vow is binding only on the non-relatives. This indicates that (a) the property was not actually given to the Temple for, if it was, it would be impossible for even the relatives to enjoy the figs, and (b) the deprivation of non-relatives by the vow[5] did not prevent others, and hence the owner, from enjoying the figs.[6]

Thus, Jesus' complaint in the Korban pericope may be paraphrased as, 'Moses commanded that parents be honoured, but if a man makes a vow depriving his parents of their dues, as if his property was dedicated to the Temple, you do not permit him to do anything for his parents'. In order to determine whether a scribal practice prohibiting benefit to parents in these circumstances, did prevail in Jesus' time, we must examine whether the following legal provisions, which are express or implicit in the complaint, then existed:

(a) That sons were liable to maintain their parents.

(b) That a vow to deprive parents of this benefit was binding, unless released by competent authority.

(c) That the scribes possessed power to release vows, but refused to release sons from vows depriving their parents.

(a) Maintenance of parents.

Although the texts read the subjunctive ὠφεληθῃs in v.11, the sense, as the translators agree, requires the removal of the subscribed iota so as to produce the indicative used in a conditional sense, 'that which you would have been entitled to'.[7] The use of ὀφειλω in this scribal context probably connotes not just moral, but legal, obligation.[8] Bauer s.v. refers to the use of ὀφειλει at Matthew 23,16,18 in the sense of being bound by an oath, and this clearly means legally.

Historically, the obligation and respect owed to parents was declared in the Commandment at Exodus 20,12,[9] and does not seem to have diminished in intensity. Ecclesiasticus 3,1-16 stresses the honour and duty owed to parents, and by the time of the Talmudic Rabbis the respect has reached extreme lengths.[10] We thus have no reason to doubt that the obligation to maintain parents was recognised in Jesus' time, and at Mark 10,19 Jesus himself includes the honour of parents amongst the most important Commandments.

(b) The binding nature of vows.

The earliest evidence suggests that all vows were legally binding. At Numbers 30,2 we read, "When a man vows a vow to the Lord, or swears an oath to bind himself by a pledge, he shall not break his word; he shall do according to all that proceeds out of his mouth." Jephthah at Judges 11,29-40 cannot take back his vow even though it involves killing his only child. Further evidence that even anti-social vows were originally considered binding, is at Judges 21 where, although the Israelites regret their vow not to give their daughters in marriage to the tribe of Benjamin, they do not attempt to dissolve the vow, but find husbands for them elsewhere. And this strict view of an oath, even though anti-social in result, apparently persisted into Jesus' day. At Matthew, 14,6-10 Herod reluctantly beheads John the Baptist following his oath to give Herodias' daughter whatever she wanted.

Philo (c.20B.C. to 50A.D.) seems to be the first writer to state explicitly that some vows by reason of their nature are not binding, and should not be performed. He writes that all oaths must be performed so long as they are "concerned with matters honourable and profitable for the better conduct of public or private affairs and are subject to the guidance of wisdom and justice and righteousness".[11] But, he claims, when oaths have the opposite objects, such as crime,[11A] then religion forbids us to perform them, for God would rather we abstain from wrongdoing than abstain from breaking oaths. There is no evidence in any of the sources, however, that a vow to deprive parents was considered invalid *ab initio* for this reason.[11AA]

(c) **Scribes' refusal to release vows depriving parents.**

Belkin[12] notes that we can trace in Philo the origin of the Mishnaic law that in some circumstances vows can be dissolved by a judge. Eusebius quotes from Philo, 'release from a promise or vow can only be in the most perfect way when the high priest discharges him from it; for he is the person to receive it in due subordination to God.'[13] It appears from the Mishnah that not later than the era of the Houses (c. A.D.20-70) the *hakamim* (Sages) had wrested this jurisdiction from the high priest, although the silence in the Mishnaic tractate, Nedarim, concerning the rôle of the high priest may be the result of polemic. It is possible that a concurrent jurisdiction in the release of vows was exercised by the Sages and the high priest from some stage until the destruction of the Temple. For Belkin[14] also refers to a dispute recorded at y. Nazir 54b and Berakoth 11b between Simeon b. Shetah and Alexander Jannaeus, which arose when Simeon dissolved the vows of some Nazirites who could not afford the sacrifices entailed in the final rites at the Temple. Belkin's interpretation of the incident is that the king's rage arose from his belief that, as high priest, he alone was entitled to dissolve vows. At least, the story shows the arrogation by a Sage of this jurisdiction near the start of the first century B.C.[15]

More persuasive evidence of the power of the Sages generally to release vows, appears in Nedarim. At 9,1 the Sages agree with R. Eliezer that the Sages may release a vow between a man and his parents since 'the way may be opened to him by reason of the honour due to his father and mother.' The Sage, acting as judge, would say to the son, 'Would you have made this vow if you had realised that you were dishonouring your parents?'.[16] If the answer were 'no', the Sage might release the vow on the ground that it was made in error and therefore was not binding: at 3,1 it is stated, 'Four kinds of vows the Sages have declared not to be binding: vows of incitement, vows of exaggeration, vows made in error, and vows (that cannot be fulfilled by reason) of constraint.' It is explained in the gemara at Nedarim 21b that such vows are not automatically invalid, but a Sage may release them.

Klausner[17] has suggested that the vow concerning the figs at Nedarim 3,2 was released because of the honour due to parents, but Manson[18] insists that it was made in error and for this reason only, declared void. As related above, a man saw others eating his figs, and said, 'May they be Korban to you!'. His father and brothers were found to be amongst the eaters; the Schools agreed that the vow was not binding on the relatives, but differed over whether the others were bound. Now this story is related under the classification of 'vows made in error', and it seems likely that the reason for the father's and brothers' freedom is that, but for his error of identity, the son would not have vowed 'Korban' regarding them. However, the honour due to a parent may well have influenced the Schools' lemma, for the fact that the vow dishonoured a parent, may have contributed to the Schools' decision that it was made in error. The honour due to parents cannot have been the substantive reason, however, since brothers also were held to be unaffected by the vow.

The evidence so far adduced suggests that the Sages *were* willing to release vows depriving parents, but a Mishnah which, at first sight, indicates the contrary, is at Nedarim 5,6. Here, a story is told to illustrate the ruling in 5,6 that, if a man was forbidden by his friend's vow to have any benefit from his friend, and he had nothing to eat, his friend may give the food to another, and the man can then eat it. It is then related that a man whose father was forbidden by the man's vow to have any benefit from him, was giving *his* son in marriage, and wanted the grandfather to be able to eat at the banquet. He therefore said to a friend, 'I give you the courtyard and the banquet, but only for my father to come and eat at the banquet.' But his friend said, 'If they are mine, I give them to the Temple.' The man complained that he had not made the gift to the friend for that purpose. The Sages ruled that a gift of property which, if the donee wishes to dedicate it to the Temple, is not to be considered dedicated, is not a valid gift. Thus, the Sages did not decide that the vower could not be released from the vow denying his father, for, far from applying to be released, he had schemed only to avoid its inconvenience on this occasion! The Sages ruled only that he could not avoid the effect of the vow by a *conditional* gift.

While the above evidence persuades us that *at some stage* in the development of the law the Sages did not refuse to release vows depriving parents, we must enquire what point in the gradual change from severity to laxity had been reached in the time of Jesus. For the positions in the Pentateuch and in the Talmud seem to be at the opposite extremes: in the former, release seems never to be possible,[19] while we read in the latter that R. Hunah and R. Judah (Babylonian Amoraim of the 3rd century)[19A] simply asked the vower, 'Are you still of the same mind?', and if he answered, 'No', they absolved him! (Nedarim 21b).

We have already noted that at Nedarim 9,1 the release of a vow between a man and his parents because of the honour due to them is agreed by R. Eliezer and the Sages to be possible; the Sages and R. Zadok only disagree with Eliezer that *any* vow (not made with parents) can be released on that ground, i.e. that the vow would bring the parents into dishonour for having so rash a son. This Eliezer is very probably b. Hyrcanus who flourished both before and after the destruction of the Temple, since he was a pupil of b. Zakkai,[20] and assisted his escape from Jerusalem before its fall.[21] Moreover, the agreement between Eliezer and the Sages over the release of vows between son and parents indicates that this law may have been established before their time. That such vows were releasable by the Sages in the generation before A.D.70 is supported by the Houses' agreement at Nedarim 3,2 that the vow about the figs is not binding on the relatives. We have no cause to doubt the evidence of the Mishnaic editor that R. Eliezer, the Sages and the Houses made the statements respectively attributed to them at Nedarim 9, 1 and 3,2; that certain vows could be released for error or similar good cause is a natural stage in the growth of the law before the Talmudic stage is reached where vows appear to be resolved on mere request. Some further slight support for the release of vows in the early first century is Philo's above statement quoted by Eusebius, for Philo was writing probably not later than 45A.D.[22] No evidence is obtainable from the Qumran Documents, for although the Damascus Rule's statutes contain strict provisions about vows and oaths, and no machinery for their release, it is unlikely that the Community's practice would much influence the scribes.

Since the activity of the Houses covered the period from the start of the first century to at least 70A.D.,[22A] and since we cannot say how long before A.D.70 R.Eliezer flourished, the state of the law concerning the release of 'parent vows' in Jesus' time is difficult to gauge. In view of the releasability of 'parent vows' being treated as established law in the time of the Houses and Eliezer, we incline to the view that the scribes did not, even in the time of Jesus, refuse to release such vows, as a matter of principle.[22B]

2. **Whether it is credible that Jesus condemned such a practice.**

Since we have decided, albeit with some diffidence, that the alleged scribal practice did not prevail in Jesus' day, we must conclude that Jesus could not have condemned such an *actual* practice. We cannot, however, proceed from this to the further conclusion that the Marcan pericope is not authentic, for it is possible that Jesus mistakenly thought that there was such a practice. Perhaps there was a particular case where release of the vow was refused, and which Jesus wrongly thought to be an example of a general scribal refusal to release vows. Probably there were refusals. As discussed above, it is clear from Nedarim 9,1 and the *gemara* at 21b that the 'way might be opened' for release by addressing a question to the son such as, 'would you have made the vow if you had realised that it would dishonour your parents?' Now, at the time, perhaps the son would have made the vow notwithstanding, and an honest son, who had later repented and wished to be released, might truthfully have answered 'yes' to that question. We think it possible that there had been some 'cause célèbre, as Rawlinson suggested,[23] in which, due to the son's affirmative reply, the scribe had refused to release him, and Jesus, since the usual practice of releasing was not well known in his day, had considered this refusal as indicative of the scribes' general practice.

That Jesus may have been mistaken as to scribal unwillingness to release such vows, accords with the alleged ignorance of Galileans concerning the niceties of the law. The general charge of b.Zakkai, 'Galilee, Galilee, you hate the Torah',[24] thought to have been uttered after eighteen years of teaching in Galilee,[25] is well known. Moreover, if Jesus is correctly placed by Vermes[26] in the tradition of the *hasidim,* then like his fellow-countryman, Hanina ben Dosa,[27] he may not have interested himself overmuch in the machinations of the lawyers. Another indication that Jesus might have misapprehended the scribal practice, arises from the third Woe of Jesus against the scribes and Pharisees in the 'M' pericope at Matthew 23,16-22, which concerns scribal practice on oaths affecting the Temple. According to Jesus, the scribes rule that an oath by the Temple, or by the altar, is not binding upon the maker, whereas an oath by the gold of the Temple, or by the gift upon the altar, does bind. There is no Talmudic authority for Jesus' allegations here, although this does not prove that those rulings did not prevail in Jesus' time. There is evidence, however, at Nedarim 2,4 that the legal effect of certain vows was different in Galilee, and that this was due to the ignorance of Galileans concerning Temple matters. Admittedly, the statements to this effect are attributed to a middle second-century Rabbi, R. Judah, but since the vows concerned relate to *terumah* of the Temple-chamber and things devoted (in the Temple) to the use of priests, the lemmas presumably prevailed before the destruction of the Temple.

Following our forensic model discussed in Chapter I our conclusions are that:—

1. The evidence of Mark that Jesus condemned a scribal practice of refusing to release sons from vows depriving their parents, is opposed by the evidence of legal history that the scribes did release such vows in the time of Jesus.

2. There is evidence that Jesus was mistaken concerning scribal practice on a kindred matter, the binding nature of oaths by the Temple or altar etc. There is also evidence that Galileans were not well-versed in the detail of Temple—connected regulations. This evidence of 'similar facts'[28] indicates that Jesus may have been mistaken with regard to the scribal practice on release of vows.

3. Mark's evidence of the condemnation by Jesus of this alleged practice, supported by the evidence of potential error by Jesus concerning the practice, outweighs in our opinion the evidence against authenticity constituted by the evidence of a contrary scribal practice. We judge that the substance of the Korban pericope is authentic Jesus-material, in that Jesus did condemn a scribal practice on Korban; however, he spoke in error because the practice which he condemned, was not, in fact, pursued by the scribes.

NOTES

1. Examples of critics favouring its authenticity are W.G. Kümmel (Jesus und der Traditionsgedanke' in **Heilsgeschehen und Geschichte,** Marburg, 1965, at p.29) and H. Hübner (**Das Gesetz in der Synoptische Tradition,** Witten, 1973, at p.146). Critics opposing authenticity include K. Berger (**Die Gezetsesauslegung Jesu. Teil I: Markus und Parallelen,** Hamburg, 1972, at p.464) and R. Bultmann (**The History of the Synoptic Tradition,** E.T. Oxford, 1972 at p.49).
1A. **Antiquities** IV, 73.
2. Op.cit. p.147f.
3. E. Haenchen, **Der Weg Jesu,** Berlin, 1966, p.263, n.2.
4. In early times, of course, the property vowed *was* actually given to the Temple, vide e.g. 1 Chronicles 26, 20,26,28. G.B. Gray (**Sacrifice in the OT,** Oxford, 1925, at p.13) notes that in Biblical usage *q-r-b-n* is only used respecting sacred gifts.

4A. Thus, at Taanith 24a the charitable R. Eleazar b. Birtah (an Amorah), desirous that his daughter should not have his stocks of wheat, said, "they shall be *to you* as devoted property, and you shall have no more right to share in them than any poor person in Israel."

5. Although the Hillelites deny that even non-relatives are bound, probably on the principle that a vow invalid in part is wholly invalid, vide Nedarim 25b.

6. J.A. Fitzmyer in **Essays on the Semitic Background of the NT**, London, 1971, argues at p.97 that the use of 'Korban' in the ossuary inscription at Jebel Hallet Et-Turi shows that the contents were reserved for sacred use. But the contents of the ossuary had presumably not been delivered to the Temple, and since the vower, being dead, could not use the bones or other contents, the use of 'Korban' in this special situation does not indicate whether the use of the contents (apart from the bones) would have been denied to the vower himself had he been living. J.D.M. Derrett in 'KOPBAN, O ESTIN DWPON, JNTS, 16, pp.364-8 at p.365 states that the votary was liable in the Temple period to pay the value of the vowed property to the Temple, and (p.366) that all vows of dedicated property prevented the owner from enjoying the property. But apparently this was not so when the votary declared the property to be 'Korban' to others than himself, as Nedarim 3,2 evidences. Derrett cites a non-existent Nedarim 4,9.

7. Vide E.J. Goodspeed, 'Text of Mark VII,11', Exp.T, Vol.XX, pp.471-2.

8. Since the Torah is the revelation of God's will, legal and moral obligations are generally co-extensive in Judaism, vide G.F. Moore, **Judaism**, New York, 1971, at Vol.II, p.79f. Derrett discusses legal enforcement of the obligation, op.cit. pp.365-6.

9. Cf. Deuteronomy, 5,16. Although the verb in both texts is Heb. *kaved* (to honour), its meaning appears to extend to material support; at Numbers 22,18 Balaam interprets Balak's promise at v.17 to do him great honour (Heb. *kabed akabed'ka)* as involving precious gifts. G. Beer (**Exodus**, Tubingen, 1939, at p.102) writes that the verb comprehends an obligation on the Israelite inter alia not to begrudge his aged parents the bread of charity. Cf. Ecclesiasticus 3,12.

10. Vide Kiddushin 31b.

11. **De Specialibus Legibus**, II,12-13.

11A. Like the Jews' vow to kill Paul (Acts 23,14).

11AA. But R. Samuel at Ned. 21b is reported as arguing that the four kinds of vows mentioned at pp.227-8 supra were invalid ab initio.

12. S. Belkin, 'Dissolution of Vows and the Problem of Anti-social Oaths

in the the Gospels and Contemporary Jewish Literature' JBL, 55(1936), pp.230-1.
13. **Praeparatio Evangelica,** VIII, vii, translated by Belkin, ibid.
14. **Op.cit.,** pp.232-4.
15. Simeon was the brother of Queen Salome Alexander who reigned over Judaea from 76 to 67 B.C.
16. Cf. H. Danby, **The Mishnah,** Oxford, 1933, p.275, n.5.
17. J. Klausner, **Jesus of Nazareth,** E.T. London, 1925, pp.289-90.
18. T.W. Manson, **The Teaching of Jesus,** Cambridge, 1935, pp.317-8.
19. Vide supra.
19A. According to Soncino Rabbinic Index to Babylonian Talmud.
20. Aboth 2,8.
21. Aboth de Rabbi Nathan, Ch.4.
22. Writing of his part in the embassy to Gaius in A.D. 39-40, he refers to ἡμεῖς οἱ γέροντες (**De Legatione ad Gaium,** I,1 Loeb edn., Vol.X).
22A. See Booth, **Jesus and the Laws of Purity,** Sheffield, 1986, p.246 n.33.
22B. It is possible that scribal practice was not uniform, and that while Hillelite Pharisaic scribes were lenient, Sadducaic scribes or Shammaites were more strict about releasing vows. Cf. J.H.A. Hart, 'Corban', *JQR,* July 1907, p.643. However, in M. Nedarim, the Shammaites are willing to release vows depriving a parent (e.g. 3,2), and only seem to vary from the Hillelites in degrees of leniency. Indeed, R. Eliezer, the protagonist of release from any vows on account of possible dishonour to parents, was, according to Shab. 130b, a Shammaite.
22C. Hart, **op.cit.** p.642, speculates that Jesus felt intensely about scribal practice on release, because on vowing himself to the Kingdom, he had by Korban deprived his mother of any benefit from him.
23. A.E.J. Rawlinson, **St Mark,** London, 1925, p.95.
24. yShab. 15d.
25. G. Vermes, **Jesus the Jew,** London, 1973, pp.56-7.
26. **Op.cit.** p.78f.
27. Cf. Vermes, **op.cit.** pp.77-8.
28. Regarding the forensic admissibility of evidence of 'similar facts', see Chapter I, p.34.

INDEX OF ANCIENT PASSAGES CITED.

Old Testament

Genesis
5,24	43
6,1-4	49,220
9,3-6	80
9,4	107
9,4(LXX)	81
14,18	67
19,1-22	42
28,1-10	48
31,30(LXX)	149
32,32	93
35,2	85,90
44,10	223

Exodus
4,6-8	131
12,4	141
12,48	76-7
13,21	44
16,3	141
20,12	226
21,18	202
22,18	49
22,21	76
23,9,12	76
23,19	93
24,3,7	131
32,6	90
32,19	108
34,16	85
34,26	93

Leviticus
1	225
2,1f	203
4	158
5,3	223
7,14,53	49
11,1-23,45	77,97
11,24-8	95
11,32-3	211-2
13,45-6	224
14,2-9	222
15,2,19,25	208
15,4	223
15,4,12,20,24,26	211
15,11	213
15,18	85
16,10	49
16,29	77
17,7	89,90
17,7-15	86-7
17,8-9,12,15	77,86
17,10-14,15	87,147
17,14	104
17,15	92,99
18,6-18	83
18,20,22-3	91
18,24-5	85
18,24-30	90
18,26	77,110
20,2	77,110
21	78
22,10	78
23,40	103
24,16	77,110
25	78

Numbers
5,14	49
9,6	224
9,7,13	225
15,15,26,29,30	76
15,37-41	144
16	155
19	102
19,10	78
19,11	224
19,12,19	207
22,17-18	228
30,2	226

Deuteronomy
5,16	232
6,4-9	144
7,3-4	85
9,13-21	144
12,2,14	155
12,21	77
14,21	77,92
16,11,14	76
18,15	169
23,20	78
29,11	76

Joshua
24,26	48

Judges
9,23	49,224
11,29-40	226

I Samuel
14,24	151
14,33-4	105,107
16,14-23	48
16,14f.	224
18,10	224
19,9	224
28	46
28,3	49

II Samuel
7,14	175
12,13	186
24,1	49

I Kings
17,8-24	54
17,12	203
22,21	48
22,23	220

II Kings
2,11	43
4,18-37	54

I Chronicles
26,20,26,28	231

Ezra
9-10	85
13,19	203

Job
1-2	65
1,6	175
2,1	175

Psalms
2,7	175
24,4	223
95, 100	154
110,1	66,191,174
113-118	144
148-150	154

Isaiah
1,13	14
2,12	195
2,12-22	58
6,1-8	42
6,5	223
10,5-6	198
35,5-6	55,59
36,24-5	90

Isaiah (cont.)				Hosea	
40,12	203	3,2	106	1,2	89,108
42,1-4	178	4	195	4,11 & 12(LXX)	106
42,6	131	13,27	85	6,6	155
43,19	109	31,31-34	125,132,157	8,5	108
45,1-7	198			13,3	58
45,7	56	Lamentations			
49,1-7	178	3,38	69	Amos	
49-8	131			3,6	46,78
49,24-5	52	Ezekiel		5,18	195
50,4-11	178	4,13	108	5,21-4	110
52,1,11	90	4,14	86,92	7,17	108
52,13-53,12	178	14,7	77		
53	61,62,67	14,9	69	Micah	
53,2-4	180	23,7,30	85,108	5,10-15	58
53,4-12	179	23,36	108		
53,10	180	23,37	85	Zephaniah	
53,13	180	36,24-5	90	3,1	84
56,3-7	100,108	44,6-9	77		
58,4	198			Zechariah	
59,3	84	Daniel		13,2	220
60,3	100	1,8	84,92		
61,1	55,59	3,25,28	175	Malachi	
63,3	84	7,13	61,66,131,181,191	1,7,12	84
		7,13-27	66,70	1,11	157
Jeremiah		7,14	131,192	4,5	67,170,180
2,23	85	7,21-2	58,66		
3,1-3	106	7,25	66		

Apocrypha and Pseudepigrapha

Assumption of Moses		46,3	192	11,1-5	50
10,1	52	48,3,6,10	192	20,7	85-90
		49,2	192	22,16	91
Baruch II		53,1-5	65	23,29	69
25-30	58	53-3	49		
		54,6	49	Judith	
Ecclesiasticus		55,4	192	12,1-2	92
3,1-16	226	56,1	49		
3,12	232	62	58	Sybilline Oracles	
		63,1	49	4	79
I Enoch		69,4,6	49		
6-7	220	69,27	192	Testament of Levi	
6-11	50			18,12	52
8-10	49	Jubilees			
8,1-4	224	4,15	50	Testament of Simeon	
9,8	224	4,22	50,217	5,3	107
10	53	5,1-2	50,220	6,6	52
10,8	221	6,7-10	81		
10,11	224	7	107	Tobit	
11,1-2	53	7,20	81	1,11-12	92
12,4	224	7,21-5	50	3,8,17	224
15,4	224	7,28-31	81	8,1-3	107
15,8-9	224	10,1-2	50,221	8,3	224
19,1	224	10,3-11	224		

Community Rule I	132	*Dead Sea Scrolls* Genesis Apocryphon		IIQ Melchisedek	67
Damascus Rule VI	132		XX 221		

New Testament

Matthew		17,2	171	1,35	142,154
4,1-11	188	17,13	180	1,39	142,143,218
4,3-4	178	17,27	102	1,40-45	55
4,3,10	51	18,1-4	160-161	1,44	102,110,155
4,5	46	18,17	30	2,3-12	69,172
4,5-7	129	19,28	66,160	2,5	185,186,220,224
4,11	181	20,20-23	160-161	2,6-10	185-7
5	102	21,10-11	69,169,170	2,10	161
5,11	185	21,26	110	2,15	142
5,18	102	21,43	74	2,16	207
5,21-48	188	22,1-10	74	2,23-8	101,173
5,33-7	110	23,23	102	3,1-6	54,78,100,102
5,47	51	23,37-9	58,191	3,11	46,175,224
6,5-13	154	24,43-44	59,191	3,13f.	72
6,9	177	25,1-12	59	3,13-19	155
6,13	60	25,31-2	191	3,14-15	223
7,21-2	53,174,218	25,41	57	3,19-20	142
8,2-5	174	26,1f.	3	3,22	54,223
8,8	91	26,26	150	3,27	52,54,59
8,10-11	73	26,26-9	115	3,28-30	183-4
8,16	218	26,28	132	3,30	54
8,20	185	26,29	136	4,13-20	57
9,19	185	26,64	181,182	5,1-13	56
10,5b-6	72	26,65	169	5,1-20	53,73,74
10,8	53,218	27,43	178	5,2f.	218,222
10,23	8,60,72,129,	27,60	22	5,3	224
	184,191	27,62-66	22	5,7	175,224
11,3	171	28,2	17	5,8	223
11,4-5	55	28,2-3	30	5,11	46
11,13	171	28,4,5,7,8,10	17-18	5,13	46,74,223
11,18	69,218	28,9	12,22	5,15	218
11,20-4	58	28,11-15	22	5,16,18	223
12,2	155	28,16-20	12,19,22	5,18-19	75,165
12,22	222			5,28,34	186,223
12,28	53	*Mark*		6,4	171
12,31-2	183	1,4	139	6,6	186
12,39-42	73	1,11	175	6,7f.	5,6,72,186,218,223
12,41-2	188	1,12-13	51	6,12,13	56,155,218,223
12,43-45	57,218,219	1,15	110	6,14f.	168,170
13,19	220	1,19	142	6,15	70,110
13,36-43	56	1,21	143	6,41,42	102,142
14,5	110,168	1,21-8	56,172	6,48-9	8
14,6-10	226	1,22	187	6,56	102
15,22	72	1,23-8	55	7,1-23	110
16,5	30	1,24	46,175,224	7,3	197,203
16,17-19	158	1,26	46,53	7,4	206-215
17,1-5,9	30	1,32-4,39	53,218	7,5	201

Mark (cont.)		13,33-37	59,136,171	10,1	159
7,9-12	102	14,1	3	10,1-12	53,56,72
7,10-13	78,201	14,3f.	168	10,13-15	58
7,11	216	14,8f.	179	10,17-19	53,56,60,
7,13	216	14,12-14	102,125		159,218
7,15	102,110,159	14,17	148	10,40	174
7,24f.	72,74,223	14,18	134	11,1-4	154,174
7,27	72	14,18-21	119	11,2	177
7,29	72,186	14,22	116,121	11,14	60,222
7,31	75	14,22-5	115	11,20	53
8,6-8	142,151	14,23	118,121	11,24	53,56,218,219
8,12	59	14,24	60,61,67,122,	11,26	219
8,27-33	61,64,170,		125,132	11,29,37,38	209
	184,185	14,25	117,123,129	11,29-31	73
8,28	168	14,28	12	11,31-2	188
8,29f.	134,154,181	14,29	53,55	11,35	191
9,2-8	29	14,31	15	11,42	101
9,7	175	14,34-41	62	12,10	183
9,12	180	14,36	177	12,35-8	136
9,17-26	222	14,37,41	33	12,37	151
9,31	64,179,184	14,50	15,32	12,40	191
9,33-5	179	14,62	32,190,191	12,50	61,128
9,38	69	14,66-72	15	12,57-9	59
9,39	160	15,1	182	13,2	186
10,1	172	15,32	178	13,28-9	73
10,2-12	96,102	15,34	62	13,32	56
10,16-21	96,173	15,39	175	13,33	110,171
10,17-18	188-189	15,46	12	14,16-24	74
10,19	226	16,1-8	12,17	15,11-32	157-8
10,33-4	64,179,184	16,7	12	16,16	171
10,42-5	147,179			17,22,24,30	184
10,45	63,68,154,	Luke		18,9-14	186
	156,179	4,1-13	51,178	19,7	209
10,47	182	4,8	181	20,11-12	30
11,2-3	174	4,9-12	128	20,16	74
11,11,15	142	4,16f.	143,144	20,19-23	18
11,15-17	155	4,25-7	73	20,26-29	18
11,16	78,102	4,33	128,218,223	21,14	70
11,25	161	4,35	218	21,36	184
11,32	70	6,4(Code D)	102	22,14	149
12,1	179	6,6	143	22,14-20	117-9,127-9,
12,1-11	74,172	6,22	185		123-4
12,14	172	7,1-10	80	22,15	61,126
12,19	172	7,6	91	22,16-18	147
12,29	111	7,16	110,169,170	22,19-30	197
12,32	172	7,19	171	22,21	134
12,33-4	102	7,21-22	55,219	22,28-30	66
12,35-7	174	7,39	70,110,168,170	22,29	130,147
13,7,10	73	8,2	219	22,30	135,147,160
13,19-27	59-60	8,12	220	22,31	65
13,20	174	9,2-4	186	22,35-7	178
13,26-32	177-8	9,31,32	30	22,37	64
13,30	191	9,38f.	222	22,42	70
13,32	189	9,58	185	22,53b	62

Luke (cont.)	
22,64	169
22,67-70	181-182
23,25	178
23,34	177
23,53-4	22
24,1-12	17,19
24,4	30
24,6	4
24,13-31	12,18,22,23
24,19	110,169,170
24,26	30
24,30-31,35	136,138,150
24,33	33
24,34	20,44
24,36-51	12,18,22,23
24,44-9	19

John	
1,21	195
1,38	172
2,6	204
4,6-26	169
4,19	109,167
4,22	102
4,23-4	140,155
4,27	102
5,14	220,223
6,32-58	148
6,51	123,124,150
6,53-6	139
6,66	121
7,20	223
7,40-1	170
8,48-52	223
8,58	167,188
9,1-34	169
9,2	220,223
9,3	186
10,20-1	223
12,31	66
Chs.13,14-17	148
13,2-18	147,179
13,5	63
13,13	195
13,14-15	147
14,6	188
14,30	66
16,11	66
18-28	91
19,42	12,21
20,1-18	17
20,14-17	12,17,22
20,19-23	12,23,32,33,161
20,20,27	22
20,26-9	12,32,33
20,68	12
21	12,19,23
21,12-13	18,22,136,138,142
21,14	12
21,15-17	161

Acts	
1,2	23,161
1,3	12,21
1,4-11	12,19,22,23
1,6,24	196
1,9	43
1,14	135,143
1,15f.	161,163
2	15
2,14f.	161
2,42	135-6,139,145
2,42-7	137
2,46	105,135-6,139,143
2,47	138
3,1	105
4,3	15
4,8f.	161
5,3f.,8f.	161
5,16	163
5,18	15
6,1-6	163
6,3,8	37
6,9	143
7,31	30
7,55-6	37,190
8,4-7	163
8,27	82
9,2	220,143
9,3f.	29
10,2	82,104
10,9-16,27	82
10,14	102,223
10,17	30
10,28	91,223
10,38	223
10,41	16
10,42	197
11,19-30,26	102
13,14	143
14,8-12	177
14,22	58
15,1,5,7-11,12,16-18,19-20,29	89
15,6-11	82,108
15,7-9	92
15,9	90
15,12	83
15,19	161
15,20,29	82,83,84,91,92,99
15,21	87
15,23	84
16	161
16,13	143
16,14	104
17,10	143
17,18	16
19,8	143
19,12-16	219
20,7	136
21,21	105
21,25	82,83,84,92
22	29
22,29	29
23,12	128
23,14	232
26	29
26,19	28

Romans	
1,24-5	90
6,3	82
6,4	139
8,34	67
10,4	105
13,8-10	95

I Corinthians	
2,8	65
5,5	66
5,11	107
7,17-19	82
8	85
8,6	193
10,7-8	108
10,16-17	120,136,137,139
10,19-21	107,140
11	137
11,17-34	108
11,23	115
11,23-6	62,109
11,24,25	116,119,121,122,124,179
11,26	117
12,3	38
15	18
15,1-11	28,38
15,4	16

I Corinthians (cont.)		*Colossians*		*James*	
15,5	20	1,15-20	110,193	5,8-9	197
15,5-8	12,27	2,8,11-13,20-21	105		
15,12-19	38	2,12	139	*II Peter*	
15,23	25			2,4	51
15,35,39-44	24-5	*I Thessalonians*		2,10	85
16,2	14	4	59,147		
		4,3-5	91	*I John*	
II Corinthians		4,15	190	3,8	68
12,1,2-4	28,109	5	147		
12,4-5	158	5,1-2	190	*Jude*	
12,7	28,50,109			6	51
15,42,50,53,54	140	*II Thessalonians*		8	85
16,22	190	1-2	190	12	108,137
		2	147		
Galatians		3	59	*Revelation*	
1,11-17	109			1,9	58
1,12-13	115	*I Timothy*		2,10	66
2,12	82,94	2,1	145	2,14,20	98,105
3,27	82,105			7,14	58
5,3	82	*II Timothy*		17,4	223
6,12-13	81	4,13	145	20,1-6	70
Ephesians		*Titus*			
5,5	223	1,10 and 14	216		
Philippians		*Hebrews*			
2,5-11	193	10,12-14,18	156		
2,9-11	67,110,173	12,8	107		

Rabbinic Literature

Mishnah

Berakoth		*Hagigah*		*Hullin*	
2,1	150	2,7	207	1-2	86
5,1	150			7,1-6	93
6,1-8	78,102	*Nedarim*		8,1-5	93
8,1-2	150	2,4	230	8,6	93
9,5	78	3,1	227-8		
9,6	101	3,2	225,228,229,233	*Tamid*	
		5,6	228	5,1	153
Shabbath		9,1	227,229,230		
2,5	221			*Kelim*	
		Eduyoth		1,8	77
Pesahim		1,3	204	2,1	217
10,2	120	7,4	217	11,1	217
				18,4-7	217
Erubin		*Abodah Zarah*		19.1	211
4,1	221	1,9	85		
				Parah	
Megillah		*Aboth*		3,2	207
1,3-4	152	1,5	102		
4,1,2	153	2,8	233	*Tohoroth*	
				8,1,2	208

Zabim			Yadaim		1,4 211
2,4		208	1,1	203,204	2,3 199,203,
5,1		208	1,2	204,211	205,206
5,12		93,217			

Tosephta

Demai			Abodah Zarah		Tohoroth
2,12		209	8,6	107	8,13 208

Palestinian Talmud

Terumoth			Ketuboth		Nazir
1,1		224	8,11	212	54b 227
Shabbath					
1,4		212			

Babylonian Talmud

Berakoth			Taanith		Kiddushin
6a		224	24a	231	31b 232
46a		150			
			Yebamoth		Sanhedrin
Shabbath			46a	79,112	56a and b 80
14b and 15a		212			
62b		204	Neḍarim		Abodah Zara
130b		233	21b	228,229,232	12b 222
			25b	231	
Pesahim					Hullin
112b and 113a		54			106a-b 203,206

Palestinian Targum			Targum of Jonathan		Targum of Onkelos
Genesis			Exodus		Genesis
9,4		81	23,19; 34,26	93	9,4 81
Leviticus			Leviticus		Exodus
17,15		87,92	17,7	89,107	23.19; 34,26 93
18,21		85	Deuteronomy		
			21,21	105	Jerusalem Fragment Targum
					Exodus
					34,26 93

Fathers according to			Mekhilta		Midrash Rabbah
Rabbi Nathan			Exodus 23,19	108	Genesis 16,6 80
4		233	Sifra		Numbers 19,8 196
8		108	Leviticus 17,15	92,106	

Other Ancient Literature

Apostolic Constitutions
VIII,12,16   117
Canon 63   99

Aristotle   176

Barnabas, Epistle of
15   14,110

Clement of Alexandria
Paedagogue 2,7   99
Stromata 4,15   99

Clement of Rome
I Clement 44   157,
                     159,166

Clementine Homilies
7,4   97
7,8   98
8,19   98

Didache
6,2   98
9   120,137,147,157
10   147,157
10,6   190
15   162

Eusebius
Ecclesiastical History
II,23   107
V,1,21   99
Praeparatio Evangelica
VII,VIII   227

Hippolytus
Apostolic Tradition
XXV,XXVI,XXVII   151
XXXV   146

Homer   205

Ignatius
Ephesians 5   157
Smyrna 8   158

Josephus
Antiquitates
IV,73   225,231
XVIII,63-4   16
XX,38-47   104
Bellum
II,454   104
V,194   104
VII,185   221
Contra Apionem
II,282   79

Justin Martyr
Apologia
1,66-7   145
63,26f.   150
63,30   125
67,29f.   14
Dialogue
6,2   195
23,3   101
18,4   197
41   157
Trypho
51,2   147

Livy   26,177

Lucian of Samosata   39,
                       54,176

Nicodemus
Gospel 15   43

Origen
Ad Celsum   176
De Principiis,
  Proem 1   157

Palladius
Historia Lausiaca   202-3

Philo
De Legatione ad
  Gaium, I,1   233
De Migratione
  Abrahami 89   79
De Somniis I,22   205
De Specialibus Legibus
II,12-13   227
IV,122   86
Leges Allegoricae
I,31   25
III,94   224

Philostratus
Life of Apollonius   176
IV,20   54
VIII,30-end   26

Pliny
Epistles 10,96-7   16,145
Natural History
  36,191   217

Plutarch   176

Pollux, Julius
Onomasticon 2,147,
  158   202

Speusippus   176

Suetonius
Claudius 25   16

Tacitus
Annales XV,44   16

Tertullian
Apology   137
1,39   137
9,13   98
De Oratione 25   145
Scorp. 15   40

Vincent of Lerinum
Adversus profanas
  etc.   156-7

Theodore of Canterbury
Penitential   99

INDEX OF MODERN AUTHORS.

A.
Alon, G. 90,108
Anderson, H. 59
Anderson, N. 5
Aquinas, T. 8,40,68

B.
Bacon, B.W. 88
Baillie, D.M. 167
Barr, J. 195
Barrett, C.K. 40,43,108,109,149
Baumgarten, J.M. 104
Beer, G. 232
Behm, J. 130,131,135,151
Belkin, S. 227,232
Berger, K. 231
Bernard, J.H. 40
Bethune-Baker, J.F. 165,194
Bettenson, H. 195
Bevan, E.R. 102
Beza, Th. 203
Blackman, P. 203
Bloch, M. 9,40
Blunt, A.W.F. 69,92,109
Bowman, J.W. 106
Bradley, F.H. 9
Branscomb, B.H. 196
Büchler, A. 217
Bultmann, R. 9,40,54,109,110,149, 152,231
Burton, E.W. 40

C.
Cadbury, H.J. 39
Cashdan, S. 204
Catchpole, D.R. 105
Charles, R.H. 49,105,224
Collingwood, R.G. 9-10
Cope, O.L. 148
Creed, J.M. 102,118,127,130,138-9, 149,154
Crusé, C.F. 109
Cullmann, O. 170,172,189

D.
Dalman, G. 135,149,150,151,224
Danby, H. 105,203,224,231
Davies, W.D. 109
Deissmann, A. 107,108,109
Delling, G. 65
Derrett, J.D.M. 232

Descartes, R. 40
De Vaux, R. 106,224
Dewey, J. II(Pref.), 39
Dibelius, M. 105
Dix, G. 14,110,125,145,146,154
Dobschütz, E.von, 42
Dodd, C.H. 17,40,57,169
Douglas, M. 109
Downing, F.G. 11
Driver, S.R. 108,109
Dugmore, C.W. 144,152,153
Dupont Sommer, A. 195,224

E.
Edersheim, A. 205
Eissfeldt, O. 81
Etheridge, J.W. 107

F.
Fey, G. II(Pref.)
Finkelstein, L. 217
Finn, T.M. 104
Fitzmyer, J.A. 67,197,232
Flemington, W.F. 109
Foerster, W. 47,107,224
Fraser, J. 152
Freyne, S. 102
Fuller, R.H. 196

G.
Geeven, H. 152
Goldberg, P.S. 153
Goodspeed, E.J. 232
Goppelt, L. 217
Gray, G.B. 231
Green, M. 68
Guttmann, A. 106

H.
Haenchen, E. 106,225,231
Harnack, A. 162
Hart, J.H.A. 233
Harvey, A.E. 196
Harvey, V.A. 5
Hastings, J. 69
Haugh, F. 223
Heinemann, J. 104,105,110
Hengel, M. 202,203
Hick, J. 39,69,110
Higgins, A.J.B. 138,150
Holmes, J. 104

Hooker, M. 64, 196
Hort, F.J.A. 163
Hoskyns, E. and Davey, F.N. 47,52
Hübner, H. 102,225,231
Hunter, A.M. 13-14, 223

I.
Inge, D. 167
Inglis, B. 43

J.
James, E.O. 47,152,165
Jastrow, M.A. 203,204
Jeremias, J. 63,103,116,123,125,128, 131,135,148,149,150,151,154, 217,223,224
Jung, C.G. 33
Jungmann, J.A. 40,149

K.
Käsemann, E. 1
Klausner, J. 104,105,228,233
Kohler, K. 152,153
Kuhn, K.G. 76
Kung, H. 40
Kümmel, W.G. 105,197,223,224,231

L.
Lake, K. 104,105,109,140
Lampe, G.W.H. 186
Langton, E. 68
Leitzmann, H. 137
Lightfoot, J. 203
Lightfoot, J.B. 164
Lindars, B. 42,165,195
Livingstone, A.R.W. 197
Lohmeyer, E. 60
Lovejoy, A.O. 7

M.
Maccoby, H. 88,95,107,153,197
Maimonides, 102,106
Mair, A. 43
Manson, T.W. 70,223,228,233
Marshall, I.H. 105
Marxsen, W. 103
McArthur, H.K. 1,3
MacQuarrie, J. 46,67
Metzger, B.M. 40,42,103,106,127, 148,211
Michaelis, W. 43
M'Neile, A.H. 103
Montefiore, H.W. 44
Moberly, R.C. 156,163

Moore, G.F. 40,104,153,232
Montgomery, J.A. 108
Moule, C.F.D. 40,149
Moulton, J.H. 48
Murray, G. 195

N.
Neusner, J. 203,212
Niebuhr, R.R. 40
North, C.R. 104

O.
Oepke, A. 224
Otto, R. 64,130,132,135,150,151, 180,185
Owen, H.P. 167

P.
Perrin, N. 4
Powell, J.E. 152
Pryke, E.J. 196

R.
Ramsay, W.M. 106,109
Rashi, 95
Rawlinson, A.E.J. 183,196,230,233
Reynolds, S.M. 205
Riches, J. 68
Robertson, A. and Plummer, A. 108
Robinson, H.W. 165
Robinson, J.M. 69
Russell, D.S. 197

S.
Sanday, W. 105
Sanders, E.P. 149
Schillebeeckx, E. 165
Schweitzer, A. 43,66,151,152
Seesemann, H. 60
Six, K. 88
Smart, N. 69
Spitta, F. 137
Staniforth, M. 40,150,152
Strauss, D.F. 9,51
Streeter, B.H. 162

T.
Taylor, V. 62,64,67,102,103,150, 185-6,195,217
Theophylact, 202
Thiessen, G. 38
Troeltsch, E. 8
Torrey, C.C. 180, 205
Turner, C.H. 202

V.
Vermes, G. 69,131,151,172,195,224, 230,233

W.
Weiss, J. 110,152,165
Wellhausen, J. 180
West, L.J. 31-3,43,68
Westerholme, S. 209
Wettstein, J. 203
Whittaker, A. 44
Williams, C.S.C. 105,152
Wilson, S.G. 103
Wrede, W. 196
Wright, A. 154

Y.
Young, F. 195

INDEX OF SUBJECTS.

A.
Abimelech,	48
Agapé (see also Meals),	90,147,154
definition of,	137
Agrath, operate on Sabbath,	54
Ahura Mazda,	47
Alexander of Abonuteichos,	38,69,176
Alexander the Great,	177
Am-haarez, female, impurity of,	208
male, impurity of,	207
Angels, fallen,	49
Angra Mainyu,	47
Anselm, St.,	68
Antiochus Epiphanes,	67
Apollonius,	26,54,176
Apostles, authority of,	159f.
Assyrians, used by God,	194
Atonement, a theory of,	155-6
Attis,	140
Augustine,	176
Authenticity, proof of,	4

B.
Baptism,	
and law observance,	82
as purification,	92
substitute for circumcision,	96
Barnabas, and Jerusalem decree,	89
Beds, immersion of,	206-11
Beelzebul,	52
Beliefs, animistic,	47
Bereavement experience,	37-8
Biology,	8f.
Bishops,	157,162-163
Body, immersion of,	206-11
Bread and Wine, as sacrifice to God,	157
Breaking of bread, is fellowship meal,	136-140

C.
Causal connection,	9
Christians,	
attitude to OT law,	71
observe, should, dietary laws and sabbath,	100f.
devotion to Jesus or Paul?	101
educated,	3
followers of Jesus,	1(Pref.)
gullible,	176
Jewish, attitude to Gentiles and law,	81
continue, should,	
agapé meals,	147
private prayer,	148
synagogue-type worship,	139f.
washing of feet at agapés,	148
Paulinists,	200
rupture with Judaism, cause of,	194
vegetarian,	97
Church,	
ministry, evolution of,	162f.
survival of, not evidence for resurrection,	13
tradition of,	156f.,199
Cloud, sign of God's presence,	30,43
Commensality, impediments to,	90f.
Covenant, bilateral at Sinai and Last Supper,	130
Criteria, authenticating,	4-5
Cybele,	140
Cyrus, used by God,	194

D.
Date of,	
Alexander the Great,	177
Apollonius,	54
Aristobulus,	102
Artapanus,	67,221
Assumption of Moses,	69
Barnabas, Epistle of,	14
Baruch II,	58
Clement of Rome,	157,159
Corinthians I,	14,137
Council of Jerusalem,	83
Council of Trent,	156
Covenant, Book of,	76
Decrees, 18,	93
Deuteronomic Code,	76
Didache,	137
'E' material,	49
Empedocles,	176
Enoch I,	49,219
Enoch II,	67
Enoch (Parables),	192
Hippolytus,	137,151
Houses' Disputes,	86,106,229
Ignatius,	157
Josephus,	16
Jubilees,	81,221
Judith,	92
Justin,	14
Juvenal,	80

Livy,	177
Malediction,	153
Mark,	215
Mishnah,	93,153
Noahide laws,	81
Philo,	79,196,221,233
Philostratus,	176
Pliny the Younger,	16
Priestly Code,	77
'Q' source,	220
Salome Alexandra,	233
Sarapion,	137
Shechitah,	86
Sybilline oracles,	79
Tacitus,	16
Targum, P.	81
Tertullian,	80,151
Thessalonians I,	190
Thessalonians II,	190
Tobit,	92
Vincent of Lerinum,	156
Zephaniah,	58
David, numbering Israel,	49
Decree of Jerusalem Council,	82f.
approval by Jeus,	96
compromise measure for commensality,	94
non-comprehensive,	90
pollution, common link of,	86
Defilement,	
association with idols, by,	84
blood, by,	85-6
fornication, by,	84f.
irrelevant after Temple,	85
marital intercourse, by,	84
strangled meat, by,	85-6
Demons,	45f.
attack from inside or outside,	53
ethically or cultically unclean?	219-223
evil attributed to,	50
belief in, widespread,	54
link between Decree's prohibitions,	88
prominence in life of Jesus,	47
recognise Jesus,	58,59,67,175
reside in cemeteries or ruins,	222
responsibility for evil,	88,186
speaking,	46-7
unclean spirits, and,	218-9
Disciples,	
believed in Jesus despite his death,	152
change of heart of, as evidence for resurrection,	15

frequented synagogue and Temple,	143
Divinity, properties of,	167-8
E.	
Ebionites,	
believed Jesus only human,	193,197
observed Eucharist annually,	150
Egypt, king of,	175
Elect, The,	59-60, 66
Elijah,	26,29,43,54,67,73,170
Elisha,	54
Elizabeth,	31
Empedocles,	176
Enoch,	26,67
Eschatology,	53,59
Evidence,	
Church tradition as,	157
circumstantial,	13-16,35
corroborating,	126
dogmatic theology as,	163-4
experiential,	8f., 51-4,178,199
Gospel statements, their weight as,	112-5
hearsay,	27,43
interpretation of timing of,	132-3
similar facts,	34-5,230-1
Evil,	
attributed to Yahweh,	47
lack of devotion, due to,	48
natural,	199
F.	
Fat of ox., not to be eaten,	93
Fence, placing around the law,	204
Fiction, in Korban,	225
Finger of God, casting out demons,	53
Finite, contemplate the infinite?	10
Forensic treatment, of NT evidence,	1f.
contains no superior wisdom,	6
Form criticism,	5
G.	
Gadarene demoniac,	46,74
Galileans, ignorance of law,	230
Gentiles,	
bodily impure,	90,108
as a corpse,	93
boil kid in mother's milk,	93
their butchers sold sacrificed food,	94
contract impurity, cannot,	91
daughters and idolatry,	85
eat kosher meat, did not,	92
land unclean,	78,207
law, and,	81

pass impurity to food, 93
Ger,
  basis of prohibitions against, in
    Jersusalem Decree, 86-7
  resident alien, application of
    laws to, 76-8
  sabbath and *Kosher* laws apply to, 77
  whether circumcised, 76-7
God-fearers, 79f.
  observance of sabbath and
    food laws, 80
Gospels,
  evidence of historic reality, 2
  statements in, their weight
    as evidence, 112-5
  words of Jesus, do not record all, 132
Gregory of Nyssa, St., 68

H.

Haberim, 201,209-10,213,215
  insisted on purity of ordinary food, 93
Hallucinations,
  group, 29,35-6
  psychological factors, 31,32-4
Hands, rinsing of, 201f.,210-1,213
Hasidim, 153,177
Heifer, Red, ashes of, 71,207
Hip, sinew of, not to be eaten, 93
Historians, secular, and lawyers,
  similar method, 6
  resurrection not mentioned
    by secular, 16
Houses' disputes, 86

I.

Impurity,
  corpse, prime source of, 222
  sickness caused by, 222,224
  sticky, 213

J.

James, and Decree, 88-89
Jargon, theological, III(Pref.)
Jerusalem, Council of, 83f.
  Luke's report, authenticity
    and text, 83f.
  reason for, 89
Jesus,
  as Christ/Messiah, 181-2
  as Judge, 191-2
  as Lord, 172-3
  as Prophet, 61,100,168-72,194
  as Ransom, 63,65-6,67-8
  as Redeemer-God, 191-192
  as Servant, 178-81
  as Son of God, Holy One, 174-8
  as Son of Man, 182,187,190
  as Teacher, Rabbi, 172-3
  as vicarious victim of Satan, 61f.
  authoritative preaching, 187
  divinity of, claim first made
    by Paul, 101
    excludes from Church, 110
  eating with sinners, 209
  explain manner and purpose of
    death, only intended to, 142
  forgiving sins, 185
  eschatology, and, 59f.
  demons, believed he expelled, 53-4
  Gentiles,
    attitude to mission to, 72f.
    observance of law by, would
      have required, 97f.
    territory of, travel to, 74
  God is like him, 167
  Hasid, 230
  Jewish law, attitude to, 71
  Kingdom of God, purpose of
    his life, 52
  message of repentance in face
    of Kingdom, 59
  mistake as to scribal practice, 230-1
  neighbours, his, of non-Jewish
    descent, 102
  priests, did not ordain, 101,155
  resurrection of,
    closeness to God, proof of, 189
    divinity, not evidence of, 188,196
  sacrifices, did not ordain, 155
  suffering, 58f.,63f.
    Servant, saw himself and
      his death as, 64,66,167
  teaching, 57,58
    on divorce, 100
  temptation of, 51,128
  washing of disciples' feet, 63
  words at Last Supper, did not
    intend repetition of, 142
  worship, would have wanted
    synagogal form of, continued, 143
Jews, creed of, 144
John, the Baptist, returned to life, 170
John, Gospel of, ancient
  tradition in, 169
Jonah, 73

K.

Karaites,	153
Kid, not boil in mother's milk,	93
Kingdom of God,	
connected with new covenant,	131-2
destruction of Satan in,	52f.
exorcisms in,	53f.
purpose of Jesus' life,	52
sacerdotal system, no place in,	153
Korban,	
condemnation by Jesus,	229-31
prevalence of practice of,	225f.

L.

Law,	
customary,	86
decided cases, English:-	
Du Bost v. Beresford,	151
Edgington v. Fitzmaurice,	103
Hart v. Lancashire and Yorkshire Railway,	41
Mood Music Publications Ltd. v. De Wolfe Ltd.,	44
R. v. Bentley,	133
don,	II(Pref.)
Laws,	
fluidity of, in Jesus' time,	100
Gentile Christians, applied to, by Decree,	87
God-fearers, Noahide applied to,	80

M.

Man, divine,	176,192-3
Mark,	
cleverness attributed to,	II(Pref.)
knowledge of purity practices,	215
malice towards Jews,	215
objection to Judaizers,	216
priority of Gospel,	115
Market, purification on return from,	203f.
Mastema,	50
Meals (see also Agapé),	
contrast between Palestinian agapé and Hellenistic Eucharist,	136-9
disciples of, after Jesus' death,	135f.
Jesus expected to return at disciples',	136
Meat,	
bad for diet, cruel and uneconomic,	101
forbidden to monks of Stam,	109
Melchisedek,	67
Men as Gods,	176-7
Merkabah,	26
Messiah, Davidic,	175,178,181
Metatron,	26,67
Method, forensic,	I(Pref.),1-11,132-3
Methodology, legal,	132
Miqveh,	91,93,95,207,210,217
Miracles,	8f.,54,69
Mithras,	140
Mohammed,	135
Moses,	29,43,67,170,189
Mystery religions,	
influence on baptism,	139
influence on interpretation of Last Supper,	139
similarity to Christianity,	139-40
Mystics, religious,	37

N.

Naaman,	73
Nature, laws of, as counter-evidence,	8f.,24f.,38,199
Nazarenes, denied Jesus' pre-existence,	193,197
Nebelah,	80,85-7
Nicaea, Creed of,	167
Noah,	50,80
Notes, function of,	II(Pref.)
NT, as evidence for resurrection,	13

O.

Orpheus, taught by Moses,	67

P.

Pandemonium,	49
Parables,	
of marriage feast,	74
of sower,	57
of vineyard,	74
of weeds,	57
Parents, sons liable to maintain,	226
Parousia,	191
Paul,	
acclaimed as Hermes,	177
attitude towards Gentiles and law,	81f.
attitude towards Jerusalem Decree,	89
freedom from law, his, contrary to Jesus' wishes,	99
impediment of,	51
Jesus, never met,	99,116
Jewish Christians, conflict with, re law,	105
visions of,	27-9
Peregrinus,	38

Peter,
   dietary laws, and, 82
   Jerusalem Decree, and, 89-90
Physics, laws of, 8f.
Pigs,
   eating of, not forbidden by Jerusalem Decree, 79f.
   gerim, not forbidden to eat, 77,95
Plato, 176
Pollutions,
   interpretations of, in Jerusalem Decree, 83f.
   rationale behind Decree, 94
Prayer,
   Book of Common, 102
      Articles of Religion, in, 31,156
   Canonical Hours, 146
   hours of prayer, 146
   Lauds and Vespers, become Morning and Evening, 146,153-4
Presley, Elvis, 44
Priests,
   Jesus did not appoint, 155f.
   monopolistic functions, 158
Prophet, 'a' and 'the', 169-70
Proteus, 38
Psychical Research, Society for, 32,44
Purity,
   laws of, 71
   needed only for Temple entry and Temple-connected things, 213-4
Pythagoras, 176

Q.
Qumran, Prophet and Messiahs of, 170

R.
Rabbis,
   Eleazar b. Birtah, 231
   Eliezer b. Hyrcanus, 79,227,229,233
   Hanina b. Dosa, 54,170,175,230
   Huna, 229
   Ishmael, 26
   Johanan b. Zakkai, 196,229,230
   Joshua b. Hananiah, 79
   Joshua, 109,208
   Judah b. Tabbai, 212
   Judah, 229,230
   Samuel, 232
   Simeon b. Shetah 212,227
   Yose b. Yo'ezer, 212
   Yose b. Yohanan, 212
   Zadok, 229
Ransom, Jesus as, 63

Reasoning, God-given faculty of, 38
Redaction criticism, 5,215
Resurrection appearances, 17f.
   disciples' change of heart, as evidence for, 15
   divinity, do not indicate, 188-9,196
   human bodily, 21-4
   nature of, 21f.
   NT evidence for, 12f.
   spiritual bodily, 24-6
   Sunday, as evidence for, 14-5
   visionary form, of, 26f.
Rome, Emperors of, 176
Romulus, 26,177
Routes, taken by Gospel traditions, 113-6

S.
Sabbath,
   relation to Lord's Day, 14,101
   work on, 54,101
Sacrifices, not ordained by Jesus, 155f.
Satan, 48
   as accuser of man, 48,65
   as bailiff or prison governor, 65
   as forces of evil or self, 200
   fall from heaven, of, 56
   rescue of men from, 52
Saul, and Witch of Endor, 46,48
Science, laws of, no longer immutable, 11
Serapis, 140
Sermon on Mount, interim ethic, as, 59
Shechitah, 86
Son of God, meaning of, 175-7
Son of Man, 60,66
   divinity attributed to, 192
   return of, 177
Souls of the dead, continued existence of, 47
Spirits, evil, 48-9
Spirit, Holy, 72
   as purification, 92
Spirits, unclean, see Demons,
Spiritualists, 46
Stephen, 37
Succession, apostolic, 159
Suffering,
   before Kingdom, 57f.
   servant, 61f.
   vicarious, of Jesus, 61
Sunday, 37
Supper, Last, 61
   covenant, new, reference to, 129f.
   cultic rite, whether Jesus intended, 124

eschatology,
- in Mark's account of, 117
- in Luke's account of, 119
- theme of, is, 134

Gospel reports of, do not contain all Jesus said, 123
- Jesus, neither eats nor drinks at, 127
- purpose of his words at, 140
- Pauline account, dominant, 120
- repetition of his words at, Jesus did not command, 126
- vicarious suffering mentioned, 122-3
- wine-before-bread order, not Luke's creation, 120
- words spoken over bread and wine, not at distribution, 121-2

Synagogue service,
- elements passed into Christian worship, 144
- nature of, 143f.

T.

Teacher, the Samaritan, 170

Temple,
- Court of Women in, 77,103
- entry to, barred to lepers but not to the sick, 222
- inscription in, about Gentiles, 103-4
- priest, blemished, not to minister in, 224

Temptations, of Jesus, 51

Terefah, 80,85-6

Theology, dogmatic, 163-4,199

Tomb, empty, evidence of, 17

Transfiguration, as internal vision, 29f.

Trent, Council of, 156

Trinity, is not monotheism, 194

V.

Vessels, immersion of, 211

Vision, may transmit truth, 189

Vows,
- abstinence, of, 128
- binding nature of, 226-7
- release of, by scribes, 227-9

W.

Washing of the hands, 201f.

Watchers, The, 53

Wine, only drunk on festive occasions, 125,136

Writing, academic, recent, II(Pref.)

Z.

Zechariah, 31

Zoroaster, 47,135

GLOSSARY.

Agapé	In our context, a fellowship meal eaten together by Jesus and the disciples, or by a group of early Christians.
Agrapha	Sayings of Jesus which are not recorded in the NT.
am-haarez (a.h.)	The ordinary people of Palestine (literally, 'the people of the land') who were not scrupulous in observing the laws of tithing and purity, as the *haberim* were.
Amorah	A teacher of the traditional law after its final compilation in written form in the Mishnah in about 200 A.D.
apocalyptic	Revealing the future, generally what will happen in the Last Days.
A.Z. (Abodah Zarah)	Idolatry. A Tractate (chapter) of the Mishnah.
Berakoth	Blessings. A chapter of the Mishnah.
c. (=circa)	About, approximately.
canonical document	A writing which has been accepted as within the canon (standard) for inclusion in the NT or OT.
cenobite	A monk who lives with others, as opposed to a hermit.
Clementina	These comprise the Homilies and Recognitions, i.e. Jewish Christian writings wrongly attributed to Clement, Bishop of Rome c.A.D. 89-97, and perhaps written c.A.D. 150.
commensality	Eating at the same table.
common prayer	Prayer by worshippers assembled together, as opposed to private prayer.
cultic	Relating to worship, often Temple worship.
demoniac	A person posessed by a demon.
empirical probability	Something which is likely, judged by past experience.
eschatological	Concerning the Last Days or End-time.
fl. (=floruit)	Flourished.
forensic	Relating to law-courts.

form criticism	The identification of the separate units of tradition (stories, sayings etc.) in the Gospels, and the study of why the units were preserved (e.g. through use in preaching, teaching etc.) and of their subsequent history until inclusion in the Gospels.
gemara	The commentary and discussion on the Mishnah which, together with the Mishnah, constitute the Babylonian Talmud.
haberim	Those Pharisees who grouped together in societies in order to observe scrupulously the laws of tithing and purity.
halakhah	A ruling by the Rabbis on a point of Jewish law.
hearsay rules	Rules which determine the circumstances in which a person may give evidence of what another person said to him.
Hasidim	Literally, 'the Pious Ones', who were devoted to the Jewish law, opposed the introduction of Greek ways in Jerusalem, and combined with the Maccabees against the attempt of Antiochus Epiphanes (ruler of Syria, 175-163 B.C.) to eradicate Judaism.
Hullin	Ordinary food, as opposed to *terumah* (priestly food) and *kodashim* (sacrificial food). The title of a chapter of the Mishnah.
infra	Below, further down (in a book).
interim	The period before something else happens, i.e. meanwhile.
ipsissima verba	Literally, the very words themselves, i.e. the exact words.
Kelim	Utensils. The title of a chapter of the Mishnah.
Kerygma	The central message of the NT. The Greek word for the proclamation of a herald.
'L'	Luke's special material, i.e. the tradition (stories, sayings etc.) which appears in Luke's Gospel only.
lemma	A proposition or ruling.
logion	A saying, usually in our context, of Jesus.
LXX (= the Septuagint)	A translation of the Hebrew Scriptures into Greek made c.250B.C. and, according to legend, in 72 days by 72 scribes.
'M'	Matthew's special material, i.e. the tradition (stories, sayings etc.) which appears in Matthew's Gospel only.

Megillah (Meg.)	A scroll (usually of the Book of Esther). The title of a chapter of the Mishnah dealing in part with the public reading of Scripture in Temple and synagogue.
Merkabah	The chariot which Ezekiel saw in a vision, and described in Ezekiel 10.
Metatron	An angel described in the Hebrew Book of Enoch as the heavenly form of Enoch 'who walked with God; and he was not, for God took him.' (Genesis 5,24).
midrash	An interpretation of Scripture in the sense of deducing new ideas or rules from it.
miqveh	The purificatory bath, being a pool of natural water in which a person who has been cultically defiled (see eg. Lev.11-15) may bathe, and then in the evening he will become clean again.
Mishnah	A collection under subjects of the oral rulings of the Scribes and Rabbis, finally compiled c.A.D. 200.
mystery cult	The worship of a God (e.g. Hermes, Diana, Mithras) whose followers believed that divine secrets, especially about the after-life, were vouchsafed to them by the God.
natural evil	Disasters which befall men through the operation of the laws of nature, not through the corrupt will of man (voluntary evil).
Nedarim (Ned.)	Vows. The title of a chapter of the Mishnah.
par. (parallel)	Reference to a verse in one Gospel which is similar to the verse just quoted in another Gospel.
parousia	In our context, the expected return of Jesus as Son of Man to judge the world.
Pentateuch	The first five books pf the OT.
Pesah (Pes.)	Passover. The title of a chapter of the Mishnah.
pericope	A separate unit of tradition (e.g. a story or piece of teaching) which is thought to have been passed down separately until incorporated in a Gospel.
Priestly Code (P)	One of the four literary sources (J,E,D and P) which were interwoven to form the Pentateuch. The Priestly Code stresses the ritual laws, and its narratives often contain legal precedents.
proleptically	Treating an event as happening before its due time.
'Q'	This abbreviation of 'Quelle' (German, source) signifies a collection (probably written) of sayings of

	Jesus upon which both Matthew and Luke drew.
R. (=Rabbah)	When written after a book of the OT, signifies the Midrash Rabbah, an explanatory commentary on the Pentateuch and five other OT books. These commentaries were of various centuries between the 4th and the 12th. R. also signifies 'Rabbi'.
redaction criticism	The identification and study of the editorial work (omissions, additions, alterations and joins) of the Evangelist when moulding the units of tradition which he had collected, into his written Gospel. To redact is to edit or revise written or oral matter.
scribes	The scholars skilled in the Biblical law and the traditional law theoretically based upon it; after the first Jewish War (A.D. 66-70) they were known as Sages or Rabbis.
second Temple	The first Temple was destroyed by the Babylonians in B.C. 586. The second Temple was built under the leadership of Zerubbabel after the return from Exile, and was re-dedicated in 516 B.C. That Temple was robbed and defiled by Antiochus Epiphanes in 168 B.C. but was re-dedicated by the Maccabees in 165 B.C. It was magnificently extended and improved by Herod the Great, but destroyed by the Romans in A.D. 70.
Seder	The order of service in the Temple or synagogue, but the term is particularly used of the procedure at the Passover Festival in the home.
Sifra	The earliest midrash (explanatory commentary) on Leviticus. Difficult to date, but perhaps c.200 A.D.
supra	Above, further back (in a book).
Synoptists	In connection with the NT signifies the Gospels of Matthew, Mark and Luke which have many similar passages. These can be placed in parallel columns and 'seen together'.
T.	An abbreviation for the Tosephta which is a collection of legal rulings traditionally thought to be supplemental to the Mishnah and compiled shortly after the Mishnah.
Talmud	Most references in this book are to the Babylonian Talmud, although there is also a Palestinian Talmud.

	The Babylonian Talmud contains the Mishnah with commentary and discussion on it, and was finally compiled c.550A.D.
tannaitic	Relating to a tanna, the name given to a teacher or transmitter of the traditional law until the publication of the Mishnah c.A.D.200; after that he was called an Amorah.
Targumim	Translations of the Hebrew Scriptures into Aramaic which were read out after the Hebrew readings in the synagogues where Hebrew was not generally understood. Since the Palestinian Targum often paraphrases Scripture and is thought to have been written pre-70 A.D., it is a useful guide as to how Scripture was interpreted in the time of Jesus and the early church.
tradents	Christians who passed on the generally unwritten tradition (e.g. teaching of Jesus and stories about him) until it was written down either by the Evangelists or earlier.
tradition	The material about Jesus (teaching, stories etc.) which was passed down by the tradents by word of mouth until embodied in the Gospels or previously written down.
type	A person who, or event which, prefigures, or is a model for, a future person or event. Thus, the Suffering Servant of Isaiah 53 is a type of Jesus, and Jonah's 3 days in the belly of the whale is a type of Jesus' 3 days in Hades after the Crucifixion.
Usha	The town in Galilee which the Rabbis made their centre after the end of the second Jewish War in A.D. 134.
voluntary evil	Suffering caused to men by the corrupt will of other men. Contrast natural evil.
water for impurity	Water mixed with the ashes of a red heifer in accordance with Numbers 19. Sprinkling with this water was necessary to cleanse persons or things which had been defiled cultically by contact with a corpse.
Yavneh	A town, North-west of Jerusalem and close to the sea, where R. Johanan b. Zakkai, after escaping from Jerusalem during the first Jewish War (A.D. 66-70) founded a new centre of Jewish learning.

Yahweh — The Tetragrammaton, one of the two separate names for God in the OT. When the Hebrew Scriptures are read aloud by Jews, the word 'Adonai' is substituted for Yahweh since that holy name must not be spoken by them.

Zabim (Zab.) — Men or women who have a flow from their body. The title of a chapter of the Mishnah.